THE CONSCIOUSNESS OF THE HISTORICAL JESUS

T&T Clark Studies in Systematic Theology

Edited by

Ian A. McFarland
Ivor Davidson
Philip G. Ziegler
John Webster†

Volume 41

THE CONSCIOUSNESS OF THE HISTORICAL JESUS

Historiography, Theology, and Metaphysics

Austin Stevenson

LONDON • NEW YORK • OXFORD • NEW DELHI • SYDNEY

T&T CLARK

Bloomsbury Publishing Plc, 50 Bedford Square, London, WC1B 3DP, UK
Bloomsbury Publishing Inc, 1359 Broadway, New York, NY 10018, USA
Bloomsbury Publishing Ireland, 29 Earlsfort Terrace, Dublin 2, D02 AY28, Ireland

BLOOMSBURY, T&T CLARK and the T&T Clark logo are trademarks of Bloomsbury Publishing Plc

First published in Great Britain 2024
Paperback edition published 2025

Copyright © Austin Stevenson, 2024

Austin Stevenson has asserted his right under the Copyright, Designs and Patents Act, 1988, to be identified as Author of this work.

Cover design: Terry Woodley

All rights reserved. No part of this publication may be: i) reproduced or transmitted in any form, electronic or mechanical, including photocopying, recording or by means of any information storage or retrieval system without prior permission in writing from the publishers; or ii) used or reproduced in any way for the training, development or operation of artificial intelligence (AI) technologies, including generative AI technologies. The rights holders expressly reserve this publication from the text and data mining exception as per Article 4(3) of the Digital Single Market Directive (EU) 2019/790.

Bloomsbury Publishing Plc does not have any control over, or responsibility for, any third-party websites referred to or in this book. All internet addresses given in this book were correct at the time of going to press. The author and publisher regret any inconvenience caused if addresses have changed or sites have ceased to exist, but can accept no responsibility for any such changes.

Every effort has been made to obtain the necessary permissions from the relevant copyright holders.

A catalogue record for this book is available from the British Library.

Library of Congress Cataloging-in-Publication Data
Names: Stevenson, Austin, author.
Title: The consciousness of the historical Jesus : historiography, theology, and metaphysics / Austin Stevenson.
Description: New York : T&T Clark, 2024. | Series: T&T Clark studies in systematic theology | Includes bibliographical references and index.
Identifiers: LCCN 2023030363 (print) | LCCN 2023030364 (ebook) | ISBN 9780567714398 (hardback) | ISBN 9780567714428 (paperback) | ISBN 9780567714404 (pdf) | ISBN 9780567714411 (epub)
Subjects: LCSH: Humanity–Religious aspects. | Jesus Christ.
Classification: LCC BV4647.S9 S77 2024 (print) | LCC BV4647.S9 (ebook) | DDC 241/.4–dc23/eng/20231016
LC record available at https://lccn.loc.gov/2023030363
LC ebook record available at https://lccn.loc.gov/2023030364

ISBN: HB: 978-0-5677-1439-8
PB: 978-0-5677-1442-8
ePDF: 978-0-5677-1440-4
eBook: 978-0-5677-1441-1

Series: T&T Clark Studies in Systematic Theology, volume 41

Typeset by Newgen KnowledgeWorks Pvt. Ltd., Chennai, India

For product safety related questions contact productsafety@bloomsbury.com.

To find out more about our authors and books visit www.bloomsbury.com and sign up for our newsletters.

For Katherine and Sophia

CONTENTS

Preface ... ix
Abbreviations, Editions, and Translations of Works of Thomas Aquinas ... x
Series Abbreviations ... xii

INTRODUCTION ... 1

Part I
CONCEPTS OF BEING

Chapter 1
THE HISTORICAL JESUS ... 19

Chapter 2
THE METAPHYSICS OF PARTICIPATION ... 41

Chapter 3
THE DOCTRINE OF THE INCARNATION ... 59

Part II
CONCEPTS OF KNOWING

Chapter 4
THE INTELLIGIBILITY OF PARTICIPATED BEING ... 99

Chapter 5
DIVINE KNOWLEDGE: AN EXCURSUS ON MK 13:32 ... 125

Chapter 6
ACQUIRED KNOWLEDGE ... 143

Chapter 7
PROPHETIC KNOWLEDGE ... 161

Chapter 8
THE BEATIFIC VISION   185

CONCLUSION: RIVAL TRADITIONS OF HISTORICAL ENQUIRY   207

Bibliography   215
Index   243

PREFACE

I am grateful to the many people who made the preparation of this book not only possible but immensely enjoyable. This project began as a doctoral dissertation at the University of Cambridge, and my thanks go first and foremost to my doctoral supervisor Andrew Davison. His attention, encouragement, and wisdom have been an invaluable gift. I am also grateful to my examiners, David Fergusson and Simon Francis Gaine, OP, as well as Ian McFarland and Catherine Pickstock, for their rigorous and insightful engagement with my work. Special thanks go to Hans Boersma, who suggested in 2015 that Thomas Aquinas might have something interesting to say with regard to my questions about Christology and historical Jesus scholarship. I have been blessed by friendships with scholars who provided generative discussions and perceptive feedback through the course of my research. In particular, I would like to thank Jesse and Iane Grenz, Alexander Abecina, Roger Revell, Jonathan Platter, Matthew Fell, Jon Thompson, Brian Dant, Daniel De Haan, Barnabas and Silvianne Aspray, Malcolm Guite, and Craig Blomberg. Thanks also to Seth Heringer and Richard Cross for correspondence about the project. Aaron Weber did an excellent job with the index.

This research benefited from those who offered substantial engagement at various conferences and seminars at the University of Cambridge, University of Oxford, University of Warwick, Nicolaus Copernicus University (Poland), the Angelicum (Rome), and Ave Maria University (Florida) where I originally presented portions of what follows. Chapters 1, 3, and 5 contain material from previously published papers. I am grateful to those who gave the appropriate permissions to make use of them.[1]

Most of all, my thanks go to my wife Katherine whose tireless work, joyful spirit, and inquisitive disposition have enriched both my life and scholarship beyond measure. Far from tolerating my research and academic pursuits, she has always shared my vision for their intrinsic and extrinsic value, motivating me and serving as a perceptive dialogue partner along the way. This is dedicated to her and our daughter Sophia, who was born two days after the completion of the first full draft.

---

1. "The Self-Understanding of Jesus," 291–307, by permission of Cambridge University Press; "The Unity of Christ and the Historical Jesus," 851–64, by permission of Wiley; "'Concerning that Day and Hour,'" 234–54, by permission of Penn State University Press.

Abbreviations, Editions, and Translations of Works of Thomas Aquinas

Latin texts are taken from the following editions: Leonine Edition (Opera Omnia. Iussu Leonis XIII, Rome: Vatican Polyglot Press, 1882–); Parma Edition (Opera Omnia, 25 vols, Parma: Fiaccadori, 1852–73); Marietti Edition (Turin: Marietti, 1953). Dating of Aquinas' works follows that of Gilles Emery in the appendix to Jean-Pierre Torrell, *Saint Thomas Aquinas*, vol. 1. Translated by Robert Royal (Washington, DC: Catholic University of America Press, 2003), 330–61, 424–38. Where no reference is given to the part of the article cited, it is to the main body or response.

Comp. Theol.	*Compendium Theologiae* (c. 1265). Leonine edition, vol. 42, 1979. English Translation ["ET"]: *Compendium of Theology*. Translated by Richard Regan. Oxford: Oxford University Press, 2009.
Contra errores Graec.	*Contra errores Graecorum ad Urbanum papam* (1263). Leonine edition, vol. 40, 1969.
De malo	*Quaestiones Disputatae de malo* (c. 1269–71). Leonine edition, vol. 23, 1982.
De Pot.	*Quaestiones Disputatae de potentia* (1266). In *Quaestiones Disputatae*, vol. 2. Marietti edition, 1949. ET: *On the Power of God*. 3 vols. Translated by Laurence Shapcote. Eugene, OR: Wipf and Stock, 2004.
De Prin. Nat.	*De Principiis Naturae* (1252–6). Leonine edition, vol. 43, 1976. ET: *On the Principles of Nature to Brother Sylvester*. Translated by R. A. Kocourek. St Paul: North Central Publishing, 1956.
De rationibus fidei	*De rationibus fidei ad Cantorem Antiochenum* (c. 1266). Leonine edition, vol. 40, 1969.
De Spir.	*Quaestiones disputata "De spiritualibus creaturis"* (1267–8). Leonine edition, vol. 24, no. 2, 2000. ET: *Saint Thomas Aquinas, On Spiritual Creatures*. Translated by M. C. Fitzpatrick and J. J. Wellmuth. Milwaukee, 1949.
De sub. Separatis	*De substantiis separatis* (1272–3). Leonine edition, vol. 40, 1968. ET: *Treatise on Separate Substances*. Translated by F. J. Lescoe. West Hartford, CT: St. Joseph's College, 1959.
De unione verbi	*Quaestio disputata "De unione Verbi incarnati"* (1272). Parma edition, vol. 8. ET: *Thomas Aquinas, De unione Verbi incarnati*. Translated by Roger W. Nutt. Dallas Medieval Texts and Translations, 21. Leuven: Peeters, 2015.

De ver.	*Quaestiones Disputate De Veritate* (1256–9). Leonine edition, vol. 22, nos. 1–3, 1970–6. ET: *Saint Thomas, On Truth*. 3 vols. Translated by R. W. Mulligan, J. V. McGlynn, and R. W. Schmidt. Chicago, 1952–4.
De virt.	*Quaestiones Disputatae De virtutibus* (1272). Marietti edition, 1953. ET: *Thomas Aquinas: Disputed Questions on the Virtues*. Edited and translated by E. M. Atkins and Thomas Williams. Cambridge: Cambridge University Press, 2005.
In Boeth. De Trin.	*Super Boethium De trinitate* (1257–9). Leonine edition, vol. 50, 1992. ET: *The Trinity and the Unicity of the Intellect*. Translated by Rose E. Brennan. St. Louis: Herder, 1946.
In De anima	*Sententia super De anima* (1268). Leonine edition, vol. 45, 1984. ET: *Commentary on Aristotle's De anima*. Translated by Robert C. Pasnau. New Haven, CT: Yale University Press, 1999.
In De Div. Nom.	*In librum Beati Dionysii De divinis nominibus exposition* (c. 1261–8). Marietti edition, 1950.
In de hebd.	*In librum Boethii De hebdomadibus expositio* (after 1259). Marietti edition, 1954. ET: *The Exposition of the "On the Hebdomads" of Boethius*. Translated by Janice L. Schultz and Edward A. Synan. Washington, DC: Catholic University of America Press, 2001.
In Epist. ad Hebr.	*Super Epistolam ad Hebraeos Lectura* (c. 1265–73), in *Super Epistolas S. Pauli Lectura*, vol. 2, edited by R. Cai, Turin: Marietti, 1953. Translated by F. R. Larcher. Edited by J. Mortensen and E. Alarcón. Lander, WY: The Aquinas Institute for the Study of Sacred Doctrine, 2012. Lander, WY: The Aquinas Institute for the Study of Sacred Doctrine, 2012.
In Epist. ad Phil.	*Super Epistolam ad Philippenses Lectura* (c. 1265–73), in *Super Epistolas S. Pauli Lectura*, vol. 2, edited by R. Cai, Turin and Rome: Marietti, 1953. Translated by F. R. Larcher. Edited by J. Mortensen and E. Alarcón. Lander, WY: The Aquinas Institute for the Study of Sacred Doctrine, 2012.
In I/II Epist. ad Tim	*Super Primum/Secundam Epistolam ad Timotheum Lectura* (c. 1265–73), in *Super Epistolas S. Pauli Lectura* vol. 2, edited by R. Cai, Turin and Rome: Marietti, 1953. Translated by F. R. Larcher. Edited by J. Mortensen and E. Alarcón. Lander, WY: The Aquinas Institute for the Study of Sacred Doctrine, 2012.
In Epist. ad Rom.	*Super Epistolam ad Romanos Lectura* (1272–3), in *Super Epistolas S. Pauli Lectura*, vol. 1, edited by R. Cai, Turin and Rome: Marietti, 1953. Translated by F. R. Larcher. Edited by J. Mortensen and E. Alarcón. Lander, WY: The Aquinas Institute for the Study of Sacred Doctrine, 2012.
In I/II Epist. ad Cor.	*Super Primum/Secundum Epistolam ad Corinthios Lectura* (c. 1265–73), in *Super Epistolas S. Pauli Lectura*, vol. 1, edited by R. Cai, Turin and Rome: Marietti, 1953. Translated by F. R. Larcher, B. Mortensen, and D. Keating. Edited by J. Mortensen and E.

	Alarcón. Lander, WY: The Aquinas Institute for the Study of Sacred Doctrine, 2012.
In Ioan.	*Super Evangelium S. Ioannis Lectura* (1272). Marietti edition, 1952. ET: *Commentary on the Gospel of John*. Translated by Fabian Larcher and James A. Weisheipl. 3 vols. Washington, DC: Catholic University of America Press, 2010.
In Iob	*Expositio super Iob ad litteram* (1261–5). Leonine Edition, vol. 26, 1965. Translated by Brian Thomas Becket Mullady and the Aquinas Institute. Lander, WY (E-text, 2018). Available online at https://aquinas.cc/la/en/~Job
In Matt.	*Super Evangelium S. Matthaei Lectura* (1270). Marietti edition, 1951. ET: *Commentary on the Gospel of Matthew*. Edited by J. Mortensen and E. Alarcón. Translated by Jeremy Holmes and Beth Mortensen. Lander, WY: The Aquinas Institute for the Study of Sacred Doctrine, 2013.
In Metaph.	*In duodecim Libros Metaphysicorum Aristotelis Expositio* (c. 1272). Marietti edition, 1950. ET: *Commentary on Aristotle's Metaphysics*. Translated by John P. Rowan. Notre Dame, IN: Dumb Ox Books, 1995.
In Sent.	*Scriptum super libros Sententiarum* (1252–6). Parma edition, vols 6–7.
QD De anima	*Quaestiones Disputate de anima* (1266–7). Leonine edition, vol. 24, no. 1, 1996. ET: *The Soul: Disputed Questions on De Anima*. Translated by John Patrick Rowan. St. Louis: B. Herder, 1949.
Quodlibet	*Quaestiones de Quolibet* (c. 1252–6 and 1268–72). Leonine edition, vol. 25, nos. 1–2, 1996.
ScG	*Summa Contra Gentiles* (1260–5). Leonine edition, vols 13–15, 1918–30. Translated by Fathers of the English Dominican Province. London: Burns Oates & Washbourne, 1934.
ST	*Summa Theologiae* (1268–73). Leonine edition, vols 4–12, 1888–1906. Translated by Fathers of the English Dominican Province. London: Burns Oates & Washbourne, 1924.
Super De causis	*Super Librum De causis expositio* (1272). Parma edition, vol. 21. ET: *Commentary on the Book of Causes*. Translated by Charles R. Hess, Richard C. Taylor, and Vincent A. Guagliardo. Washington, DC: Catholic University of America Press, 1996.

Series Abbreviations

CCSL	*Corpus Christianorum Series Latina*
NICNT	*New International Commentary on the New Testament*
NPNF	*Nicene and Post-Nicene Fathers*
PG	*Patrologia Graeca*
PL	*Patrologia Latina*

INTRODUCTION

Modern historical consciousness has transformed academic thinking about theology and religion, and its significance and value cannot be overstated. And yet, it has also been a notable factor in the rise of religious fundamentalism.[1] When applied to religious traditions, critical history often imposes metaphysical assumptions that clash with fundamental elements of those traditions. As a result, many religious communities have rejected critical historiography in an effort to safeguard their traditions from its skepticism and naturalism. However, this need not be the case. Developing an approach that ameliorates these tendencies would both strengthen our grasp of history and better allow religious communities to engage receptively with critical historiography. Something similar stands behind the perennial enmity between historical biblical scholarship and theology. The two disciplines have not only approached Scripture with different aims and methods, but they have also held fundamentally different assumptions about reality. If, as I will claim, the antipathy between theology and history is not a clash between dogmatism and objectivity, but rather a conflict between theistic ontology and metaphysical naturalism, then this division could be eased through the development of a critical approach to history that assumes within its foundations a nonnaturalistic construal of reality. A key element of the conflicts between theology and historical criticism is ongoing disagreement about how those conflicts are to be characterized. It is not simply that each advances views that the other rejects, but that they do not agree on the standards by which a position might be advanced or refuted. As such, to discuss their ongoing conflict is unavoidably to participate in it. In doing so, I do not enter as a neutral party, and a key part of my claim in what follows is that it could not be otherwise.

In this book, I undertake a theological and philosophical exploration of the historical study of Jesus. I consider the philosophical conditions of the discipline in a modern academic context, the metaphysical constraints built into the methods employed, and the ways in which particular ideological aims in the modern period have impacted what can and cannot be said about Jesus from a historical perspective. The horizon concern of this study is the question of what counts as a historical perspective when it comes to Jesus and why. I argue that

---

1. See, e.g., Marsden, *Fundamentalism and American Culture*, 150.

classical Christology and historical Jesus scholarship should be characterized as rival traditions of historical enquiry. Establishing this thesis involves two primary tasks. The first is to show that the methods and conclusions of historical Jesus scholarship are impacted in nontrivial ways by implicit metaphysical assumptions that are neither neutral nor adequately defended. Therefore, it should not be treated as a value-neutral or scientific discipline whose function is to release us from the ideological strictures of "tradition" and reveal to us what really happened in the past. Historical Jesus scholarship, despite its great diversity, should instead be characterized as a tradition, with strict, if implicit, metaphysical and even doctrinal commitments that have a notable impact on what can and cannot be said about the past. Here I am using "tradition" in the sense employed by Alasdair MacIntyre:

> A tradition is an argument extended through time in which certain fundamental agreements are defined and redefined in terms of two kinds of conflict: those with critics and enemies external to the tradition who reject all or at least key parts of those fundamental agreements, and those internal, interpretative debates through which the meaning and rationale of the fundamental agreements come to be expressed and by whose progress a tradition is constituted.[2]

MacIntyre notes that "to appeal to tradition is to insist that we cannot adequately identify either our own commitments or those of others in the argumentative conflicts of the present except by situating them within those histories which made them what they have now become."[3] I take it that this is why narrating the history of historical Jesus scholarship plays such a prominent role in books on the historical Jesus. To say that historical Jesus scholarship is a tradition, in this sense, is also to say that the views it advances are not simply the "results" of a scientific method but are in part constructed by and received from and within a history of thought and argumentation, and that members of that tradition are inducted into modes of reasoning that include basic beliefs about reality that make sense in light of that history. In failing to recognize their tradition *as a tradition*, historical Jesus scholars are liable to be blinded to this fact. That certain kinds of views advanced by historical Jesus scholars exhibit great diversity is not surprising, given the centrality of internal conflict to this concept of tradition. To be part of a tradition in this sense is not to be homogeneous, but to share fundamental agreements about a common task such that the degree and type of ideological diversity will be constrained in important ways by the nature of the ongoing argument that constitutes the tradition. In what follows, I focus especially on one area of agreement that constitutes this tradition: a particular view about the nature of and limits to human knowledge and self-understanding.

---

2. MacIntyre, *Whose Justice? Which Rationality?*, 12.
3. Ibid., 13.

The second task is to establish that the classical Christological tradition, here represented by Thomas Aquinas (c. 1225–74), should be considered a legitimate tradition of historical enquiry. To do this, I show that Aquinas' Christology coherently upholds the historical and fully human existence of Jesus in a way that both vindicates and necessitates critical historical research, and I explore the ways in which his rival metaphysical claims impact the task of thinking about Jesus as a historical figure. By showing the theological criticisms of historical Jesus scholarship to be unjustified, I demonstrate that this Christological tradition need not adopt the metaphysical or theological views of historical Jesus scholarship in order to adapt and develop critical historical methods and undertake genuine historical research. There is much more scope for this tradition to employ critical historical methods than it has done thus far, and I hope that my argument will encourage and enable it to do so. This does not undermine its legitimacy as a tradition of historical enquiry, but rather points to its need to expand and develop the practices that constitute the ongoing enquiries and conversations of which it is constituted.

The critical perspective represented by this study might be summarized as follows. I will argue that the discipline of historical Jesus studies has, often unwittingly, served to establish an Ebionite Christology under the guise of critical history.[4] Of course, I am not the first to raise issues about this field of study. Criticisms of historical Jesus scholarship have been published regularly for decades.[5] In one way or another, each of these critics is an heir of Martin Kähler, who maintained that "the Jesus of the 'Life-of-Jesus movement' is merely a modern example of human creativity, and not an iota better than the notorious dogmatic Christ of Byzantine Christology."[6] He had little patience for either approach and, eschewing both critical history and conciliar Christology, he focused instead on the kerygmatic preaching of the risen Christ.[7] Despite the shortcomings of his

---

4. Ebionitism refers to the Christological tendency to reject the divine nature of Christ, which can issue in a purely human conception of Jesus or some form of adoptionism. In what follows, I use heresiological terms in a synchronic or ahistorical manner. It is important to recognize the difficulties surrounding historical appellations of heresy to particular groups of Christians. The terms Ebionitism, Arianism, adoptionism, docetism, monophysitism, Eutychianism, monothelitism, and Nestorianism are the widely accepted terms to refer to theological conceptions of Christ that do not cohere with conciliar orthodoxy, and their use should not necessarily be taken as a condemnation of the particular Christian individuals or communities historically associated with them.

5. E.g., Kähler, *The So-Called Historical Jesus and the Historic Biblical Christ*; Schweitzer, *Von Reimarus Zu Wrede* (1906). ET: *The Quest of the Historical Jesus*; Johnson, *The Real Jesus*; Adams, *The Reality of God and Historical Method*; Heringer, *Uniting History and Theology*; Rowlands, "The Metaphysics of Historical Jesus Research."

6. Kähler, *The So-Called Historical Jesus and the Historic Biblical Christ*.

7. For Kähler, the value of Jesus' life "lies in the church that has been going throughout the centuries, in the confessing word and life of the brothers, in one's own powerful faith" (ibid., 25–6).

constructive proposal, Kähler's critique is evocative, and its full force has yet to be worked out in sufficient detail. It is still underappreciated just how far the Jesus of modern historiography is the product of scholarly imagination, rather than simply an objective or scientific reconstruction of the past.[8] In particular, the metaphysical presuppositions that contemporary historiography has retained from its roots in nineteenth-century German historicism remain largely uninterrogated, and they play an outsized role in the conclusions of the discipline.[9]

Another way of describing historical Jesus scholarship is to say that it is an attempt to understand and explain Jesus within conceptual frameworks deliberately at odds with Christian theology: to tell a different story and provide an alternative interpretation of Jesus' life, identity, purpose, and significance.[10] Scholars have invested considerable rhetorical effort into connecting these aims with "history," which has done much to obscure the fact that Christian theology itself possesses a powerful set of resources for thinking about Jesus as a historical figure. As a result, many today are unaware that the Christian tradition is deeply interested in historical questions relating to Jesus' life and teaching, and that its theological frameworks are not, in themselves, antithetical to that task. Just because critical historians became hostile toward classical Christology (as they understood it), that does not mean that classical Christology is inimical to the task of critical history.[11]

The preponderance of what follows is not, however, deflationary. While critiques of Jesus scholarship abound, there has been considerably less constructive work done to open an alternative historiographical path forward. Theologians frequently reject critical historiography altogether, rather than attempting to resituate historical methodology within a broader theological or metaphysical framework. Meanwhile, Christian historians have often attempted to build a new theology out of the "results" of critical history, assuming that the shortcomings of the discipline arise from a lack of theological will, rather than fundamental methodological

---

8. I am using "historiography" to refer to the practice of writing about the past and the discourse it produces. I refer to methodological questions relating to historiography with the term "historical method" and deeper philosophical questions relating to the nature of the historical task with the term "philosophy of history."

9. See esp. Beiser, *The German Historicist Tradition*; Howard, *Religion and the Rise of Historicism*; Howard, *Protestant Theology and the Making of the Modern German University*; Zachhuber, *Theology as Science in Nineteenth-Century Germany*. In what follows I am not making a genealogical argument about the various direct and indirect philosophical influences on modern historicism. I am interested in the theological and metaphysical presuppositions that are reflexively deployed or tacitly assumed by contemporary historians. Thus, rather than providing a detailed diachronic study of the discipline, I provide a synchronic engagement with various historians on these issues.

10. See Wright, *Jesus and the Victory of God*, 17. Henceforth *JVG*.

11. Not only does the classical Christological tradition evidence a keen interest in history, the Christological principles themselves, adopted in a contemporary context, direct us toward, rather than away from, critical historical investigation.

problems. Wanting in all this is sustained reflection on the implications of a nonnaturalistic construal of reality for the historical task. Within this reflection, a further subset of questions arises: what are the implications of classical Christology for thinking about Jesus as a historical figure? What resources do we possess within the Christian tradition for illuminating the historical figure of Jesus, and what space does the doctrine of Christ leave—or, rather, open up—for Christians to engage with history? It is my contention that the classical Christological tradition contains the conceptual tools to expand the horizon of possibilities available to historical Jesus scholarship in a way that will augment their access to the historical figure of Jesus. Chalcedonian Christology should make us more interested in history, not less. At the same time, adopting historical methodology into a theistic metaphysical framework will have important implications for the nature and methods of the discipline.

Theological Interpretation

This project builds upon an ongoing conversation regarding theological interpretation of Scripture. In his book *Reading the Bible Theologically*, Darren Sarisky argues that "theological reading does not exist in contradistinction to a historically grounded approach to reading, but rather to one that is driven by metaphysical naturalism."[12] He demonstrates the impact of a theological construal of reality on the process of biblical interpretation, focusing on the reader, the text, and the process of interpretation and engaging questions of interpretation from the vantage of what he calls "theological ontology." Opposing any dualism between doctrine and history, he seeks to provide an account of doctrine as a description of reality that makes a difference for practices of interpretation. Sarisky's book is essential reading for anyone interested in theological interpretation of Scripture, and his hermeneutical arguments are sharp and compelling. One shortcoming of the work, however, is the way in which the "results" of historical criticism seem to emerge unscathed from the hermeneutical gauntlet that he constructs. If theological reading is opposed not to historical reading, but rather to metaphysical naturalism, then that must mean that a theological construal of reality should be able to deliver a historical reading driven instead by theological ontology. In what follows, I extend Sarisky's argument to consider how a nonnaturalistic construal of reality will impact not only a theological approach to Scripture that makes judicious use of historical criticism but also the process of historical criticism itself.

Seth Heringer has pointed out the value of such an approach. In his book, *Uniting History and Theology: A Theological Critique of the Historical Method*, he notes that "theological interpretation is normally done on Scripture, not history."[13]

---

12. Sarisky, *Reading the Bible Theologically*, 72.
13. This originated as his PhD dissertation from Fuller Theological Seminary in 2016, titled "Worlds Colliding: A Theological Critique of the Historical Method." Citations are from the dissertation. Quotation from "Worlds Colliding," 188.

He considers this to be a mistake that stems from the acceptance of a problematic historical method. Heringer outlines the ways in which historicism—stemming especially from Ernst Troeltsch and Leopold von Ranke—separated history and theology, and how this division was solidified in historical study of the New Testament.[14] He critiques the attempts of theologians such as Martin Kähler, Wolfhart Pannenberg, and N. T. Wright to overcome this division, and outlines how constructivist historical theorists such as Arthur Danto, Roland Barthes, Hayden White, and Frank Ankersmit have called this tradition of historiography into question.[15] "History," notes Heringer, "is the combination of events we live and the stories we tell about them."[16] Modern historical method assumes that both events and narratives exist outside the mind of the historian and determine how historiography should be written. Postmodern thinkers, however, insist that only events exist in the past, though they are significantly shaped by the mind, and that historical narratives are entirely constructed by historians. These latter thinkers have made a convincing case that the Rankean tradition of historicism fails in its foundation (the removal of the self in service of "objectivity"),[17] means (to relate the narrative of history "as it really was"), and end (the "Ideal Chronicle" with no biases or perspectives added).[18] Heringer suggests that, in spite of these damning criticisms, the Rankean approach remains prevalent in modern biblical studies "because ignoring these problems is easier than trying to overcome them."[19] He

---

14. Heringer also shows how the application of this method in biblical studies has largely followed a misreading of German historicism that "focuses only on its scientific and naturalistic aspects, to the detriment of its idealism and aesthetic concerns" (ibid., 244).

15.

> Arthur C. Danto aids the critique of the historical method by showing that even the perfect recitation of facts is not enough for a work to be history. Roland Barthes furthers the critique by unmasking the "reality effect" of the historical method and undermining its claim to be speaking directly about reality. Hayden White continues this challenge by looking at the tropes historians use to construct history. The precognitive understandings we use to figure the world, he argues, are more important than historical events. Frank Ankersmit changes White's discussion of narratives to one of representations. By doing so, he tries to awaken historians to the importance of experience in historical theory (ibid., 244).

16. Ibid., viii.

17. "Objectivity" is a term used to ameliorate the exercise of power that excludes those who do not share the beliefs, biases, and practices of those who determine what it is acceptable to believe in a given community. In an important sense, those seeking objective history are doing something similar to those seeking theological history, for both are making epistemological and ontological claims about the world. Each offers a vision that is incompatible with the other" (ibid., 189).

18. Ibid., 186.

19. Ibid.

urges Christian historians to abandon this method and follow theorists like White and Ankersmit who have revealed the subjective, constructed nature of history in a way that creates space for a distinctively Christian approach.

Heringer has ably demonstrated the metaphysical determinism of modern historicism, and the ways in which this historical method dogmatically militates against historical narratives that do not fit its preconceived notions about reality. Insofar as this is the case, modern historical method has failed as "a public space from which all historians can work together."[20] While I agree with Heringer's assessment on this score, I remain unconvinced that constructivism is the best path forward. These reader-response theories may open a promising space for "boldly Christian history," but they also remove the possibility that historic Christian texts can speak for themselves with any real authority.[21] Having extricated Christian historians from the metaphysical entailments of enlightenment historicism, these proposals trap them anew in the confines of relativism, putting them at odds with the core epistemic convictions of the Christian tradition. As we will see in Chapter 4, Aquinas' epistemic claims provide a stronger basis for understanding how historical reality presses against us from the outside. Furthermore, Thomas insists on the possibility of rational argumentation between these divergent metaphysical frameworks, offering hope for constructive dialogue about the philosophical conceptions that prove decisive for our understanding of the past.

Just before I completed this project, Jonathan Rowlands defended a PhD thesis at the University of Nottingham titled "The Metaphysics of Historical Jesus Research: An Argument for Increasing the Plurality of Metaphysical Frameworks within Historical Jesus Research."[22] Rowlands is sensitive to the impact of what he calls "secular metaphysics" on contemporary historiography, and he argues that "a genuine plurality of metaphysical frameworks for undertaking historiographical work is not only desirable, but encouraged by the ideals of academia itself."[23] I concur with this assessment in part, though I argue for it on rather different grounds. I would suggest that a mere plurality of frameworks is not the goal, certainly not at the level of individual scholars, but rather an expansion of disciplinary boundaries to make space for diverse traditions of historical enquiry. This is not so much about the personal preferences and beliefs we each bring with us to the historical task, but about the history of argumentative conflicts and basic assumptions that give substance to how the historical task is understood and pursued. The upshot of Rowlands' argument is that someone's historiography is secular if they do not let belief in the historicity of Jesus' resurrection explicitly drive their historical scholarship. Despite the lengthy exercise of definition, it seems that "metaphysics" quickly comes to mean "doctrine." Paradoxically, he criticizes the critical realism of Bernard Lonergan as if it were the source of these problems for historians like

20. Ibid., 18.
21. Ibid., 229.
22. Now published as *The Metaphysics of Historical Jesus Research*.
23. Rowlands, "Metaphysics of Historical Jesus," 26.

N. T. Wright, whereas it seems to me that it is in part the failure of Wright and others to understand Lonergan that leads to methodological shortcomings.[24] In what follows, I argue instead that metaphysical presuppositions should be argued for rationally, and their claim to influence historical method stands on different grounds from theology proper. A historian can be faulted for assuming that metaphysical naturalism is an objective stance from which to do history, but they cannot be faulted in the same way for refusing to place belief in Jesus' resurrection at the foundation of their method.[25]

Classical Christology

Historical Jesus scholars have frequently assumed that theologians are concerned with attaching supernatural predicates to the human person of Jesus in an attempt to paint him as a divine figure, thereby placing him safely out of reach of historical scholarship and insulating him from his first-century cultural setting. While there is no doubt that much mischief has been managed in the name of "Christology," and that some theologians have effectively dehistoricized Jesus in an attempt to universalize his significance for humanity,[26] the classical Christological tradition, grounded in the first seven ecumenical councils—Nicaea I (325), Constantinople I (381), Ephesus (431), Chalcedon (451), Constantinople II (553), Constantinople III (680–1), and Nicaea II (787)—has very different aims.[27] This ancient tradition was concerned to develop a theological vocabulary that would allow them to speak of the personal active presence of God within the historical human life of Jesus of Nazareth. The concern that runs through the center of this tradition is the need to

---

24. See Losch, "Wright's Version of Critical Realism," 101–14; Wilkins, *Before Truth*.

25. This is not to deny that there is an important complexity here, which different theologians will understand differently. For instance, I do not think that a historian can be faulted for letting their belief in the resurrection impact their historical method—as if a distinctly nonreligious stance is more "historical." Indeed, when theologians engage in historical reflection, they should assume this belief within their methods. But they should also allow for an open and genuine space for the work of historians who do not believe in the resurrection, without allowing their metaphysical naturalism to control the terms of the conversation. Kavin Rowe offers an evocative discussion of this issue in *One True Life*. This also has important interreligious implications, as nonnaturalistic historiography can be just as significant for Muslim and Jewish thought.

26. This tendency was widespread during the enlightenment, and we might think of the Jesus of Kant or Hegel as prominent examples.

27. I use the terms "classical Christology" and "Chalcedonian Christology" interchangeably to refer to this tradition. I do not intend by the use of these terms to criticize ancient non-Chalcedonian Christian traditions, but to distinguish this dominant strand of theological reflection from contemporary streams of thought that seek to depart anew from historic Christian approaches to Christology.

affirm the integrally finite historical human existence of Jesus and to find ways of speaking about his personal identity that attribute his words and actions wholly to God. The theological conundrum was to uphold the unity of the person of Christ in a way that establishes and perfects the integral difference of his humanity.[28] This is no easy task. As Rowan Williams writes:

> To speak of God's action in Jesus is to claim not merely that God brings about a particular historical result by means of natural agency—as a writer of Hebrew Scripture might claim is happening when King David defeats the Philistines—but that some result that is *not just another* episode in history is brought about through the historical doings of finite agency ... So when—as people who believe that the world has changed comprehensively because of him—we look for adequate language to tell the truth about Jesus, we shall need a model for the union of divine and human action in Christ that sees Christ as the historical and bodily *location* of unlimited active freedom, the place where God is active with an intensity that is nowhere else to be found.[29]

Williams finds vital resources for this theological task in the thought of Thomas Aquinas (1224–75), whose Christology he considers "a watershed in the doctrinal story."[30] While Williams refrains from touting Aquinas' approach as a perfect and timeless statement of the doctrine of Christ, he does suggest that it is "the point at which the broadest range of theoretical questions was brought into view and a robust and consistent vocabulary developed for integrating these questions. So often in this area of theology, later puzzles and apparent dead ends in doctrinal reflection can be transformed by a better understanding of what we discover that Aquinas has already discussed."[31] The breadth and consistency of Aquinas' approach make him an ideal interlocutor in this area.

---

28. Here I follow Riches and Grillmeier in seeing Chalcedon not as a developmental milestone in the church's theology or a compromise document seeking to reconcile conflicting opinions, as it is commonly understood in contemporary scholarship, but as a radical return to the biblical and Nicene affirmation of the "one Lord Jesus Christ" (1 Cor. 8:6). It is a reaffirmation, in the face of theological innovation, of the early confessions of the Christian faith.

> The dogma of Chalcedon must always be taken against the background of scripture and the whole patristic tradition ... Few councils have been so rooted in tradition as the Council of Chalcedon. The dogma of Chalcedon is ancient tradition in a formula corresponding to the needs of the hour. So we cannot say that the Chalcedonian Definition marks a great turning point in the Christological belief of the early church (Grillmeier, *Christ in Christian Tradition*, 550).

See Riches, *Ecce Homo*, 58–63, esp. 61n21.
29. Williams, *Christ the Heart of Creation*, 5.
30. Ibid., 7.
31. Ibid.

Beyond this, there are three elements in particular that make Aquinas well suited for this study. First, Aquinas is widely recognized as one of the most adept and nuanced philosophers in the Christian tradition, and his synthesis of metaphysics and theology remains a high point of Christian reflection on God and all things as they relate to God.[32] Because of the centrality of metaphysics in this study, Aquinas was a clear choice of dialogue partner. In addition, Aquinas' Aristotelian philosophical anthropology and cognitive psychology have gained significant scholarly attention in recent years, and they provide a robust alternative to contemporary approaches that, as we will see, cause significant problems for both Christology and historiography. Second, I consider Aquinas' Christology to represent the final flowering of the patristic Christological tradition.[33] He is rigorously faithful to the concerns and logic of the Christological councils, and, as the first Western scholastic theologian known to have quoted directly from the conciliar documents of Ephesus, Chalcedon, and Constantinople II and III, he was uniquely versed in the history of the patristic debates and the relevant texts that stand in the background of those conciliar decisions.[34] Unlike many theologians soon after his time and into our own, Aquinas did not abandon the patristic approach in an attempt to forge an alternative Christological paradigm. As a result, he provides us with an opportunity to engage critically with a fully formed Chalcedonian Christology and ask detailed questions about the implications of such an approach for thinking about Jesus as a historical figure. Finally, Aquinas offers what is arguably the most detailed and compelling treatment of the doctrine of Jesus' knowledge in the Christian tradition. In doing so, he provides important resources for connecting Christology directly to historiographical issues such as intention, motivation, and self understanding.

I am not concerned to establish Aquinas' approach as the only possible nonnaturalistic alternative or to argue that a Thomistic metaphysic is necessary in principle to uphold orthodox Christology. It is my hope to encourage historians and theologians from a variety of confessional and philosophical backgrounds to engage critically with metaphysical questions in relation to history, and one need not agree with Aquinas in detail to acknowledge the significance of the philosophical and theological questions raised herein. Nonetheless, it is my conviction that projects like this one are best done in conversation with specific traditions of theological reflection. I hope to show the value of Aquinas' thought in relation to these issues to commend him to those engaged in this discussion. I am under no illusion that by outlining what I see to be the reasons for the ongoing conflict between different traditions of reasoning about the historical Jesus, and

---

32. *ST* I.1.7.

33. As Andrew Louth puts it, "it makes a good deal of sense to see the original unity of the Patristic vision not collapsing with the rise of scholasticism, but finding there its final flowering. St. Thomas Aquinas and St. Bonaventure, in different ways, can be seen to bear witness to this. Such is the view of Henri de Lubac" (Louth, *Discerning the Mystery*, 6).

34. Riches, *Ecce Homo*, 16. See Barnes, *Christ's Two Wills in Scholastic Thought*, 113–17.

by contending for one point of view among them, I will be able to secure general agreement. My intention is rather to transform our disagreements into something more constructive.

As the title of this book implies, the primary focus is on the mental life of Christ. For many historical Jesus scholars, especially those of the so-called "third quest," questions of identity, intention, and motivation stand at the core of their project. The central aim is to reconstruct who Jesus thought he was, what he intended to accomplish through his actions, and what motivated him to undertake them. Therefore, knowledge is not one of various relevant issues that could equally have been chosen as the focus of this study, but the central guiding issue that determines the shape of the discipline more than any other. It is here, in particular, that the charge of naturalism is most focused. Darren Sarisky takes Benedict de Spinoza (1632–77) as an important example of a historically grounded approach to biblical interpretation that is driven by metaphysical naturalism. He writes that:

> Naturalism refers to an ontology in which what exists is a single substance. As Jonathan Israel explains, this entails "conflating body and mind into one, reducing God and nature to the same thing, excluding all miracles and spirits separate from bodies, and invoking reason as the sole guide in human life, jettisoning tradition."[35]

Spinoza was aware of the close connection between metaphysics and biblical interpretation, and he explicitly advanced a naturalistic metaphysic for the purpose of transforming biblical scholarship into an empirical undertaking that serves political ends.[36] Spinoza's achievement laid the foundations for higher biblical criticism which, as we will see, has retained many of the same naturalistic assumptions. And yet, as Sarisky argues, "naturalism is one way to underline the value of historical consciousness, but it is by no means the only way."[37] My primary concern is to show that *when it comes to issues of interiority and knowledge, naturalistic assumptions have been retained by historical Jesus scholars of otherwise diverse theological and philosophical persuasion.* In arguing this, I am not suggesting that the personal beliefs of these scholars are naturalistic, nor am I claiming that they hold to a coherent or explicit naturalistic metaphysic that can

---

35. Sarisky, *Reading the Bible Theologically*, 163. Quoting Israel, *A Revolution of the Mind*, 242, 245.

36. For further discussion, see also Boersma, *Scripture as Real Presence*, 7–9. Richard H. Popkin maintains that this is Spinoza's main contribution to history ("Spinoza and Bible Scholarship," 404).

37. Sarisky, *Reading the Bible Theologically*, 171. In what follows, I am not concerned to defeat naturalism, but to show that it is not necessary to do genuine history, and that it is not neutral, which means that historians are not justified in simply assuming it as part of their method.

be reconstructed in detail.[38] For this reason, naturalism is an intentionally broad concept in this book, just as it is in contemporary philosophy more broadly.[39] It does not look the same for every historian, and it is not necessarily to be found intact as a comprehensive framework. Rather, it shows up as an assortment of assumptions in various places with more or less consistency.[40]

It is no surprise that the mind of Christ is a similarly prominent topic within the discipline of theology. However, in the twentieth century, many theologians abandoned the doctrine of two natures to focus on Jesus' consciousness *instead of* ontology.[41] Often, they were driven to do so as a result of the supposed results of historical Jesus scholarship.[42] I am critical of this approach, and much of what follows is an argument for the reordering of these emphases into an integrated doctrinal whole. This is for two reasons. First, as Thomas Joseph White comments, "in the very structure of personal being, ontology is more fundamental than consciousness. Self-awareness is only one dimension of human being, and ultimately needs to be explained in terms of the latter."[43] As we will see in Chapter 3, the filial consciousness of Jesus must be grounded in the ontology

---

38. Philosophers frequently distinguish between metaphysical naturalism—the denial of the existence of supernatural entities—and methodological naturalism—the refusal to appeal to supernatural entities to explain the phenomena in question. This is useful insofar as it illustrates the possibility of employing naturalistic methods without holding naturalistic beliefs, and it is the latter ("methodological naturalism") that is in view in what follows. It is potentially misleading, however, given that methodological naturalism is still a metaphysical issue. See, e.g., Draper, "God, Science, and Naturalism," 272–303.

39. "The term "naturalism" has no very precise meaning in contemporary philosophy. Its current usage derives from debates in America in the first half of the last century. These philosophers aimed to ally philosophy more closely with science. They urged that reality is exhausted by nature, containing nothing "supernatural," and that the scientific method should be used to investigate all areas of reality, including the "human spirit" (Papineau, "Naturalism"). See also Kim, "The American Origins of Philosophical Naturalism," 83–98.

40. Unearthing the implicit metaphysics of historical Jesus scholarship is a complex task, and it would be a mistake to pin it down with undue precision. I am interested in the fact that, despite endless differences, these scholars share the same basic naturalistic assumptions when it comes to knowledge and intentionality, and that this significantly impacts the historical task. In what follows, I also show how various nonnaturalistic metaphysical assumptions nonetheless undermine these historians' understanding of classical Christology. Constructively, I show how explicit, coherent reflection on metaphysics matters for the discipline of history, particularly when Jesus is in view.

41. This is due in part to Karl Rahner's essay "Dogmatic Reflections on the Knowledge and Self-Consciousness of Christ," 193–215. For a historical overview see Moloney, *The Knowledge of Christ*.

42. See, e.g., Gutwenger, "The Problem of Christ's Knowledge," 91–105; Hanson, "Two Consciousnesses," 471–83.

43. White, *The Incarnate Lord*, 237.

of the hypostatic union because of the relationship between consciousness and substantial being. Second, Christological approaches grounded in consciousness create myriad problems for historical reconstruction, and I will argue that they are to blame for some of the antagonism between theology and history in the contemporary academy. An ontological approach to Christology protects both the unity of Christ's personhood and the integrity of his humanity in a way that provides the requisite grounds for historical inquiry. When ordered rightly, the consciousness and ontology of Christ are "mutually self-interpreting"—Christ's transcendent identity is manifest in his consciousness, which is grounded in his ontological being.[44] In this way, Aquinas' approach to Jesus' knowledge is shown to be a powerful outworking of the principles of Jesus' identity, brought into the sphere of knowledge and intentionality, rather than vice versa.[45] This, in turn, further highlights the relevance of metaphysics for historical questions of interiority.

From a theological perspective, it is my contention that theology needs historical research, but it needs a method of historiography not beholden to metaphysical naturalism. The incarnational claims at the heart of the Christian faith are an affirmation of history as much as physicality. God took on flesh not only in space but also in time, and Christian theology should reflect this. Indeed, as I will argue, historical research into the life of Jesus plays a vital role in Christology, broadly speaking. Understanding Jesus requires a nuanced understanding of first-century (Hellenistic) Judaism, alongside the social, political, religious, and economic realities of the broader Greco-Roman world of the time. Without attempting to be exhaustive, we might note that this research unearths points of reference for understanding Jesus' teachings, or for how he and his followers might have been perceived by the political and religious leaders of the time. It has already contributed greatly to overcoming the latent anti-Judaism within various forms of Christian thought.[46] Paying close historical attention to the first century, to the gospels and other relevant historical texts, and to the early development of Christianity, as well as the continuity and discontinuity between these, is a central task for Christian theology. However, that is not the same thing as giving the metaphysical presuppositions of modern historicism free rein to redefine Christian doctrine.

At the same time, academic historical study of Jesus should make space for rival traditions of historical enquiry to reflect a genuine diversity of metaphysical perspectives. As an academic discipline, it is not surprising or inherently problematic that historical Jesus studies often stands in tension with Christian

---

44. Ibid., 236–7.

45. I have avoided rehashing debates with a variety of alternative theological approaches to Jesus' knowledge, which have already been engaged in detail by scholars such as Simon Gaine and Thomas Joseph White.

46. As an example of a Thomist theologian engaging this task, see Levering, *Engaging the Doctrine of Israel*.

theology, but this relationship need not be entirely antagonistic. By recognizing that historical research stemming from a theistic metaphysic is no less "objective" than one stemming from naturalism, the discipline can become more rigorously critical by accounting for its own perspective to a greater degree. As MacIntyre writes, "Generally only when traditions either fail and disintegrate or are challenged do their adherents become aware of them as traditions and begin to theorize about them."[47] By characterizing historical Jesus scholarship as a tradition of historical enquiry, my hope is that historical Jesus scholars will take up the task of exploring, developing, and critiquing the metaphysical foundations of their own tradition so that they can better contend for its perspective against rival traditions, or else recognize it to be incoherent and abandon it for some alternative.

Argument in Outline

To unpack these claims, I will advance arguments on two levels: metaphysics and theology. On the level of metaphysics, I am concerned with (a) the range of possibilities when it comes to the nature of human thought and intention, and this has to do with philosophical anthropology, cognitive theory, and philosophical realism; (b) the frameworks for making sense of human motivation, focusing on ethical concepts of desire and the good, as well as the role of vices like avarice in shaping modern understandings of universal human motivations; and (c) the way that metaphysical presuppositions (such as competitive accounts of the finite/infinite or psychological accounts of personhood) undermine historical Jesus scholars' understanding of theology. On a metaphysical level, Aquinas' participatory metaphysic and philosophical anthropology expand the range of possibilities open to the historian and provide a basis for a more accurate interpretation of classical Christology. The main work of these arguments happens in Chapters 2 and 4.

On the level of theology, I make four interrelated arguments: (a) historical Jesus scholars frequently misunderstand (or else caricature) Christology and one of the most effective ways of responding to their criticisms is by correcting their misapprehensions and misrepresentations; (b) non-Chalcedonian Christologies "from below" are often assumed to be better for historical study, but are actually worse; (c) Chalcedon, often assumed to make historiography impossible, is actually fully compatible with historical study of Jesus; and (d) a metaphysically informed Christology possesses the tools to provide a more nuanced and faithful conception of Christ's knowledge, which would illuminate, rather than obscure, the historical figure of Jesus of Nazareth. The main work of these arguments happens in Chapters 3, 6, 7, and 8.

The argument unfolds as follows. In Part I, I argue that the quests for the historical Jesus have largely operated with an understanding of history hindered by a severely constricted range of divine and human possibilities. By outlining

---

47. MacIntyre, *Whose Justice? Which Rationality?*, 8.

human "self-understanding" as a historiographical question, I emphasize the determinative role played by the historian's assumptions about the range of possibility available to the processes of human thought. Delineating three concerns that historians tend to connect to "docetism," I explicate the implicit metaphysical assumptions that underlie their grasp of what is at stake theologically, comparing these with trends in modern theological reflection.

Having outlined certain metaphysical presuppositions operative in historical Jesus scholarship, I then turn to explore the participatory metaphysics of Thomas Aquinas and the doctrine of the Incarnation. In Chapter 2, I emphasize the centrality of noncompetition to participatory accounts of being and unpack the ontological and semantic connection between participation and analogy. For Thomas, God is being itself, utterly simple and transcendent in a way that does not jeopardize his active presence within creation.[48] Creatures are qualitatively different from God, existing by participation in him, which means they cannot relate to God in a competitive or mutually exclusive fashion. In Chapter 3, I consider how a Chalcedonian Christology, understood in light of participatory metaphysics, maintains the unity of Christ's personhood and the properly finite reality of his human nature such that Jesus can be considered the subject of historical investigation, and I argue that Aquinas' Christology in particular offers resources to augment our access to the historical figure of Jesus. This includes a critical discussion of philosophical concepts of personhood and their bearing on the oneness of Christ, a consideration of accidental forms of union as they are employed in various Christologies "from below," and a Thomistic approach to "Spirit Christology" that holds together ontological and narrative depictions of Jesus' identity.

In Part II, the focus of our attention turns to concepts of knowledge and their role in historical and theological understandings of Jesus. In Chapter 4 I outline Aquinas' understanding of the powers and ways of knowing proper to God, angels, and humans. In Chapter 5 I consider the patristic background of the doctrine of Jesus' knowledge and the Fathers' interpretations of Mk 13:32. In Chapter 6 I outline Aquinas' unique argument for Jesus' acquired or empiric knowledge and how this connects with Jesus' priestly office. In Chapter 7, I discuss the nature of prophetic knowledge, its role in Jesus' prophetic office, and some of the reasons why it might not be sufficient to account for some of the things Jesus is presented as knowing in the gospels. Finally, in Chapter 8, I discuss Aquinas' argument that Jesus possessed the beatific vision, emphasizing the role of this vision in upholding the unity of his personhood. I also suggest a connection between the genre/worldview of "Apocalyptic" and the theological concept of the beatific vision, noting how Aquinas' argument on this score helps to fill out our understanding of Jesus' messianic office as presented in the Gospels.

---

48. In following the tradition of using masculine pronouns of God, I do not mean to imply that God is male. For an insightful discussion of the gendered imagery used to speak of God, see Soskice, *The Kindness of God*.

In this way, I argue that conceptions of the nature of and limits to human thought and intention are inevitably determinative of historical judgments regarding Jesus' self-understanding, which are themselves central to historical reconstruction. If history is about the events we live and the stories we tell about them, then we embed within our reconstruction of the past our fundamental beliefs about the nature of human thought and intention: about what is possible in a human life, and what is plausible about the lives of those in question. The simple assertion that Jesus was fully human does nothing to establish that his knowledge must have been limited to those ways of knowing assumed within post-enlightenment naturalistic historiography. There is nothing "docetic" or ahistorical about attributing to Jesus prophetic knowledge or an apocalyptic vision of God. Rather, these forms of knowing clash with the assumptions of metaphysical naturalism. Normative philosophical and theological assumptions create a rigid hermeneutical horizon for Jesus scholars' engagement with the past. By interrogating and challenging these assumptions, the scope of the discipline can be expanded to include approaches to Jesus that are genuinely historical, but not naturalistic.

Part I

CONCEPTS OF BEING

Traditional, orthodox christologies have assumed that Jesus was fully aware of his own godhead and spoke accordingly, whereas modern criticism has, in the judgment of many of us, exterminated this possibility.

—Dale Allison Jr.[1]

---

1. Allison Jr., *The Historical Christ and the Theological Jesus*, 89.

Chapter 1

THE HISTORICAL JESUS

The "quests" for the historical Jesus have largely operated with an understanding of history hindered by a severely constricted range of divine and human possibilities. While this assessment will no doubt prove controversial to some, there are many—including members of the quests themselves—who will recognize it to be true.[1] This evaluation is not limited to those historians of the so-called "old quest" whom Schweitzer so convincingly showed to have remade Jesus in their own image.[2] Rather, it is my contention that this restricted sphere of possibilities remains intact among much Jesus scholarship today, and that it is detrimental to the historical task. One of the areas where this scotoma is most acutely manifest is the question of Jesus' self-understanding.

Among the hallmarks of historical criticism is the methodological necessity to inquire after intention and motivation in order to illuminate the self-understanding of a historical individual. This is what the philosopher of history R. G. Collingwood (1889–1943) called the "inside" of history, and it is a vital piece of the historical task.[3] If history is to be more than a list of dates or "external" facts about the past, then we must inquire into the *meaning* of the actions of historical subjects, which requires the investigation of both the outside and the inside of events. History is not a simple chain of cause and effect, nor is the study of history about determining general formulas or natural laws that govern the flow of events through time. This is because, as Collingwood says, historical processes "are not processes of mere events but processes of actions, which have an inner

---

1. See arguments to this effect in, e.g., Meyer, *The Aims of Jesus*, 58; Evans, "Methodological Naturalism in Historical Biblical Scholarship," 180–205; Schillebeeckx, *Jesus*, 64–76; Kähler, *So-Called Historical Jesus*; Hays, "Knowing Jesus," 41–61; Wright, *JVG*, 18; Adams, *The Reality of God and Historical Method*; Anderson, *The Fourth Gospel and the Quest for Jesus*, 177–9; Zahrnt, *The Historical Jesus*, 48.

2. Schweitzer, *Quest*, 4.

3. Collingwood, *The Idea of History*, 213. This only plays a notable role in historical Jesus studies for those scholars who believe the sources are such that a significant amount can be known about Jesus, such as R. A. Horsley, M. Borg, H. Boers, J. Charlesworth, M. de Jonge, R. Leivestad, B. Meyer, B. Witherington, N. T. Wright, and B. Pitre.

side, consisting of processes of thought."[4] If, therefore, "all history is the history of thought," then the range of potential historical interpretations will be determined in part by what the historian considers to be the horizon of possibility with regard to processes of human thought.[5]

When this question is applied to Jesus, it provides a particularly clear lens into the range of divine and human possibilities presupposed by the historian. Herman Samuel Reimarus (1694–1786) began his inquiry by asking this question of Jesus— "What sort of purpose did Jesus himself see in his teaching and deeds?"—and over the course of two centuries many historical Jesus scholars have followed suit. My purpose in this chapter is to illuminate the background and methodological context of the question of Jesus' self-understanding and show the prevalence of this issue in contemporary historical Jesus scholarship that calls for philosophical and dogmatic analysis. This discussion will lead us into theological territory in the final section, considering how the concept of "Docetism" is understood and used by historical Jesus scholars, along with the question of what it means to affirm Jesus as fully human.

A Brief History of Historical Jesus Scholarship

Given the immense scope of the discipline of historical Jesus studies, it is necessary at the outset to place our conversation within the history of the "quests." Standard histories of modern Jesus studies typically divide the discipline into four distinct periods. The "old quest" is said to have begun in 1778 with the posthumous publication of H. S. Reimarus' notorious "Wolfenbüttel Fragments," and it included notable works by D. F. Strauss, E. Renan, H. J. Holtzmann, and J. Weiss.[6] The "old quest" ended in 1901 with the simultaneous appearance of William Wrede's (1859–1907) *Das Messiasgeheimnis in den Evangelein* and Albert Schweitzer's *Das Messianitäts- und Leidensgeheimnis*.[7] Wrede and Schweitzer offered two alternative approaches to Jesus scholarship: Wrede proposed thoroughgoing skepticism, which assumes the essential unreliability of the gospels and emphasizes literary criticism, while Schweitzer opted for thoroughgoing eschatology, wherein

---

4. Ibid., 215.

5. Ibid. Collingwood has long been a key resource on the philosophy of history for historical Jesus scholars and his insights can be seen at work both implicitly and explicitly in the work of numerous members of both the new quest and the third quest. See Merkley, "New Quests for Old: One Historian's Observations on a Bad Bargain," 203–18; Meyer, *Critical Realism and the New Testament*, 148.

6. Reimarus, *Von Dem Zwecke Jesu Und Seiner Jünger*. ET: *Reimarus: Fragments*.

7. Wrede, *Das Messiasgeheimnis in den Evangelein* (1901). ET: *The Messianic Secret*; Schweitzer, *The Mystery of the Kingdom of God*.

Jesus is conceived along apocalyptic lines in an attempt to understand him as he is presented in the gospels.[8]

Despite the arrival of two proposals for renewed inquiry at the outset of the twentieth century, the subsequent fifty years are generally considered a period of "no quest." The reasons for this, it is often said, are threefold: Martin Kähler's insightful critique of the *historisch* enterprise (1896),[9] Albert Schweitzer's demolition of the portraits of the "old quest" in *Von Reimarus zu Wrede*,[10] and the theological criticisms of Karl Barth and Rudolf Bultmann.[11] Despite being an obvious misnomer,[12] the term "no quest" highlights the temporary attenuation of German interest and the fact that the enduring relevance of the work of this period is not widely endorsed.[13] One of the hallmarks of the "no quest" era is the number of books questioning whether Jesus had even existed.[14] In 1953, the "new quest" was inaugurated with Ernst Käsemann's programmatic address to a gathering of Bultmann's students.[15] The "new quest" was conceived in part as a necessary corrective to modern Docetism, and it tended to follow in Wrede's footsteps methodologically.[16] Notable members of the "new quest" include G. Bornkamm, J. Jeremias, E. Schillebeeckx, and the so-called "Jesus Seminar." A little over a

---

8. The terms "thoroughgoing skepticism" and "thoroughgoing eschatology" are the ones Schweitzer used to characterize his and Wrede's alternative approaches (*Quest*, 328).

9. "I regard the entire Life-of-Jesus movement as a blind alley" (Kähler, *So-Called Historical Jesus*, 46). In 1953 Käsemann noted the enduring need to reckon with Kähler's critique, "which still, after sixty years, is hardly dated and, in spite of many attacks and many possible reservations, has never really been refuted" (Käsemann, "The Problem of the Historical Jesus," 15–47, at 16).

10. "But it was not only each epoch that found its reflection in Jesus; each individual created Him in accordance with his own character" (Schweitzer, *Quest*, 4).

11. Bultmann, *Jesus and the Word*, 14.

12. Walter Weaver has devoted nearly four hundred pages to outlining serious contributions to historical Jesus studies during this period (*The Historical Jesus in the Twentieth Century*). See bibliography for this period in Evans, *Life of Jesus Research*, 19–26.

13. See Wright, *JVG*, 22–3. Dale Allison maintains that there was sufficient work done between 1906 and 1953 for us to view historical Jesus studies as a continuous venture since its inception ("The Secularizing of the Historical Jesus," 135–51).

14. See Weaver, *Historical Jesus*, 49–62. Maurice Casey rejects the term "no quest" and highlights the anti-Semitic cast of much work in this period. See his section titled "The Nazi Period" in *Jesus of Nazareth: An Independent Historian's Account of His Life and Teaching*, 4–8.

15. "It is one of the marks of the upheaval in German work on the New Testament in this last generation that the old question about the Jesus of history has receded rather noticeably into the background" (Käsemann, "Problem of the Historical Jesus," 15).

16. "We also cannot do away with the identity between the exalted and the earthly Lord without falling into docetism and depriving ourselves of the possibility of drawing a line between the Easter faith of the community and myth" (ibid., 34).

decade later the "third quest" emerged as a movement distinct from the "new quest"—partially due to its likeness to Schweitzer—and was given its name by N. T. Wright in the 1980s.[17]

Histories of the "quests" abound.[18] Despite the heuristic value of the "old quest, no quest, new quest, third quest" narrative, many have noted that it often proves simplistic or misleading. Those who champion the enduring relevance and complexity of nineteenth-century Jesus scholarship object to the chronological snobbery and homogeneity implied by the term "old quest." Further, although scholars like Wright conceive of the difference between the "new quest" and the "third quest" along primarily methodological lines, the nomenclature inaccurately implies a succession or even supersession.[19] It also fails to account for a significant number of scholars who do not fit neatly into either group.[20] The overall impression of linear progress is possibly the most misleading element, for so much of the research has proven repetitive and cyclical.[21] Despite these shortcomings, these designations have become

---

17. Neill and Wright, *The Interpretation of the New Testament 1861–1986*, 379. Cf. Wright, "Doing Justice to Jesus: A Response to J. D. Crossan," 345. Note that the "third quest" is thus the *fourth* stage of the quests. According to some, members of the "third quest" include, e.g., B. F. Meyer, A. E. Harvey, E. P. Sanders, N. T. Wright, B. Chilton, R. Horsley, and R. Theissen. Elisabeth Schüssler Fiorenza is typically considered part of the "third quest" though she offers significant criticisms of its dominant methodological approaches. See esp. *Jesus and the Politics of Interpretation* and discussion of her work in Walters, "Elisabeth Schüssler Fiorenza and the Quest for the Historical Jesus," 468–74.

18. In addition to those noted above, see, e.g., Borg, *Jesus in Contemporary Scholarship*; Brown, "Historical Jesus, Quest Of," 337; Bond, *The Historical Jesus: A Guide for the Perplexed*, 7–36; Hagner, "An Analysis of Recent 'Historical Jesus' Studies"; Luke Timothy Johnson offers a survey that is highly critical of the entire enterprise in *The Real Jesus*; Clive Marsh offers a ninefold division of the quests in "Quests of the Historical Jesus in New Historicist Perspective"; Paget, "Quests for the Historical Jesus"; Powell, *Jesus as a Figure in History*. The classic history of the "old quest" is that of Schweitzer, *The Quest of the Historical Jesus*. Simpson, *Recent Research on the Historical Jesus*; Tatum, *In Quest of Jesus*; Telford, "Major Trends and Interpretive Issues in the Study of Jesus"; Theissen and Merz offer a thorough treatment of the relevant issues in *The Historical Jesus*; Witherington III, *The Jesus Quest*; Wright, *JVG*, 3–125; Wright, "Jesus, Quest for the Historical," 796–802. For detailed bibliography see Evans, *Life of Jesus Research*.

19. See Crossan, "Straining Gnats, Swallowing Camels: A Review of *Who Was Jesus?* By N.T. Wright." For this reason, there are many who simply refer to all contemporary Jesus scholarship as the "third quest." E.g., Witherington, *The Jesus Quest*, passim.

20. Wright, for example, notes that Géza Vermes, Marcus Borg, J. D. Crossan, and Richard Horsley all defy this categorization (*JVG*, 83). Even the so-called "Jesus Seminar" is put in different groups by different scholars. Compare Wright, *JVG*, 30, with Meier, "The Present State of the 'Third Quest' for the Historical Jesus: Loss and Gain," 459.

21. See Paget, "Quests," 149.

somewhat standard and remain the simplest terminology for discussing historical Jesus studies in broad terms.

Despite vigorous methodological debates among contemporary scholars, deeper discussions of hermeneutics and the philosophy of history are markedly rare in the literature.[22] Historical Jesus scholars tend to conceive of their differences according to issues such as form-critical criteria of authenticity or divergent conceptions of Second-Temple Jewish apocalypticism.[23] And yet, it is evident that one of the most fruitful methods of delineating the quests would be according to their diverse philosophical and hermeneutical positions, which inevitably influence the historiographical outcome.[24] It was something like this recognition that made Schweitzer's book, *Von Reimarus zu Wrede*, so formidable and, despite being explored fruitfully by a few others, it has not always been a primary category for the historiography of the quests.

Jesus' Intentions and Motivations

If philosophy of history and hermeneutics have been underdiscussed in the literature, one area that has tended to receive priority, both in histories of the "quests" and in the historiographical methods of the historical Jesus scholars, is the question of Jesus' own understanding of his identity and purpose.[25] G. E. Lessing's (1729–81) publication of the *Fragmente eines Ungenannten* may not have been quite the epoch-making act that Schweitzer made it out to be, but in the seventh fragment, entitled *Von dem Zwecke Jesu und seiner Jünger*, Reimarus

---

22. For books that include this level of discussion see: Adams, *The Reality of God and Historical Method*; Childs, *The Myth of the Historical Jesus and the Evolution of Consciousness*; Denton Jr., *Historiography and Hermeneutics in Jesus Studies*; Meyer, *Critical Realism and the New Testament*; Stewart, *The Quest of the Hermeneutical Jesus*. Wright notes that "the same cultural presuppositions which have shaped Enlightenment thought as a whole have also shaped the practice of history itself, and with it the historical study of Jesus" (*History and Eschatology*, 55). His Gifford Lectures helpfully discuss, largely at a cultural level, some of the issues under discussion in this thesis. And yet, he still refrains from dealing in detail with the actual metaphysical questions that I argue are relevant to the task at hand.

23. See bibliography for "criteria of authenticity" in Evans, *Jesus Research*, 127–47. For discussions of "Apocalyptic" see esp. Collins, *The Apocalyptic Imagination*; Wright, *The New Testament and the People of God*, 280–99 [henceforth *NTPG*]; Crossan, "What Victory? What God? A Review Debate with N. T. Wright on Jesus and the Victory of God," 352–3.

24. "It can make a difference that Reimarus wrote with certain Enlightenment presuppositions; that Strauss was a Hegelian; that Harnack was a liberal Protestant; that Schweitzer had read Nietzsche …; and that members of the Jesus Seminar operate in a country where Christian fundamentalism of an apocalyptic colour is so influential" (Paget, "Quests," 149).

25. See *NTPG*, 110–11.

managed to raise certain questions so forcefully that they remain alive and well today.[26] Assuming the essential reliability of the accounts of Jesus' *teaching* in the four gospels ("the integrity of their reports is not to be doubted"), but skeptical of everything else, Reimarus set out to reconstruct Jesus' true intentions.[27] For Reimarus, Jesus was a political revolutionary intent on building up "a worldly kingdom" who became increasingly radicalized and reckoned too confidently on the approval of the crowds who then abandoned him to his death.[28] Jesus' final words on the cross expressed his disillusionment with the God who had failed him. After his death, Jesus' disciples (with motives "aimed at worldly wealth and power") engineered the narratives of his resurrection and promise to return to establish the Messianic kingdom.[29] In so doing, they infused Jesus' death with salvific and religious significance.[30]

Reimarus exhibited a preference for sayings material that, however uncritical, bears some similarity to Wrede's skepticism and to the form-critical approaches of the "new quest."[31] The rejection of Jesus' divine self-understanding is an a priori in Reimarus' project. He began with the assumption that Jesus did not possess a divine identity and designed his investigation to generate an alternative explanation. Both forms of skepticism would spawn parallel, though often overlapping, approaches: on the one hand, skepticism with regard to the authenticity of the gospel materials would continue to grow, leading first to a rejection of John,[32] and eventually to a mistrust of all four gospels following Strauss' concept of mythologization[33] and Wrede's critique of Mark.[34] This trajectory, often associated most with Bultmann, redirected a significant portion of historical Jesus studies away from the study of Jesus himself to focus on the literary forms of the Gospels and the history of the

---

26. Schweitzer hailed it as "one of the greatest events in the history of criticism" (Schweitzer, *Quest*, 15). However, see discussion highlighting Reimarus' indebtedness to Spinoza and English Deism in Brown, *Jesus in European Protestant Thought*, 1–55, esp. 50–5.

27. Reimarus, *Fragments*, §I.3, p. 65.

28. Ibid., §II.8, pp. 148, 150.

29. Ibid., §II.53; pp. 242–3.

30. "In a few days they alter their entire doctrine and make of Jesus a suffering savior for all mankind; then they change their facts accordingly" (ibid., §I.33, p. 134).

31. "Uncritical" because, although Reimarus shows a preference for certain material, his judgments are not based on any explicit criteria of authenticity. See him wrestling with a version of the criterion of dissimilarity at the beginning of Part II (§II.1, p. 135).

32. This process began in earnest with D. F. Strauss and became an essentially unassailable position through the work of F. C. Baur. See Schweitzer, *Quest*, 87.

33. Strauss understood the gospels to be the result of a (partly unconscious) process of mythologization through which genuine religious convictions became clothed with historical narratives. See Strauss, *Das Leben Jesu, kritisch bearbeitet*; ET: *The Life of Jesus Critically Examined*.

34. Wrede, *Messianic Secret*.

traditions that had supposedly fabricated the gospel narratives.[35] On the other hand, some continued to assume certain elements of historicity in the gospels and, following Reimarus' a priori rejection of Jesus' divine self-understanding, sought to develop alternative explanations for how Jesus understood his identity and purpose.

What Collingwood calls the "inside" of history played a substantial role in historiography long before he elucidated its explicit methodological function. In historical Jesus studies it was framed primarily in terms of the origin of the Christological beliefs of the early church and focused on the "titles" that Jesus is reported to have used of himself: especially "Messiah," "Son of God," and "Son of Man."[36] Although many in the "old quest" insisted that Jesus saw himself as the Messiah (in a purely "political" sense), much historical Jesus scholarship now assumes there is no reliable evidence to confirm that Jesus possessed a messianic self-understanding.[37] Closely related to this is the sense that Jesus did not attribute any redemptive significance to his own death.[38] The same goes for "Son of God": Reimarus maintained that for Jesus this simply meant "beloved of God," but many now reject the possibility that Jesus referred to himself in this way.[39] Of the three, the title "Son of Man" has fared the best in terms of its assumed historicity, while eliciting the least agreement as to its origin and meaning.[40] In the end, even

---

35. N. T. Wright maintains that "much of the impetus for form-critical and redaction-critical study came from the presupposition that this or that piece of synoptic material about Jesus *could not* be historical; in other words, that *an historical hypothesis about Jesus could already be presupposed* which demanded a further tradition-historical hypothesis to explain the evidence" (*JVG*, 87).

36. In other words, did the early Christians' belief in the divinity of Christ derive from Jesus' own words and actions, or was it something that they developed after his death? The question of self-understanding is a way of examining the continuity between Jesus and Second-Temple Judaism on the one hand, and between Jesus and the rise of the early church on the other. Meyer maintains that "thematic Christology either did or did not originate earlier than Easter. Between these contradictory alternatives there can be no middle ground or third position" (Meyer, *Critical Realism*, 159).

37. In response to this state of scholarship Martin Hengel argued that "the unmessianic Jesus has almost become a dogma among many New Testament scholars" (Hengel, *Studies in Early Christology*, 16). See discussion in Pitre, *Jesus and the Last Supper*, 9–14. Some recent exceptions to this include Allison Jr., *Constructing Jesus*, 221ff; Bauer, "Son of David," 166–9; Bird, *Are You the One Who Is to Come?*; Meyer, *The Aims of Jesus*, 178–80.

38. See discussion in McKnight, *Jesus and His Death*, 47–75; Balla, "What Did Jesus Think about His Approaching Death?," 239–58; Howard, "Did Jesus Speak about His Own Death?," 515–27.

39. Reimarus, *Fragments*, §I.10–13, pp. 76–88.

40. Boring describes research in this area as "a veritable mine field" (Boring, *Sayings of the Risen Jesus*, 239). Evans lists over forty books and articles published in the past fifty years written specifically about Jesus' usage of, and the meaning of, "son of man" (*Life of Jesus Research*, 195–210). See discussion in Burkett, *The Son of Man Debate*.

among those who find in favor of Jesus using these titles of himself, many agree with Sanders' sense that they tell us little about what Jesus thought of his identity and mission because "there were no hard definitions of 'Messiah,' 'Son of God,' or 'Son of Man' in the Judaism of Jesus' day."[41]

Although there is a diversity of opinion regarding Jesus' self-understanding as Messiah, Son of God, or Son of Man, there has long remained a broad consensus in this scholarship that Jesus did not "know he was God."[42] Consider, for example, the following quotations:

> Did [Jesus] call himself the messiah? … And did he call himself God? Here I want to stake out a clear position: messiah, yes; God, no … What we can know with relative certainty about Jesus is that his public ministry and proclamation … were not about his divinity at all.[43] (Bart Ehrman)

> Often theologians prefer to study the problem of Jesus' knowledge of his divinity in terms of the question: "Did Jesus know he was God?" From a biblical viewpoint this question is so badly phrased that it cannot be answered and should not be posed.[44] (Raymond Brown)

> But if we are to submit our speculations to the text and build our theology only with the bricks provided by careful exegesis we cannot say with any confidence that Jesus knew himself to be divine, the pre-existent Son of God.[45] (James Dunn)

> Jesus did not, in other words, "know that he was God" in the same way that one knows one is male or female, hungry or thirsty, or that one ate an orange an hour ago. His "knowledge" was of a more risky, but perhaps more significant, sort: like knowing one is loved. One cannot "prove" it except by living it.[46] (N. T. Wright)

---

41. Sanders, *The Historical Figure of Jesus*, 248. See Allison Jr., *Constructing Jesus*, 221–3.

42. There are a couple of scholars who stand out from this consensus, including J. C. O'Neill who concludes that "Jesus did in fact hold that he was the eternal Son of God" (O'Neill, *Who Did Jesus Think He Was?*, 189). Similarly, François Dreyfus concludes that the real Jesus of Nazareth was "Son of Man and Son of God, God himself, knowing that he was and saying it" (Dreyfus, *Did Jesus Know He Was God?*, 128).

43. Ehrman, *How Jesus Became God*.

44. Brown, *Jesus God and Man*, 86. Brown goes on in a later article to say: "Yet, if I judge unsatisfactorily obscure the question, 'Did Jesus know he was God?', I am more disconcerted when Christians give the answer 'No.' Some who give that answer think they are being alert to the historical problem; in my judgment their denial is more false to the historical evidence of Jesus' self-awareness than the response 'Yes'" (Brown, "Did Jesus Know He Was God?," 78).

45. Dunn, *Christology in the Making*, 33.

46. Wright, *JVG*, 653. Elsewhere Wright unpacks this further, suggesting that Jesus did not sit back and say "Well I never! I'm the second person of the Trinity!," but that "as a part of his human vocation, grasped in faith, sustained in prayer, tested in confrontation, agonized over in further prayer and doubt, and implemented in action, he believed that he

It would interfere with all human treatment of the subject and Christ would be a completely ghostly figure if we were to ascribe to him either the recollection of a consciousness of a prehuman state of being ... or a parallel awareness of his divinity and his humanity.[47] (Friedrich Schleiermacher)

I, for one, simply cannot imagine a sane human being, of any historical period or culture, entertaining the thoughts about himself which the Gospels, as they stand, often attribute to [Jesus].[48] (John Knox)

We can, strictly speaking, know nothing of the personality of Jesus.[49] (Rudolf Bultmann)

[First], in all likelihood, the pre-Easter Jesus did not think of himself as the Messiah or *in any exalted terms in which he is spoken of*. Second, we can say with almost complete certainty that he did not see his own mission or purpose as dying for the sins of the world. Third and finally, again with almost complete certainty, we can say that his message was not about himself or the importance of believing in him.[50] (Marcus Borg)

As these quotations show, there are, broadly speaking, four approaches. For some, the question is out of bounds altogether, as is seen most clearly in Bultmann.[51] Others want to affirm the possibility of divine self-understanding in some sense, but not in a straightforward way, and certainly not in the theological terms of the Christian tradition (e.g., Brown and Witherington). Others, such as N. T. Wright, answer in the negative and argue that we know Jesus did not think of himself as God.[52] The final group (e.g., Marcus Borg) provides an even stronger negative answer: we know that Jesus *knew he was not God*.

had to do and be, for Israel and the world, that which according to Scripture only YHWH himself could do and be" ("Jesus and the Identity of God," 54). For Wright, Jesus possessed this awareness of his vocation "with the knowledge that he could be making a terrible, lunatic mistake" ("Jesus' Self-Understanding," 59).

47. Schleiermacher, *The Life of Jesus*, 269.
48. Knox, *The Death of Christ*, 58.
49. Bultmann, *Jesus and the Word*, 8.
50. Borg, "Portraits of Jesus," 87. Emphasis added. Sanders writes, "Jesus seems to have been quite reluctant to adopt a title for himself. I think that even 'king' is not precisely correct, since Jesus regarded God as king. My own favorite term for his conception of himself is 'viceroy'. God was king, but Jesus represented him" (*Historical Figure*, 248). Robert Funk claims, "[Jesus] had nothing to say about himself, other than that he had no permanent address, no bed to sleep in, no respect on his home turf" (*Honest to Jesus*, 320). See similar comments in Robinson, "Theological Autobiography," 144–5.
51. That is not to say they find the question uninteresting or irrelevant, just that they believe the nature of the sources are such that they provide us no data from which to determine an answer. See discussion in Robinson, "The Last Tabu? The Self-Consciousness of Jesus," 553–66.
52. See also Wright, "Jesus and the Identity of God," 42–56.

Closely related to the questions of intention and self-understanding is that of motivation. When we look at the actions of individuals, we want to know what drove them to do the things they did, and we want to know what they expected to achieve or gain thereby. Again, since Reimarus, much historical Jesus research has centered on the question of what motivated Jesus to undertake the characteristic actions attributed to him in the gospels. For those scholars who believe the gospels largely reflect the intentions of the later communities that constructed the narratives therein, the question has little to do with Jesus and focuses instead on the motivations of the various authors of the gospels. Reimarus attempted to answer both questions: Jesus himself was motivated by revolutionary political aspirations, his followers were after worldly wealth and power.

While the complexity of this reconstructive task on a historical level is widely acknowledged, I have yet to come across a discussion in the literature of the relevant philosophical questions regarding human motivation.[53] In contemporary philosophy, there is by no means any broad agreement regarding ethical concepts of rationality, desire, and the good, or those virtues and vices that variously drive our motivations.[54] Indeed, Hume continues to loom large in contemporary approaches, having maintained that "Avarice, or the desire of gain, is an universal passion, which operates at all times, in all places, and upon all persons."[55] Hume argued that reason is and must be the slave of the passions and concluded that all people at all times cannot but rationally pursue the increase of power and riches.[56] His particular view of the relationship between practical reasoning and desire led him to transform what had hitherto been considered a vice and make it the controlling virtue of human action. By cutting off ethics from teleology and metaphysical questions of "the good," Hume took a description of the typical desires of the eighteenth-century European elite and inscribed it as universal to human nature.[57] As Alasdair MacIntyre notes, "The difference between Aristotle and Hume is that while, on Aristotle's view, desires for objects that attract only because they are pleasing to the agent who desires them are to be distinguished from desires for objects taken to be good, on Hume's there can … be no such distinction."[58] Thus, Aristotle's emphasis on the shared recognition of standards of practical reasoning is replaced by a notion of universal sentiments—avarice being

---

53. Wright defines motivation as "the specific sense, on one specific occasion, that a certain action or set of actions is appropriate and desirable" and he briefly mentions Aristotle's treatment of the problem that arises when motivations clash with aims and intentions (JVG, 110).

54. See esp. MacIntyre, *Ethics in the Conflicts of Modernity*.

55. Hume, *A Treatise of Human Nature*, ii, 2, 5.

56. Gregory, *The Unintended Reformation*, 284–7. Cambridge economist Ha-Joon Chang discusses this in *23 Things They Don't Tell You about Capitalism*, 41–50. "Thing 5: Assume the worst about people and you get the worst."

57. MacIntyre, *Conflicts of Modernity*, 92; Gregory, *Unintended Reformation*, 87.

58. MacIntyre, *Conflicts of Modernity*, 80.

chief among them. Here we no longer have an account of the virtues contextualized within a vision of human flourishing that directs social relationships toward individual and common goods. Instead, we are left with an atomized individualism that considers only which activities and relationships will be agreeable or useful to the agent in question.[59]

Without drawing a clear line of influence from Hume to specific historians, this contrast between Aristotle and Hume illustrates how metaphysical questions, which in part determine debates about ethics, also influence historiography. This can be seen most clearly in the way that the arguments of historical figures and the discussions they undertake with their peers about the good and those standards of practical reasoning necessary to achieve human flourishing are taken into account by historians seeking to reconstruct those figures' motivations. In other words, one reason we might have for discounting certain source material as ahistorical is because it attributes motivations to a character that does not match our vision of how human motivation works. We might, for example, discount the arguments we encounter in a speech or a sermon, maintaining instead that some set of universal passions will be likely to motivate a person more than the beliefs they hold about the good and goods.[60] My point is not that history should indulge in long-distance psychology.[61] Rather, I am suggesting that the broader philosophical discussion that seeks to describe how motivation relates to virtue, vice, passion, and reason is relevant to the question at hand. In fact, it provides the fundamental framework within which questions of motivation are formulated, and it determines the range of possibilities brought to bear in answering them.

This issue also relates directly to the theological question of Jesus' impeccability. The attribution of vice to Jesus on the assumption that such passions drive all human action drives a wedge between historical reconstruction and theology.[62] Similarly, to insist that Jesus' disciples were driven primarily by avarice is entirely to discount their claims about the sanctifying work of the Spirit among them after Pentecost.[63] This is not to say that historians must always assume the

---

59. Ibid., 82–4. MacIntyre argues "not only that some of Hume's claims were mistaken, but also that one effect of his advancing them in the way that he did was to conceal and disguise from his readers the importance of certain facts about the condition of their social and economic order" (ibid., 84).

60. "A more fruitful scholarly suggestion is that Jesus' treatment of his opponents shows that he did not really love his enemies" (Maurice Casey, *Jesus of Nazareth*, 311).

61. See Wright, *JVG*, 111. Cf. Miller, *Jesus at Thirty*; Capps, *Jesus*. Cf., van Os, *Psychological Analyses and the Historical Jesus*.

62. One of the most common vices attributed to Jesus is his apocalyptic fervor—a set of misguided beliefs that led him to inordinate agitation against the ruling powers, with disastrous results.

63. "When the early Christians spoke of their motivation, they regularly did so in terms of the divine spirit" (Wright, *NTPG*, 446). The ways of being witnessed to by ascetics and saints expand the horizon of possibilities for those historians who take these traditions seriously.

best of historical figures, or that they must always believe those figures' claims to virtue and integrity. Rather, it is to note that metaphysical and theological presuppositions will drive historians to discount certain evidence that does not fit with their perception of what typically motivates people to act in certain ways. When the historians are intent on disproving the historical claims of the Christian tradition, as Reimarus was, they will sometimes go so far as to attribute malicious motivations to those historical figures whom they wish to malign.

The Problem of "Docetism"

N. T. Wright has argued that "the 'Quest' began as an explicitly anti-theological, anti-Christian, anti-dogmatic movement. Its initial agenda was *not* to find a Jesus upon whom Christian faith might be based, but to show that the faith of the church (as it was then conceived) could not in fact be based on the real Jesus of Nazareth."[64] This is as true of some contemporary scholars as it was of Reimarus, Paulus, and Strauss. However, it is not universally the case, and there are a number of scholars who understand the "quest" to be a vital task for theology, aimed at connecting the Christian faith to its historical roots. For these historians, the task is frequently perceived as an antidote to Docetism.

In the lecture that inaugurated the "new quest," Käsemann argued that losing the link between the faith of the kerygma and the historical Jesus (what he calls "the identity between the exalted and the humiliated Lord") would result in Docetism.[65] Wright interprets Käsemann's warning as the insistence that "if Jesus was not earthed in history then he might be pulled in any direction, might be made the hero of any theological or political programme."[66] Wright, therefore, uses the term Docetism to refer to any Christology insufficiently grounded in the historical Jesus.[67] Witherington concurs—"a faith that does not ground the Christ of personal experience in the Jesus of history is a form of docetic or gnostic heresy"—and numerous others, including Meier, Borg, Crossan, and Dunn, have advanced similar arguments.[68]

---

64. Wright, *JVG*, 17.

65. Käsemann, "Problem of the Historical Jesus," 34. This is an argument on at least two fronts: against Bultmann, it is a belief that Jesus *as he actually was* is theologically relevant (not just the faith of the kerygma). It is also an assertion that Jesus *as he can be reconstructed by historians* is necessary for theology.

66. Wright, *JVG*, 23. He notes the un-Jewish Jesus of the Nazis as a pertinent example.

67. See for example, *JVG*, 653, 661; Wright, "A Biblical Portrait of God," 27–8; Wright, *The Challenge of Jesus*, 121.

68. Witherington, *The Jesus Quest*, 11; Meier, *A Marginal Jew*, 199; Meyer, *Critical Realism*, 148; Borg, *Jesus in Contemporary Scholarship*, 196; Meyer, "Faith and History Revisited," 82; Crossan, "Jesus at 2000 Debate"; Dunn, *Jesus Remembered, Christianity in the Making*, 102; Schweizer, "Die Frage Nach Dem Historischen Jesus," 403–19; Schillebeeckx, *Jesus in Our Western Culture*, 13; Allison Jr., *The Historical Christ and the Theological Jesus*, 84–5. Cf.

As various scholars have noted, "Docetism" in this context is evidently not being used in quite the same way as in classical Christological discourse.[69] In the Patristic era, "Docetism" (the idea that Christ only appeared [*dokein*] to live in the flesh) emerged as a sense that Christ was not what he seemed to be.[70] This problem was typically understood on an ontological level, and docetic heresies met opposition for the way they undermined or cheapened the suffering and full human consubstantiality of Christ. In other words, Docetism characteristically stemmed from a gnostic denial or deprecation of the physical (i.e., "matter"). On this ontological register, it is doubtful that historical criticism has much to offer as a dogmatic corrective. As A. K. M. Adam has argued:

> What would constitute historical evidence regarding whether Christ was divine on Chalcedonian terms or simply a divine being inhabiting a human appearance? Or whether Christ had a *physical* or *spiritual* body? Here historical critics lack the sorts of evidence and arguments that permit them to draw the conclusions that would, presumably, help confound Docetism.[71]

While historical Jesus scholars may indeed be concerned by the classical problem of Docetism, they most often use the term to refer instead to high Christologies that they deem incompatible with historical methodology. There are three issues in particular that Käsemann et al. appear to connect with "Docetism" in this way.

The first issue arises from a sense that an insistence on Jesus' "divinity" undermines historians' access to the "inside" of history. If history is not only about events and data but about intentionality, perspective, and meaning, then part of the historical task is to discern the thoughts to which historical actions give expression. For Collingwood, there is only one way for the historian to discover these thoughts and that is "by re-thinking them in his own mind."[72] To do so, historians rely on concepts of similarity and analogy.[73] We must assume that any historical character thinks in a way that is, in principle, intelligible to us. This is the reason that historians and judicial systems alike have supreme difficulty with people who suffer from insanity: it removes the possibility of establishing intention or motive. Furthermore, we can only reconstruct a plausible hypothesis regarding

---

discussion in Johnson, "The Humanity of Jesus," 15–16; Jüngel, "The Dogmatic Significance of the Question of the Historical Jesus," 82–119; Adam, "Why Historical Criticism Can't Protect Christological Orthodoxy," 37–56; Pannenberg, *Jesus, God and Man*, 307–64.

69. See Adam, "Historical Criticism," 37–56; Johnson, "Humanity of Jesus," 3–28.

70. See Slusser, "Docetism: A Historical Definition," 163–72; Brox, "'Doketismus'—Eine Problemanzeige," 301–14.

71. Adam, "Historical Criticism," 43.

72. Collingwood, *The Idea of History*, 215.

73. This is the second of Ernst Troeltsch's (1865–1923) three "principles of critical history." See Troeltsch, *Gesammelte Schriften*, II, 729–53. Because of Jesus' sinlessness, Kähler maintains that such analogy is impossible (*So-Called Historical Jesus*, 53–4).

a historical figure's aims and intentions by comparing them with other related scenarios and by drawing on a predetermined range of possible explanations. If Jesus did not possess human intentions and motivations like we do—as many historians appear to believe would be the case were he "divine"—then the possibility of historical analogy is undermined, and Jesus is excluded from the purview of historical reconstruction.

The second closely related issue comes from a recognition that some conceptions of Jesus undercut the historical emphasis on context. Historians insist that the consciousness and human experience of a historical figure must stand in significant continuity with their cultural and historical setting. Therefore, Jesus must be contextualized with reference to the language and concepts of Second-Temple Judaism. Wright gives this particularly detailed expression, arguing that Jesus must have possessed a "mindset" that was a basic variation on the broader first-century Jewish "worldview," which, like all mindsets, was confined to the limitations of a critical realist epistemology.[74] This focus on historical particularity opposes the presumed universalizing tendency of Christology, insisting that Jesus must have experienced the same limited, historical perspective as all other humans if we are to understand him as a first-century Jew.

Another facet of this second issue can be understood in terms of what historians typically see as the cardinal sin against their discipline: anachronism.[75] Raymond Brown refuses to approach the issue of Jesus' self-understanding in terms of the question "Did Jesus know he was God?" because he believes that without a developed Trinitarian framework the idea is nonsensical. "When we ask whether during his ministry Jesus, a Palestinian Jew, knew that he was God, we are asking whether he identified himself and the Father—and, of course, he did not" (see Mk 10:18).[76] The question of self-understanding is complicated by the fact that we are attempting to locate a judgment in the mind of a historical figure, even though we understand that judgment in conceptual terms that are foreign to that figure's historical milieu.[77] It would be anachronistic to suggest that the content of Jesus' self-understanding would have been structured in terms of our own Nicene expressions of Trinitarian theology. In this sense, a "docetic" insistence that Jesus knew he was the second person of the triune God undermines the prime imperative of historiography.

The third issue has to do with the veracity of certain historical sources that, by presenting Jesus as somehow "divine," subvert the accepted forms of narrative discourse. In his seminal book *The Testament of Jesus*, Käsemann characterized the

---

74. See Wright, *JVG*, 137–44; Wright, *NTPG*, 31–77.

75. See Fasolt, *The Limits of History*, esp. 3–45.

76. Brown, *Jesus God and Man*, 87. See similar arguments in e.g., Harvey, *Jesus and the Constraints of History*, 154–73; Vermes, *Jesus the Jew*; Vermes, *The Religion of Jesus the Jew*; Bird, *How God Became Jesus*, 52.

77. See discussion of concepts and judgments in Yeago, "The New Testament and the Nicene Dogma," 152–64. Cf. Sarisky, "Judgments in Scripture and the Creed."

Christology of the Gospel of John as "naïve Docetism," and argued that the church had misjudged it by declaring it to be orthodox.[78] Kasper Larsen has suggested that what Käsemann took issue with was the "touch of 'irreality'" that John's depiction of Jesus throws onto the narrative world of the Fourth Gospel.[79] Relying on Greimas' theory of narrative discourse,[80] Larsen highlights what happens when omniscience is applied to one of the participating actors in a narrative. Jesus' extraordinary knowledge of himself and others results in him being "elevated into a sphere of his own," which makes him a kind of stranger in the narrative world.[81] Elevated thus, Jesus is never really in danger from his antagonists: even their treachery serves Jesus' purposes (see Jn 10:17-18, 13:27, 18:4-9). Narrative tension is typically dependent on the limited knowledge and perspective of the characters. By including a character with neither limitation, John reaches beyond the perimeters of narrative convention in unexpected ways.[82] In this sense, "narrative Docetism" is understood as a literary phenomenon in which the significance of pragmatic narrative functions is subordinated when cognitive processes are in focus. "Narrative Docetism" causes unique problems for historians for whom pragmatic narrative functions are a priority.[83]

In response to Käsemann's critique of John's gospel, Marianne Meye Thompson rightly argues that not only in docetic Christologies but in any Christology with roots in orthodoxy, Jesus transcends the limits of typical humanity so that in addition to his likeness to us, his *unlikeness* is fundamental to his identity as Christ.[84] Although these issues may pose a threat to contemporary historical methodology, it remains to be seen if they are a "docetic" threat to theology. At the same time, they invite a similar question in the opposite direction: Is the historical Jesus scholars' alternative to Docetism simply a form of Ebionitism? For Jesus to be *fully* human, must he be *merely* or *typically* human? Wright describes Docetism as a sense that Jesus was "so 'divine' that he only seemed to be human but wasn't really so,"[85] and Meier maintains that a non-docetic Jesus must be understood to

---

78. Käsemann, *The Testament of Jesus*, 26, 76.

79. Larsen, "Narrative Docetism," 354.

80. See Greimas and Courtés, "The Cognitive Dimension of Narrative Discourse."

81. Larsen, "Narrative Docetism," 352.

82. See Ashley, "Jesus' Human Knowledge According to the Fourth Gospel," 241-53.

83. T. E. Pollard picks up on this tension between a preference for external details and a methodological focus on internal motivations. He maintains that "the Synoptists see Jesus and his words and actions from the outside through the eyes of the disciples: John 'enters sympathetically into the mind' of Jesus, or 'puts himself into the shoes' of Jesus. [Therefore,] on Collingwood's definition of the real task of the historian, it could well be argued that John is a better historian than the Synoptists" (From his inaugural lecture given at Knox Theological Hall, Dunedin, in 1964, quoted in Robinson, "The Last Tabu?" 560).

84. Thompson, *The Incarnate Word*, 7-8, 117-28. See related discussion in Voorwinde, *Jesus' Emotions in the Fourth Gospel*.

85. Wright, *The Challenge of Jesus*, 3.

be "as truly and fully human—with all the galling limitations that involves—as any other human being."[86] One gets the impression from such statements that a dichotomy is being assumed wherein two mutually exclusive natures (human and divine) are in competition. Analyzed in terms of Christological doctrine, Jesus is located squarely on the side of humanity (resulting in Ebionitism) or on the side of divinity (resulting in Docetism), or he is judiciously placed along a spectrum between the two (resulting in Eutychianism). This differs quite radically from the Christian tradition, which confesses that Jesus is *fully* divine and *fully* human. In that context, Docetism is understood to result not from Jesus being too divine (one cannot be more than *fully* divine) but from a gnostic denial of his humanity.

Historical Jesus studies, as with historical biblical scholarship more broadly, tends to operate with Kantian or post-Kantian anti-metaphysical assumptions and, for the most part, these scholars intentionally limit their investigation to the realm of the "phenomenal." The result, however, is not that metaphysical suppositions are removed from the inquiry. They continue to play a role but avoid critical investigation or justification. Wright argues that "rigorous history ... and rigorous theology ... belong together, and never more so than in discussion of Jesus. If this means that we end up needing a new metaphysic, so be it."[87] The problem is that this "new metaphysic" is never worked out in detail, it is simply assumed, and although it is difficult to pin down with much precision, it appears to include a commitment to the mutual exclusivity (or a quantitative delineation) of the finite and the infinite, along with a restricted understanding of divine transcendence.[88] Only if we posit a competitive relationship between humanity and divinity or suppose a truncated view of the human capacity for union with God do we end up with the Christological polarities noted above. Fortunately, we have good philosophical and theological reasons to question these assumptions, and by doing so we can help to free the historians from the metaphysical restrictions that so often hamper their investigations.

As we have seen, philosophical and theological assumptions about what it means for Jesus to be *fully* human play a seminal role from the outset of historical investigation. This is made especially clear when Dale Allison Jr., Marcus Borg, and others argue explicitly that a fully human Jesus could not possess a divine self-understanding.[89] There is no doubt that this metaphysical (even theological) judgment impacts the historiographical outcome. At the same time, it is no

---

86. Meier, *Marginal Jew*, vol. 1, 199.

87. *JVG*, 8.

88. An explicit example of a quantitative delineation of divinity and humanity can be found in Bart Ehrman's work. He argues that the Gospels should be read against a background in which humanity and divinity were not thought of as qualitatively distinct, but as existing along a continuum (Ehrman, *How Jesus Became God*). Cf. Bauckham, *God of Israel*.

89. Allison Jr., *The Historical Christ and the Theological Jesus*, 89; Borg, *Jesus a New Vision*, 4–8; Wright, "A Biblical Portrait of God," 27; Wright, *The Challenge of Jesus*, 3.

wonder that, when restricted to these terms, those who want to affirm that Jesus possessed some sort of divine identity find themselves grasping for conceptual tools and coming up empty.[90] The influence of these scholars' understandings of philosophical anthropology, Christology (e.g., "Docetism"), and the nature of divine and human knowledge and consciousness is significant enough to warrant explicit theological appraisal.

Theological Parallels

Christology is arguably the area of theological reflection where metaphysical ideas of the relationship between the finite and the infinite, transcendence and immanence, nature and grace, and a host of other questions come most fully to the fore. At the same time, it is the doctrinal locus where Christians often look for the fullest revelation of each of these realities. This means there is a dialectical relationship between Christology and metaphysics, neither of them wholly prior to nor independent from the other.[91] This complex relationship has led a number of theologians into the same dead ends as the historical Jesus scholars that we outlined above, and it is worth discussing some of the theological parallels to the ideas we have been discussing.

There exists a widespread misconception that, even if Jesus was "divine" in some sense, he could have been truly human only if his divinity was evacuated of its divine properties in the manner of so-called *kenotic* Christology.[92] There are various *kenotic* approaches, but one of the most influential is that associated with P. T. Forsyth and H. R. Mackintosh.[93] Building upon a particular reading of

---

90. Witherington concludes his book-length study on Jesus' self-understanding somewhat vaguely, writing that "I think [Jesus] implied that he should be seen not merely as a greater king than David but in a higher and more transcendent category" (*The Christology of Jesus*, 276). This reveals quite clearly the need for richer language and terminology around this issue. Cf. Wright, *JVG*, 121.

91. As Rowan Williams writes,

> Chicken and egg, you may rightly say: the pressures that shape the language of traditional doctrine push forward an exploration of the metaphysical structure that alone will make sense of it ... Christology is not just one example of a theological theme or topic that is illuminated by a general metaphysical axiom about finite and infinite; it is, I shall argue, the major theological enterprise that itself shapes and clarifies that axiom. (Williams, *Christ the Heart*, 6)

92. For an example of this assumption at work among biblical scholars, see O'Neill, *Who Did Jesus Think He Was?*, 189–90.

93. Forsyth, *The Person and Place of Jesus Christ*; Mackintosh, *The Doctrine of the Person of Christ*. See discussion in McCormack, "Kenoticism in Modern Christology," 444–57. Nineteenth-Century "kenoticists" on the Continent included Thomasius, Hofmann,

the words ἑαυτὸν ἐκένωσεν in the so-called "Christ hymn" of Phil. 2:6-11, they conceive of God divesting himself of his divine properties in order to live and act humanly: God literally becomes the subject of a human life, his divine *nature* becoming subject to all of the "galling" limitations of typical human existence.[94] This is often worked out in terms of a version of the *communicatio idiomatum*—referred to as the *genus tapeinoticum* or *genus majestaticum*—in which, rather than ascribing the attributes of each nature to the one person of Christ, the properties of each nature are cross-attributed to each other.[95] By ascribing the attributes of Christ's humanity to his divinity, the "divinity" of the Word essentially becomes a human nature through the Incarnation.[96] Viewing divine transcendence as incompatible with the Incarnation, these theologians insist that God must give up elements of his divinity in order to become human.[97] This view is often used as theological justification for the idea that Jesus could have been "divine" in some sense without necessarily possessing extraordinary knowledge, or even a divine self-understanding.

Most Reformed and Roman Catholic theologians reject *kenotic* Christology.[98] That is not to say that they ignore Philippians 2, which has always been a central Christological text. Rather, *kenosis* has typically been understood as "taking [λαβών] the form [μορφήν] of a slave, being born in human likeness [ὁμοιώματι]"

Liebner, Frank, Ebrard, Martensen, and Gess (see Welch, *Protestant Thought in the Nineteenth Century*, 233–40). In Britain it included Gore, Fairbairn, Weston, and Gifford, in addition to Forsyth and Mackintosh (see Ramsey, *From Gore to Temple*, 30–43). Cf. Thompson, "Nineteenth-Century Kenotic Christology," 74–111.

94. Stephen Sykes argues that this abandons a two-natures approach altogether ("The Strange Persistence of Kenotic Christology," 349–75).

95. The former involves ascribing attributes of the human nature to the divine nature, the latter ascribes attributes of his divinity to his humanity.

96. Stephen Sykes, "Strange Persistence," 349–75; Evans (ed.), *Exploring Kenotic Christology*, 354–6. Sykes calls the ideas behind the nineteenth-century development of *kenosis* "grotesquely anthropomorphic." He continues, "It is surely odd that they were not perceived as such at the time, and that they have not been consistently, and by every thoughtful theologian similarly perceived" ("Strange Persistence," 357).

97. For exegetical discussions see Gorman, *Inhabiting the Cruciform God*, 21–2; Witherington, *Friendship and Finances in Philippi*, 66–7.

98. See, e.g., Barth, *Erklärung Des Philipperbriefes*. ET: *The Epistle to the Philippians*, 60–4; Barth, *CD* IV/1, 180–4; Pope Pius XII, "Sempiternus Rex Christus" (September 8, 1951): §29, accessed May 1, 2018, http://w2.vatican.va/content/pius-xii/en/encyclicals/documents/hf_p-xii_enc_08091951_sempiternus-rex-christus.html. While Barth rejects kenotic Christology, he later employs a version of the *genus tapeinoticum* in *Church Dogmatics* IV/1 and IV/2 as he works out his understanding of the meaning of *Deus pro nobis* (see, e.g., *Church Dogmatics* IV/1, 215). See discussion in White, "The Crucified Lord," 157–92.

(Phil. 2:7),[99] which is how Paul explains it in context.[100] The *kenosis* of the divine Son involves the addition of a human nature—he "emptied" himself by *taking up* (λαβών) the form of a slave—not the diminution of his divinity. As Aquinas notes, "[The Son of God] is called 'emptied' ... not because anything was subtracted from his fullness or the greatness of his divinity, but because he took up our exile and our smallness."[101] Aquinas picks up on Paul's use of the word "form" (Greek: μορφή; Latin: *formae*),[102] noting that "it is necessary to say that in Christ there are two forms (*formae*), even after the union ... But it cannot be said that the form of God

---

99. Quotations are taken from the New Revised Standard Version (NRSV), copyright 1989, National Council of the Churches of Christ in the United States of America. Used by permission. All rights reserved. Greek text from GNT28-T.

100. Thus, Sykes notes that "kenosis" refers to the quality of God's love in becoming human. "In this sense the word has no technical [ontological] Christological connotation" ("Strange Persistence," 356).

101. *In Rom.* c. 9, lect. 5, §805. See *ScG* IV, c. 8. "But since he was filled with divinity, did he empty himself of divinity? No, because he remained what he was, and he assumed what he was not ... For as he descended from heaven (not that he ceased to be in heaven, but that he began to be in a new mode on earth), so also he emptied himself (not by laying down his divine nature but by assuming a human nature)" (*In Epist. ad Phil.* c. 2, lect. 2, §57). Here, in the first parenthetical aside, Aquinas affirms Augustine's position that the Word of God did not cease to govern the universe in taking on human flesh in the Incarnation, thereby advocating what the Lutheran tradition refers to as the *extra Calvinisticum*: a position Calvin shared with the Patristic (esp. Athanasius, Augustine, and Gregory Nazianzus), and medieval tradition, which Luther rejected. See *ST* III, a. 10, q. 1 *ad 2*; *In Heb.* I, lect. 2, 30–6; *In Epist. ad Phil.* ch. 2, lect. 2, §57; Calvin, *Institutes of the Christian Religion*, II, c. 13, n. 4. See recent discussion in Gordon, *The Holy One in Our Midst*; McGinnis, *The Son of God Beyond the Flesh*.

102. Gordon Fee notes that, contrasted with σχῆμα ("fashion": emphasizing external features), μορφή is identified more closely with the essence of a thing, denoting "those characteristics and qualities that are essential to it" (Fee, *Paul's Letter to the Philippians*, 204). The word for Christ's transfiguration on the mountain is μετεμορφώθη (Mt. 17:2), and after the resurrection he is said to have appeared to the disciples "in another form (μορφή)" (Mk 16:12). Compare this with Rom. 12:2 ("be not conformed [συσχηματίζεσθε] to this world") or 2 Cor. 11:13 ("deceitful workmen, disguising [μετασχηματιζόμενοι] themselves as apostles of Christ"). In the Vulgate, these words are translated as *effigie* and *formae*, which demarcate a similar distinction: both can be translated as "form" but the former has the sense of imitation and appearance, while the latter is more essential. See *Deferrari*, s.v. "*effigies*" (p. 353); *Deferrari*, s.v. "*forma*" (p. 433). Markus Bockmuehl takes μορφή to refer to something visible or perceptible about an object, but still more essential than σχῆμα. He therefore associates the "form of God" with the visible glory of God from LXX texts such as Job 4:16, Isa. 44:13, and Dan. 3:1 ("'The Form of God' [Phil. 2.6]," 1–23). Obviously, the contrast between these terms cannot be overstated, and μορφή is not fully synonymous with φύσις either way. This is a highly metaphorical passage and grammatical nuances are unlikely to yield sufficient theological fruit. Nonetheless, Aquinas' interpretation in terms of

and the form of a slave are the same, since nothing 'takes' (*accipit*) what it already has (*habet*)."[103] He maintains further that the form of God in Christ cannot be said to have been corrupted by the union, and neither can the form of a slave, nor can they be mixed together, because then he would be neither God nor the form of a slave.[104] The very possibility of the divine Word taking on flesh to experience the limitations of finite human existence depends on the infinitude of his divine nature.[105] Otherwise we are forced into the absurd task of positing the union of two finite natures within the one person of Christ.[106] As Austin Farrer argued, "the finite excludes another finite of incompatible nature."[107] Transforming the divine agency into a finite activity would result in two comparable (univocal) natures jostling for space within the incarnate Christ.[108] The impulse toward a strong *kenotic* Christology derives from a misunderstanding of divine transcendence and of the radically noncompetitive relationship that exists between the finite and the

---

"nature" does no violence to the text and accords quite well with one probable grammatical sense of the passage. So Moisés Silva notes,

> We may want to dispute that the passage speaks primarily to ontological issues regarding the nature of the Trinity, but it would appear futile to deny that Phil. 2:5-7 has some strong implications for these issues. These verses cannot serve as the total basis for a formula regarding the two natures of Christ, but the description of Christ in this passage reflects certain ontological commitments that lead rather naturally to the later orthodox formulations. (*Philippians*, 114)

103. *ScG* IV, c. 35.
104. *ScG* IV, c. 35. As Michael Gorman puts it, "the parallel phrases 'form of God' and 'form of a slave' mean that to the extent that this one really took on the form of a slave, he also really was in the form of God—and vice versa" (Gorman, *Cruciform God*, 22). Gorman challenges concessive translations of the participle ὑπάρχων in Phil. 2:6 ("*though* being in the form of God"), noting that the sacrificial act of the Incarnation is the outworking of divine identity, rather than its abrogation. It is *because* he was in the form of God that he took the form of a servant.
105. "Descent into man's lowly position is a supreme example of power—of a power which is not bounded by circumstances contrary to its nature" (Gregory of Nyssa, "Address on Religious Instruction," 300–1).
106. "How beautiful that it says he 'emptied himself.' For the empty is opposed to the full. But the divine nature is amply full, because every perfection of goodness is there ... But human nature and the soul, is not full, but is in potency to fullness, because it is made like a blank slate. Human nature is therefore empty. Thus, it says he 'emptied himself' because he assumed a human nature" (*In Epist. ad. Phil.* c. 2, lect. 2, §57).
107. Farrer, *Scripture, Metaphysics, and Poetry*, 35.
108. This imagery of natures "jostling for space" comes from Rowan Williams' 2016 Hulsean Lectures: http://www.divinity.cam.ac.uk/events/the-hulsean-lectures-2016-christ-and-the-logic-of-creation.

infinite. To borrow a phrase from Kähler, I regard *kenotic* Christology as a blind alley.[109]

Recognizing *kenotic* Christology as a failure to grasp the relationship between transcendence and immanence leads us quite naturally to a second theological approach, which finds its roots in the thought of G. F. W. Hegel (1770–1831). The historicizing Christologies of twentieth-century theologians such as Wolfhart Pannenberg (1928–2014), Jürgen Moltmann (b. 1926), and Robert Jenson (1930–2017) attempt to resolve the presumed tension between humanity and divinity by defining God in terms of key characteristics of human existence, including temporality and suffering.[110] As Kathryn Tanner explains, for these theologians "God becomes Godself in and through our history."[111] Similar to proponents of *kenotic* Christologies, these theologians consider transcendence, as classically conceived, to be incompatible with the Incarnation. The difference is that, rather than suggesting that God gave up aspects of his divinity to become human, they instead redefine divinity in historical terms.[112] There is a particular affinity between historicizing Christologies and historical Jesus studies insofar as theologically minded practitioners of the latter have sometimes attempted to adapt the doctrine of God to fit with the human characteristics of the life of Christ.[113] The result is an erosion of the difference between divinity and humanity through the incarnation: God is approached as a being among beings who exists in a competitive relationship with created reality. As we will see in the next chapter, the classical Christian tradition conceives of the relationship between transcendence and immanence rather differently. In other words, they have very different understandings of metaphysics or "being." The Christian confession that Jesus is fully human is not the same as an insistence that Jesus must be conformed to a reductive post-enlightenment philosophical anthropology.

Conclusion

To critique the metaphysical and theological assumptions of historians is not to replace historical rigor with a priori dogmatic claims. Rather, on the one hand, it is to say that metaphysical presuppositions shape our thinking in deep and enduring ways, and it is incumbent upon us as scholars to engage with those

---

109. See also Weinandy, *In the Likeness of Sinful Flesh*, esp. 8–11.

110. See, e.g., Pannenberg, *Systematic Theology*, 327; Moltmann, *The Crucified God*, 187, 227; Jenson, *God After God*, 123.

111. Tanner, *Jesus, Humanity and the Trinity*, 10.

112. Pannenberg writes, "The dependence of the deity of the Father upon the course of events in the world of creation was first worked out by Jüngel and then by Moltmann, who illustrated it by the crucifixion of Jesus" (*Systematic Theology*, 329). Cf. Jüngel, *God as the Mystery of the World*.

113. See Wright, "Jesus and the Identity of God," 44, 54–5.

concepts critically,[114] and on the other hand it is to say that historiography is about plausibility[115] and plausibility is about worldviews.[116] Only if we understand the meaning and implications of theological claims can we venture to say how they stand in relation to "history." The point, then, is not that a Christian historian will possess only naïve credulity when it comes to studying Jesus. Rather, hard-won, nuanced, and clearly expressed philosophical and theological understandings of the world should be brought to bear on all areas of knowledge, especially in the field of history. To introduce a metaphysical grammar into this discussion is not to dehistoricize it, but to recognize that it is *already inherently metaphysical*, only confusedly so. By undertaking the task of clarifying and correcting these assumptions—thereby rendering them coherent and intelligible—we stand only to gain increased access to the historical figure of Jesus.

---

114. "When the existence of metaphysical commitments is ignored or denied, their grip only tightens" (Kerr, *Theology after Wittgenstein*, 187).

115. Many historical Jesus scholars explicitly frame their projects in terms of plausibility. See, e.g., Theissen and Winter, *The Quest for the Plausible Jesus*, esp. 37; Pitre, *Jesus and the Last Supper*, esp. 31–52. See Rowlands, "Historical Jesus," 109–14.

116. John P. Meier is right to note that "Whether we call it a bias, a *Tendenz*, and worldview, or a faith stance, everyone who writes on the Historical Jesus writes from some ideological vantage point; no critic is exempt" (*A Marginal Jew*, 6). However, his solution is inadequate: "The solution is to admit honestly one's own standpoint, to try to exclude its influence in making scholarly judgments by adhering to certain commonly held criteria, and to invite the correction of other scholars when one's vigilance inevitably slips" (ibid.). It is naïve to assume that briefly stating one's background ("I'm Roman Catholic," or "I've been disillusioned by Evangelicalism") will allay the influence of metaphysical presuppositions on the historical task. Unfortunately, this seems to be what the "critical" part of "critical realism" amounts to in much contemporary New Testament scholarship.

Chapter 2

THE METAPHYSICS OF PARTICIPATION

I have suggested that there are ways of thinking about being that differ from those typical among most historical Jesus scholars, and that some of these may prove more appropriate to the historiographical task, especially when it comes to the figure of Jesus. If we want to make sense of Jesus as a historical figure, we require a conception of being that accounts for the radically noncompetitive relationship that exists between the finite and the infinite: between creator and creature. In order to avoid the kind of competitive metaphysics that tends to hamper the more theologically minded historical Jesus scholars on the one hand, and the reductive anthropology that inhibits the more *a*-theological scholars on the other, the clearest way forward is a retrieval of classical metaphysics in some form. In order to speak with any sort of coherence about Jesus, we require a grammar of ontology.[1]

To say this is simply to recapitulate one of the central insights of the early church. There are good reasons why the early Christians articulated their faith in Christ in an ontological manner,[2] and those reasons went well beyond simply the influence of Greek metaphysics on their thought.[3] They recognized the fact that speaking of Jesus inevitably involved them in conversations of ontological significance, and that when faced with the mystery of the incarnation, they could not avoid speaking at the level of being. Importantly, it is precisely through reflection on the doctrine of Christ that the Christian tradition developed a particular way of thinking and speaking about created being and its relation to God. As Rowan Williams

---

1. I am using ontology and metaphysics as synonyms, to refer to the study of being.
2. As opposed to merely a narrative depiction of Jesus' divine identity, for example.
3. "Early Christians could not have worshipped Jesus as they did, and simultaneously followed the prohibition of worshipping other deities, without considering Jesus, in a sense that needs to be specified precisely, to be on the same ontological level as God" (Sarisky, *Reading the Bible*, 316). See Rowe, "Biblical Pressure and Trinitarian Hermeneutics," 295–312. Greek metaphysics may have helped them answer questions raised by the biblical text, but the questions themselves were not driven by Greek metaphysics. It is more historically appropriate to follow Robert Louis Wilken and speak of the "Christianization of Hellenism," now that "the notion that the development of early Christian thought represented a hellenization of Christianity has outlived its usefulness" (*The Spirit of Early Christian Thought: Seeking the Face of God*, xvi).

has argued, "the pressures that shape the language of traditional [Christological] doctrine push forward an exploration of the metaphysical structure that alone will make sense of it."[4] The incarnation has metaphysical implications, and if that is the case, then we should expect that certain ways of speaking about being will be more appropriate to the task than others.

Because of the non-metaphysical (or anti-metaphysical) nature of much modern thought, especially in the field of history, it has become difficult to grasp the ways that ontological presuppositions shape how we think about things such as human nature, cognition, and historiography.[5] As a result, it is necessary to explore alternative metaphysical approaches in order to clarify what is at stake.[6] For Aquinas, this begins with the idea of creation. In this chapter I will begin by considering Aquinas' understanding of the doctrine of *creatio ex nihilo* in terms of the ontology of participation, highlighting the centrality of noncompetition to participatory accounts of being.[7] I will then unpack the ontological and semantic

---

4. Williams, *Christ the Heart*, 6.

> Christology, so far from requiring a rethinking of the classical account of divine perfections (impassibility, immutability and so on), actually provides the fullest possible rationale for them. And conversely, the classical modes of characterizing divine life, so far from being abstract and alien importations into a properly scriptural and/or experientially grounded theology, allow created existence its own integrity and dignity, and deliver us from a theology in which God is in danger of being seen simply as a very important or uniquely powerful agent in the universe competing with other agents in the universe for space or control. (Ibid., 11)

See a similar argument in Burrell, "The Act of Creation with Its Theological Consequences," 40–52.

5. "Whether consciously or unconsciously, we all work with a particular ontology; unfortunately, usually the ontology of those who plead for the abolition of ontology turns out to be the nominalist ontology of modernity" (Boersma, *Heavenly Participation*, 20).

6. As we will see, one of the fundamental claims of Thomistic philosophy is the fundamental role of *esse* in both existence and knowledge. This claim entails that, contrary to post-Kantian philosophical tendencies, it is better to begin with metaphysics and then turn to epistemology (which we will consider in Chapter 4). As Jacques Maritain notes, "Although in the interests of exterior order in a written treatise … it is convenient to place the critique [of knowledge] at the beginning of metaphysics, like a sort of introductory apologetic—in reality, criticism, ontology and natural theology all grow together … since they are integrated into one and the same specific whole" (*The Degrees of Knowledge*, 97). For a defense of realism see Maritain, *Degrees of Knowledge*; Gilson, *Thomist Realism and the Critique of Knowledge*).

7. In recent years, this return to a noncompetitive (or "non-contrastive") ontology has been central to a number of theological works from a broad spectrum of theologians. Concerned with the relationship between nature and supernature—between sacramental sign and reality—the theologians associated with the *nouvelle théologie* movement sought to recover the noncompetitive ontology of the premodern Christian tradition. See, e.g.,

2. The Metaphysics of Participation

connection between participation and analogy. By way of contrast with the implicit metaphysical presuppositions outlined in the previous chapter, this discussion will provide us with an ontological grammar capable of doing justice to the infinite difference and intimate relationship that exist between God and creatures, which is itself essential to the task of Christology.[8]

Creation

For Saint Thomas, one way of saying that the world is God's good creation is to say that God is the cause of all things by means of participation.[9] This is not

---

Boersma, *Nouvelle Théologie & Sacramental Ontology*. A noncompetitive participatory ontology is also central to the thought of those theologians related to the Radical Orthodoxy movement (see Milbank, Pickstock, and Ward, eds., *Radical Orthodoxy: A New Theology*, 1–20). Kathryn Tanner develops the principle of noncompetition between creatures and God, which underlies her radical interpretation of divine transcendence in *Jesus, Humanity and the Trinity*. Katherine Sonderegger outlines an account of "compatibalism of Divine Nearness," which attempts to establish a non-contrastive ontology while rejecting the language of participation as employed by Radical Orthodoxy (see esp. comments on p. 108) and attempting to remain "looser and more commonsensical than scholastic architecture demands" (*Systematic Theology, Volume 1*, 111). John Webster comments on noncompetition, discussing how "omnipotent power creates and perfects creaturely capacity and movement" in, among other places, "'Love Is also a Lover of Life,'" 170. One distinguishing characteristic of Aquinas' approach in comparison with all of these is that it is far more detailed and comprehensive. Sonderegger and Tanner, in particular, prefer an ad hoc approach to metaphysics that presents a stark contrast with the nuanced and thoroughgoing vision offered by Aquinas. Despite overlap between these approaches, differences remain. On the differences between participation and compatibilism, see Davison, *Participation in God*, 228–35.

8. Participation has become a major theme in contemporary NT studies, in large part thanks to the so-called New Perspective on Paul, following the release of Sanders' *Paul in Palestinian Judaism*. However, these discussions have often focused on the redemptive dimension of participatory language without attending to the related ontological relationship between creator and creature. At the conclusion of his study, Sanders comes to the telling conclusion that "We seem to lack a category of 'reality'—real participation in Christ, real possession of the Spirit—which lies between naïve cosmological speculation and belief in magical transference on the one hand and a revised self-understanding on the other. I must confess that I do not have a new category of perception to propose here" (ibid., 522). See Eastman, "Participation in Christ"; MaCaskill, *Union with Christ in the New Testament*. For critical comments on Wright in this connection, see Finlan, "Can We Speak of *Theosis* in Paul?", 68–80 esp. at 71.

9. The concept and terminology of participation appears with increasing regularity over the course of Aquinas' writing career (see Velde, *Participation and Substantiality in*

so much a statement about cosmology and the origins of the universe as it is a structuring principle for the entirety of how the created order is understood in relation to God.[10] Moreover, the fact that all things exist by participation in God who is existence itself (*ipsum esse subsistens*) structures the analogical nature of our knowledge of God.[11] For Aquinas, such knowledge begins with the sensible understanding of created things; God is known to us by his effects in creation.[12] And yet, because all creatures receive their *esse* from the one who is *ipsum esse*, their existence can only be understood analogically in relation to the existence of God. Thus, recovering Aquinas' participatory ontology, which is the ground of the analogy of being, is the first step to understanding the insights he has to offer when it comes to thinking about existence.

Janet Soskice writes that "*creatio ex nihilo* is a central teaching in Jewish, Christian and Muslim thought—in fact, the only teaching that the medieval Jewish philosopher Moses Maimonides thought that all three traditions shared."[13] Furthermore, the belief that God created all things "from nothing" is present in some of the earliest Christian sources we possess, its explicit articulation in the early church evidently driven by reflection on the pervasive biblical theme of the

---

Thomas Aquinas, 3–4; Koterski, "The Doctrine of Participation in Thomistic Metaphysics," 185–7). Participation was often overlooked in Thomist scholarship until two influential studies by Cornelio Fabro and Louis-Bertrand Geiger placed it back on the agenda in the twentieth century (Fabro, *La Nozione Metafisica di Partecipazione; Secondo San Tommaso D'Aquino*; Geiger, *La Participation dans la Philosophie de S. Thomas d'Aquin*). Since then, English-speaking Thomists have picked up the theme. See, e.g., Clarke, "The Meaning of Participation in St. Thomas," 147–57; Wippel, "Thomas Aquinas and Participation," 117–58; Koterski, "Participation" (1992); Velde, *Participation* (1995); Velde, "God and the Language of Participation," 19–36; Davison, *Participation in God*.

10. Étienne Gilson comments that for Aquinas, the world "is a sacred world, impregnated to its inmost fibers with the presence of a God whose supreme existence saves it constantly from nothingness" (*Le Thomisme* [Sixth Edition, 1965]. ET: *Thomism: The Philosophy of Thomas Aquinas*, 103).

11. *ST* I.3.4.

12. *ST* I.12.12. This has as much to do with revealed theology as it does with so-called natural theology—in other words, the fact that our knowledge of God begins with sensible knowledge of created things is determinative of the nature of divine revelation, regardless of whether or not it also points to the possibility of knowing God by natural reason (a possibility that Aquinas views as arduous and prone to error, but nonetheless possible). See *De ver.* q. 19, a. 1; *ScG* I.4; *ST* I.1.1; and discussion in White, *Wisdom in the Face of Modernity*.

13. Soskice, "*Creatio ex nihilo*: Its Jewish and Cristian Foundations," 24. See her argument that the church Fathers did not simply baptize Aristotle, for their metaphysic is the result of a particular Judeo-Christian understanding of creation in "Athens and Jerusalem, Alexandria and Edessa: Is There a Metaphysics of Scripture?" 149–62.

2. The Metaphysics of Participation

dependence of all things on the creating and sustaining power of the one God:[14] "For thus says the LORD who created the heavens ... I am the LORD, and there is no other" (Isa. 45:18).[15] It is an affirmation that God freely created the world out of nothing—"no pre-existent matter, space or time"—that draws an absolute metaphysical distinction between the one God and everything else that exists and is not God.[16] This distinction is not simply about separation, however, for it is a distinction that structures the relationship and order that exists between God and creation: "Creation in the creature," writes Aquinas, "is only a certain relation to the Creator as to the principle of its being [*principium sui esse*]."[17] The doctrine of creation is foundational to our understanding of both God and creatures, and the relation that endures between them.

Aquinas writes that "every being in any way existing is from God. For whatever is found in anything by participation [*per participationem*], must be caused in it by that to which it belongs essentially [*essentialiter*], as iron becomes ignited by fire [*ignitum ab igne*]."[18] Now, existence cannot belong to creatures essentially because a thing's being cannot be caused by its own essential principles: "Nothing can be

---

14. See, e.g., the *The Shepherd of Hermas*, in *The Apostolic Fathers*. For an exegetical discussion of *creatio ex nihilo*, see McFarland, *From Nothing*, 1–10. On later patristic treatments of *creatio ex nihilo*, see Blowers, *Drama of the Divine Economy*.

15. "The meaning and substance of the doctrine, though not the terminology, is firmly rooted in scripture and pre-Christian Jewish literature" ("*Creatio ex nihilo* in Palestinian Judaism and Early Christianity," 270). See *Creation Ex Nihilo; Creation and the God of Abraham*.

16. Soskice, "*Ex nihilo*," 24. Aquinas makes clear that in the phrase *creatio ex nihilo*, *ex* ("from") "does not signify a material cause, but only order; as when we say, *from morning comes midday*—i.e., after morning is midday" (*ST* I.45.1). Today we often find conceptions of "nothing" as a kind of potency that allows physicists to dispense with metaphysical questions of the provenance of being. For Aquinas, nothing is not the kind of thing that could be productive of anything; nothing is not something out of which the universe could spontaneously emerge. See Davison, "Looking Back toward the Origin: Scientific Cosmology as Creation *ex nihilo* Considered 'from the Inside,'" 367–89.

17. *ST* I.45.3. See *ST* I.47.1.

18. *ST* I.44.1. Aquinas emphasizes that created beings do not take a part of God's *esse* but possess a participated similitude to the divine *esse*, a similitude to which he refers as *esse commune*. In this sense the divine essence itself remains uncommunicated and unparticipated: it does not enter into composition with the creature. See *In De div. nom.*, c. 2, lect. 3, n. 158; *De ver.*, q. 2, a. 3, ad 20; *ST* I.3.8; Wippel, *The Metaphysical Thought of Thomas Aquinas*, 120–2. Aquinas denies that *esse commune* can be identified with *ipsum esse subsistens* (i.e., God), because *esse commune* is a creative effect of God's agency—unlike God, *esse commune* is not self-subsistent. See *De ente*, c. 5; *In I Sent.*, d. 8, q. 4, a. 1, *ad* 1; *ScG* I.26; *De Pot.* q. 7, a. 2, *ad* 4, 6; *ST* I.3.4, *ad* 1, and discussion in Te Velde, *Participation and Substantiality*, 188–94; Fran O'Rourke, *Pseudo-Dionysius and the Metaphysics of Aquinas*, 148–55; Beiler, "The Theological Importance of a Philosophy of Being," 295–326 at 314–15.

the sufficient cause of its own existence."[19] If the question of essence pertains to *what* a thing is, and the question of existence to *whether* a thing is, then to affirm that all things are created is to say that all things are composed of essence and being (*esse*), and that they receive being by participation in God.[20] All created things are contingent; it is not of their essence necessarily to exist. This is not the case for God, however, because his essence is not caused by any exterior agent. If God is the first efficient cause, then he cannot exist by participation in another, but must possess existence essentially. In God, *what* and *whether* coincide: "*sua essentia est suum esse.*"[21] Unlike creatures, God is not contingent: he cannot not exist, for his very essence is the act of existence itself.[22]

Perhaps the clearest lens through which to explore the details of Aquinas' doctrine of participation is the concept of God as the cause of all things.[23] Aristotle (384–322 BC) influentially discerned four different ways in which the term "cause" is used: (1) a material cause is "that from which a thing comes into being;" (2) a formal cause is "the form or pattern;" (3) an efficient cause is "that from which the change … first begins;" and (4) a final cause is "that for the sake of which a thing is."[24] Taking the example of a house, we might say that the material cause

---

19. *ST* I.3.4. See also *ScG* II.15; II.52.

20. "What a man is and that a man is are different" (Aristotle, *Posterior Analytics*, in *Complete Works*, 2.7 [92b11]). In other words, because we can conceive of the essence of something (e.g., a woman or a phoenix) without knowing whether it actually exists, then essence must be something other than existence. It is worth noting that, for Aquinas (but not necessarily for Aristotle), the question of existence is not so much a yes or no fact as it is an act. Rowan Williams comments that "*esse* means active existence, and so denotes all that is involved in actively being the particular kind of substance that a thing is," not in the abstract sense of *essentia* but in terms of "the actual *presence in the world* of this particular thing" (*Christ the Heart*, 26–7). On essence/*esse* composition in creatures see esp. Wippel, *Metaphysical Thought*, 132–76. For medieval controversy on this issue see Gilson, *History of Christian Philosophy in the Middle Ages*, 420–7; Wippel, "Essence and Existence," 385–410. The thematization of this distinction between essence and existence, based on Aristotle's remark, was first suggested by the Muslim philosopher Alfarabi (d. 950). See discussion in Gilson, *Christian Philosophy*, 185–7.

21. *ST* I.3.4. This is the foundation of the doctrine of divine simplicity for Aquinas. See *ST* I.3, aa. 1–8; *Comp. Theol.* I, cc. 9–25; *ScG* I.18–28; Stump, *Aquinas*, 92–130; White, "Divine Simplicity," 66–93; Wittman, "'Not a God of Confusion but of Peace,'" 151–69.

22. Gilson, *Thomisme*, 144, 85–97, 137–73; Gilson, *God and Philosophy*.

23. Gilson comments that "Thomas Aquinas … began by changing the Platonic notion of participation into an existential notion of causality" (*Le Thomisme*, 73). "To participate and to be caused are one and the same thing" (Gilson, "Causality and Participation," 89–100). See esp., Davison, *Participation in God*; Fabro, *Partecipazione e Causalità secondo S. Tommaso d'Aquino*.

24. Aristotle, *Metaphysics*, in *Complete Works*, V.2 (1013a24-1013b4); Aristotle, *Physics*, II.3 (194b16-195a3).

2. The Metaphysics of Participation

is the wood, the formal cause is the blueprints, the efficient cause is the builder, and the final cause is shelter. Aquinas uses this Aristotelian insight to explore the Pauline confession of God that "from him and through him and to him are all things" (Rom. 11:36).[25] In the rest of this section, we will follow Aquinas' close grammatical commentary on this passage to explore the way that his doctrine of participation emerges from his meditation on Scripture, leading him to speak of God as the efficient ("from him"), formal ("through him"), and final ("to him") cause of creation.[26]

In his commentary on Paul's letter to the Romans, Aquinas notes that, grammatically, "from" (Greek: ἐκ; Latin: *ex*) can be taken in multiple ways. Although it can be taken as referring to that *out of which* something is made, the world is not made out of God. In other words, God is not the material cause of creation, though he is the cause of all matter.[27] The preposition "from" must therefore denote not the material but the efficient cause: "All things are from God as from their first maker."[28] The world is not a necessary emanation from the divine essence, for the act of creation is the result of the will of God: *voluntas Dei est causa rerum*.[29] Furthermore, as we noted above, creation is primarily about the relationship between God and creatures: "Creation imports a relation [*habitudinem*] of the creature to the Creator, with a certain newness [*novitate*] or beginning [*incoeptione*]."[30] This relation, however, is radically asymmetrical: "The relation whereby the creature is referred to the Creator must be a real relation [*sit*

---

25. Andrew Davison makes much of this verse in his extensive treatment of participatory metaphysics (see Davison, *Participation in God*, esp. 13–132). What I offer here is more concisely focused on those elements most relevant for my overall argument and is more specifically driven by Aquinas' commentary on this passage.

26. *ST* I.44.1. Aquinas also interprets this in a Trinitarian fashion, writing that although all three prepositions "can be applied to each of the three persons, ... by appropriation we can say: from him, namely, from the Father, through him, namely, through the Son, in him, namely, in the Holy Spirit, are all things" (*In Epist. ad Rom.* §949). See, e.g., Emery, "Trinity and Creation," 58–76.

27. *In Epist. ad Rom.* §943. "God is the efficient, the exemplar and the final cause of all things, and ... primary matter is from him" (*ST* I, q. 44, a. 4). See Augustine, *Confessions*, XII.7, 298.

28. *In Epist. ad Rom.* §943. Citing 1 Cor. 11:12.

29. *ST* I.19.4. "There remains for [God], then, a free judgment [*liberum iudicium*] for willing this or that, as there is also in us," although "free choice [*liberum arbitrum*] ... is found in Him in a different way [*alio modo*] than in angels and in men" (*De ver.*, q. 24, a. 3; See *ST* I.19.10). Deliberative creation distinguishes Christian thought from the emanative creation of Neoplatonism (Boland, *Ideas in God According to Saint Thomas Aquinas*, 138; Dodds, *Proclus*, 290).

30. *ST* I.45.3, *ad* 3. Aquinas argues that although we know from divine revelation that the world did not exist eternally (*ST* I, q. 46, a. 2), even if it had, it would not in any way undermine the belief that it is created. Creation could exist eternally in a participatory relationship of contingent reliance on the creating and sustaining power of God just as

realis], while in God it is only a logical relation [*relatio secundum rationem*]."[31] This is often called a "mixed" relation, because it denies the existence of the relational accident to one of the subjects of the relation. In this case, the relational accident is denied of God because God cannot be the subject of accidents and because nothing of God's being is constituted by his relationship to his creation—creation fulfills no needs of God's, for he has none.[32] As Herbert McCabe puts it, "God simply does not have any relation of dependence on his creatures but he understands, with an understanding more intimate than any knowledge from experience, the truth about the dependence of creatures on his knowledge and love."[33] The ground of all of God's effects in creation is his efficient causation of the being of all things, for as Gilson notes, "There is nothing the creature itself can receive without first receiving being."[34] And as long as a thing has being, God must be present to it; "hence, it must be that God is in all things, and most intimately [*intime*]."[35]

Turning to the second preposition, Aquinas notes, citing Jn 1:3, that "all things are said to have been made by the Father *through* [Greek: διά; Latin: *per*] the Son."[36] For Aquinas, to say that God is the formal cause of things is to say that all of creation comes forth in an ordered way bearing a likeness to its creator and that all things were made through Christ, who is "the image [εἰκών] of the invisible God, the firstborn [πρωτότοκος] of all creation" (Col. 1:15). Therefore, God is an extrinsic formal (or exemplar) cause, not an intrinsic formal cause.[37] This is an affirmation of what Aquinas calls God's "self-communicative goodness," which sees God imparting to creatures something of himself.[38] Aquinas writes that "every substance circumscribed by the limits of its own nature has a limited and confined existence [*esse limitatum et coarctatum*]."[39] Creatures do not bear a uniform likeness to their cause, because "the 'similitude' of the divine essence," explains Te Velde, "is multiplied and distinguished into many and diverse effects, each of them

---

it could exist from a beginning in the same fashion "because to be from another is not inconsistent with being from eternity" (*De Pot.*, III.14).

31. *De Pot.*, III.3. Cf. *ST* I.13.7. A real relation involves boundedness and contrast. Tanner writes that "a God who transcends the world must also ... transcend the distinctions by contrast appropriate there. A God who genuinely transcends the world must not be characterized, therefore, by a direct contrast with it" (*God and Creation*, 42–6).

32. Matthew R. McWhorter defends Aquinas against the objections of William Lane Craig in "Aquinas on God's Relation to the World," 3–19. See discussions in Gorman, *Aquinas on the Metaphysics of the Hypostatic Union*, 57–72; Webster, "Non ex aequo," 115–26; Stump, *Aquinas*, 92–115.

33. McCabe, *God Matters*, 45.

34. Gilson, *Christian Philosophy*, 97.

35. *ST* I.8.1.

36. *In Epist. ad Rom.*, c. 11, lect. 5, §946. See Gen. 1:26; Jas 3:9 (*ST* I.4.3 s.c.).

37. *De ver.*, q. 3, a. 1.

38. See Davison, *Participation in God*, 84–112.

39. *De Spir.*, 1.15.

bearing a likeness in a distinct and partial way."[40] Accordingly, creatures are said to participate in God formally both as an imitation of the divine ideas[41] and as diverse participations in the divine perfections.[42] Aquinas speaks of all creation bearing a trace of God, while intellectual creatures are said to be made in his image.[43] On the flip side, evil is understood as a failure to participate: a breakdown in the act of characterful existence as the kind of thing one has been created to be.[44]

The third preposition "to" (Greek: εἰς; Latin: *in*)[45] "designates a relationship of final cause, in that the entire good of a thing and its preservation consists in its own greatest good."[46] Final causation has to do with direction, meaning, and purpose. All creatures are constituted with a fundamental orientation toward their fulfillment, not only in a temporal sense but also in an ontological, even existential sense. God is that "for which" creation exists (Acts 17:28) and, insofar as that teleological relationship of potentiality constitutes its existence even now, we say that it participates in God. Importantly, in connection with God's extrinsic formal causality, the destiny of all things to be united with God is not one of annihilation or obscurity. Rather, it is to attain the fulfillment of what they were created to be, to fill out the likeness to God that their nature was uniquely fashioned to achieve.[47] For humans, union with God makes us most fully and truly

---

40. Te Velde, *Participation and Substantiality*, 94. Aquinas writes: "Hence it is evident that it is not incompatible with a thing's simplicity to have many relations towards other things: indeed the more simple a thing is the greater the number of its concomitant relations: since its power is so much the less limited and consequently its causality so much the more extended" (*De Pot.*, VII.8).

41. *ST* I.15.2.

42. *ScG* I.54.4. See also *De Pot.*, VII.7 *ad obj. 6*.

43. *ST* I.93.1, *resp*; *ST* I.93.1, *ad* 3.

44. "The term 'evil' [*mali*] signifies nothing else than privation of perfect being [*privatio esse perfecti*]" (*Comp. Theol.* I.114). See *ST* I.49; *ScG* II.41.10; and Davison, *Participation in God*, 239–59. Augustine writes: "No one, therefore, need seek for an efficient cause of an evil will. Since the 'effect' is, in fact, a deficiency, the cause should be called 'deficient'" (Augustine, *City of God*, XII.7).

45. Although εἰς typically has the sense of "into" or "to," while the Latin "*in*" with the ablative typically does not have the sense of "to," Aquinas still recognizes the teleological direction of Paul's wording with the help of Col. 1:17.

46. *In Epist. ad Rom.*, §947. Translation adjusted.

47. "Nature does not attain to goodness in its universal aspect, but only to this particular good which is its perfection" (*ScG* II.23.10). Note that this involves more than creatures simply willing themselves to perfection, because their perfection, while proper to their nature, also transcends their nature. Although the ultimate good of humans, the beatific vision, involves their highest function (*operatio intellectus*), they are not by nature capable of attaining this intellectual vision. It is thus by grace that the created intellect is provided with the capacity for the blessed vision of God, through the *lumen gloriae* (*ST* I, q. 12, a. 4). It is important to recognize that an emphasis on the substantiality of creatures does not undermine their reliance on grace any more than it undercuts the meaning of participation.

what we are by forming us into the likeness of Christ, who is the image of God and the firstborn of all creation. Here we see the basis for an important principle in Aquinas' thought: "grace does not destroy nature but perfects it."[48] Because of its relationship to God as final cause, Aquinas understands human nature to have an obediential potency, rather than a natural passive potency, toward grace, such that nature can be taken up and transformed by the divine initiative of grace without either a superadded accident that makes it more suitable for grace, or a transformation that undermines or corrupts the nature.[49] We might summarize the foregoing picture of participation as follows: "The conceptuality of God's work of creation, like that of any 'intelligent' work, exhibits a threefold structure of bringing forth into existence, in an ordered way, and for the sake of some good."[50]

Because Aquinas conceives of the relationship between God and creation in terms of participation, he avoids the view that God is a being among beings. This allows him to uphold the radically noncompetitive relationship between the infinite and the finite and to conceive of their difference in qualitative, rather than quantitative terms. Aquinas typically approaches this qualitative difference in light of the modus principle: "The received is in the receiver according to the mode of the receiver."[51] When one thing is received into another it does not maintain the mode of existence proper to its source but comes to be present in the mode of the recipient. The clearest illustration of this principle comes from the sphere of sense perception. Aquinas, commenting on Aristotle, explains that, in the case of some physical changes, the form of one material object is received into the matter of another by means of a physical agent (e.g., when air is heated and thereby receives, in a material mode, the form of fire).[52] However, in the case of perception, the form of a material object is received into the senses *immaterially*. In this way, the form comes to exist in a new mode (*esse intentionale et spirituale*) according to the power that received it (i.e., the senses).[53] We will return to the application of this principle to sense perception and cognition in Chapter 4, but here we are interested in its broader metaphysical implications.

Aquinas employs the modus principle on the level of being to affirm that, by participation in God who is self-subsisting being itself, the creature receives the act of being *in a creaturely mode*. He puts it as follows: "The beings which share being from the First Being, do not share in it according to a universal mode of being as it is found in the First Principle; they participate in it in a particular way, according to a certain determinate mode of being which belongs to this given genus or this given species."[54] God and creatures are not two kinds of beings, for

---

48. ST I.1.8.
49. ST III.2.12 s.c. See Garrigues, "'Natural Grace' of Christ," 103–15.
50. Velde, *Aquinas on God: The "Divine Science" of the Summa Theologiae*, 125.
51. ST I.84.1.
52. *In De anima*, II, c. 12, §551.
53. *In De anima*, II, c. 12.
54. *De sub. Separatis*, §43. Aquinas speaks of there being present in creatures "a definite manner of being [*determinatum modum essendi*] which is founded upon the very existence

2. The Metaphysics of Participation

God is being itself, while creatures receive their being from another. By using the language of "mode," Aquinas avoids quantitative terminology and opens up a way for judgments to apply to diverse predicates in different ways without losing their meaning. This is the ground of analogy, to which we will turn shortly. He also gives us the conceptual framework within which to explore what it means that creator and creaturely agencies are noncompetitive. God and creatures cannot exist in a mutually exclusive relationship because the presence of God is the very ground of the existence, essence, power, and operations of creatures.

Aquinas notes that "things were made like God not only in being but also in acting."[55] Thomas typically approaches creaturely activity in terms of secondary causation, by which he means that God, the first cause, has created all creatures to exercise the operations belonging to their nature in such a way that their ability to cause anything is dependent on an antecedent operation of God.[56] It is of human nature to be free; in exercising freedom we express our natures, and in expressing our natures we express the activity of our first cause, which caused (and causes) our nature and its freedom.[57] Aquinas writes:

> But just as God has not only given being to things when they first began to exist, and also causes being in them [*esse in eis causat*] as long as they exist, conserving things in being, as we have shown, so also has He not merely granted operative powers [*virtutes operativas*] to them when they were originally created, but He always causes these powers in things. Hence, if this divine influence were to cease, every operation would cease. Therefore, every operation of a thing is traced back [*reducitur*] to Him as to its cause.[58]

Indeed, every movement of a will in which powers are applied toward some operation must be traced back to God (*reducitur in Deum*) as the "first agent of willing [*primum volentem*]."[59]

---

of the thing" (*De ver.*, q. 21, a. 1 *resp.*). A creature's particularity depends on the fact that its form is not infinite; rather, "it has determined principles without which it cannot exist, and a determined mode of existence" (*De Pot.*, q. 3, a. 16, *resp.*).

55. *De Pot.*, III.7. See *In Epist. ad Hebr.*, ch. 1, lect. 2, §31.

56. Antecedent metaphysically, moment by moment. Creatures only participate in being, while God is his own being: "That is why contingent beings are never more than second causes; they are never more than second beings" (Gilson, *The Spirit of Mediæval Philosophy*, 90). "Physical causality is to the act of creation what beings are to Being, and time to eternity" (ibid., 101). See also Clarke, "Causality and Time," 27–38.

57. To paraphrase Farrer, *Glass of Vision*, 17.

58. *ScG* III.67.3. "[By] the immensity of His goodness ... He has willed to communicate His likeness to things, not only so that they might exist, but also that they might be causes for other things" (*ScG* III.70.7).

59. *ScG*, III.67.4. Here Aquinas cites Jn 15:5, "for apart from me you can do nothing" and Phil. 2:13, "It is God who works in you, both to will and to work for his good pleasure." See more detailed discussion in *In Ioan.* §1993; *In Epist. ad Phil.*, c. 2.3.

This does not mean that second causes are therefore illusory, rendered superfluous by the superior efficacy of the first cause. Rather, Aquinas is suggesting that it is the very nature of divine causality to create and perfect creaturely capacities for action, endowing them with real powers that they exercise as created agents.[60] Unlike God's action, it is inherent to the nature of finite causality that it must always displace other finite causes. As Austin Farrer (1904–68) puts it, "The finite excludes another finite of incompatible nature ... I am enacting my life, you are enacting yours: I cannot enact yours nor you mine. But in some true sense the creature and the Creator are both enacting the creature's life, though in different ways and at different depths: in the second cause the first cause operates."[61] Divine causality does not exclude other causes; it is so efficacious that it can cause in creatures the full, free capacity to act in a way that does not compete with the infinite power that sustains it in being.[62] The action of God does not deprive creatures of movement, for his action is the very power of their movement. Were he to withdraw from them their freedom would not increase, rather, they would cease to exist altogether.[63]

It is this particular issue that Rowan Williams has taken up in his recent monograph *Christ the Heart of Creation*. Following the work of Austin Farrer, Williams argues:

> If God is truly the source, the ground and the context of every limited, finite state of affairs, if God is the action or agency that makes everything else active, then God cannot be spoken of as one item in a list of the forces active in the world. God's action cannot be added to the action of some other agent in order to make a more effective force. And this also means that God's action is never in *competition* with any particular activity inside the universe.[64]

---

60. "God makes the world to be *itself*, to have an integrity and completeness and goodness that is—by God's gift—its own. At the same time, God makes the world to be open to a relation with God's own infinite life that can enlarge and transfigure the created order without destroying it" (Williams, *Heart of Creation*, xiii).

61. Farrer, *Glass of Vision*, 35.

62. See ST I-II.6.2 *ad* 3.

63. It is this non-contrastive relationship, in particular, that absolves Aquinas of the critique of ontotheology. See, e.g., David Bentley Hart's argument that Heidegger does not understand this relationship in the theologies he critiques when expanding his criticism from Hegel to "the schoolmen" and the classical Christian tradition (Heidegger, "The Onto-Theo-Logical Constitution of Metaphysics," 42–74; Bentley Hart, *The Beauty of the Infinite*, 183–4). Jean-Luc Marion retracts his previous critique of Aquinas in his essay "Thomas Aquinas and Onto-Theo-Logy," 38–74. See also Ricoeur, "From Interpretation to Translation," 331–64.

64. Williams, *Heart of Creation*, xii.

The system of second causes that exists in the world is the proper effect of the first cause. Whenever infinite causality is conceived of as a remarkable instance of finite causality, it is transformed into a second cause. That is not to say that God cannot work through second causes to produce effects that transcend the natural efficacy of those causes (something like what we typically call miracles).[65] To be sure, Aquinas believes this is one way in which we experience God's action in history.[66] However, any approach that places God into gaps within a system of finite causes or considers divine action to be in competition with creaturely activity has thereby transformed the first cause into a second cause. Williams illustrates the ways in which Christological questions helped Christians over the course of the centuries to clarify and sharpen their grasp of the grammar of finite being and its relationship to God. The most complex and significant Christological questions turn on getting this relationship right. We will be in constant danger of transforming the divine nature into a created being unless we keep the notion of God as creator, and the resulting participatory ontology, at the center of our talk about Christ.

Analogy

Aquinas associates the fundamental ontological structure of reality with the function of language through his understanding of analogy.[67] In this vein, he writes that "the likeness (*similitude*) of creatures to God … [is affirmed] solely according to analogy, inasmuch as God is being by his very essence (*ens per essentiam*), whereas other things are beings by participation (*ens per participationem*)."[68] Cornelio Fabro notes that, in contrast to theories emphasizing formal univocity, the Thomistic notion of participation makes possible analogical discourse, "which has in participation its beginning, middle, and conclusion."[69] So, we might say that for Aquinas, analogy is the semantics of participation, while participation provides the formula for analogy.[70] It is for this reason that a number

---

65. Cf. Farrer, *Glass of Vision*, 22; Williams, *Christ the Heart*, 3.

66. ST I.105.6–8.

67. George Klubertanz provides a collection of many of the relevant texts on analogy in *St. Thomas Aquinas on Analogy*, 157–294. Technically, in the triangle of things, concepts, words, Aquinas is concerned more with the realm of concepts/*verba*, from which the analogical nature of language stems.

68. *ST* I.4.3 *ad* 3.

69. Fabro, "The Intensive Hermeneutics of Thomistic Philosophy," 481.

70. Ibid., 468. It should be noted that there are Thomists who object to this relationship between logic and metaphysics, arguing that analogy belongs to logic alone (see esp. McInerny, *Aquinas and Analogy*). Without entering that debate here, it is worth signaling my general agreement with the critique of McInerny's position advanced by Dewan ("St. Thomas and Analogy," 81–95). For Aquinas, the science of logic depends on metaphysics.

of contemporary Thomists refer to Aquinas' model of analogy as the "analogy of participation."[71]

Although Aquinas never wrote a treatise on analogy, it plays a central role in his thinking, and it matured into a complex and nuanced approach over the course of his writings. For a diachronic account of the development of analogy in Aquinas, I refer the reader to the meticulous studies of Hampus Lyttkens, George P. Klubertanz, John F. Wippel, and Gregory P. Rocca.[72] In what follows, I offer a general account of Thomas' mature doctrine of analogy with particular reference to the transition from predicamental analogy to transcendental analogy by way of participation.[73]

Aquinas explains that things cannot be predicated univocally of God and creatures because of the fact that creatures participate in God. God is what he is simply and universally while creatures receive what they are compositely and partially.[74] Again we see the modus principle at work: "An effect ... will not receive the univocal predication of the name unless it receives the same specific form according to the same mode of being."[75] Univocal predication requires that the predicate in question apply to both subjects according to the same *modus essendi*. Univocity applies only when the difference between the predicates is one of degree (e.g., when "white" is predicated of snow and of a wall); it does not function when the difference is qualitative (e.g., when "white" is predicated of snow and of whiteness itself).[76] So Aquinas concludes that "although the form in the agent and

---

Therefore, the logician's notions of univocity and analogy are more bounded than that of the metaphysician's and always retain the character of "stand-ins" for metaphysical conceptions. Analogy, especially on the transcendental level, implies a judgment with relation to a reality, rather than a mere proportion between concepts. See discussion of this last point in Rocca, *Speaking the Incomprehensible God*, 146–53.

71. See, e.g., Klubertzna, *Aquinas on Analogy*, 29; Clarke, *The One and the Many*, 56. See Rocca's summary of what makes Aquinas' approach distinctive in *Speaking*, 92.

72. Lyttkens, *The Analogy between God and the World*; Klubertanz, *Aquinas on Analogy*; Wippel, *Metaphysical Thought*; Rocca, *Speaking*.

73. Some scholars use "predicamental" analogy to refer to the level of finite being (or to more purely logical uses of analogy) and "transcendental" (and sometimes "theological") analogy to refer to analogy between God and creatures, but this should not be taken as a denial of the metaphysical nature of inter-categorical uses of analogy. Predicamental analogy of one-to-another is present from the early *De principiis naturae* and *De ente et essentia* (1252–6) to the late commentary on Aristotle's *Metaphysics* (1270–1). The more participatory strand of analogy is evident in the *Summa Contra Gentiles* (1259–65), *Summa Theologiae* (1265–73), *De Pot.* (1265–6), and *De substantiis separatis* (1271). See discussion in Montagnes, *Doctrine of Analogy* and, following Montagnes, Hütter, "Attending to the Wisdom of God—from Effect to Cause, from Creation to God," 209–45.

74. *ScG* I.32.2; I.32.6.

75. *ScG* I.32.3. See also *De Prin. Nat.* 6.

76. *ST* I.13.5.

the form in the effect have a common ratio, the fact that they have different modes of existence (*diversus modus existendi*) precludes their univocal predication."[77]

This does not, however, mean that names applied to God and creatures are merely equivocal, for in that case "we would know nothing about God except empty expressions (*nomina tantum vana*) to which nothing corresponds in reality."[78] Aquinas says that such a conception has been disproved by the philosophers and would go against the teaching of Scripture: "Ever since the creation of the world his eternal power [ἀΐδιος δύναμις] and divine nature [θειότης], invisible though they are, have been understood and seen through the things he has made [ποιήμασιν]" (Rom. 1:20).[79] Equivocity implies an absolute dissolution of the connection between God and creatures that cannot be squared with the doctrine of creation. As Aquinas maintains, "The effect must in some way be like its cause, wherefore nothing is predicated equivocally of cause and effect."[80] If, therefore, things are not predicated univocally or equivocally of God and creatures, then they must be understood in an analogical sense, "i.e., according to proportion [*idest proportionem*]."[81]

Aquinas distinguishes two different ways of speaking analogically. The first, analogy of many-to-one, is when something is predicated of two things with respect to something prior to both, in which they share. Aquinas rejects the application of this kind of analogy to God and creatures for the same reason that he rejected univocity, because there is nothing prior to God in which he shares.[82] The second, analogy of one-to-another, is when something is predicated of two things by reason of the relationship between them.[83] In this case nothing precedes the two, "but one of the two must precede [*esse prius*] the other."[84] Because God precedes the creature, and because the creature bears a likeness to God by means of participation, analogy of one-to-another is possible between God and

---

77. *De Pot.*, VII.7.
78. *De Pot.*, VII.7.
79. *ST* I.13.5.
80. *De Pot.*, VII.7.
81. *ST* I.13.5.
82. *ST* I.3.5 s.c.
83. *ST* I.13.5. The primary instance of such predication on the level of finite being is between substances and their accidents, for the former give causal order and unity to the latter within a particular being. Thus, accidents relate proportionately to each other, but also by way of causality of the substance. This is often illustrated with Aristotle's example of health (cf. *De Prin. Nat.* §366). In Aquinas' comments on this example (an example of *extrinsic* analogy) we can see how proportionality is dependent on unity of order: causality is given ontological primacy over proportionality. In other words, analogy of one-to-another—what Wippel calls "analogy by reference to a first" and Rocca calls "analogy of referential multivocity"—is more basic than analogy of many-to-one (Wippel, *Metaphysical Themes*, 82–6; Rocca, *Speaking*, 124–7, 141–3).
84. *De Pot.*, VII.7.

creatures.[85] In this way, names are predicated *per prius et posterius* by reference to an individual reality.[86] Metaphorical names apply primarily to creatures and only by similitude[87] to God (e.g., "God is a lion" or "God is a rock"), while analogical names belong primarily to God rather than creatures (e.g., "God is good"), because God is not only the cause of creaturely perfections such as goodness, but is himself good essentially.[88] However, because we first come to know such analogical names in and through creatures, they retain a creaturely *modus significandi* in our usage.[89]

At this point we circle back around to apply analogy on the transcendental level with reference to being, a conception often referred to as the "analogy of being." Aquinas writes that "when something receives in a particular way that which belongs to another in a universal way, the former is said to participate in the latter."[90] This definition of participation determines Aquinas' account of the analogy of being, the key to which is his notion of being as the "act of existence." If we simply consider being in terms of a yes or no question (does the chair exist? does God exist?), then we might be tempted to suggest that "being" is a univocal concept. However, such an approach would be far too reductive. Be-ing is not a simple fact; it is an act (the Latin word for being, *esse*, is the infinitive form of the verb "to be"), a standing forth from non-being that always takes a particular shape.[91] For this reason, it cannot be treated as a genus under which God and

---

85. *ScG* I.34.6. Aquinas will appeal to both types of analogy in relation to being, but only on the predicamental level (see *In IV Metaph.*, lect. 1, §539-43).

86. See Klubertanz, *Aquinas on Analogy*, 29-31.

87. From the Latin *similitudo*, which is often translated as "likeness." As Eleonore Stump notes, "That translation, however, often leads people into supposing that a *similitudo* is a pictorial representation or that it is supposed to resemble whatever it is a *similitudo* of. These are very misleading impressions" (*Aquinas*, 246n4). It is common in much Thomist writing, therefore, to anglicize the Latin to retain "similitude" as a technical term with a broader range of meaning than "likeness." See Deferrari, *A Lexicon of Saint Thomas Aquinas Based on the Summa Theologica and Selected Passages of His Other Works*, s.v. "similitudo."

88. *ST* I.13.6. See Rocca, *Speaking*, 139-41.

89. *ST* I.13.3. The fact that we may nonetheless speak truly of God is not because the *res significata* is a univocal core at the center of the concepts employed. Burrell notes that "Scotus uses a distinction Aquinas will also employ but it is more at home with Scotus. When any predicate is applied to God, the *res significata* can be affirmed of God, for it is arrived at by prescinding from every indigenous this-worldly *modus significandi*" (Burrell, *Analogy and Philosophical Language*, 116-17). The *res/modus* distinction functions differently for the two scholastics, and Aquinas' approach is often misunderstood when read according to Scotus' subsequent usage. See ibid., 136-9.

90. *In de hebd.* 2.71.

91. Aquinas notes that "act, however, is twofold; first, and second. The first act is the form and integrity (*forma et integritas*) of a thing; the second act is its operation (*operatio*)" (*ST* I, q. 48, a. 5 *resp*). See Gilson, *Mediaeval Philosophy*, 90.

creatures might be placed; "rather, 'being' is predicated analogically."[92] In this way, we can see that, on a theological register, the analogy of being is first of all a refusal to treat God as a being among beings,[93] and second an insistence on the derived likeness of creatures to the creator from whom they receive their being by participation.[94]

Conclusion

In contrast to the implicit metaphysical conceptions outlined in the previous chapter, Aquinas provides a robust and compelling understanding of God as being itself. In this way, God is understood to be utterly simple and transcendent in a way that does not jeopardize his active presence within creation. There is no gradation of being that reaches up to God as the greatest of all beings, for God is qualitatively different from all things, which exist by participation in him. This also means that God cannot be placed in a competitive or mutually exclusive relationship with humanity, for his presence is the ground of their existence and the source of their freedom for rational, willful action. Furthermore, our language, if it is to be true, must conform to this reality, and our ability to make faithful theological judgments will hinge on the appropriate use of analogy and metaphor when speaking about the mysteries of the faith and the relationship between created and uncreated being. This metaphysical picture has significant implications for philosophical anthropology, cognitive theory, and epistemology, as well as doctrinal loci such as Christology. Before unpacking the philosophical implications in detail, we will begin with a discussion of Christology. As we will see, we can only speak with any coherence about the hypostatic union of divinity and humanity in the person of Christ if we avoid collapsing these two natures into one another in a competitive fashion.

---

92. *De Prin. Nat.* 48. As Hütter notes, "Behind this approach is an axiomatic belief that the structure of the conceptual syntax that arises from the analysis of the way we predicate reality is isomorphic to this very reality. Hence the very predication of being discloses and renders intelligible the structures of being itself" ("Wisdom of God," 215).

93. See Clarke, "What Cannot Be Said in Saint Thomas's Essence-Existence Doctrine," 193.

94. For an influential modern approach to the analogy of being, see Przywara, *Analogia Entis*.

Chapter 3

THE DOCTRINE OF THE INCARNATION

Albert Schweitzer wrote that, at Chalcedon, the "doctrine of the two natures dissolved the unity of the Person, and thereby cut off the last possibility of a return to the historical Jesus."[1] He continued, "That the historic Jesus is something different from the Jesus Christ of the doctrine of the Two Natures seems to us now self-evident. We can, at the present day, scarcely imagine the long agony in which the historical view of the life of Jesus came to birth."[2] Schweitzer is not alone in his sense that the dogmatic confession of Christ's two natures is incompatible with historical inquiry into the figure of Jesus of Nazareth.[3] And it was not only the historical Jesus scholars who rejected the possibility of speaking of Jesus as a historical person with two "natures," for many theologians then and now have argued similarly.[4]

In this chapter I would like to address two closely related issues. One is a modern trajectory of theological reflection that has rejected ontological Christology in favor of what is often termed a "Christology from below," in which Jesus' divinity is accounted for by means of the perfection of some characteristic of his humanity,

---

1. Schweitzer, *The Quest of the Historical Jesus*, 3.
2. Ibid., 4. "He was still, like Lazarus of old, bound hand and foot with the grave-clothes … of the dogma of the Dual Natures" (ibid.).
3. "Chalcedon, I think, always smelled a bit like a confidence trick, celebrating in Tertullian-like fashion the absurdity of what is believed" (Wright, "Jesus and the Identity of God," 46). See also Strauss, *The Life of Jesus Critically Examined*, §146 (pp. 409–14), §151 (pp. 437–40); Wrede, "The Task and Methods of 'New Testament Theology,'" 68–116, at 69; von Harnack, *What Is Christianity?*, 204; Troeltsch, "The Dogmatics of the History-of-Religions School," 87–108; Bultmann, "The Christological Confession of the World Council of Churches," 273–90, esp. 287; Schillebeeckx, *Interim Report on the Books "Jesus" and "Christ,"* esp. 140–3; Schillebeeckx, *Jesus, an Experiment in Christology*, 656 (cf. Runia, *The Present-Day Christological Debate*, 53–8); Hollenbach, "The Historical Jesus Question in North America Today," 11–22, at 19–20; Vermes, *Christian Beginnings*, 234; Wilson, *Jesus*, xiii; Allison Jr., *The Historical Christ and the Theological Jesus*, 82–5. See Weaver, *The Historical Jesus in the Twentieth Century, 1900–1950*, 72–5.
4. See especially the various Christologies "from below" discussed in this chapter.

such as his God-consciousness or archetypal receptivity of the Spirit.[5] Many have supposed that this reversal of aspect, which begins with narrative, intention, and operation rather than ontology, is more amenable to historical treatments of Jesus. The other issue is historical Jesus scholars' conviction that treating Jesus as the subject of critical historical investigation necessitates the denial of Chalcedon. I contend that both elements rest on a mistake, due in large part to fundamental misunderstandings of classical Christological discourse, which are, in turn, often due to problematic metaphysical presuppositions, further highlighting the relevance of the previous chapter.[6] Compared with the various Christologies "from below," I want to suggest that classical Christology is better suited to maintain the properly finite reality of Christ's human nature and the unity of his person such that Jesus can be considered the subject of historical investigation, and that Aquinas' Christology in particular offers resources to augment our access to the historical figure of Jesus.[7] I will begin this argument with a critical discussion of philosophical concepts of personhood and their bearing on the oneness of Christ. Following that, the core of the chapter will provide a constructive account of Aquinas' doctrine of the hypostatic union, which includes discussion of a Thomist "Spirit Christology" that unites ontological and narrative accounts of Jesus' divine identity, affording common ground for dialogue between metaphysical and historical treatments of Christ.

Hypostasis and Personal Identity

Recent scholarship has noted a marked tendency in modern Christological reflection toward Nestorianism: a conception of the Incarnation as the accidental union of a human person with a divine person.[8] This tendency underwrites a persistent dualism that frequently leads scholars into conceptual gridlocks like those we discussed in Chapter 1, confronting them with insurmountable dichotomies that drive them to reject basic elements of classical theism, such as divine simplicity, impassibility, and so on.[9] This tendency is acutely manifest

---

5. Ian McFarland notes that the terminology of Christology from "above" and "below" likely originated with F. H. R. Frank in 1891 (*Word Made Flesh*, 5n11). Nicholas Lash argues convincingly that this above/below distinction is typically used to oppose Christologies "from above" and serves to obscure significant methodological and conceptual differences in "Up and Down in Christology," 31–46.

6. Not all of these disagreements result from misunderstandings. Some have understood and nonetheless chosen to reject the classical approach, in which case I am arguing that the classical tradition provides greater coherence than their alternatives.

7. These Christologies "from below" include especially the kenotic and historicizing Christologies discussed in Chapter 1 and the "consciousness Christologies" and non-Trinitarian "Spirit Christologies" discussed in this chapter.

8. See esp., Riches, *Ecce Homo*; White, *The Incarnate Lord*.

9. E.g., Allison, *Historical Christ*, 82–5.

among historical Jesus scholars, and their discussions of traditional Christological concepts belie a common assumption that the Christian tradition endorses a Christology in which a divine nature is united to the human person of Jesus.[10] By way of contrast, Aaron Riches rightly notes that the unity of Christ is traditionally maintained by affirming that "the human nature of Jesus exists only as subsisting in the divine Son such that, in the Son, the human Jesus and the Lord God are 'one and the same' (*unus et idem*)" (see 1 Cor. 8:6).[11] In other words, there is no human person in Christ; the human nature of Jesus only exists insofar as it is united to the divine person of the Word.[12] To unpack the significance of this approach for historical study of Jesus, we will begin by addressing common misconceptions about the kind of unity envisaged in classical Christology.

The Chalcedonian definition confesses that Christ is truly God and truly man, and that the distinction of natures is not taken away by the hypostatic union, "but rather the property of each nature [is] preserved, and concur[s] in one Person [πρόσωπον] and one *hypostasis* [ὑπόστασιν], not parted or divided into two persons [πρόσωπα], but one and the same Son, and only begotten, God the Word, the Lord Jesus Christ."[13] The terms used to describe the oneness of Christ, the Greek nouns *prosopon* and *hypostasis*, are typically translated into Latin as *persona*, and English as "person." However, "person" has come to have a different meaning in contemporary thought than it did for the church fathers, and this confusion has led not a few theologians and historians astray in their understanding of Chalcedon. Rather than attempting a detailed genealogical account of the philosophical influences on specific theologians, I want to discuss an idea that seems to have been "in the air," so to speak, by the eighteenth century

---

10. For instance, while Edward Schillebeeckx is aware that this is not the case for the Chalcedonian tradition, he argues in favor of it: "*Anhypostasis*, as privation or loss of the human person, must therefore be denied, of course, in Jesus" (*Jesus*, 656–7). Certain advocates of *kenotic* Christology also defend this approach: "No real meaning could be attached to a human 'nature' which is not simply one aspect of the concrete life of a human person" (Mackintosh, *The Doctrine of the Person of Jesus Christ*, 207). It has become standard to use the terms *anhypostasis-enhypostasis* to refer to the lack of a human hypostasis in Christ (*anhypostasis*) and the uniting of his human nature to the divine hypostasis (*enhypostasis*), even though that is not quite what they meant in patristic usage. See Shults in "A Dubious Christological Formula," 431–46; Gleede, *The Development of the Term* ἐνυπόστατος *from Origen to John of Damascus*; Riches, *Ecce Homo*, 107–27.

11. Riches, *Ecce Homo*, 3. This is because *unus* is founded on *esse* (In III *Sent.* d. 6, q. 2, a. 2).

12. "Although [Christ's] human nature is a certain individual in the genus of substance, nonetheless, because it does not exist separately through itself, but rather in something more perfect, namely, in the person of the Word of God, it follows that it would not have its own personhood. And thus the union was made in the person" (*ST* III.2.2 *ad 2*). See *ST* III.4.2; *ST* III.17.2.

13. "The Symbol of Chalcedon," 62.

and remains highly influential today. This is an account of personhood grounded in consciousness and memory: an approach originally proposed by the English philosopher John Locke.

Around the mid-seventeenth century, the question of personal identity began to shift away from ontology toward a more subjective approach. No longer understood as something inscribed in things themselves, it was now thought of as arising from our concepts or ideas of things. Alongside this shift, the concept of personhood began to serve a different purpose philosophically. For Boethius, a person was a particular type of *supposit*, and it was a concept that answered questions related to individuation.[14] But virtually all of the prominent English philosophers in the seventeenth century were nominalists, and nominalists need not account for individuation.[15] As a result, they began to consider the question of personhood as an inquiry into what preserves personal identity across time and change. When Locke published his chapter on identity in the second edition of his *Essay Concerning Human Understanding* in 1694, he forged a new direction for this conversation, arguing that personal identity across time is a function of continuity of consciousness, rather than substance-identity. "For the same consciousness being preserv'd," he wrote, "whether in the same or different Substances, the personal Identity is preserv'd."[16] Locke's account is about diachronic personal identity, *not* synchronic individuation—he argues that bare existence is sufficient to account for individuation[17]—and it remains a leading approach in the literature, despite centuries of critical response.[18] Locke distinguishes between three abstract ideas under which we can consider human subjects: soul, man, and person.[19] "Soul" refers to the thinking substance, and Locke remains agnostic about its immateriality; though, notably, many subsequent thinkers pick up his approach because of its compatibility with a materialist philosophy of mind.[20] "Man" essentially refers to the human body, though the exact referent of these terms will depend on one's broader anthropology.[21] The importance of the concept of "Person," in this triad, is that it indicates the aspect of a human subject with respect to which it can be

---

14. Boethius, *Contra Eutychen*, III.5-4 (p. 85).

15. "Nominalism (or the view that everything that exists is individual) reigned supreme in the English-speaking world. At least, all of the seventeenth-century English philosophers who are still well known today—Bacon, Hobbes, Locke—adopted some form of nominalism" (Thiel, *The Early Modern Subject*, 23). See ibid., 72.

16. Locke, *An Essay Concerning Human Understanding*, II.xxvii.13.

17. See early critical discussion in Lee, *Anti-Skepticism*, 121-2. See Thiel, *Early Modern Subject*, 163.

18. In other words, this is not about what distinguishes one individual from another, but what sustains the continuity of individual identity over time. Contemporary advocates of the Lockean account include John Perry, David Lewis, Sydney Shoemaker, and Derek Parfit.

19. Locke, *Essay*, II.xxvii.15.

20. Locke, *Essay*, II.xxvii.25.

21. Locke, *Essay*, II.xxvii.8. See also ibid., II.i.11, and II.xxvii.21.

judged from a legal or moral perspective.[22] The question of personal identity is the ground of law and morality. Whom can we hold accountable for their actions? Not the "Soul" or the "Man," but the "Person," which Locke grounds in a relatively novel concept of consciousness.[23]

In the English-speaking world, the first philosopher to use the term "consciousness" with a particular technical meaning was the Cambridge Platonist Ralph Cudworth (1617–88). Drawing on Neoplatonic sources, he used the term to indicate an awareness of one's own thoughts and actions, and in his usage it is closely related to the more widely used concept of conscience: *conscience* is the term for moral judgments of the self, based on internal *conscious* reflection.[24] Consciousness thus refers to that piece of the conscience that precedes moral judgment and enables reflection. Notably, Cudworth only ascribes to consciousness a role in knowledge, and he holds that personal identity is secured by the immaterial substance of the soul.[25] Locke takes up this concept of consciousness, which is distinct from two closely related notions: reflection and memory. Reflection occurs when our mental acts become objects of observation: it is a higher-order mental act directed toward other mental acts.[26] Memory is the way our consciousness relates to the past: it is the avenue for acts of thinking linked to the past, to which consciousness attends, and it is through this relation to past experiences that personal identity is preserved over time. Consciousness, on the other hand, is understood as a presence of the mind to itself, an immediate awareness that attends all acts of thinking but is not itself a distinct or higher-order act of thinking.[27] For Locke, consciousness does not account for the individuation of substances; it presupposes a thinking substance and adds a particular abstract idea under which it is to be considered.[28] While conscious memory can span gaps of unconsciousness, loss of memory can mean that I am still the same "Man" as before, but no longer the same "Person," and in this way personhood floats entirely free of substance.[29]

---

22. Locke, *Essay*, II.xxvii.26, II.xxviii.30.

23. See LoLordo, "Persons," 154–81.

24. See, e.g., Ralph Cudworth, *The True Intellectual System of the Universe* (1678), 159–60.

25. Ibid., 751.

26. Locke, *Essay*, II.i.8.

27. This is especially important for avoiding Leibniz's critique of an eternal regress: "it is impossible," writes Leibniz, "that we should always reflect explicitly on all our thoughts; for if we did, the mind would reflect on each reflection, ad infinitum, without ever being able to move on to a new thought" (Leibniz, *New Essays on Human Understanding*, 118).

28. Thiel, *Early Modern Subject*, 122.

29. Locke affirms the reverse is also the case, "That if the same consciousness … can be transferr'd from one thinking Substance to another, it will be possible, that two thinking Substances may make but one Person" (Locke, *Essay*, 2.xxvii.13). For further discussion of Locke's approach, see, e.g., Martin and Barresi, *Naturalization of the Soul*, esp. 12–29; Martin and Barresi, *The Rise and Fall of Soul and Self*; Stuart, *Locke's Metaphysics*, 340–80.

Locke's approach was developed in various ways by Leibniz and Wolff, attacked by Hume, and reestablished on different grounds by Kant. Its influence is also perceptible in the reflection on *das Gefühl* ("feeling" or "sentiment") in the German Romantic movement. Schleiermacher (1768–1834) transformed this broader Romantic concept into the distinctive notion of the "feeling of absolute dependence," which stood at the foundation of his dogmatic project.[30] By grounding dogma in religious consciousness, he established an alternative basis for theological speech that was broadly empirical. Further, because he developed a Christology out of human subjectivity, Schleiermacher has been referred to as the "father of consciousness Christology."[31] While Schleiermacher is directly influenced far more by Kant than Locke, the concept of personal identity grounded in consciousness stands at the heart of his Christological project and appears to contribute to his rejection of Chalcedon.

In his mature work, *The Christian Faith*, Schleiermacher interrogates the Chalcedonian approach, asking: "how, then, is the unity of a person's life to endure with the duality of natures without one yielding to the other … or, without the two natures blending into each other?"[32] He believed that the starting point of Chalcedon inevitably results in either Eutychianism or one of the twin errors of Apollinarianism and Nestorianism. Furthermore, he opposed the dyothelitism[33] of the Christian tradition, concluding that "if Christ has two wills, then the unity of the person is no more than apparent."[34] This led Schleiermacher to reconceive divine transcendence and human existence, as well as the unity of the two in Christ, in a radically new fashion. For him, Christ brings the divine to full expression within history through his perfect god-consciousness—that is, his arrival at a complete consciousness of the self as dependent on God. This is not a divine consciousness in Christ, but a human consciousness fully aware of its dependence on the divine; Jesus calls himself the Son "insofar as the Father is in him, but not insofar as something divine, which is called Son, dwells in him as a man."[35] As Thomas Joseph White has noted, a number of more recent theologians have followed a similar trajectory, and scholars such as Karl Rahner,[36] Jacques Dupuis, Jon Sobrino, and, in a different sense, N. T. Wright and Hans Urs von Balthasar, have sought to ground the unity of Christ in a form of consciousness, thus interpreting the personal union of God and man in the Incarnation through the

---

30. Schleiermacher, *The Christian Faith*, §4.3, p. 23. See McGrath, *The Making of Modern German Christology*, 19.

31. Vass, *A Pattern of Doctrines 1*, 193n78.

32. Schleiermacher, *Christian Faith*, §96.1, 585.

33. Greek for "two wills," *dyothelitism* became the official orthodox position at the Third Council of Constantinople in AD 681.

34. *Christian Faith*, §96.1, 586.

35. Schleiermacher, *Life of Jesus*, 100.

36. Rahner, "Self-Consciousness of Christ," 193–215 at 203–5.

medium of Christ's human spiritual operations.[37] Even scholars not intending to develop a "consciousness Christology" often intuitively assume that the confession of one "person" amounts to, or is reducible to, positing one consciousness in Christ. Keith Ward stands as a representative example. In his book, *Christ and the Cosmos*, he states erroneously that "in what was to become Patristic orthodoxy, it was asserted that the human consciousness of Jesus was identical with the divine consciousness of the eternal Logos."[38] Ward reflexively interprets the patristic language of hypostatic union *in terms of consciousness*, and he is not alone in this.[39]

The fact that our theological terms do not necessarily align with the meaning they have acquired within our broader culture is a perennial issue in Christological reflection. In his 1960 book *L'Incarnation*, Francis Ferrier wrote of the term "person" that "It may be true that certain philosophers use these terms in the context of their philosophical systems, but when the Church uses them in her official definitions she does not necessarily use them in the specialized senses in

---

37. See White, *Incarnate Lord*, 111; von Balthasar, *Theo-Drama: Theological Dramatic Theory*, 149–79, 207; *JVG*, 653.

38. Ward, *Christ and the Cosmos*, 37.

39. To offer just three examples of this pervasive tendency, Bentley Hart writes of

> the so-called enhypostatic union: the doctrine, that is, that there is but one person in Jesus, that he is not an amalgamation of two distinct centers of consciousness in extrinsic association, and that this one person, who possesses at once a wholly divine and a wholly human nature, is none other than the hypostasis, the divine Person, of the eternal son. (*That All Shall Be Saved*, 189)

Wickham maintains that Cyril of Alexandria "meant to preserve a unity of consciousness in Christ" ("The Ignorance of Christ: A Problem for the Ancient Theology," 224). And, following Friedrich Loofs' misreading of Leontius of Byzantium on *enhypostasis*, Relton praises Leontius for anticipating the "modern understanding" that consciousness gives substantial existence to intellectual natures, and that "the Ego of the God-Man was the divine unlimited Logos" (*A Study in Christology*, 225). It is worth noting that scholars occasionally assume the opposite as well, which is equally inaccurate: "The Council of Constantinople in 680 CE drew out the consequences of this assertion, affirming that in Christ there are two centers of consciousness" (McCord Adams, *What Sort of Human Nature?*, 8). The council does not include any discussion of consciousness that, as we have seen, is a modern concept. It proclaims "two natural volitions or wills in him and two natural principles of action." Even some English translations of Aquinas have anachronistically rendered terms like *considerationem* as "consciousness": "Christ is always engaged in the act of thinking according to His uncreated knowledge. But, since the two activities belong to Him by reason of two natures, this actual consciousness does not therefore exclude the added consciousness of created knowledge" (*De ver.*, q. 20, a. 1 *ad* 6, trans. James V. McGlynn, S.J. [Chicago: Henry Regnery Company, 1953]). To the contrary, Aquinas explains that "*Considerationem* signifies the act of the intellect in considering the truth about something" (*ST* II-II, q. 52, a. 4 *resp.*). See *Deferrari*, s.v. "consideratio" (p. 216).

which a particular school of philosophers habitually uses them."[40] In the sixth century, Leontius of Byzantium argued similarly: "What is at issue for us is not a matter of phrasing, but the manner in which the whole mystery of Christ exists. So we cannot make judgments or decisions here simply on the basis of this or that expression, or of certain phrases, but on the basis of its fundamental principles."[41] What we are after is the judgment at the heart of the Christological tradition, not simply its terminology. While this should be obvious to theologians, it is not always so.[42]

By way of contrast, Aquinas, following Boethius, offers a substantial account of personhood.[43] Michael Gorman helpfully unpacks Aquinas' understanding of substance as follows: "substances are all *individuals*; they all *subsist* [meaning they exist through themselves and not in another]; they all *stand under* non-subsisting beings [such as accidents]; [and] they are all *unified* [unlike a pile of sand, they are just one thing]."[44] "Person" adds to this concept of substance a determinate nature: "rational."[45] A substance with a rational nature has dominion over their actions, and this is why they have a special name over other substances.[46] The scholastic approach, therefore,

---

40. Ferrier, *What Is the Incarnation?*, 78.

41. *Deprehensio et Triumphus super Nestorianos* 42 (PG 86:1380 B). ET: Daley, "'A Richer Union,'" 246.

42. For examples of theologians who have made note of this problem, though without treating it in detail, see Pohle, *The Divine Trinity*, 224–7; Ferrier, *What Is the Incarnation?*, 78; Williams, "A Programme for Christology," 513–24 at 517; Sturch, *The Word and the Christ*, 269–74; Mongeau, "The Human and Divine Knowing of the Incarnate Word," 34; Pawl, *In Defense of Conciliar Christology*, 218ff; Hart, *In Him Was Life*, 98–9.

43. Scott M. Williams has recently argued that, while Aquinas did cite Boethius, he did not accept his definition on its own terms, but interpreted it in line with later interpreters who criticized Boethius' approach, especially Gilbert of Poitiers, William of Auxerre, and Richard of St. Victor ("Persons in Patristic and Medieval Christian Theology," 52–84, at 66). Joseph W. Koterski also argues that Aquinas finds the Boethian definition lacking and that he corrects it in *ST* III, q. 16, a. 2 *ad* 2 ("Boethius and the Theological Origins of the Concept of Person," 203–24). However, it seems that Michael Gorman is right to say that, *pace* Koterski, "in this place (and others) Aquinas means to explicate Boethius's meaning rather than correct it" (Gorman, *Aquinas on the Metaphysics of the Hypostatic Union*, 36). Whether Aquinas' explication is indebted to those interpreters highlighted by Williams is hard to say, though Aquinas' emphasis on subsistence points in this direction.

44. Gorman, *Aquinas on the Metaphysics of the Hypostatic Union*, 16. "Individual" signifies that this is a first substance, not a second substance, the latter of which means something like "nature" in Aristotle's usage (*ST* I.29.1 *ad* 2). Cf. Koterski, "Concept of Person," 203–24.

45. *De Pot.* q. 9, a. 1 resp.

46. *ST* I.29.1 *resp.*

denies Locke's distinction between substance, man, and person. The "man" is the same as the "person" for a realist, because consciousness is conceived of as a power of the substance and thus accidental to it. A substantial account of personhood, which grounds both synchronic individuation and diachronic identity, cannot be reduced to accidents.[47] If we are only discussing our ideas or "naming" of things, then we can parse out such accidental features and make them constitutive of our concepts, but that will only *replace* our understanding of things themselves if we are skeptical about knowledge of essences, which, as we will see in Chapter 4, we have good reason not to be. As Henry Felton (1679–1740), an early critic of Locke, noted, we may distinguish between the idea of soul, man, and person in our minds, but they are not separate in things themselves.[48] Delimiting our understanding of the human person to a concept of consciousness is tremendously reductive,[49] something that Locke was well aware of.[50] Personhood is not simply one of various ideas we can apply to a substance in terms of its psychological powers. Rather, it signifies a particular substance "as it is in its completeness (*in suo complemento*):"[51] it refers to a subject of active existence in its entirety.[52] That is not to say that human subjectivity is therefore

---

47. This gives us good reason to affirm, for example, that a dementia patient is the same person they were before.

48. Henry Felton, *The Resurrection of the Same Numerical Body, and Its Reunion to the Same Soul; Asserted in a Sermon Preached before the University of Oxford, at St. Mary's on Easter-Monday, 1725. In which Mr. Lock's Notions of Personality and Identity Are Confuted. And the Author of the Naked Gospel Is Answered* (1725), 67. See *De Pot.* q. 9, a. 2 *ad 2*. This is not to say that a person is ontologically identical with their soul, which is hylomorphically distinguished as the intrinsic formal cause of their substantial existence. But neither is the person separable from their soul in reality.

49. "The problem is that, ontologically speaking, any process of human consciousness—while it truly exists or has being—cannot be said to be all that a person is, for it is only an 'accidental' characteristic of a substantial human being, albeit a quite important characteristic" (White, *Incarnate Lord*, 42).

50. Recall that Locke limits the concept by distinguishing it from the man and soul—meaning that he recognizes that his new conception of personhood is not sufficient to account for a human in its entirety. Also note that it grounds only diachronic identity and thus assumes synchronic individuation by some other means (i.e., existence).

51. *ST* III.2.3 *ad* 2. "Hence the suppositum is taken to be a whole which has the nature as its formal part to perfect it" (*ST* III.2.2 *resp.*).

52. See *ST* III.2.2. In *DQ De Unione*, a. 4, *resp.*, Aquinas notes that *esse* cannot be recognized without a corresponding suppositum (and vice versa). "Now if there were two supposita in Christ, then each suppositum would have its own principle of being. And thus there would be a two-fold being in Christ simply."

unimportant to Aquinas,[53] but it is insufficient to account fully for the nature of personhood.[54]

In the *tertia pars*, Aquinas writes that "to the hypostasis alone are attributed the operations and the natural properties, and whatever belongs to the nature in the concrete."[55] The person is not reducible to the operations of its nature. This is why the Christian tradition is able coherently to attribute two wills to Christ, why Aquinas attributes two "knowledges," and why theologians such as Bernard Lonergan extrapolate two consciousnesses from these attributions.[56] Insofar as these are properties of the natures, they are not *constitutive* of the hypostasis, but are *attributed* to it, through the communication of idioms. And, therefore, "the human nature in Christ," writes Aquinas, "cannot be called a hypostasis or suppositum … but the complete being with which it concurs is said to be a hypostasis or suppositum."[57] In order to grasp the central judgment inscribed in classical accounts of Christ's personhood—that is, the affirmation of the substantial, personal presence of God in Christ—we cannot reduce the predicate

---

53. It is often assumed that the "turn to the subject" is a distinctly modern development beginning with Descartes, and that premodern thinkers fail to grasp that human minds are self-knowing. In reality, Aquinas had a sophisticated theory of human self-knowledge and a robust conception of the human person as a self-aware agent. See Scarpelli Cory, *Aquinas on Human Self-Knowledge*; de Libera, "When Did the Modern Subject Emerge?" 181–220.

54. Jean Galot, without mentioning Locke, argues that, because it is through consciousness that we perceive ourselves as persons, it is tempting to confuse our perception of personhood with personhood itself. "The person is the subject and object of consciousness, but he is not consciousness itself. Becoming conscious of oneself is an activity which, although emanating from the person and redirected to the person, belongs to the realm of nature" (*La Personne du Christ*. ET: *The Person of Christ*, 45).

55. *ST* III.2.3 *resp*. Note that Aquinas uses "concrete" here not in the typical contemporary sense (wherein "concrete" denotes something not abstract), but in the scholastic sense (wherein concrete terms refer to the person of Christ, while abstract terms refer to one of the natures). See Pawl, *In Defense of Conciliar Christology*, 34–8.

56. "We shall then conclude that Christ is one subject, ontologically of two natures and psychologically of two consciousnesses" (Lonergan, *De Constitutione Christi Ontologica et Psychologica*, 7). See also, e.g., Galot, *La Conscience de Jésus*. Andrew Ter Ern Loke critiques two-consciousness models of the Incarnation on the grounds that they result in Nestorianism. Without defending his conflation of consciousness with personhood, he states simply that "there are good grounds for agreeing with scholars who think that each discrete range of consciousness would be a person" (Ern Loke, *A Kryptic Model of the Incarnation*, 49). This assumption plays an outsized role in the overall logic of his proposal. It is also key to his critical review of Simon Gaine (*Journal of Theological Studies*, 465–8).

57. *ST* III.2.3 *ad* 2.

in view to a power of one or both natures, because it would render the union accidental.[58]

In fact, the mistake of many who have rejected the Chalcedonian approach is to assume that the fathers were interested in discussing the action of two natures, whereas what is in view is the assumption of a human nature by a divine person. Aquinas notes in an objection that "to act befits a person, not a nature [*agere convenit personae, non naturae*]," so that while he is clear that "the principle of the assumption belongs to the divine nature itself," he also maintains that "the term of the assumption belongs not to the Nature in itself, but by reason of the Person."[59] The divine nature is, of course, inseparable from the divine person, no less so in the Incarnation than from all eternity,[60] but that does not mean that Christology is about parsing out which bits of Jesus' appearance, words, or actions are the result of his divine "nature" and which are from his humanity. Rather, Chalcedonian Christology preserves the ancient Jewish confession of the invisibility of God: "no one shall see me and live" (Exod. 33:20; cf. 1 Tim. 6:16, Jn 1:18), which means that the Incarnation is not about transforming the divine nature to make it available to our senses.[61] Every*thing* we perceive in Christ is created and human,[62] but it is a human nature taken up and transformed by the active existence of the divine person of the Word. As Rowan Williams writes, this is

> an act of being which "enacts" its personal distinctiveness by comprehensively shaping the finite actions of a human subject in such a way that the real and concrete distinctiveness of that subject cannot be spoken of without reference to the Word. Finite agency becomes a real communication of more than it is (abstractly considered) in itself.[63]

---

58. So White argues:

> "Jesus is one with God/the Logos only insofar as he is remarkably conscious of God" can readily be interpreted as "Jesus is a subject distinct from God/the Logos with whom he is united in virtue of his consciousness of God/the Logos." The second idea follows logically from the first once we realistically concede that a human being is not his or her consciousness, but is an entity who possesses human consciousness. (White, *Incarnate Lord*, 112)

To make the point explicit vis-à-vis Locke, we should say "a *person* is not his or her consciousness," noting again the substantialist rejection of Locke's distinction between the human being (soul/man) and the person.

59. *ST* III.3.2 *resp.*
60. *ST* III.2.2 *ad 1*.
61. See *ST* I.12, qq. 3 and 11. Ian McFarland puts this in stark terms: "although the one *whom* we see in Jesus is none other than the Son of God, *what* we see in Jesus is simply and exhaustively human flesh and blood" (*The Word Made Flesh*, 8).
62. "No created likeness is sufficient to represent the Divine essence" (*ST* I.56.3 *resp.*).
63. Williams, *Christ the Heart of Creation*, 26.

Unity at the level of *hypostasis* and act of being are both far grander claims than can be grasped by the concept of consciousness. The transcendent mystery of the divine hypostasis, constituted through subsistent relations, giving a specificity to the eternal act of being of the Word (proceeding from the Father in the eternal unity of the triune Godhead), hypostatically united to a human nature in the Incarnation, is otherwise reduced to a strikingly mundane conception of a precognitive awareness of mental acts.

Thinking of personhood in terms of consciousness leads us to think of God and humanity in a competitive paradigm and encourages us to conceive of the unity of Christ by way of the addition of predicates, as if divinity plus humanity *adds up* to something. By placing divinity and humanity on the same plane, it sets up a quantitative paradigm between them where elements of one can be added to elements of the other. There is an Apollinarian caste to this,[64] where we look to replace a feature of Jesus' humanity with a feature of his "divinity": in this case not necessarily the whole mind but the consciousness. This goes hand in hand with a conception of the Incarnation as a divine nature being united with the human supposit of Jesus. In this way, Jesus' "divinity" is accounted for by the addition of certain divine predicates to a preexisting human person. Conceiving of personhood in terms of consciousness led Schweitzer et al. to understand classical Christology as a form of Nestorianism that rendered Christ a ghostly ahistorical figure, a schizophrenically divided jumble of divinity and humanity, far removed from the first-century Jewish man named Jesus of Nazareth. It was this approach they felt compelled to abandon.

Contrary to this whole picture, Aquinas argues that there is no human "person" in Christ, but that his human nature is hypostatically united to the divine person of the "Word." It is not personhood itself that his humanity lacks, but a person *other than the Word*.[65] In other words, there is no finite act of being in virtue of which Christ is who he is, but the act of being of the Word is the sole ground of Jesus of Nazareth's active agency.[66] This is arguably the central, distinctive insight of Aquinas' Christology. While the hypostatic union brings about, by the work of the Spirit, certain perfections of Jesus' human nature,[67] it in no way involves the

---

64. Apollinarianism has become known as the claim that in the Incarnation the Logos replaced the human mind (νοῦς) of Jesus. See the extant fragments of Apollinarius' writings in *Apollinarius von Laodicea und seine Schule*. See cautionary comments about judging Apollinarius himself in *The Case against Diodore and Theodore*, 9–10. Cf. Grillmeier, *Christ in Christian Tradition*, vol. 1, 329–40.

65. Mascall, *Via Media*, 103.

66. *ST* III.4.2 *resp*. See Barnes, "Albert the Great and Thomas Aquinas on Person, Hypostasis and Hypostatic Union," 107–46. Therefore, the human nature of Christ did not exist before it was assumed by the Word (*ScG* IV.43). Alfred Freddoso compares Aquinas' position on this point with Scotus and Ockham in "Human Nature, Potency, and the Incarnation," 27–53.

67. *ST* III.7.

addition of divine predicates to the humanity of Christ, nor the transformation of his human nature into something else.[68] Rather, as Williams articulates, it is an affirmation that the active presence of the Word "makes the humanity what it is, in the sense that it makes it to be the *way* it actively is (not in the sense that it makes it to be the *sort* of thing it is)."[69] As we will see, Aquinas understands this in instrumental terms: Christ's humanity is the instrument of his divinity.[70] As a result of Aquinas' metaphysical distinction between essence and existence in created things, he is able to attribute a single act of being to Christ—that is, the *esse* of the eternal Word—thereby securing the unity of Christ's personhood without recourse to predicates of essence, such as consciousness.

This discussion illustrates the importance of metaphysics for theological reflection by highlighting how our ideas about the individuation and knowledge of essences transform our theology.[71] If we cannot speak of things in themselves, then we will render properly ontological dogmatic judgments in terms of empirical phenomena, as Schleiermacher does.[72] In Christology, if we can no longer talk about substances and natures, then we are left with psychological descriptions of what it must have felt like to be God incarnate. Ironically, such metaphysical skepticism often leaves us with a perniciously speculative form of theology. As Eric Mascall noted in 1956:

> I am convinced that the early Church was right in seeing the problem of the Incarnation as primarily a metaphysical one. I am frankly amazed to find how often the problem of the Incarnation is taken as simply the problem of describing the mental life and consciousness of the Incarnate Lord, for this problem seems to me to be strictly insoluble. If I am asked what I conceive to be the metaphysical relation between the human and the divine in Christ, I can at least make some sort of attempt at an answer; but if I am asked to say what I believe it feels like to

---

68. "The flesh of Jesus Christ has not received the Word of God as one of its predicates" (Neder, *Participation in Christ*, 6).

69. Williams, *Christ the Heart*, 25.

70. *ST* III.19.1 *resp*.

71. In particular, it is here that nominalism has a notable impact. For a discussion of the nominalism underlying modern historicism, see Beiser, *The German Historicist Tradition*, 5–6.

72. I am not arguing that nominalism always inevitably leads to the approaches outlined here, as counterexamples in late medieval thought are readily available. Rather, I am suggesting that the overall nominalist caste of modern thought has led to a state of affairs where a dominant approach, and many people's automatic impulse, is to reject knowledge of essences and interpret personhood in terms of empirical phenomena. Nominalism, as a metaphysic that points its adherents away from asking metaphysical questions, thus contributes to an uncritical tendency in this direction while also concealing the fact that it does so.

be God incarnate I can only reply that I have not the slightest idea and I should not expect to have it.[73]

Whether or not Neo-Lockean accounts of personhood in terms of consciousness are adequate to serve as phenomenological descriptions of personal identity and provide sufficient grounds for ethics and law—something we have good reason to question[74]—we must recognize that this emphasis stems from a broader metaphysic. While discussions of consciousness expand our range of idioms for treating philosophical and theological questions, there is no reason to allow such subjective approaches to *substitute* for substantial accounts of personhood, not least in Christology. In other words, psychological, phenomenological, and historical approaches to philosophical and theological questions are, at times, valuable and appropriate to the task at hand, but they do not carry within themselves sufficient grounds to reject an attendant consideration of ontology. Furthermore, a substantial account of the unity of Christ provides greater space for historical approaches to Jesus because it alone protects the integrity and properly finite reality of Christ's human nature.

Aquinas on the Doctrine of the Hypostatic Union

In the previous section, we sketched an outline of Christology by way of a discussion of personhood. We now turn to a more systematic discussion of the doctrine of the hypostatic union in order to substantiate further the ways in which classical Christology protects the integrity of Christ's humanity for the sake of historical research. As much recent historical scholarship has shown, the Christian articulation of Christology in ontological terms is not driven by an aberrant obsession with Greek metaphysics, but by the insight that the mystery of Christ can finally be upheld consistently only through predication at the level of being—something Aquinas accomplishes with particular clarity. Anything short of this relies on "accidental" predicates at the level of nature, which admit only of separation or mixing. To speak in this mode is not to delimit what can be said of Christ in other modes: historical, narratival, existential, affective, ethical, and so on. Rather, it is, at the deepest level, to uphold the mystery of Christ in the face of various intentional and unintentional attempts to dissolve that mystery. In this way, classical Christology protects the integrity of Christ's humanity and the unity of his personhood in a way that much modern Christology fails to do. I would like to illustrate this fact by outlining Aquinas' Christology in dialogue with a variety of modern approaches. This will set the scene for our discussion of the mind of Christ in Chapters 5 through 7.

---

73. Mascall, *Via Media*, 118.
74. See, e.g., Flew, "Locke and the Problem of Personal Identity," 155–78; Mackie, *Problems from Locke*, 155–73; Williams, "Personal Identity and Individuation," 1–18.

We have already seen how Aquinas understands "person"; what, then, is a nature? Aquinas defines nature as "the 'whatness' (*quiddity*) of a species."[75] A nature is the intrinsic principle of its supposit by virtue of which it possesses its essential features and has its simple existence as a supposit: Aristotle is human by virtue of his humanity; humanity is that by which he exists as a supposit, for without his humanity he would not exist at all.[76] In light of this understanding of nature, Aquinas explains three ways that unity in nature could be understood, highlighting how each is unable to account for the unity of Christ. The first is found in artifacts, where two things are brought together untransformed to make up a third thing—like steel and wood in an axe. While this seems promising at first glance, in the end it can only amount to a juxtaposition; it is not a true union.[77] The second is by confusion, where the two are transformed into a third thing that is no longer either of them. This union of mutual transformation is impossible in Christ because the divine nature is immutable and infinite, so nothing can be added to it to make it something else.[78] The third involves the combination of two things incomplete in themselves, which become a complete thing through their union (such as a body and soul). Aquinas notes that this is impossible in Christ, (a) because divinity and humanity are each complete natures, (b) because there is no quantitative difference between them, such that they could add up to a whole, and (c) because just as a "human" is neither fully soul nor fully body, so Christ would be neither fully divine nor fully human.

Aquinas' understanding of "nature" is important in one further respect. As Michael Gorman has noted, Christology involves talking about Christ's human nature a lot, which tempts us to reify it, as if it were a thing in itself. But this is a serious mistake, and surely part of the reason why Nestorianism is such a perennial issue in modern thought. Affirming the reality of Jesus' humanity should not involve treating it as a thing, which is tantamount to hypostatizing

---

75. Aquinas notes that *natura* comes from *nascendo* ("nativity"), first signifying the begetting of living things and then coming to signify the principle of their begetting, which was taken to be the intrinsic principle of motion. Since the end of generation is the essence of the species, he identifies nature with essence, which points to the idea that "*Natura est unamquamque rem informans specifica differentia, quae scilicet complet definitionem speciei*" (*ST* III.2.1). Here he follows both Aristotle and Boethius.

76. For further discussion see, e.g., Gorman, "Uses of the Person–Nature Distinction in Thomas's Christology," 58–79; Gorman, *Metaphysics of the Hypostatic Union*, 45, 73–100; West, "The Real Distinction between Supposit and Nature," 85–106. West explains that, while Giles of Rome asserted that a real distinction resulted in multiple *res*, and Scotus held separability as both necessary and sufficient for a real distinction, Aquinas believes that positing a real distinction between essence and existence, or between nature and supposit, does not entail that the two could ever exist apart from each other (ibid., 93). That is not, however, to say an essence need be united to its own proper *esse*.

77. *ST* III.2.1 *resp*.

78. *ST* III.2.1.

it: treating it as a person.[79] While it is tempting to assume, as Schillebeeckx does, that only by denying the *anhypostasis* of Jesus' humanity can we affirm that he was really, truly a first-century Jewish man who lived and died in history, to do so is a fundamental Christological mistake, which rests on a misunderstanding of ontology. If we recall the modus principle once more, we can say that a nature is not a thing, rather, it is that by which something exists in a certain way: it is the principle of their particular mode of being. As such, to say that the Word assumed a human nature is to say that the person of the Word took up, in the Incarnation, that in virtue of which he exists in a human mode, without being multiplied into two supposits.

In the standard theological text of Aquinas' day, Peter Lombard's *Sentences*, the nature of the hypostatic union was addressed in terms of three common "opinions."[80] Because of his extensive recovery of Greek patristic conciliar documents, Aquinas came to reject the first and third of these opinions as versions of Nestorianism.[81] Many medieval commentators opted for the first opinion, known as the *homo assumptus* theory, which affirmed the substantial reality of Christ's humanity by arguing that, while there is one person (*persona*) in Christ, there are two hypostases or supposits: the humanity of Christ, body and soul, was a supposit that was assumed by the Word. Aquinas had already established in *ST* III.2.3 that a hypostasis or supposit *is* a person ("person only adds to hypostasis a determinate nature ... hence it is the same to attribute to the human nature in Christ a proper hypostasis and a proper person"), and therefore, he maintains, the *homo assumptus* theory posits two persons.[82] If there is a second hypostasis or supposit in Christ, then whatever pertains to humanity will be predicated not of the Word but of that supposit to which it belongs—which means we can no longer affirm that the Word of God was born of a virgin, suffered, died, and rose again.[83] Like those we discussed in the previous section,

---

79. Gorman, *Hypostatic Union*, 34.

80. Peter Lombard, *Sentences* III, d. 6, c. 2.

81. See discussion of Aquinas' development on this question in West, "Aquinas on Peter Lombard and the Metaphysical Status of Christ's Human Nature," 557–86. Aquinas' historical research in Orvieto resulted in his recovery of texts from the councils of Ephesus, Chalcedon, and Constantinople II and III, which were otherwise unknown in the thirteenth century. See discussion in Morard, "Thomas d'Aquin lecteur des conciles," 211–365; Geenen, "The Council of Chalcedon in the Theology of St. Thomas," 172–217; Barnes, *Christ's Two Wills in Scholastic Thought*.

82. He cites Constantinople III in his response (*ST* III.2.3 *resp.*). See also *De Pot.* q. 9, aa. 1–2. For his relation to earlier medieval commentators on this point, see Barnes, "Albert the Great and Thomas Aquinas on Person, Hypostasis, and Hypostatic Union," 107–46, esp. 114–19.

83. "And this, too, was condemned with the approval of the Council of Ephesus" (*ST* III.2.3 *resp.*).

this theory falls into error *per ignorantiam*, because it misunderstands the nature of personhood.[84]

In rejecting the third opinion, known as the *habitus* theory, Aquinas was in common company with many other thirteenth-century authors who viewed it as problematic.[85] This opinion, in an attempt to avoid Nestorianism, denied that the humanity of Christ could be considered something substantially distinct from the Word by maintaining that, rather than coming together in a substantial unity like they do in us, the body and soul of Christ were each united to the Word as accidents. To this theory, Aquinas responds that such an accidental union amounts to the same position as Nestorius, "for there is no difference in saying that the Word of God is united to the Man Christ by indwelling, as in His temple (as Nestorius said), or by putting on man, as a garment, which is the third opinion."[86] As with many reactionary theological positions, the extremity of this view pushes it into incoherence. Here the most anti-Nestorian attempt falls ironically back into Nestorianism by positing the accidental union of two substances as a result of "a shared quality or set of habitual relations" instead of a common hypostatic identity.[87] The problem with this, Aquinas argues, is that whatever truly adheres to a person is united to it in person: "Hence, if the human nature is not united to God the Word in person, it is nowise united to Him and thus belief in the Incarnation is altogether done away with."[88] This theory renders Christ's humanity illusory, which equally undermines our ability to affirm that the Word of God lived and died as a human. Therefore, Aquinas opts for the second theory, known as the *subsistence theory*. This view maintains the nonaccidental assumption of a complete human nature (body and soul integrated), which does not possess its own subsistence or *esse* (act of being), but is assumed into personhood by a higher, already-existing hypostasis.[89]

---

84. This theory can be found in Hugh of St. Victor, for example. The kind of error Aquinas pinpoints here is a mistake in reason's effort to comprehend the faith. The conciliar documents, as definitions of the faith, do not define the terms "nature" and "person"—to do so is the task of reason as it seeks to comprehend the mysteries of the faith. Faulty metaphysical understandings of the relevant theological terms result in faulty theology, not because of any intention to err theologically, but through ignorance of the relevant metaphysical issues.

85. This position came to be known as Christological Nihilianism because it denies that Christ's humanity could be called "something" (*aliquid*), and a version of it had been condemned by Pope Alexander III in 1177. See discussion in Colish, "Christological Nihilianism in the Second Half of the Twelfth Century," 146–55. The terminology is somewhat unhelpful insofar as, like we noted above, a nature on its own is not a "thing." What it is intending to express is a discontent with accidental or partible views of Christ's humanity.

86. *ST* III.2.6 *resp.*

87. White, *Incarnate Lord*, 86. If it is not united substantially to the Word, then it will have its own finite supposit, resulting in multiple persons.

88. *ST* III.2.2 *resp.*

89. "Already-existing" from our temporal perspective. This is not to say that in God's eternity, there is a narrative to be told about the Word existing pre-, during, and

Following on his insight that Nestorianism is a Christology of accidental union, Aquinas outlines five modes of accidental union that have commonly been suggested: (1) unity by indwelling, such that the Word dwells within the man as in a temple; (2) unity of intention, such that the will of the man was united with the will of God; (3) unity by operation, such that the man was an instrument of the Word; (4) unity by greatness of honor, such that the honor due to God was equally shown to the man; (5) unity by equivocation, or the communication of names.[90] This list of accidental modes of union is striking for its resemblance to contemporary Christology. (1) Non-Chalcedonian Spirit Christologies posit a unity by indwelling; (2) Consciousness Christology is a sophisticated version of the unity of intention; (3) Christologies of "mission consciousness" suggest a unity of operation; (4) mythological approaches emphasize unity by greatness of honor, and (5) unity by equivocation might be seen in those who posit the late development of high Christology, such that over time Christians came to worship and ascribe divine attributes to a purely human Jesus. As such, it might be more accurate to describe most Christologies "from below" as Christologies of accidental union.

Just as important, however, is the fact that Aquinas does not reject any of these modes of accidental union in his own Christology. He affirms (1) that the Spirit, though not the Word, dwells within Jesus' humanity as in a temple;[91] (2) that Jesus' human will was united with his divine will;[92] (3) that Jesus' humanity is an instrument of his divinity;[93] (4) that the honor due to God is shown to Jesus in his humanity;[94] and (5) that we should employ the communication of names. Aquinas' point is that these kinds of unity are too reductive to account adequately for the personal presence of the Word in Christ. These accidental forms of union must be grounded in and flow from substantial union in order to maintain Christ's hypostatic identity and the reality of his humanity. As a result, this theology of substantial union provides a structure for interrelating methods of inquiry that typically focus on accidental forms of union. In light of this, I would like to discuss

---

post-Incarnation. As Herbert McCabe helpfully articulates, "From the point of view of God, then, *sub specie eternitatis*, no sense can be given to the idea that at some point in God's life-story the Son became incarnate." He continues, "Moses could certainly have said 'It is true now that the Son of God exists' but he could not have said truly 'The Son of God exists now.'" *That* proposition, which attributes *temporal* existence ("now") to the Son of God, is the one that became true when Jesus was conceived in the womb of Mary. The simple truth is that apart from the Incarnation the Son of God exists at no time at all, at no "now," but in eternity, in which he acts upon all time but is not himself "measured by it," as Aquinas would say. "Before Abraham was, I am," 50.

90. *ST* III.2.6 *resp.*
91. *ST* III.16.
92. *ST* III.18.
93. *ST* III.19.1.
94. *ST* III.25.1.

how a Christology of substantial union allows us to integrate, compare, and assess Christological insights coming from historical, liberationist, existentialist, religious pluralist, apocalyptic, and other perspectives.

Procedural differences lead some to begin their enquiry into the identity and nature of Christ by way of narrative and operation before proceeding to the attendant ontological implications, while others (including most of the classical Christian tradition) begin with ontology, in the light of which they proceed to explore the historical, intentional, and operational questions. This divide is not, in itself, necessarily problematic, as it mirrors the division between the order of being and the order of knowing, which should always issue in a hermeneutical spiral. The problem arises when a procedural order that begins with history and narrative becomes a methodological restriction that denounces ontology or reduces it to empirical and historical phenomena (such as those historicizing and kenotic Christologies we discussed in Chapter 1),[95] or when an ontological Christology fails to engage with narrative and history (such as the decidedly a-historical Christ of Hegel or Kant, for example). Both errors impoverish our Christology.[96] Accidental modes of union are vital in our understanding of Christ, but they are insufficient as explanations of his substantial identity. Aquinas argues that this is because, "whatever is predicated accidentally, predicates, not substance, but quantity, or quality, or some other mode of being."[97] If our treatment of accidental modes of union is not ordered to, or does not arise from, an affirmation of hypostatic union, then we will not escape Nestorianism, with all of its attendant consequences. In the following chapter, we will address more fully the questions of epistemology that drive these divides, but first, it is worth discussing the role given by Aquinas to these modes of accidental union within a properly incarnational Christology and how it relates to prominent contemporary approaches.

---

95. For an excellent Thomist response to these lines of thinking, see McCabe, *God Matters*, 39–51. See also criticisms in Murphy, *God Is Not a Story*.

96. In this connection, the way Aquinas structured the *tertia pars* is noteworthy—in a break from the theological manuals of his day, Aquinas offers a twofold structure: the mystery of the Incarnation (qq. 1–26) and those things done and suffered by the Savior (qq. 27–59). In an effort to allow Scripture to interpret Scripture, Aquinas prioritizes questions about the identity of Christ (that he answers by way of detailed engagement with Scripture), which stand as the principles for interpreting the history of his incarnate life. See discussion in Boyle, "The Twofold Division of St. Thomas's Christology in the *Tertia Pars*," 439–47. On the other hand, Aquinas' doctrinal works flow from his commentaries on Scripture, so there is a real sense in which historical, exegetical questions are given a kind of priority in his thought. The key here is his theological approach to exegesis, which keeps these two poles from being mutually exclusive in the way that they often are today.

97. *ST* III.2.6 s.c.

Unity by Indwelling

Arguably the most noteworthy Christology centered on unity by indwelling is known as "Spirit Christology," which is often set in opposition to the "Logos Christology" of the Christian tradition.[98] The Jesuit theologian Roger Haight is an influential proponent of this approach. He characterizes it as proceeding "from below" in three senses: it is historical, genetic, and experiential, meaning that it relies on historical reconstruction, traces the development of beliefs about Jesus, and appeals to the Christian experience of grace for its Christological grammar.[99] As a result, Haight writes that the "foundational metaphor" underlying his spirit Christology is empowerment. Here he departs from various alternatives within Spirit Christology: John Hick's symbol of *inspiration*, Paul Tillich's metaphor of *possession*, Jürgen Moltmann's image of *incarnation*, and Shailer Mathews' metaphor of *indwelling*. Haight sees the metaphor of empowerment as more interactive and dynamic than these. He makes it clear that "God as Spirit is not present as the subject of Jesus' being and action," and, indeed, the focus here is on Jesus' activity, rather than his identity.[100] Haight writes that "Empowerment presumes the indwelling of God as Spirit to the human person of Jesus."[101] Jesus is to be thought of as the location or symbol of the Spirit's action: "where God acts, God is" writes Haight, "in this empowerment Christology Jesus is the reality of God."[102] There seem to be three reasons in particular why Haight finds this approach preferable—he thinks it is warranted exegetically (here relying on James Dunn in particular), he finds that the resulting "pioneer soteriology" emphasizing Jesus as second Adam makes Christ more imitable, and it allows for religious pluralism. As he writes, "Jesus … is constitutive and the cause of the salvation of Christians because he is the mediator of Christian awareness of life in the Spirit. But Jesus is not constitutive of salvation universally" because the Spirit is operative elsewhere as well.[103]

Dominic Legge has argued persuasively that Aquinas evidences his own balanced Spirit Christology.[104] Legge explores how, for Aquinas, the eternal processions of the Son from the Father (cf. Jn 8:42) and of the Spirit from the Father and Son (cf. Jn 15:26) are extended into time in the divine missions. The key here is that "a

---

98. See esp. Mackey, *Jesus, the Man and the Myth*; Mackey, *The Christian Experience of God as Trinity*; Dunn, *The Christ and the Spirit*; Dunn, *Jesus and the Spirit*; Dunn, *Christology in the Making*; Dunn and Mackey, *New Testament Theology in Dialogue*.

99. Haight, *Jesus Symbol of God*, 447.

100. Ibid., 455. He denies, among other things, the communication of properties (ibid., 456n60).

101. Ibid., 455.

102. Ibid.

103. Ibid., 456.

104. Legge, *The Trinitarian Christology of Thomas Aquinas*. See my review in *Reviews in Religion and Theology*, 526–8. This is contra Rahner, Balthasar, Weinandy, and others who have argued that Aquinas divorced Christology from the Trinity in his theology. See, e.g., Rahner, *The Trinity*, 30.

3. The Doctrine of the Incarnation 79

mission includes the eternal procession, with the addition of a temporal effect."[105] While every divine action is efficiently caused by the whole Trinity, the effect (or "terminus") of a divine mission is properly related to a single divine person who is made uniquely present therein.[106] In their invisible missions the Son and Spirit produce in rational creatures, through habitual grace, a likeness to their processions by which they dwell within the creature and lead it back to the Father.[107] In these cases, creatures are drawn into the divine persons as a "terminus" according to exemplar causality.[108] Within their visible missions the presence of the Spirit is only *signified* visibly by a sign (e.g., the dove in Jn 1:32), while the divine person of the Son is truly and uniquely *made visible* as the Word made flesh.[109] In the Incarnation, the human nature of Christ is drawn into the second person of the Trinity in a wholly unique way, as a terminus according to being (*esse*).[110]

Aquinas distinguishes between the one *esse* of the three divine persons and their threefold mode of existing (*modum existendi*), delineated according to the relations of origin.[111] The three persons exist as subsistent relations within the one divine nature, such that when we speak of the "personal *esse*" ("act of being") of the Son, we are referring to the proper supposit of the Son whose *esse* just is the one divine nature *as it is received from the Father*.[112] As a result, Christ's human nature is not united to the divine being in general, but specifically to the personal *esse* of the Son. In this way, the single personhood or "act of being" of the Word incarnate exists in a distinctly "filial" mode of being, such that everything he is and does comes from the Father and makes Him known (cf. Jn 14:9). Jesus humanly manifests the Son as the one who proceeds eternally from the Father, and thereby reveals the Father as his principle.[113]

---

105. *ST* I.43.2 *ad* 3.

106. *In I Sent*, d. 30, q. 1, a. 2 *ad* 3. For a discussion of these themes of the inseparability and appropriation of Trinitarian operations among pro-Nicene theology, see Ayres, *Nicaea and Its Legacy*, 297–300.

107. *Contra errores Graec.* I, c. 14.

108. "This occurs … according to exemplar causality, as … in the infusion of charity there is a termination to a likeness of the personal procession of the Holy Spirit" (*I Sent.* d. 30, q. 1, a. 2). See also *ScG* IV.21, and discussion in Legge, *Trinitarian Christology*, 38–9 and Doolan, *Aquinas on the Divine Ideas as Exemplar Causes*, 156–90.

109. *In I Sent.* d. 16, q. 1, a. 1 *ad* 1; *ST* I.43.7.

110. "There is a termination according to being [*esse*], and this mode belongs uniquely to the incarnation, through which the human nature is assumed into the being [*esse*] and unity of the divine person" (*I Sent.* d. 30, q. 1, a. 2). See *In Epist. ad Hebr.* c. 1, lect. 1 (no. 52); *ST* III, q. 17, a. 2.

111. *De Pot.*, q. 3, a. 15 *ad* 17; *ST* I.33.1; *ST* I.42.3. Cf. Emery, OP, "The Personal Mode of Trinitarian Action in Saint Thomas Aquinas," 31–77; Emery, *The Trinitarian Theology of Thomas Aquinas*, 71.

112. *ST* I.27.2 *ad* 3; *De Pot.*, q. 9, a. 5 *ad* 23.

113. *In Ioan.* c. 16, lect. 4, §2107. See Legge, *Trinitarian Christology*, 116.

One of the views that Aquinas shares with certain contemporary proponents of Spirit Christology is that, in order to avoid a confusion of natures, we cannot simply say that the hypostatic union divinizes Christ's humanity.[114] As St. Thomas puts it, "the soul of Christ is not essentially Divine. Hence it behooves it to be Divine by participation (*fiat divina per participationem*), which is by grace."[115] The invisible mission of the Holy Spirit is present through habitual grace in the human soul of Christ, fully sanctifying Christ's human nature and preparing it with the "habitus" to function as an instrument of the Word.[116] Aquinas says that Christ receives "the whole Spirit" (*totum spiritum*),[117] and Legge notes three key implications of this: Jesus receives the gifts of the Spirit to the fullest extent;[118] he perpetually possesses the fullness of the Spirit's power to work miracles and prophesy;[119] and he has the infinite capacity to pour out the gifts of the Spirit, and the Holy Spirit himself, upon others.[120]

For Aquinas, because the Spirit proceeds eternally from the Father and the Son, the humanity of Christ receives the habitual grace of the Spirit from the font of the Word, to which he is united in person. As Legge notes, Aquinas thus

> offers an authentic Spirit-Christology, [which] preserves the Trinitarian order of processions ... while accounting for the absolute uniqueness of Christ ... The humanity of Christ is not mixed with the divine nature, but is supremely sanctified by the Holy Spirit's gift of grace in accordance with his human

---

114. See, e.g., Liston, "Christology," 77.
115. *ST* III.7.1 *ad* 1.
116. *ST* III.7.2. Legge maintains, against those Thomists of the "substantial holiness" position (Toletus, Suarez, and others), that in order to avoid a confusion of natures, we cannot simply say that the hypostatic union divinizes Christ's humanity. The mediation of a created form is necessary, which is habitual grace: the invisible mission of the Spirit to Christ. At the same time, Legge disagrees with Jean-Pierre Torrell, who argues that habitual grace is only fitting, and not a necessary consequence of the hypostatic union. Legge agrees with Torrell that Christ's habitual grace is formally distinct from the grace of union, but he maintains that it is nonetheless entailed by it. He concludes,

> both of these modes of divine presence in Christ are efficiently caused by all three persons of the Trinity, a fact that does not diminish in any way the reality of Christ's identity as the son, or the reality of the Spirit's presence in his humanity. As Thomas suggests elsewhere, the important thing is not to distinguish different actions belonging to different persons, but to distinguish the divine persons within the one divine action. (Legge, *Christology*, 135–59, at 158)

117. *In Matt.*, c. 12, lect. 1, §1000; Legge, *Christology*, 162–3.
118. *ST* III.7, aa. 10–11.
119. *In Ioan.* c. 14, lect. 4, §1915.
120. *ST* III.7.10 *ad* 1.

condition, so that the Holy Spirit is present in that humanity according to the full capacity of a human nature for union with God.[121]

Aquinas' approach encourages us to delineate the different depths and modes of the causality and presence of the Word and the Spirit within the person and work of Christ. Not only is this important for consistently upholding Trinitarian doctrine, it also allows us to discern the patterns of the eternal processions *within* the created effects of the divine missions, patterns that provide what Legge calls the "vectors" for our own return to God.[122] Furthermore, it protects the integrity of Jesus' humanity by emphasizing the filial *theandric* actions of Jesus as divine actions in a fully human "mode of being." The grace of the Holy Spirit does not destroy the integrity of Jesus' human finitude any more than does the work of the Spirit among the patriarchs, prophets, and disciples, even if the nature or degree of this work is wholly unique in the person of Christ.

For Aquinas, the humanity of Christ is the created effect of the visible mission of the Son (a terminus according to being), by which he is made visible in person, *and* it is the recipient of the invisible mission of the Spirit. For Haight, by contrast, the human *person* of Christ is the visible sign that signifies the Spirit's presence. Much like the dove, the humanity of Christ retains its own proper supposit—its own finite human identity—but becomes the place, signifier, or "symbol" of the Spirit's activity. To my mind, the strongest exegetical arguments in Haight's favor support the role of the Spirit in Christ's saving mission but do not rule out the filial identity and Incarnation of the Son. As such, Haight's constructive aim to speak of Christ's human existence using the grammar of the Christian experience of grace can be fruitfully integrated into a Thomistic account. It is primarily his negative aim, to deny Christ's hypostatic identity in pursuit of religious pluralism, which stands at odds with Aquinas' approach. Somewhat ironically, Haight claims that "Logos Christology ... tended to place other christologies in a shadow," whereas his Spirit Christology provides a basis for considering, interpreting, and appropriating other Christological approaches.[123] And yet, while Aquinas' approach can account for the positive aims of Haight's Spirit Christology, Haight explicitly rules out the positive aims of much of the classical tradition.

Before turning to the second form of accidental union, it is worth pausing here to explore briefly how Aquinas' "Spirit Christology" bears on the question of Jesus' knowledge, which will occupy our focus in Chapters 5 to 7. In qq. 9–12 of the *Tertia pars*, Aquinas argues that Christ possessed divine knowledge and a threefold human knowledge: beatific, infused (i.e., prophetic), and acquired. Here, I would like to note how the crucial pneumatological elements of Thomas' Christology reveal connections between his ontological reflections on Christ and his focus on Scripture's larger narrative of salvation history. Aquinas draws a connection

---

121. Legge, *Trinitarian Christology*, 167–8.
122. Legge, *Trinitarian Christology*, 105.
123. Haight, *Jesus Symbol of God*, 451.

between Christ's threefold human knowledge, his threefold office (*munus triplex*), and his fulfillment of the threefold law (*lex triplex*).[124] He notes that "Wherefore as to others, one is a lawgiver [*legislator*], another is a priest [*sacerdos*], another is a king [*rex*]; but all these concur [*concurrunt*] in Christ."[125] In this connection, he highlights the fact that, by his flesh, Christ belongs to the people of Israel and is born a son of Abraham and of David. It was to these two patriarchs that God's great promises were made (cf. Gen. 22:18; Ps. 132:11), and as prophet,[126] priest, and king, Christ fulfills their roles in salvation history so that God's promises might flow out to all creation.[127] Christ fulfills the moral precepts of the Old Law as prophet, the ceremonial precepts as priest, and the judicial precepts as king.[128] But note that these titles describe Jesus' human nature: Christ *as man* fulfills the roles of the patriarchs.[129] This brings us to the role of the Spirit, anointing and sanctifying Jesus' humanity, enabling him *humanly* to fulfill the roles of prophet, priest, and king that God entrusted to his chosen people, and thereby releasing them from bondage: "For the Lord is our judge, the Lord is our lawgiver, the Lord is our king; he will save us" (Isa. 33:22).[130]

Quoting Heb. 5:8, Aquinas connects Jesus' priestly office with his acquired knowledge: "Although he was a son, he learned obedience through what he suffered [ἔπαθεν]." Thomas references a gloss that says "through what he experienced," reflecting on the necessity of Jesus' authentically human experiences for his priestly mediatorial role.[131] For Aquinas, Christ is the true mediator because, while he was God incarnate, he learned obedience in the way that we do, through the physical working of his senses and imagination in concert with his intellect. In addition, Aquinas maintains that Jesus is the prophet like Moses foretold in Deuteronomy

---

124. For discussion of the three eschatological figures (prophetic, priestly, and royal) mentioned in the Dead Sea Scrolls, in particular in *1QRule of the Community*, see Pitre, *Jesus and the Last Supper*, 64.

125. *ST* III.22.1. On Jesus' threefold office, see, e.g., *In Epist. ad Rom.*, c. 1, lect. 2, §40; Ibid., c. 4, lect. 2, §352; Ibid., c. 9, lect. 2, §752; *In Epist. ad Hebr.*, c. 3, lect. 5; ibid., c. 3, lect. 9; *In Epist. ad Phil.*, c. 3, lect. 1. The concurrence of these three offices in one figure appears to be in line with widespread expectation in the first century of a priestly Messiah who would be the prophet like Moses foretold in Deuteronomy 18.

126. Aquinas uses "lawgiver" and "prophet" interchangeably: a prophet teaches the people how to live according to God's law.

127. *ST* III.31.2. Aquinas maintains that Abraham was a prophet and priest, David a prophet and king. See, *In Matt.*, c. 1, lect. 1, §19.

128. See discussion in Levering, *Christ's Fulfillment of Torah and Temple*, 69.

129. "Because of the hypostatic union, these attributes in a real sense 'belong to' the divine Word as subject; but they are nonetheless attributes of Christ *as man*" (Levering, *Torah and Temple*, 70).

130. *In Matt.*, c. 1, lect. 4, §99.

131. *ST* III.9.4 s.c. Aquinas' text has *passus* for "suffered" and the gloss provides *expertus est*.

18, who through infused species (i.e., knowledge supernaturally infused in Jesus' possible intellect by the grace of the Spirit) taught the New Law: the supernatural end of the Old Law, which he brought about in his ministry and, ultimately, through his passion. Like Moses, Jesus' prophetic vocation was to redeem God's people, and by his saving work on the cross his teaching came to be written, not in stone but on the flesh of the heart by the indwelling of the Spirit (2 Cor. 3:3).[132] Finally, Aquinas maintains that Christ's kingship is founded upon his possession of the beatific vision in his human soul.[133] This is how "he that was born King of the Jews" shares in the Father's rule.[134] Citing Rom. 2:16, Aquinas explains that because he is the Word incarnate, Christ as man receives the "whole Spirit," which flows from the Word and imparts to his soul the supernatural *habitus* of the light of Glory "under which" (*sub quo*)[135] he sees the essence of God directly.[136] This is divine knowledge possessed in a human manner in Christ's soul: the received is in the receiver according to the mode of the receiver. In this way, Christ, as man, holds a human royal office, but reigns therein as the divine king—and this can be traced to the invisible mission of the Spirit to his human soul *by virtue* of the divine Word to whom he is hypostatically united in person.

Aquinas' Spirit Christology can help us connect the narrative presentation of Jesus' distinctiveness—something akin to what Richard Bauckham calls a theology of divine identity—with a metaphysically informed Christology that reveals the presence and causality of all three divine persons within the words and actions of the Incarnate Christ.[137] We will engage this task in greater detail in the final three chapters.

Unity by Intention

In positing the presence of God in Christ through Jesus' God-consciousness, Friedrich Schleiermacher offers one of the most prominent modern approaches to unity by intention. To put his approach in Thomistic terms: because Jesus' God-consciousness is a property of his human nature, the dignity that accrues to Christ by virtue of this "existence of God in him"[138] must be an accidental quality derived from the "habitual grace" of Christ (rather than the grace of union). This unity of intention thus leads to a kind of unity by indwelling, such that God indwells the human Christ by virtue of his consciousness.

Aquinas also affirms that there is a unity of intention in Christ but conceives of it differently because it is grounded in Jesus' hypostatic identity. The doctrine of the

132. *ST* III.42.4 *ad* 4.
133. *ST* III.58.4, *ad* 2.
134. *ST* III.36.8.
135. *ST* I.12.5.
136. *ST* III.10. Cf. *ST* III.10.2 *resp.*
137. See Bauckham, *Jesus and the God of Israel*, esp. 57–9.
138. *Christian Faith* §94, 385.

two wills of Christ—referred to by the Greek word *dyothelitism*—was the last major piece of Chalcedonian orthodoxy to come into place in the early Christological councils.[139] The two central elements of the doctrine are that the will belongs to the nature, not the supposit—willing is only proper to certain natures, and, from a Trinitarian perspective, the opposite would result in three wills in the Godhead—and that the will belongs to the perfection of human nature,[140] so that had Christ not assumed a human will, his humanity would have been incomplete.[141] The great champion of *dyothelitism*, Maximus the Confessor, made it clear that what is at stake is the true humanity of Jesus: "If the Word made flesh does not himself will naturally as a human being and perform things in accordance with nature, how can he willingly undergo hunger and thirst, labour and weariness, sleep and all the rest?"[142] As he goes on to say, Christ "did not come to debase the nature which he himself, as God and Word, had made," rather, he came that it might be deified by uniting to himself "everything that naturally belongs to it, apart from sin."[143] In line with Maximus, Aquinas affirms a twofold mode of operation in Christ that follows from an affirmation of his twofold mode of being.[144] However, he explains that these two modes of operating are not simply divine and human modes—rather, one is divine, the other is a composite *theandric* operation.[145] In the Incarnation, the Word retains his eternal divine operation, which he has in common with the Father and the Spirit (the "Extra-Calvinisticum"). But he also has a mode of operation in which he does divine things humanly and human things divinely: "inasmuch as His Divine operation employs the human, and His human operation shares in the power of the Divine."[146] In this way, there is a synergy of

---

139. See Louth, *Maximus the Confessor*, 1–18.

140. "For everything that is rational by nature, certainly also possesses a will by nature" (Maximus the Confessor, "Opuscule 7" in Louth, *Maximus the Confessor*, 183).

141. Ibid., 181. Otherwise, Maximus notes, either "we melt down the two essential wills ... and recast them by composition as one will ... as in the myths," something like the Eutychian approach, or else "we preserve unblemished the natural will of the divine nature of the Incarnate Word ... and remove and reject them from the nature of its humanity ... [such that] the flesh endowed with a rational soul and mind, that is of our nature and substance, is not at all preserved sound and whole in the Word," not unlike the Apollinarianism (ibid., 181–2).

142. Ibid., 182.

143. Ibid., 184.

144. Barnes, *Christ's Two Wills*.

145. For his understanding of this principle Aquinas is indebted to John Damascene's *On the Orthodox Faith* (see esp. 3.13-3.19), which mediated to him Maximus' approach (esp. *Ambiguum* 5) to interpreting Dionysius. See discussion in Hofer, "Dionysian Elements in Thomas Aquinas's Christology," 409–42. For more on Dionysius' Christology itself, see Mahoney, "A Note on the Importance of the Incarnation in Dionysius the Areopagite," 49–53; Perczel, "The Christology of Pseudo-Dionysius the Areopagite," 409–46.

146. *ST* III.19.1 *ad 1*.

divine and human action—and an instrumental unity between divine and human will—in the person of Christ.

Maximus distinguished between *Logos*, which signifies nature according to its defining principles, and *Tropos*, which signifies the mode according to which a nature is actualized. As such, he maintained that Christ shared the *Logos* of our nature, but a different *Tropos* according to the concrete act of existence of the Word. In particular, Maximus maintains that Jesus possessed a natural will (θέλημα φυσικόν), but not the *Tropos* of a gnomic will (γνώμη), which involves deliberation in light of ignorance and uncertainty and is intimately connected with the possibility of sin.[147] Maximus' argument was mediated to Thomas by John of Damascus, who alters it slightly. Nonetheless, Aquinas affirms something similar, and, citing Eph. 1:4, he notes that doubt is not necessary for free choice, "since it belongs even to God Himself to choose."[148] Jesus' natural will is perfectly attuned and surrendered to the divine will—"not my will, but yours be done" (Lk. 22:43)[149]—revealing to us the action of a human will set free to act in perfect concert with the will of God.[150]

To put this in Schleiermacher's terms, this is a human consciousness fully aware of its dependence on the divine. Schleiermacher rightly departs from most historical Jesus scholarship in his insistence that (to put it in classical terms) Christ does not share the same *Tropos* or economic mode of existence as we do, because his humanity (at least his human consciousness) is perfected by grace. If he is to be understood by historical analogy, it will be according to the highest experiences of "God-consciousness," rather than a universal post-enlightenment anthropology. Therefore, it seems to me that Aquinas' approach can accommodate many of Schleiermacher's constructive aims, whereas Schleiermacher explicitly denies the classical approach. Where Aquinas differs from Schleiermacher is that he sees this habitual grace flowing from the grace of union, because it is fitting to Christ's personal identity and saving mission. Christ's humanity is perfected *in virtue of* the Incarnation of the Word, whereas for Schleiermacher, the perfection of Christ's humanity itself *just is* the presence of God in history.

Unity of Operation

For a prominent modern example of unity of operation, I want to consider N. T. Wright's Christology. Wright might be said to account for Jesus' "divinity" by the

---

147. *Opusculum* III, 45D.

148. *ST* III.18.4 *ad 1*.

149. Some contend that "Yours" in this passage refers to the will of the Father, rather than Jesus' divine will, but the will is constitutive of nature, not person, so there is only one will in God. In other words, the will of the Father *is the divine will of the Son*.

150. For defense of dyothelitism against a number of contemporary objections raised by J. P. Moreland, William Lane Craig, P. T. Forsyth, H. R. Mackintosh, Wolfhart Pannenberg, Schleiermacher, and John Macquarrie, see Watts, "Two Wills in Christ?," 455–87.

fact that "as a part of his human vocation, grasped in faith, sustained in prayer, tested in confrontation, agonized over in further prayer and doubt, and implemented in action, he believed that he had to do and be, for Israel and the world, that which according to Scripture only YHWH himself could do and be."[151] Jesus is said to have possessed this awareness "with the knowledge that he could be making a terrible, lunatic mistake."[152] It is consistently the case that the most exalted terms Wright uses to speak of Jesus have to do with this "mission consciousness" (a concept reminiscent of Hans Urs von Balthasar's Christology).[153] It is not always clear what Wright has in mind, but he does speak of Jesus slowly coming to view himself as possibly having a job to do; one that—if he succeeds—will see him exalted and glorified in quite an unprecedented manner. It is striking just how little Wright's Jesus knows, and Wright typically gives natural explanations for moments when Jesus seems to possess extraordinary knowledge. For instance, Jesus' prediction of his own death "did not, actually, take a great deal of 'supernatural' insight, any more than it took much more than ordinary common sense to predict that, if Israel continued to attempt rebellion against Rome, Rome would eventually do to her as a nation what she was now going to do to this strange would-be Messiah."[154] Even Jesus' own identity remained opaque to him. As we have seen, Wright maintains that

> Jesus did not, in other words, "know that he was God" in the same way that one knows one is male or female, hungry or thirsty, or that one ate an orange an hour ago. His "knowledge" was of a more risky, but perhaps more significant, sort: like knowing one is loved. One cannot "prove" it except by living it.[155]

Like others we have discussed thus far, Wright pursues his positive aims in part by denying what he sees to be the traditional alternative. However, his sense of what that alternative might look like is revealing. Jesus did not sit back and say "Well I never! I'm the second person of the Trinity!" nor did he "[wander] around with a faraway look, listening to the music of the angels, remembering the time when he was sitting up in heaven with the other members of the Trinity."[156] Wright says that, "Chalcedon, I think, always smelled a bit like a confidence trick, celebrating

---

151. Wright, "Jesus' Self-Understanding," 54.
152. Ibid., 59.
153. Wright argues that Jesus was conscious of a vocation "given him by the one he knew as 'father,' to enact in himself what, in Israel's scriptures, God had promised to accomplish all by himself," with the caveat that "awareness of vocation is by no means the same thing as Jesus having the sort of 'supernatural' awareness of himself, of Israel's God, and of the relation between the two of them" such as those who hold to a "Docetic" high Christology (*JVG*, 653).
154. *JVG*, 610.
155. Wright, *JVG*, 653.
156. Wright, *Challenge*, 164–5.

in Tertullian-like fashion the absurdity of what is believed."[157] He considers it a "de-Judaizing of the Gospels" that leads theologians to ignore the fact that the Gospels' incarnational claim is that "this is Israel's God in person coming to claim the sovereignty promised to the Messiah."[158] Clearly, Wright wants to distance his approach from the ontological terms common to the classical Christian tradition—and he thinks doing so is necessary in order to do "serious history."

For his part, Aquinas understands the unity of operation in Christ not only in terms of mission consciousness, but in a more robust sense that he calls instrumentality,[159] a concept that depends on his noncompetitive metaphysic and his attendant conviction that God is able to move interiorly in all rational creatures without overriding their freedom.[160] This insight is applied to Christ through the language of *instrumentum Divinitatis*—which brings us to the second form of accidental union.[161] Aquinas writes that "the humanity of Christ is the instrument of the Godhead—not, indeed, an inanimate instrument, which nowise acts, but is merely acted upon; but an instrument animated by a rational soul, which is so acted upon as to act."[162] By applying the concept of instrumental causality to Christ's human nature, Aquinas upholds the *anhypostasis* of his humanity while affirming that it retains its active integrity and freedom.[163] Unlike an inanimate instrument (an axe, for example) Jesus' humanity is a conjoined instrument (analogous to how the body is the instrument of the soul), such that its action is not distinct from the action of the principal agent (the Word), even while it retains its proper operation through its own form.[164] The operation of the human nature is subordinate to and moved by the divine operation in such a way that its actions remain unified under a fully human will that acts freely. This plurality of operations, each proper to its own principle, is not incompatible with the unity of the person, because "operation is an effect of the person by reason of a form or nature."[165] And, as such, both operations concur in one action "inasmuch as one nature acts in union with the other."[166]

---

157. Wright, "Jesus and the Identity of God," 46.

158. Wright, "Whence and Whither," 133-4 (italics deleted). See *NTPG*, 137. See further comments critical of traditional Christology in Wright, "Response to Richard Hays," 64 and *JVG*, 613.

159. *In Sent. III*, dist. 18, q. 1, a. 1; *De ver.*, q. 20, a. 1; *De unione verbi*, aa. 1, 4, and 5; *ST* III.19.1.

160. *ST* I.83.1 *ad 3*.

161. *In Sent. III*, dist. 18, q. 1, a. 1; *De ver.*, q. 20, a. 1; *De unione verbi*, aa. 1, 4, and 5; *ST* III.19.1.

162. *ST* III.7.1 *ad 3*.

163. "The human nature in Christ is … a principle of action insofar as it has dominion over its own acts" (*De unione verbi*, a. 5 *ad 4*). See White, *Incarnate Lord*, 119-21, and related discussion in Tanner, *Jesus, Humanity, and the Trinity*, 24.

164. *De unione verbi*, a. 5 *ad 5*; *ST* III.19.1 *ad 2*.

165. *ST* III.19.1 *ad 4*.

166. *ST* III.19.11 *ad 5*.

It should be evident how a competitive metaphysic undermines this picture, by forcing us to say that it was *really* his humanity or *really* his divinity that was operative at this or that moment. In fact, Aquinas argues that this is what led the monothelites into their problematic position: they failed to recognize that when something is moved by another, its action is twofold according to the principles of its own form and by virtue of the movement that originated in its mover.[167] While the operation of an axe is to chop, its operation in the hands of a craftsman is to make benches, and such an operation is unified, for it is not properly attributed to either the axe or the craftsman independently of one another. Rather, each share in the proper operation of the other, even though the operation of the axe is subordinate to and dependent on that of the craftsman. So, by analogy, is the humanity of Christ to the divine hypostasis of the Word, except that in place of the passivity of the axe is the fully active freedom of the human operation. Paul Crowley puts it as follows:

> The operations remain specifically distinct, but united; working in relation with each other, they find their unity in the subsisting hypostasis of the Word. The Word acts as principal agent, or first moving cause, of the human nature of Christ. The human nature, while utterly integral and possessing a self-determining will, receives the grace of the Word and freely exercises operations proper to a human nature, in communion with the saving end of the Word of God. In this order of causality, therefore, the human nature is subordinate to the Word, but not passive to the Word. Precisely as a conjoined, animate and rational instrument of the Word, the human nature possesses dominion over the full range of operations proper to it as a human nature.[168]

It is precisely for this reason that the Fathers opposed Docetism so forcefully, because it is in and through the full operation of his humanity that Christ's divinity is made manifest: "In the second cause, the first cause operates."[169] If his humanity becomes passive, then his saving work is undermined, and if it is somehow separate, acting on its own, then it is not the action of the person of the Word, the divine incarnate Son. Aquinas concurs. As Dominic Legge notes, "Thomas's appropriation of instrumental causality permits him to give a supreme importance and salvific significance to everything that the man Christ did and suffered" and he emphasizes the history of Christ's human life rather more than most of his contemporaries.[170] Both unity of intention (the unity of Christ's wills) and unity of operation (the instrumentality of Christ's humanity) must stem from a hypostatic unity so that they are *theandric* and not just human. Christ's human actions

---

167. *ST* III.19.1 *resp.*
168. Crowley, "*Instrumentum Divinitatis* in Thomas Aquinas," 451–75, at 473.
169. Farrer, *Glass of Vision*, 35. Cf. *ST* III.19.1; *ST* I.8.1.
170. Legge, *Trinitarian Christology*, 218.

constitute genuine revelation of God first and foremost because their principle of movement is the hypostasis of the Word.

Returning to Wright, then, if everything Jesus does comes from a position of inference, hope, and faith—knowing that "he could be making a terrible, lunatic mistake" but doing his best nonetheless—in what sense can we say that his every word and action is that of the divine Son? Either the Word must bypass his human intellect to direct his human will (resulting in Docetism), or his will must follow where his ignorance leads (resulting in Nestorianism). We will return to this issue in the final chapter. What is at stake here is not simply the ontological reality of Christ's humanity and divinity, but his actual life and actions in history. Aquinas' understanding of the instrumentality of Christ's humanity points us continually back to history itself, for it is the human life of Christ that reveals and unites us to God. Aquinas insists that Jesus was not a human supposit with a special calling. He is God himself, existing in a fully human mode of being, and profound ignorance is not compatible with the instrumental freedom of his humanity.

As I noted, I see a strong similarity between Wright's treatment of Jesus' mission consciousness and that of Hans Urs von Balthasar, who argues for an absolute identity between person and mission in Christ—his identity is his mission.[171] Von Balthasar calls this a "Christology from below," but it is one with "an eye open for the possibility that an answer may eventually come from a 'Christology from above.'"[172] In other words, he presents first a "Christology of consciousness" that leads to a "Christology of being."[173] And it is here that his approach differs significantly from Haight, Schleiermacher, and Wright, each of whom denies that a Christology articulated in ontological terms might provide final coherence to their understanding of Christ.

Unity by Greatness of Honor

For the third mode of accidental union, we turn to the prominent twentieth-century idea of myth. Rudolf Bultmann was concerned to translate what he saw to be the core message of the New Testament out of a falsely objective form of expression and into an existential mode more appropriate to his contemporaries. For Bultmann, what is valuable is not the worldview of the New Testament authors or their particular concepts or modes of expression, but the call to commit

---

171. Balthasar, *Theo-Drama III*, 149.

172. Balthasar, *Theo-Drama III*, 150. Here Balthasar is referencing the general distinction between a "historical" and "theological" Christology, or between a Christology that attends to Jesus' "overt function" vs. his "covert being" (149). He defines a Christology from above as one that "goes beyond all the anthropological facts and all the events of salvation history to date" and has to do with *being* (150). A Christology from below is thus the opposite of that, focusing on the anthropological and historical facts and asking about *behaviors* and *actions*.

173. Balthasar, *Theo-Drama III*, 163.

ourselves to Christ in a particular way. This call must be demythologized, in order to shed its embeddedness in an outdated understanding of the world no longer palatable to modern people. As Bultmann famously wrote, "It is impossible to use electric light and the wireless and to avail ourselves of modern medical and surgical discoveries, and at the same time to believe in the New Testament world of spirits and miracles."[174]

Bultmann defined myth as "the presentation of the otherworldly in terms of this world, and the divine in terms of human life."[175] Aquinas wrote similarly: "we know God from creatures as their principle, and also by way of excellence and remotion. In this way therefore He can be named by us from creatures, yet not so that the name which signifies Him expresses the divine essence in itself."[176] Many of the enduring insights of Bultmann's program of demythologization had been expounded by Aquinas in his treatment of analogy, though Bultmann's approach is anthropological and existential, while Aquinas' is ontological. It is no surprise to Christian theology that we present the divine in the terms of this world, but that does not mean that it can be reduced to the terms in which it is represented. The essentially Feuerbachian move of Bultmann to discount such analogical language as myth and reduce the divinity of Christ to the faith statements of the kerygma depends for its force on a conflation of technological development with philosophical progress and an absolutization of the reductive metaphysical claims of twentieth-century German historicism.[177] Existential claims about the genuine decision evoked by the gospel do not carry within them sufficient reasons to reject ontology, any more than Bultmann's repeated claims that people today are incapable of adopting the "world picture" of the Bible prove that modern secularism offers a more faithful representation of reality.[178] For Bultmann, what

---

174. Bultmann, *Kerygma and Mythos*, vol. 1, 5.

175. Bultmann, *Kerygma and Mythos*, vol. 1, 22n2.

176. ST I.13.1 *resp.* In his review of *The Myth of God Incarnate*, McCabe writes that

> it is not at all clear whether a myth is always meant to be an untruth. Sometimes the authors merely seem to mean by "mythical" the same as "subject to the limitations of religious language." I do not think they have any very clear analysis or critique of religious language (they do not, for instance, distinguish between analogy and metaphor) and I do not find their use of "myth" here particularly helpful or illuminating, but if all they are trying to say boils down to the assertion that the doctrine of the incarnation is a religious or theological statement like any other, then, of course what they say is right though not very interesting. ("The Myth of God Incarnate," 350–7

177. Karl Barth claimed that Bultmann's existential way of speaking about God reduces theological propositions to affirmations of the inner life of man (Barth, *Church Dogmatics* 3/2, 445–6). Bultmann attempts to overcome Feuerbach in "The Problem of Natural Theology," 319ff; Bultmann, *Kerygma and Myth*, 199–200.

178. See Bultmann, "New Testament and Mythology."

matters is that the honor due to God is shown to Jesus in the preaching of the kerygma, which in turn calls us to decision. We need not adopt the mythology of Scripture or necessarily concern ourselves with all of the events depicted—what matters is the existential import of the preaching of the resurrected Christ.

By contrast, Aquinas writes that "We may consider two things in a person to whom honor is given: the person himself, and the cause of his being honored." He applies this to Christ as follows:

> Since, therefore, in Christ there is but one Person of the Divine and human natures, and one hypostasis, and one suppositum, He is given one adoration and one honor on the part of the Person adored: but on the part of the cause for which He is honored, we can say that there are several adorations, for instance that He receives one honor on account of His uncreated knowledge, and another on account of His created knowledge.[179]

When it comes to Christ, the root of honor lies in that which is honored, rather in the perspective of those doing the honoring. It is a central pillar of the Christian faith that the honor due to Christ is reserved for the one God (Deut. 6:4-9, 1 Cor. 8:6).[180] For all that Bultmann wanted to reach his contemporaries, there is good reason to think that people find existentially significant that which they have reason to believe is real.[181] It is the cause of Christ being honored, rather than the honor itself, that holds the greatest significance, and the latter can only be sustained through the substantial personal presence of God.[182]

---

179. *ST* III.16.1 *resp.*
180. *ScG* III.120.
181.
> Bultmann's approach is bound in as much with Heideggerian philosophy and with a Lutheran understanding of the relative importance of human imagining or arguing on the one hand and divine manifestation in freedom on the other as it is with strict considerations of literary history: Christology for Bultmann is most emphatically not and cannot be about anything for which we could supply "evidence." But subsequent scholarship has been uneasy with the philosophical over-determination of his readings; and theologians have not been comfortable with the reduction of Christology to the bare event of proclamation, the Word uttered out of an impenetrable historical silence and darkness. Surely theology claims something more, something about an embodied *narrative* that displays God's action rather than a naked demand for the obedience of faith? (Williams, *Christ the Heart*, 44–5)

182. *ST* III.25.

Unity by Equivocation

The fifth mode of accidental union might be seen most prominently in the work of those who posit the late development of high Christology, such that over time Christians came to worship and ascribe divine attributes to a purely human Jesus. A popular example of unity by equivocation comes from Bart Ehrman. For Ehrman, Jesus was a human person who, after his death, was gradually elevated to the status of a divine being through the incremental growth of his followers' religious devotion. "The Christians exalted him to the divine realm in their theology, but in my opinion," writes Ehrman, "he was, and always has been, a human."[183] Ehrman suggests that for most ancient people, humanity and divinity existed on two overlapping continuums.[184] He argues that the Gospel of Mark views Jesus as a human person who was elevated to the level of divinity by an act of God. This supports his opinion that the earliest Christians viewed Jesus through the lens of exaltation rather than Incarnation.[185]

Of course, the questions raised by Ehrman are historical rather than doctrinal, and this is not the context to adjudicate those historical questions, except to say that Ehrman's methods have rightly been widely criticized and his arguments have been convincingly shown to fall far short of those offered by scholars such as Martin Hengel, Larry Hurtado, and Richard Bauckham. Hengel did much to dismantle older versions of the evolutionary hypothesis of Christological development and, in comparison to Hurtado's studies of early Christian devotional practices and Bauckham's exploration of Jewish monotheism, Ehrman's claims remain unconvincing.

While Ehrman is correct that there were various ancient views about intermediary figures, he wrongly ignores the significant differences between such figures and Christian views about Jesus. As Michael Bird argues, "Jesus was regarded as part of God's own identity but without thereby compromising the strict nature of Jewish monotheism. In the end, mighty angels and exalted persons serve God, but they do not share his rule, nor do they receive his worship, but Jesus does."[186] One of the central ways that the Christian tradition carries forward this view is through the doctrine of the *communicatio idiomatum*. The purpose of this doctrine is to emphasize the unity of Christ while maintaining the qualitative dissimilarity of his natures.[187] Aquinas explains that, because an operation is an effect of the person by reason of the nature, the predicates proper to each nature are attributed to the one person, but not cross-attributed to each other.[188] This is a necessary implication of the fact that natures do not exist in the abstract; they

---

183. Ehrman, *How Jesus Became God*, 353–4.
184. Ehrman, *How Jesus Became God*, 4.
185. Ibid., 8.
186. Bird, *How God Became Jesus*, 24.
187. *ST* III.16.
188. *ST* III.16.5.

3. The Doctrine of the Incarnation

only occur in reality as the natural determinations of persons, to whom their properties are attributed. This allows us to say things like "God is man," because we can rightly predicate words signifying a nature to the suppost of that nature.[189] We can also affirm that "man is God" because "man" refers to any hypostasis of a human nature, and the divine Word is the hypostasis of Christ's human nature.[190] The precision of this Christological language allows Aquinas to treat the natures of Christ as distinct grammatical subjects without suggesting that they exist as separate ontological subjects.[191]

Ehrman envisions Christ as a human suppost to whom supernatural predicates were applied over time, thereby nudging him up the spectrum from human to divine. And yet, from the earliest days, Christians have insisted that our beliefs about Jesus do not involve placing him somewhere on a spectrum between divinity and humanity. Affirming the divinity of Christ is not a matter of attaching divine properties to a human person. Doing so leads, at best, to monophysitism, the mythology of a demi-god. Rather, the integrity of Jesus' humanity and divinity are preserved, and the relation between the two is upheld through the twofold communication of names to the one person of Christ.

Nestorianism is typically thought of in terms of dual personhood, but Aquinas helpfully shows that Nestorianism frequently shows up in places where explicit discussions of two persons are not in view. Rather, as we have seen, he has shown that Christologies relying on forms of accidental union result in Nestorianism because natures must always inhere substantially in a suppost. If they are only accidentally united to the divine suppost, then they must inhere substantially in a human suppost, resulting in two persons. Furthermore, when forced to account for the unity of Christ on its own, accidental union replaces elements of one nature with the other, thereby corrupting or transforming one or both natures. This is because accidental union relies on predicates of essence rather than being. If, on the other hand, these forms of accidental union are understood to flow from the substantial, personal union of divinity and humanity in Christ, then they uphold both the integrity of the two natures and the true unity of the person. For Aquinas, these modes of accidental union, when properly ordered within an incarnational Christology, are not about attributing divine predicates to Jesus' humanity, or transforming it into something else. Rather, they are about the perfection of his humanity by grace. Prioritizing ontology does not require us to ignore historical, narrative, or existential analysis. Rather, it provides each a fruitful place, outlining

---

189. *ST* III.16.1.

190. *ST* III.16.1. "This word *God* is predicated of man not on account of the human nature, but by reason of the suppositum" (*ST* III.16.1 *ad3*).

191. See the debate between Thomas Joseph White and Thomas Weinandy on this topic: Weinandy, "Jesus' Filial Vision of the Father," 189–201; White, "The Voluntary Action of the Earthly Christ and the Necessity of the Beatific Vision," 497–534; Weinandy, "The Beatific Vision and the Incarnate Son," 605–15; White, "Dyothelitism and the Instrumental Human Consciousness of Jesus," 396–422. See also Gaine, *Did the Savior See*, 44–5.

a coherent framework for the coordination of their diverse insights. Ideally, this might ease the stress that each of these modes of union is forced to bear, because they need not account for the divine identity of Christ, but rather for the instrumental perfection of his human nature in a way that is fitting to his personal identity and saving mission.

Conclusion

N. T. Wright has criticized the Christological doctrine of two natures, calling it a "de-Judaizing of the Gospels" that leads theologians to ignore the fact that the Gospels' incarnational claim is that "this is Israel's God in person coming to claim the sovereignty promised to the Messiah."[192] Our exploration of this connection between narrative and ontological approaches to Christology reveals Wright's claim to be unwarranted. For Aquinas, as for many others, these two always go hand in hand. Belief in the full divinity of Christ is always a confession that Jesus is Lord, God in person come to claim the sovereignty of the Messiah. The story of redemption hinges not only on the actions of Christ but on his *identity*, which is why talking about his "hypostasis" is an integral part of announcing the good news of his coming as Messiah. Furthermore, the developed Christological grammar of the Christian tradition need not be set over against the more narrative-oriented categories in which the earliest Christians rendered judgments about the identity of Jesus. We will say more on this in the chapters to come.

In the Christological terms outlined in this chapter, Docetism takes on a particular character, and the theological significance of Jesus' humanity comes into sharp relief. As Crowley puts it:

> To the degree that the human nature of Christ is realized, precisely according to its nature as a conjoined, animate and rational instrument of the divinity, that nature will be fully human. The converse is also true: To the degree that the human nature of Christ is perceived differently—separate or simply passive—that nature will be less than fully human. But the divinity of Christ can only be shown through a full humanity. Thomas' doctrine of instrumental causality retrieves the uncompromising significance, not only of the full humanity of Christ, but also of the divinity of Christ, by focusing on what together they accomplish in relation with each other: the saving work of God.[193]

---

192. Wright, "Whence and Whither" in Jesus, *Paul and the People of God*, 133–4 (italics deleted). See *NTPG*, 137. See further comments denigrating the Christology of the Christian tradition in Wright, "Response to Richard Hays," in ibid., 64 and *JVG*, 613.

193. Crowley, "*Instrumentum Divinitatis*," 474.

3. The Doctrine of the Incarnation

The reason historical Jesus scholars' opposition to Docetism tends to result in Ebionitism is that their conception of Jesus as "fully human" appears to require that Jesus be a human supposit. As we have shown, such a conception rests on an ontological mistake, which serves only to deny the possibility of Jesus' full divinity—it does nothing to make him more human. For Aquinas, we can only affirm Jesus' full humanity by upholding his full divinity; the two go hand in hand because the integrity of his humanity depends on its status as a conjoined, animate, rational instrument of the divine person. Docetism results from separating Jesus' humanity from the divine person or rendering it passive in the actions of the Son of Man. Avoiding Docetism requires a noncompetitive grasp of the composite *theandric* agency of Christ, wherein the Word is the principle of action and humanity is its mode.[194] To apply the insights from the previous chapter: "the creature and the Creator are both enacting the creature's life, though in different ways and at different depths."[195] Though this action comes about in a qualitatively different fashion in Christ—God does not "enact" our life through a hypostatic union—it nonetheless does not corrupt the paradigm of the Creator/creature relation to do so.[196]

The doctrine of the hypostatic union is a sophisticated way of holding together these claims while insisting on the reality and integrity of Jesus' humanity. By contrast, anti-metaphysical Christologies "from below" show themselves to be an impediment to historians because of how they blur the lines between humanity and divinity, associating God with aspects of Jesus' humanity in a way that corrupts his human nature and renders it passive to his divinity. Historical Jesus scholars need not reject Chalcedon in order to clear a space for historical reconstruction. The fact that they have done so has limited them needlessly and polemically skewed their conclusions away from Christian orthodoxy. The Chalcedonian picture of Christ is fully compatible with historical study of Jesus.[197] Furthermore, I want

---

194. "In many respects, [Aquinas's] defense [against Docetism] remains unsurpassed to this day" (Gondreau, "The Humanity of Christ, the Incarnate Word," 252–76, at 253). See Gondreau, *The Passions of Christ's Soul in the Theology of St. Thomas Aquinas*.

195. Farrer, *Glass of Vision*, 35.

196. *ST* I-II.10.4.

197. White makes a similar argument focused on Aquinas' doctrine of Jesus' knowledge, to which we will turn in Chapter 5. "A nuanced appreciation of Aquinas's doctrine of the human knowledge of Christ may permit us to assimilate many of the legitimate aspirations of modern historical-Jesus studies while still retaining a high doctrine of the infused knowledge of the Lord as the greatest of the prophets" (White, "Infused Science," 619). See also Coakley's discussion:

> One has to surmount the challenge of modern historical-critical approaches to the biblical Jesus, yet also acknowledge that metaphysical discussions of the person of Christ need not be accounted incompatible with these, but seen as

to suggest that the Chalcedonian framework will both encourage and enable our historical efforts.

two (non-competing) perspectives on the same reality. If one drives a wedge between them it is exceedingly difficult to recover any convincing christology in the Chalcedonian tradition at all, let alone in Thomas' form. Thomas of course knew nothing of these modern historiographical developments; but, as we have seen, his probing account of the human sufferings and mental development of Jesus eschews all docetism and invites a creative metaphysical response. ("The Person of Christ," in *The Cambridge Companion to the Summa Theologiae*, 222–39 at 238).

Part II

CONCEPTS OF KNOWING

Truth is a mode of being that "pertains to every being as such."

—Josef Pieper[1]

---

1. *The Silence of St Thomas*, 54.

Chapter 4

THE INTELLIGIBILITY OF PARTICIPATED BEING

One recurring theme of the previous chapters has been how our conceptions of knowledge bear on historical and theological questions related to the identity of Jesus of Nazareth. Before advancing the theological arguments further, therefore, we must grasp the nettle and address the nature of knowledge and cognition because of its decisive influence on multiple relevant areas of inquiry. There are three issues in particular that I would like to address in this chapter. The first has to do with the epistemic status of history as a form of knowledge. As Bernard Lonergan explains:

> The precise object of historical inquiry and the precise nature of historical investigation are matters of not a little obscurity. This is not because there are no good historians. It is not because good historians have not by and large learnt what to do. It is mainly because historical knowledge is an instance of knowledge, and few people are in possession of a satisfactory cognitional theory.[1]

Despite cursory discussions of critical realism among certain historical Jesus scholars, the nature of historical knowledge *as knowledge* has not been adequately scrutinized, in particular in relation to questions of cognitive theory, which, as we will see, helpfully connect the relevant epistemological issues more directly to metaphysics. While it is beyond the scope of this study to provide a full account of the nature of historical knowledge, opportunities will arise to gesture toward the implications this discussion might have for such an account.

Not only is this discussion relevant to how we understand history as a form of knowledge, it also impacts the ways of knowing that we attribute to historical figures in the process of interrogating their aims and beliefs. As Lonergan has noted, Collingwood's conception of history as reenactment—the process by which a historian discerns the thoughts to which historical actions give expression "by re-thinking them in his own mind"—is complicated by the problems of idealism and depends for its force on a very particular conception of knowledge.[2] Our

---

1. Lonergan, *Method in Theology*, 175.

2. Collingwood, *The Idea of History*, 215. "A more concrete illustration of the matter may be had by reading the *Epilogomena* in Collingwood, *The Idea of History*. The first three sections on Nature and History, The Historical Imagination, and Historical evidence, are

understanding of both the nature of our knowledge as historians and the nature of the knowing of historical figures depends to some degree on our theory of cognition.

The second issue has to do with metaphysical realism and the nature of our mind's grasp of reality. This is particularly important for how we approach the theological questions in view, a point that has been well-illustrated by our discussion of how the denial of the knowledge of essences directs us toward a Christological approach that is perniciously speculative and consistently threatens to undermine the integrity of Jesus' humanity. As a result, it is important to outline the impact of participatory metaphysics on our conceptions of knowledge, thereby highlighting how our conceptions of being impact our acceptance or rejection of metaphysical realism.[3] I will not offer a detailed epistemological defense of realism against modern objections, a task that would take us too far afield from our main concern. I direct the reader to the detailed work of Jacques Maritain and Étienne Gilson for arguments of that kind.[4] Cognitional theory is one piece in a much larger ontological puzzle, the anthropological pole of a metaphysic that extends from the ground of being into its variegated, concrete, historical instantiations. In this chapter I will seek to show the coherence of the doctrine of creation and participatory metaphysics with a particular philosophical anthropology and theory of cognition that will lend cumulative weight to the strength of adopting a realist position.

---

right on the point. The fourth on History as a Re-enactment is complicated by the problems of idealism" (Lonergan, *Method in Theology*, 175n1). It is primarily the fourth section that gets picked up by historical Jesus scholars, such as Meyer and Wright.

3. "Critical Realism has been used with different epistemological positions, because the term has been constantly reinvented" (Losch, "The Origins of Critical Realism," 85–106, at 98). Historical Jesus scholars, such as Ben Meyer, N. T. Wright, James Dunn, and others, who have sought to appropriate critical realism into their projects, have frequently confused and conflated divergent accounts of critical realism, including those of Bernard Lonergan, Ian Barbour, Roy Bhaskar, R. W. Sellars, and A. O. Lovejoy. For example, Losch has argued persuasively that N. T. Wright's approach to critical realism follows Ian Barbour rather than Lonergan (via Ben Meyer), despite Wright's suggestions to the contrary, and that Wright failed to recognize the differences between Lonergan's and Barbour's accounts. Most notably, Wright means "realism" in the Kantian sense of the existence of the spatiotemporal world, not in the scholastic sense of the reality of both the external world and of essences. Wright also characterizes critical realism as a middle way between positivism and cultural relativism, rather than between naïve realism and idealism, as Lonergan does. As a result, it is not always possible to distinguish Wright's critical realism from idealism, which is itself a middle way between positivism and relativism. Losch notes that, for his part, Dunn references Bhaskar in his discussion of Meyer without noting the divergences between their accounts. See Losch, "Wright's Version of Critical Realism," 101–14, at 110–11.

4. See esp. Maritain, *The Degrees of Knowledge*; Gilson, *Thomist Realism and the Critique of Knowledge*; Gilson, *Methodological Realism*.

4. The Intelligibility of Participated Being

The third issue is the doctrine of Jesus' knowledge, which will occupy the final four chapters. As we will see, the details of Aquinas' cognitive theory serve as the raw material for his theology of Jesus' knowledge and self-understanding. In fact, Aquinas' unprecedented affirmation of Jesus' humanity is due in part to his complex philosophical anthropology and cognitive psychology. In addition to the anthropological implications, rival accounts of being result in contrasting conceptions of God, and, following from that, of divine knowledge. Given the Christian claim that Jesus is fully God and fully man, the Christological question of the nature of divine knowing and its relationship to human knowing in the hypostatic union is relevant to the question of Jesus as a historical figure. As we noted in Chapter 1, historical Jesus scholars frequently discuss this issue and their dismissive rejections of the possibility of Jesus possessing extraordinary knowledge betray very specific theological conceptions of Christology and of human and divine modes of knowledge. Before accepting their denials, if behooves us to take a deeper look at the issues at play.

The idealist cast of most modern philosophy of history has kept the discipline from developing a cognitional theory sufficient to fully theorize an account of critical historical method.[5] Similarly, philosophical psychology in the twentieth century has long proceeded without regard for the ontology of mind,[6] while the discipline of neuroscience has, since its conception, focused its analysis on the sub-psychological level: the biological systems of information processing that are observable with experimental methods.[7] Until recently, what has been left out of these disciplines is an approach to the ontology of the psychological powers of cognition—an inquiry that stood at the heart of philosophical anthropology for much of the history of Western thought. When the conversation has strayed into this territory, it has often assumed a reductive materialism, but rarely has it mounted an adequate defense of this view. The critical question for our purposes is in what way the understanding of participated being outlined in Chapter 2 impacts our conception of cognition, and what effect that might have on the historical study of Jesus and Christology.

***

In the *Disputed Questions on Truth*, Aquinas considers whether truth is found principally in the intellect, or in things. He begins to construct an answer by arguing that "a natural thing is placed [*consituta (est)*] between two intellects

---

5. See comments in Ebeling, *Word and Faith*, 49; Lonergan, *Method in Theology*, 175.

6. That is, a philosophical anthropology that includes an ontological account of the psychological powers of cognition and intellection.

7. Daniel De Haan discusses this hylomorphic distinction between psychological powers, and the sub-psychological systems that materially constitute and enable them in "Hylomorphic Animalism, Emergentism, and the Challenge of the New Mechanist Philosophy of Neuroscience," 9–38. See also comments in Haldane, "The Metaphysics of Intellect(ion)," 39–55.

[*duos intellectus*]," that is, between the creative, productive divine intellect and the receptive human intellect.[8] In light of this, he develops a twofold notion of truth: "a thing ... is called *true* in so far as it conforms to either."[9] Truth, with respect to the divine intellect, is a correlate of extrinsic formal causation: "The truth of anything is a property of the act of being which has been established for it."[10] With respect to the human intellect, something is true when "it is such as to cause [*facere*] a true estimate [*veram aestimationem*] about itself."[11] As Josef Pieper explains, "the first denotes the creative fashioning of things by God; the second their intrinsic knowability for the human mind."[12] For Aquinas, the fact that all things are created is the ground of their intelligibility. The truth of things, while not dependent on the limited ability of our minds to grasp it, is nonetheless lucid and open to us to behold.[13] If being is communicative, then it must be capable of retaining its "truthfulness" across different modes of existence. This notion of reality existing "between two minds" helps elucidate how Aquinas connects being to truth ("the reality of things is itself their light")[14] and insists on an isomorphism between our faculties for making meaning and the reality of the world outside of our minds.[15] To grasp this picture as a whole, we begin where all things originate, in the mind of God.

Divine Knowledge

One significant recurring theme of the Hebrew Scriptures is the surpassing knowledge of the God of Israel. He knows all things, from the foundations of the world to the innermost thoughts of our hearts (see Jer. 23:23-24; Job 7:17-20; 2 Kgs 19.27).[16] There is nowhere we can go to escape his gaze; his knowledge is far above ours, mysterious and inscrutable (Job 11:7-10). "Such knowledge is too wonderful for me," writes the Psalmist, "it is so high that I cannot attain it" (Ps. 139). Here the Psalmist connects God's knowledge to his acts of creation: "Even before a word is on my tongue, O LORD, you know it completely ... For it was you who formed my inward parts; you knit me together in my mother's womb." This meditation on the works of God leads the Psalmist to praise him, not for his strength but for his

---

8. *De ver.* q. 1, a. 2 *solutio*.
9. Ibid.
10. Ibid.
11. Ibid.
12. Pieper, *The Silence of St Thomas*, 54.
13. "It signifies that things can be known by us because God has creatively thought them; *as* creatively thought by God, things have not only their *own* nature ('for themselves alone'); but as creatively thought by God, things have also a reality 'for us'" (ibid., 55).
14. *Super De causis* I, 6.
15. *De ver.* q. 1, a. 5 *ad* 2. See Pieper, *Living the Truth*.
16. See *In Iob*, c. 7, lesson 4.

4. The Intelligibility of Participated Being

thoughts: "How precious to me are your thoughts, O God! How vast is the sum of them!"[17] This ancient tradition of reflecting on the mind of God finds echo and amplification in the New Testament—"Oh, the depth of the riches and wisdom and knowledge of God!" (Rom. 11:33)—with the result that divine knowledge and the divine ideas have become a key piece of much Christian talk about God.

Aquinas argues, citing Rom. 11:33, that "in God there exists the most perfect knowledge [*perfectissime scientia*]," and he begins by extrapolating this fact from the definition of knowledge itself.[18] Thomas argues, following Aristotle, that to know something is to possess the form of that thing within the mind.[19] The pre-Socratic philosopher Empedocles believed that by being materially constituted of all the elements, the soul can know all things: we, being earth, know earth; we, being water, know water, and so on.[20] Having divided bodies into underlying elemental matter and accidental forms, the ancients assumed the matter was the basic and enduring element, thereby prioritizing potentiality over actuality as the first principle.[21] Aristotle, on the other hand, insists on the priority of actuality: "What we seek is the cause, i.e. the form, by reason of which the matter is some definite thing."[22] Therefore, Aristotle, and Aquinas after him, agree that the soul (i.e., mind) becomes that which it knows, but not according to the determined act of existence (*determinatum esse*) proper to that object: "It is not the stone which is present in the soul but its form."[23] In coming to know a material object, the intellect receives the form of that object immaterially. In line with the modus principle, the form comes to exist in a new mode of being according to the power that receives it, no longer *esse naturale*, but now *esse intentionale*.[24]

By possessing the forms of things, the intellect "becomes" that which it knows: "intellect in act *is* what it understands; the form of the object *is* the form of the mind in act."[25] The result is that intellectual beings have greater "amplitude" and "extension" because they are not limited to possessing only their own forms, but can also have (or, indeed, "become") the forms of other things. This is why Aristotle says, "the soul is, in a sense, all things which exist."[26] This ability, according

---

17. See Isa. 33:6.
18. *ST* I.14.1.
19. *In Boeth. De Trin.*, q. 5, a. 2; *De ver.* q. 2, a. 6. "*Quaelibet cognitio sit secundum modum formae quae est in cognoscente*" (*De ver.* q. 2, a. 6 resp.). To be precise, in human cognition, to know something is to receive into the mind the intelligible species, which is an intentional *similitude* of the essence of the thing known.
20. See *ScG* II.49.11; Aristotle, *de Anima*, I.2 [404b 15]; Pasnau, *Thomas Aquinas on Human Nature*, 30–4.
21. See Pasnau, *Human Nature*, 34.
22. Aristotle, *Metaphysics*, VII.17 [1041b7-8].
23. Aristotle, *On the Soul*, III.8 [431b28-29]. See *De ver.*, q. 2, a. 2, solutio.
24. *In II De anima*, §553.
25. *In III De anima*, §788 (emphasis added). Cf. Spruit, *Species Intelligibilis*, 38.
26. Aristotle, *de Anima* III.8 [431b20-21]. Aquinas explains that by "in a sense" Aristotle means the soul is *potentially* all things, though not actually (*In III De anima*, §788).

to Aquinas, is what separates intelligent and nonintelligent beings: "the latter possess only their own form," while the former are "naturally adapted to have also the form of some other thing."[27] If we ask what accounts for the difference between these two kinds of beings, Aquinas answers that it is matter. Thus, we can outline a gradation of cognitive being, from those which are wholly material and incapable of knowledge (such as plants),[28] to those capable of sense (animals and humans) and intellect (humans), to those wholly immaterial who possess the highest degree of knowledge (the angels and, preeminently, God).[29] "The immateriality of a thing is the reason why it is cognitive; and according to the mode of immateriality is the mode of knowledge (*cognitionis*)."[30] If the mode of one's knowledge is determined by their mode of immateriality, then God must occupy the "highest place in knowledge."[31]

The fact that there is knowledge in God does not mean that his knowing is like ours. Again, we find the modus principle at work, now adapted to the context of knowledge: "the known (*scitum*) is in the knower (*sciente*) according to the mode of the knower (*scientis*)."[32] Because God's mode of being is higher than the creature's, so is his mode of knowledge. This difference can be described in the first place in terms of two elements of cognition: first, for humans to feel or know something, our senses or intellect must be informed by sensible or intelligible species. However, God is absolutely simple, which means that the intelligible species of divine intellection do not differ from the divine essence.[33] Thus, it must be the case that

27. *ST* I.14.1.

28. *On the Soul*, II.12 [424a24-34].

29. *De ver.*, q. 10, a. 4–6; q. 2, a. 1–5. This is not to place God's knowledge univocally at the top of a quantitative spectrum. God's knowledge is *qualitatively* different from creaturely knowledge (including angelic knowledge), a fact that can be seen especially in that his knowledge is not receptive but productive (see discussion of Augustine, *De Trinitate*, XV.13 below). See also Rosemann, *Omne Agens Agit Sibit Simile*, 253–78.

30. *ST* I.14.1. See *ScG* I.44.5.

31. *ST* I.14.1. See *In I Sent.*, 35.1; *XII Metaph.* lect. 8, §2542. As Boland notes, in addition to this argument that follows the *via negativa*, Aquinas offers two further arguments (*Ideas in God*, 196–7). Following the *via per causalitatem*, we know that God is intelligent and purposive because of his conscious act of creation. Every agent acts for some purpose, and intellect is integral to intention (*De ver.*, q. 2, a. 3; *ScG* 1.44.2). Following the *via per eminentiam*, Aquinas repeats the Anselmian contention that, since no perfection in created things is lacking in God, and intelligence is the greatest perfection, God must be intelligent (Anselm, *Proslogion*, 6; *ScG* I.44.6).

32. *ST* I.14.1 repl. 3. See *De ver.*, q. 2, a. 13 ad 3.

33. Aquinas makes a distinction between two modes in which a form can exist in the intellect: as the *principle* of the act of understanding, and as its *terminus* (*De ver.* q. 3, a. 2). Doolan argues, with reference to the divine ideas, that "although Thomas does not explicitly state it, one can infer from what he said earlier that the divine essence is presented to God's intellect in this respect as the terminus of his act of understanding rather than as the principle of that act" (Doolan, *Aquinas on the Divine Ideas as Exemplar Causes*, 89–90).

"the intelligible species itself is the divine intellect itself."[34] Among other things, this means that God does not come to know things either through physical senses or by discursive reasoning.[35] Second, the creaturely act of understanding involves a change from a state of potentiality to actuality occasioned by the informing act of the intelligible species.[36] Aquinas, expounding on 1 Cor. 2:11, maintains that God is pure act, containing no potentiality,[37] and that therefore, the intellect of God and its object, along with the intelligible species and the act of understanding itself, are all one and the same.[38] God understands himself through himself, and comprehends himself, for, in being free from all matter and potentiality, he is most fully and perfectly knowable.[39] This is a deeply apophatic doctrine for Aquinas, which primarily involves denying of God's knowledge the finite and material elements of creaturely modes of knowing.

Because of the biblical witness to divine providence (e.g., Heb. 4:19) Aquinas argues that not only does God know creation in general through his essence, he knows each particular individual thing.[40] To do so, Aquinas returns to the idea of participation: "Inasmuch as God knows his essence perfectly, He knows it according to every mode in which it can be known [*omnem modum quo cognoscibilis est*]. Now it can be known not only as it is in itself, but as it can be participated in by creatures according to some degree of likeness [*modum similitudinis*]."[41] This is where the divine ideas come in, which, as Gregory Doolan explains, are "the 'participabilities' of the likeness of the divine nature as it is known by God," or, in other words, "[God's] knowledge of the ways in which the likeness of his essence can be participated."[42] The divine ideas are not only of universal forms but also of individuals. In contrast to Aristotle, Aquinas maintains that the divine ideas include not only the forms of things but also the matter that individuates the forms, thus extending God's knowledge to the particular essence of each and every created thing.[43]

---

34. *ST* I.14.2. See arguments for divine simplicity in *ST* I.3.1–8; *Comp. Theol.* I, cc. 9–25; *ScG* I.18–28; and discussion in Stump, *Aquinas*, 92–130; White, "Divine Simplicity and the Holy Trinity," 66–93; Wittman, "'Not a God of Confusion but of Peace," 151–69.

35. *De ver.* q. 2, a. 4 *ad* 5; *ST* I.14.7; *ScG* 1.55–57.

36. Scarpelli Cory, *Aquinas on Human Self-Knowledge*, 69–70.

37. *ST* I.14.2. This is the first of Aquinas' "Five Ways," see *ST* I.2.3; *ScG* I.16; *Comp. Theol.* I, cc. 2–4; Wippel, *Metaphysical Thought*, 444–59; Gilson, *Thomisme*, 53–62.

38. *ST* I.14.4.

39. *ST* I.14.3; *ScG* I.47.

40. *De ver.*, q. 2, a. 11; *ST* I.13.5; I.14.1; *ScG* I.32–34, 44.

41. *ST* I.15.2; *In I Sent.*, d. 36, q. 1, a. 1.

42. Doolan, *Divine Ideas*, 249.

43. Contra Plato, who posited ideas only of species, Aquinas argues that "since, however, we hold matter to be created by God, though not apart from form, matter has its idea in God, though not apart from the idea of the composite; for matter itself can neither exist, nor be known" (*ST* I.15.3 *ad* 3). Cf. *De ver.*, q. 3, a. 8. Thus, as exemplars, the divine ideas are the formal causes of the entire essence of the creature.

God's knowledge has a few notable characteristics. First, God knows all things as particulars because their perfection consists not only in what they share in common (namely, being) but also in what distinguishes them, and all such distinguishing perfections exist preeminently in God.[44] Second, Aquinas quotes Augustine: "It is true of all his creatures, both spiritual and corporeal, that he does not know them because they are, but that they are because he knows them."[45] The knowledge of God, maintains Thomas, is the cause of things and "his knowledge extends as far as his causality extends."[46] It also extends to things that are not, for he knows all things actual and all things possible.[47] Here Aquinas points to the eternity of God: "The present glance (*intuitus*) of God extends over all time, and to all things which exist in any time, as to objects present to him."[48] This knowledge includes future contingent things that result from human free will. Such things are not actually "future" to God, but they are contingent insofar as they are not determined.[49] Finally, citing Jas 1:17, Aquinas explains that, as God's knowledge and essence are one, and as his essence is immutable, so his knowledge must be unchangeable (*invariabilem*).[50]

The species of divine intellection is none other than the divine essence, but the intention (the willed terminus of an act of understanding) is the Word of God, in whom and through whom all things actual and intelligible come into being. Recalling our discussion in Chapter 2, this has to do with God's extrinsic formal causation of creation and the multiplication of the similitude of the divine essence in which things diversely participate.[51] "In this way, therefore, through one intelligible species, which is the divine essence, and through one understood intention, which is the divine Word, God can understand many things."[52] Although we have outlined a distinctly philosophical conception of creation and divine knowledge, Aquinas also explores this understanding theologically in a robustly

---

44. *ST* I.14.6; *De ver.*, q. 2, a. 4; *ScG* I.50; *De Causis*, lect. 10; *Comp. Theol.*, I, cc. 132–5; *De sub. separatis*, c. 14.

45. Augustine, *De Trinitate*, XV.13. Cf. *ST* I.14.8.

46. *ST* I.14.11. See *ST* I.14.8; *De ver.*, q. 2, a. 14; *In I Sent.*, d. 38, q. 1, a. 1. Among the divine ideas, these are called extrinsic formal causes, which are referred to as exemplars: the ideas of individual things that God makes at some point in time. See Doolan, *Divine Ideas*, 147.

47. Here Aquinas distinguishes between practical knowledge (which includes exemplars) and speculative knowledge, the latter pertaining to knowledge of possibles. See *ST* I.15.3; Boland, *Ideas in God*, 252; Doolan, *Divine Ideas*, 1–43, 124–33.

48. *ST* I.14.9; 1.10.1–6. In *ST* I.10.1 Aquinas affirms the Boethian definition of eternity: "The whole [*tota*], simultaneous [*simul*] and perfect possession of boundless life [*interminabilis vitae*]" (Boethius, *The Consolation of Philosophy*, V.6 [422.9-11]).

49. *ST* I.14.13; *ST* I.86.4; *De ver.*, q. 2, a. 12; *ScG* I.67.

50. *ST* I.14.15; *De ver.*, q. 2, a. 13; q. 1, a. 5 *ad 11*; q. 1, a. 7; *ScG* I.58–59; *In I Sent.*, d. 38, q. 1, aa. 2–3; d. 39, q. 1, aa. 1–2; d. 41, q. 1, a. 5. See Augustine, *City of God*, XI.21.

51. Cf. Te Velde, *Participation and Substantiality*, 94.

52. *ScG* I.53.5.

Trinitarian fashion. Divine simplicity and the ontology of participation are simply two sides of the same coin for Aquinas, and his understanding of God's knowledge of all things follows directly from his understanding of finite being and its relation to its source, the one in whom essence and existence coincide. As we will see in the following chapters, these principles will prove decisive for our conceptions of Jesus' knowledge.

Angelic Knowledge

The knowledge of creatures is qualitatively different from divine knowing because it is receptive, and yet Aquinas maintains that not all creatures receive knowledge by *observing* what already is. Rather, he argues that when creating the angels, God infused the intelligible species of all created things into their intellects, meaning that they receive their knowledge from God, rather than from sensory input from their environment. The highest form of creaturely knowledge is that of separate substances (i.e., angels) because their knowledge is due solely to the inherent intelligibility of the divine ideas, which ensure by formal causation the intelligibility of creation: their mind does not work to "make intelligible" things that are not.[53] So, Aquinas writes:

> Now, the order of intelligibles is in keeping with the order of intellects. Now, in the order of intelligibles, things that are intelligible in themselves *rank above things whose intelligibility is due solely to our own making*. And all intelligibles derived from sensibles must be of the latter sort, because sensibles are not intelligible in themselves. Therefore, the separate substance's intellect, being superior to ours, has not as the object of its understanding intelligibles received from sensibles, but those which are in themselves intelligible in act.[54]

The objects of the angelic intellect are actually intelligible species derived from the divine ideas themselves, which preexisted eternally in the Word and came forth into substantial and intelligible being in the creation of the universe. Bernard Lonergan writes that "the pure Thomist theory of intellect is to be sought in the Thomist account of angelic knowledge."[55] As such, Aquinas' treatment of the angelic intellect helps to distinguish between rationality and the intellect, and illuminate how the intellect functions differently when allied to embodied forms of sensation and cognition: "Now, just as human intellect is mainly reason, because it operates from sense as a starting point, so the quiddity known by the human intellect is

---

53. Aquinas' supreme authority in discussing separate substances is Ps. Dionysius (See *De sub. separatis*, c.18, §91).

54. *ScG* II.96.4 (emphasis added).

55. Lonergan, *Verbum*, 46. See Aristotle, *On the Soul* III.4 [430a 3]; *ST* I.87.1 *ad* 3; *De ver.*, q. 8, aa. 6–7; *De sub. separatis*, c. 3; *In IX Metaph.* lect. 11, §1904.

different in kind from that known by the angelic."⁵⁶ In this way, Aquinas' treatment of angels provides a number of principles that help illuminate his understanding of both anthropology and Christology.⁵⁷

The angels are not divine but are created by God, which means that they, like all other created things, are composed of essence and existence.⁵⁸ Aquinas notes that this means an angel's act of understanding cannot be its substance, as is the case in God, because "the action of anything differs more from its substance than does its existence."⁵⁹ In other words, if the substance of something differs from its existence, then its action must differ from its substance, for its action follows from its powers, which follow from the actualization of its substance. Because angels are not simple, they must know by means of powers that are ordered to operations with proper objects. This fact gives us the procedure by which we as philosophers come to know the natures of things: Objects → Operations → Powers → Nature.⁶⁰

For Aquinas, angels are composed of essence and *esse* (being), but they are not composed of form and matter the way all other creatures are. Rather, they are incorporeal separate substances. They thereby lack any operations exercised by physical organs, such as the external and internal senses.⁶¹ "Now the angels have no bodies naturally joined to them ... hence of the soul's powers only intellect and will can belong to them."⁶² Because angels do not receive their knowledge from sensible things,⁶³ phantasms (i.e., formal objects of perception, to be discussed below) play no role in their intellection, and thus there is no distinction between agent (active) and possible (passive) intellect in angels.⁶⁴ In fact, "knowledge is

---

56. Lonergan, *Verbum*, 32.
57.

> The angelic operations of knowing and willing served as a test case for anthropological speculations in medieval thought. According to the Pseudo-Dionysian hierarchy of being, which most medieval scholars accepted, the top of each inferior level of being touches upon the bottom of the superior level without blurring the discontinuity between the two. For example, the highest human powers, *viz.* intellect and will, are similar to the intellectual operations of angels while remaining fundamentally distinct from the latter. In this way, angelology makes up a kind of philosophical laboratory to carry out thought experiments in which angelic knowledge and will serve either as contrasting counterexamples or as idealized forms of human knowledge and human will. (Goris, "The Angelic Doctor and Angelic Speech," 88)

58. *De sub. separatis*, c. 9, §46.
59. *ST* I.54.1 *s.c.*
60. *ST* I.77.3; I.54.3.
61. *ST* I.55.2 *ad 2*.
62. *ST* I.54.5.
63. *ScG* II.96; *ST* I.55.2.
64. *ST* I.54.4 *s.c.*; *ScG* II.96.8; *ScG* II.96.3.

not generated in the angels, but is present naturally."[65] As Augustine argues, "such things as pre-existed from eternity in the Word of God, came forth from Him in two ways: first, into the angelic mind; and secondly, so as to subsist in their own natures."[66] In this way, the angels know all things by impressed species (*species impressas*) according to the angels' proper mode of being. Because intelligible species reach our intellects in contrary ways—a difference Aquinas characterizes as analysis (*resolutionis*) in humans vs. synthesis (*compositionis*) in angels[67]—angels are capable of knowing both universals and singulars through their intellect.[68]

There are a number of salient features of angelic knowledge worth noting. First, Aquinas argues that angels do not know the future in the same way that God does,[69] and "although the angel's intellect is above that time according to which corporeal movements are reckoned, yet there is time in his mind according to the succession of intelligible concepts."[70] Similarly, angels are not able to "read the secrets of hearts," for God alone can do so. Here, Aquinas cites Jer. 17:9: "I the Lord, test the mind and search the heart."[71] Further, "the angelic nature is itself a kind of mirror representing the Divine image."[72] Aquinas notes that a thing is known in three ways: (1) when its essence is present in the knower, as light in the eye; (2) when its similitude is present to the power of the knower, like the image of a stone in the eye; (3) when the image appears in something else, like a reflection in a mirror. Our knowledge of God in this life is limited to the third—seeing God's image reflected through creation—and in heaven it will be of the first type (through the light of the *lumen gloriae* in the beatific vision). The angels' knowledge of God is, by nature, the second type, "for since God's image is impressed on the very nature of the angel in his essence, the angel knows God in as much as he is the image of God,"[73] and by grace, the first type: "and he has a knowledge of glory whereby he knows the Word through His essence."[74]

The interesting thing about this account is the way that Aquinas conceives of angelic being itself as always actually intelligible—unlike humans, angels know themselves directly by means of their own forms. And since God's image is impressed upon the essence of the angel, it is also able to know God through itself, its essence functioning as something akin to an intelligible species or "mirror."[75]

---

65. *ST* I.54.4 *ad 1*; *ST* I.55.2 *ad 1*.

66. This is Aquinas' summary of Augustine. *ST* I.56.2, citing Augustine, *The Literal Meaning of Genesis*, 2.8.16 (p. 200).

67. *ScG* II.100.4. Synthesis proceeds from cause to effect, analysis from effect to cause (*ST* I-II.14.5).

68. *De sub separatis*, ch. 13; *ST* I.57.2; *ScG* II.100.3-4.

69. *ST* I.57.3 *s.c.*, citing Isa. 41:23.

70. *ST* I.57.3 *ad 2*; *ScG* II.96.9-10.

71. *ST* I.57.4.

72. *ST* I.56.3.

73. *ST* I.56.3; *ST* I.55.1-3.

74. *ST* I.62.1 *ad 3*. See *In Matt.*, ch. 24, lect. 3 (§1982).

75. *ST* I.56.3.

Also noteworthy is that Aquinas argues that angels do not by nature possess the beatific vision—"yet [the angel] does not behold God's essence."[76] Aquinas applies to the angels Augustine's enigmatic distinction between "morning" and "evening" knowledge,[77] thus distinguishing between their natural and supernatural knowledge.[78] The latter is a direct vision of the divine essence, while the former is a reception of intelligible species from the Word, who is the "intention" of the divine intellect and the creative principle of God's production of all things.

Human Knowledge

Turning finally to human cognition, we must begin by noting that contemporary cognitive theories tend to focus on unifying phenomenological accounts that emphasize the psychological and neurological processes involved in knowing. Aquinas, on the other hand, is interested in an ontological account of the various powers of cognition that enable us to know diverse things. As we saw above, for Aquinas, natures are differentiated by their potencies, potencies are identified by their acts, and acts are specified by their objects.[79] The fact that Aquinas never provides a synthetic, phenomenological description of the unity of conscious experience[80] does not in itself make his approach incompatible with modern theories, any more than the fact that contemporary accounts often ignore ontology.[81] The first step in making sense of Aquinas' cognitive theory is to emphasize its distinctly ontological nature.[82] Far from an exhaustive treatment,

---

76. *ST* I.56.3.
77. See Augustine, *Genesis*, 2.8.16-19 (pp. 200–1).
78. *ST* I.62.1 *ad* 3.
79. Cf. *On the Soul*, II.4 [415a 14-20].
80. As Pasnau notes, the search for a distinct "faculty of consciousness" is a peculiarly Cartesian enterprise that assumes the questions of sensation, cognition, and consciousness to be separate. If Aquinas developed a theory of consciousness it would likely be in terms of a complex interrelation of the various powers of the soul. See Pasnau, *Human Nature*, 197–9.
81. I am grateful to Daniel De Haan for helping me grasp the significance of this, and for his help in various conversations regarding the content of this section. For a Thomist approach that is much more explicitly phenomenological, see esp. Lonergan, *Insight*.
82. This is not to deny that there is a perceptive and quite sophisticated phenomenological element to Aquinas' approach, but to acknowledge that "if Aristotle and Aquinas used introspection and did so brilliantly, it remains that they did not thematize their use, did not elevate it into a reflectively elaborated technique, did not work out a proper method for psychology" (Lonergan, *Verbum*, 6). Spruit cautions against "distinguishing sharply in Aristotle and his medieval and Renaissance followers between psychology and theory of knowledge" (Spruit, *Species*, 37n38). Herein, I am using terms such as "cognitive theory" and "theory of knowledge" to highlight ontology ("the powers of the soul"), while phenomenology has to do with the experience of knowing, and epistemology refers to the theory of the validity and scope of knowledge. However, it is important to avoid

the following summary of Aquinas' theory of cognition is designed to highlight those elements most relevant to the chapters to follow.[83]

It has long been noted that cognition and epistemology are two areas where the impact of metaphysical presuppositions on our understanding of the world is most clearly manifest. On the one hand, a materialist philosophy of mind is itself the result of a materialist metaphysic. On the other hand, those who maintain dualist understandings of the relationship between mind and body have to address the perceptual and intellectual transition from physical sensory data to immaterial cognitive content and functions.[84] The way that they do so is determinatively shaped by their understanding of being, of the relationship between spirit and matter, soul and body, and so on. Importantly, Aquinas is neither a materialist nor a Cartesian dualist, and he holds something of a middle position between the two. In this connection, Leen Spruit notes that

> The metaphysical framework of Thomas' doctrine of the intelligible species is constituted by his theory of participation, which eliminates any radical cleavage between the material and spiritual realms, as well as between the ideas of mental receptivity and activity; according to his view of the active potentiality of the intellect, there is no absolute passivity or autonomous spontaneity.[85]

Aquinas' cognitional theory is structured throughout by his participatory metaphysics, seen especially in his use of the modus principle, and it follows upon his hylomorphic anthropology:[86] if one's mode of knowledge follows one's mode of

---

anachronistically drawing any hard lines between these constellations of concepts. It is also important to keep in mind the hylomorphic distinction I noted above between psychological (powers of the soul) and sub-psychological (the physical organs and biological processes that embody these powers).

83. I am leaving discussion of the passions out of this account, but a complete treatment would include a discussion of their divisions and connections with the powers of sense, intellect, and will. See discussion in, e.g., Miner, *Thomas Aquinas on the Passions*.

84. For a fuller introduction to these issues, see Feser, *Philosophy of Mind*; Kretzmann, "Philosophy of Mind," 128–59. Stump distances Aquinas' "dualism" from a Cartesian or Platonic "dualism," showing how his hylomorphism makes better sense of embodied existence than Descartes or Plato while also eschewing reductive materialism (Stump, *Aquinas*, 191–216). See a related discussion of the "mind-world" gap in Aquinas in Scarpelli Cory, "Knowing as Being?," 333–5.

85. Spruit, *Species*, 170.

86.

> Although the various modes of being for intellect, species and object may change, they are identical with respect to their formal structure in the cognitive act. Hence, according to Thomas, humans do not know a deformed "spiritualized" object: they are capable of grasping the intelligible structure of sensible objects, for material beings naturally tend toward an "*esse spirituale*"—in the same way

being, then the mode of cognition of a human soul will be appropriate to its status as the form of a material body.[87]

As with so many other areas of Aquinas' work, his philosophical anthropology is a synthesis of Platonic and Aristotelian strands of thought that offers elegant and satisfying solutions to debates that spanned centuries up to his time. One such debate has to do with the ontological status of the human soul, which Plato understood to be a substance while Aristotle argued that it was a substantial form. While many patristic authors were uncomfortable with the way that Platonic anthropology undermined the unity of the person and relegated the body to a secondary element of human nature, most of them nonetheless accepted some form of the thesis that the soul is a substance.[88] Certain medieval Latin and Arabic thinkers developed an eclectic dualistic approach that attempted to conceive of the soul as both form and substance, but relied on equivocal predication (Averroes),[89] or instrumentalism (Avicenna and Peter of Spain),[90] both of which undermined the hylomorphic principles they attempted to apply because the union of form and matter for these thinkers remained accidental.

In contrast to these currents of thought, Aquinas maintains that the intellectual soul is the substantial form of the physical body.[91] As the form of the body, the soul is subsistent and immaterial, has the ability dynamically to configure matter, and only realizes the perfection of its nature when it is united to the body.[92] Aquinas writes that:

> The [human] soul has subsistent being [*esse subsistens*], insofar as its being does not depend on the body but is rather elevated above corporeal matter. Nevertheless, the body receives a share [*communionem*] in its being, in such a way that there is one being of soul and body [*unum esse animae et corporis*], and this is the being of a human.[93]

This mode of existence is reflected in the human mode of cognition, which is naturally inclined toward the essences of material objects that it accesses by way of the physical senses. There is thus an isomorphism between the nature of

> the human mind is capable of containing more forms than just its own. (Spruit, *Species*, 171)

See *ST* I.14.1; Aristotle, *On the Soul*, II.12 [424a17f]; Owens, "Cognition a Way of Being," 1–11; Aristotle, "Cognition as Existence," 74–85; Paolozzi, "Hylomorphic Dualism," 271–82.

87. *QD De anima*, a. 9. On the continuing viability of hylomorphism, see, e.g., *Neo-Aristotelian Perspectives on Contemporary Science*.

88. See discussion of Nemesius, Eunomius, Augustine, and John Damascene in Bazán, "The Human Soul," 101–3.

89. Cordubensis, *Commentarium magnum in Aristotelis De anima libros*, , II, 5, 134–5.

90. Avicenna, *Liber de anima seu sextus de naturalibus*, V, 1 (80, 59–60); Hispanus, *Scientia libri De anima*, tr. I, c. 2 (17, 18–31).

91. See Wippel, "Thomas Aquinas and the Unity of Substantial Form," 117–54.

92. See *ST* I.75.6; I.76.1; *De Spir.*, a. 2 *ad* 5; Pasnau, *Human Nature*, esp. 25–95.

93. *De Spir.*, a. 2 *ad* 3 (translation by Stump, *Aquinas*, 201).

4. The Intelligibility of Participated Being　　　　　　　　113

created reality and the structure of the senses and intellect. To understand this structure, Aquinas suggests a complex process of dematerialization undertaken by a hierarchy of cognitive powers. Commenting on Aristotle's maxim that "nothing is in the intellect that was not previously in the sense" Aquinas notes that "a thing is led by gradual steps from its own material conditions to the immateriality of the intellect through the mediation of the immateriality of sense."[94] This involves a transition from the external senses, which are embodied in physical organs, to the four internal senses, which are embodied in the brain, and finally to the powers of the intellect, which are not embodied in a physical organ (see Figure 1).

Aquinas' cognitive psychology can thus be descriptively broken down into three stages, each having to do with the intention under the same formal aspect but under an increasingly immaterial mode of being: (1) sensory cognition, which takes place in material cognitive powers using bodily organs (including the five external and four internal senses) and is common to both humans and nonrational animals;[95] (2) apprehension of single essences, which involves the "light" of the agent intellect abstracting the intelligible species from the phantasms, allowing the intellect to grasp not just the individual object of perception but the universal form of that object; and (3) discursive reasoning, wherein the possible intellect (understood as pure intellectual potency) is "informed" by the intelligible species and, being "turned toward the phantasms," cooperates with the imagination and cogitative power to perform intellectual acts of deliberation, judgment, and reasoning.[96] Let us briefly consider each of these elements in greater detail.

To begin with, each of the external senses receives information about the sensible attributes of a physical object and relays this sensory data (known as "sensible species") to the internal sensory powers embodied in the brain.[97] For

---

94. *De ver.*, 2.3, arg. 19; cf. *ScG* II.92.10. Pickavé comments: "What Aquinas means is rather that the senses provide the intellect with the basic 'raw material' for higher-level cognitive activity" ("Human Knowledge," in *The Oxford Handbook of Aquinas*, 314). Aquinas stresses that the *De anima*'s "blank slate" analogy applies only to the possible intellect (*In III De anima* 9.39-60, 10.128-66; cf. Pasnau, *Human Nature*, 308).

95. Sensory cognition is not *qualitatively* different in humans and nonrational animals, and the powers of the external senses in animals often supersede the human senses (e.g., the sight of an eagle or the olfaction of a dog). However, nonrational animals possess a power of "estimation" rather than "cogitation," which is a natural instinct restricted to apprehending particular intentions here and now. See *ST* I.78.4, I-II.6.2; *In II De anima*, lect. 13, §398.

96. "When the mind is actively aware of anything it is necessarily aware of it along with an image; for images are like sensuous contents except in that they contain no matter" (Aristotle, *de Anima* III, 423a7-9).

97. See Aquinas' argument for the number of exterior senses in *ST* I.78.3. In recent years, some philosophers and neuroscientists have argued that there could be between twenty-two and thirty-three senses (see *The Oxford Handbook of Philosophy of Perception*,). However, much of what is being termed "senses" have to do with different phenomena than what Aquinas is defining as sense powers here. See also *In II De anima*, lect. 13-24; bk. 3, lect. 1-6; *QD De anima* a. 13.

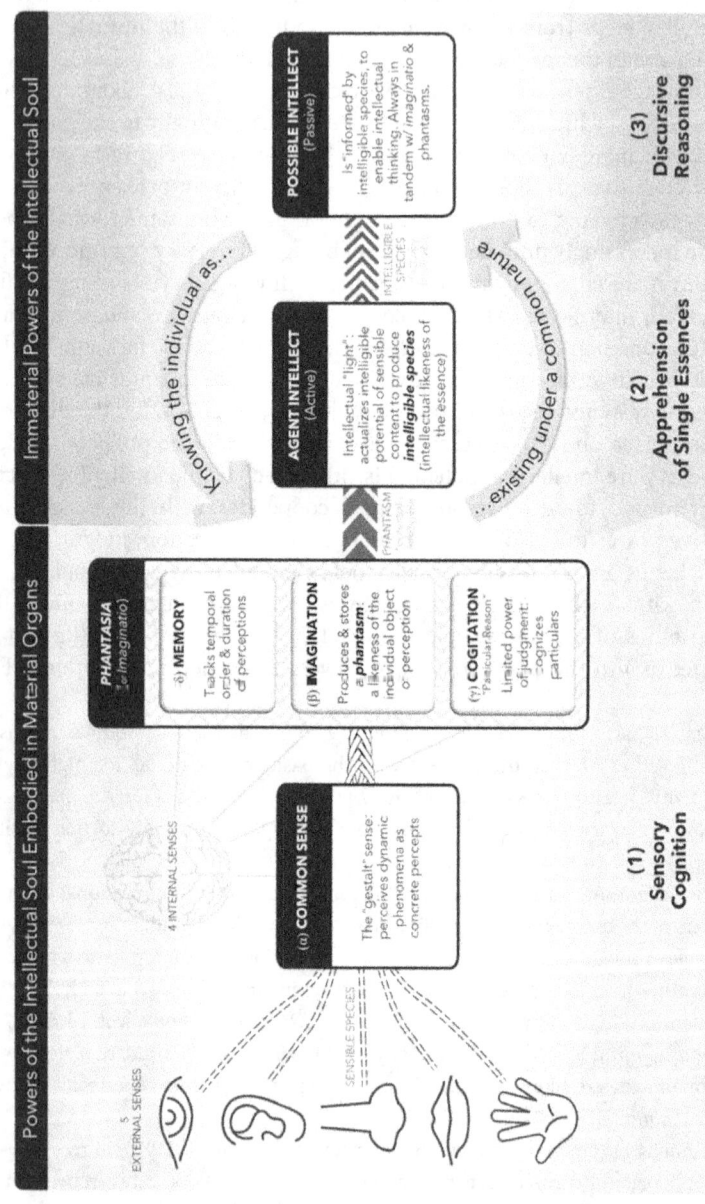

Figure 1 Thomas Aquinas' Cognitive Psychology.

Aquinas, the sensible species is not the object of perception; it is "not what [*quod*] is perceived, but rather that *by which* [*quo*] sense perceives."[98] The sensible species are received and transformed by the four inner senses of the brain to produce and store a "phantasm" of the individual object. (α) The common sense is a kind of gestalt sense:[99] it is a power of perception and discrimination, perceiving the objects of the individual senses as unified wholes. The common sense is thus responsible for the state of communication between the external sense powers and the power of common sense. Aquinas sees the common sense as both the source and terminating point of acts of sensation: "the common root and principle of the exterior senses."[100] (β) The imagination or *phantasia* is "as it were, a storehouse of forms received through the senses," which produces and stores a similitude of the individual object of perception known as a "phantasm."[101] The imagination thus retains per se sensibles, which include proper sensibles (color, sound, odor, flavor, tangibles: each of which is proper to one of the senses) and common sensibles (movement/rest, number, shape, dimension: each of which is common to multiple senses),[102] but not *per accidens* sensibles.[103] (γ) Cogitation, also known as particular reason, is a limited power of judgment that apprehends or cognizes individuals to form phantasms.[104] Michael Stock notes that the cogitative power "must be subject

---

98. *ST* I.85.2 *s.c.* (emphasis added). See *De unitate intellectus*, ch. 3, §66; *In I De anima*, lect. 14, §418; *In Metaph.* bk. 5, lect. 7, §860; *ST* I.83.3; Spruit, *Species*, 159; De Anna, "Aquinas on Sensible Forms and Semimaterialism," 43–63; Pasnau, *Theories of Cognition in the Later Middle Ages*, esp. 31–62.

99. See De Haan, "Perception and the *Vis Cogitativa*," 397–437.

100. *ST* I.84.4 *ad 1*. See *ST* I.78.4 *ad 2*; *QD De anima*, q. 13 ["*sic igitur*"]; *In II De anima*, lect. 13, §390; *In III De anima*, lect. 3, §602.

101. *ST* I.78.4. Aquinas also uses "*phantasia*" as a genus description of how common sense, imagination, and memory work together as they move from sensation to perception. See *In De memoria*, lect. 2, §322; *In De memoria*, lect. 2, §321; *ScG* II.73.14; *QD De anima* 20; *ST* I.89.5.

102. Note that common sensibles are not the special object of common sense, which "is the faculty whereat the modifications affecting all the particular senses terminate" (*In II De anima*, c. 6, lect. 13, §390).

103. One way to conceive of the difference between *per se* sensibles and *per accidens* sensibles is that if the former involve "seeing" then the latter involve "seeing as." De Haan explains that "these incidental sensibles are in themselves essentially cognoscible realities, even though they are by definition accidental to sensibles *qua* sensibles. Following Avicenna, Aquinas calls these cognoscible realities *intentions*" (Daniel De Haan, "Linguistic Apprehension as Incidental Sensation in Thomas Aquinas" *Proceedings of the ACPA* 84 [2011]: 187, citing *ST* I, q. 78, a. 4). See *In II De anima*, c. 6, lect. 13: "We speak of a sense-object in three ways: two [kinds of sense-objects] are perceptible essentially; one incidentally. Of the two former, one is proper to each sense, the other common to all."

104. *ScG* II.60.1. See *ST* I.78.4; *In II De anima* lect. 13, §396. De Haan develops some of the groundwork for a philosophy of perception based on the Thomistic account of the cogitative power in "Vis Cogitativa," 398.

to direction from the intellect, so that its own activity will be conformed to the purposes of the higher power, and not vice versa."[105] In other words, the cogitative power is not simply instinctual, as if it functioned separately from the intellect, even though its action has ontological priority in the order of knowing.[106] The cogitative faculty knows individuals "as existing under a common nature" because of its unity with the intellect, thus enabling it to recognize *this* tree as this *tree*.[107] (δ) The memory apprehends the temporal order and interval of acts of perception, thus pertaining to particular intentions under the aspect of pastness.[108] Aquinas characterizes human memory as not only a "sudden recollection of the past," as in animals, but also as *reminiscentiam* (reminiscence).[109]

Aquinas quotes Aristotle saying that "phantasms are to the intellect what sensible things are to sense," and explains that "just as colors are made actually visible by light, so phantasms are made actually intelligible only by the agent intellect."[110] Phantasms are, in other words, potentially intelligible sensory content, still singular (as opposed to universal) and contextualized in matter (though existing immaterially).[111] The production of phantasms is subject to the individual's conditions of learning and knowing, which makes Aquinas' approach amenable to contemporary discussions of concept formation.[112] St. Thomas writes that "the intellective soul is related to phantasms as to its objects."[113] However, because phantasms are *potentially* intelligible content—just as color and sound are *potentially* sensible content—they require a power that is active in the relevant way to abstract from them the intelligible essence of the sensible object. So Aquinas writes,

> Now nothing is reduced from potentiality to act except by something in act; as the senses are made actual by what is actually sensible. We must therefore assign on the part of the intellect some power to make things actually intelligible [*faceret intelligibilia in actu*], by abstraction of the species from material conditions. And such is the necessity for an agent intellect [*intellectum agentem*].[114]

105. Stock, "Sense Consciousness According to St. Thomas," 433. "This same particular reason is naturally guided and moved according to the universal reason" (*ST* I, q. 81, a. 3 resp.).

106. See *QD De anima*, q. 13.

107. *In II De anima* lect. 13, §398.

108. *De ver.*, q. 10, a. 2 s.c.

109. *ST* I.78.4. See *De memoria*, esp., e.g., lect. 3, §320.

110. *On the Soul*, III.7 [431a14]; *QD De anima*, a. 15. The "agent intellect" is often translated as the "active intellect." Cf. Haldane, "Aquinas and the Active Intellect," 199–210.

111. *ScG* II.59.13.

112. For a related discussion, see De Haan, "Linguistic Apprehension," 179–96.

113. *De ver.*, q. 18, a. 8, ad 4; *De ver.*, q. 10, a. 2, ad7. Although Aquinas refers to phantasms as "objects" of understanding, it is best not to reify them, and if we are to imagine them, they are probably better thought of as words than as pictures.

114. *ST* I.79.3. See Lee, "Agent Intellect," 41–61.

Aquinas describes the agent intellect as an intellectual "light"[115] that has the power to abstract the intelligible species from the phantasm.[116] In other words, the agent intellect is able to "take into consideration the specific nature without the conditions of individuality, the image of which informs the possible intellect."[117] Despite Aquinas' phrase *sine individualibus conditionibus*, Spruit notes that, for Aquinas, "abstraction is not an unveiling; it is an actualization or determination of the intelligible potential of sensible contents. Illumination consists in assigning a higher actuality to these contents, such that the agent intellect makes available the essential structure of sensory representations."[118] Here Aquinas draws an analogy between sensing and intellection: colors, he argues, are not actually visible themselves because they make no contact with our eyes. Rather, light, which is actually visible, enters our eyes and enables us to perceive colors. In the same way, phantasms are not intelligible because they do not enter our intellect, rather the "light" of the agent intellect makes the phantasms actually intelligible, such that they can move the possible intellect.[119] While one could define the intelligible species as a similitude of the universal *form* of the object,[120] it is more often spoken of as a similitude of the *essence*, which would include the element of materiality.[121] The species, unlike phantasms, are abstracted from *individual* intelligible matter, but they remain contextualized within *common* intelligible matter. As Aquinas explains, the species of a man, for example, "includes matter … flesh and bones, but does not denote *this* flesh and *these* bones."[122] Not only this, but, as noted above, the intellect never relies on the species alone, for thinking always involves turning to the phantasms: knowing the individual as existing under a common nature. After all, to discern causal priority in the order of knowing is not to isolate functions into a strict temporal succession.[123]

---

115. *QD De anima*, a. 15 *ad 19*. See Boland, *Ideas in God*, 280; Scarpelli Cory, "Rethinking Abstractionism," 607–46.

116. See Cory, "Averroes and Aquinas on the Agent Intellect's Causation of the Intelligible," 1–60.

117. *ST* I.85.1 *ad 4* (my translation). See Baltuta, "Aquinas on Intellectual Cognition," 589–602; Bower and Brower-Toland, "Aquinas on Mental Representation," 193–243.

118. Spruit, *Species*, 168.

119. *ScG* II.59.14.

120. *De ver.*, q. 10, a. 4; q. 10, a. 4 *ad 2b*.

121. *ST* I.85.1 *ad 2*. Spruit notes that there are a number of possible sources Aquinas used to develop his theory of species, including Aristotle, Augustine, Averroes, Alexander of Hales, Peter of Spain, and Albert the Great, but that "Thomas offers a fundamentally new interpretation of this notion" (Spruit, *Species*, 157, cf. fn. 216).

122. *ScG* II.92.9. See Spruit, *Species*, 170. Cf. *ST* I.84.7; I.85.1 *ad* 5; *ScG* I.30.277.

123. *De ver.* q. 18, a. 8, ad 4. See Scarpelli Cory, "What Is an Intellectual 'Turn'?," 129–62. For further discussion of sensation in Aquinas, see, e.g., Stock, O.P. "Sense Consciousness According to St. Thomas," 415–86; Simon, "An Essay on Sensation," 55–95; White, "The Picture Theory of the Phantasm," 131–56; White, "Why the Cogitative Power?" 213–27; MacDonald, "Direct Realism and Aquinas's Account of Sensory Cognition," 348–78.

All of this leads us to the function of the possible intellect (*intellectus possibilis*), which is sometimes mistranslated as "passive intellect."[124] The possible intellect is a pure intellectual potency that is actualized by the "informing" presence of the intelligible species. Aquinas explains that

> In the reception through which the possible intellect [*intellectus possibilis*] receives species from phantasms, the phantasms act as instrumental and secondary agents. The agent intellect acts as the principal and first agent. Therefore, the effect of the action is received [*relinquitur*] in the possible intellect according to the condition of both, and not according to the condition of either one alone. *Therefore, the possible intellect receives forms whose actual intelligibility is due to the power* [virtute] *of the agent intellect* [intellectus agens], *but whose determinate likeness* [similitudines] *to things is due to cognition of the phantasms.* These actually intelligible forms do not, of themselves, exist either in the imagination [*phantasia*] or the agent intellect, but only in the possible intellect.[125]

Aquinas believes that, in order to cognize universals, we must possess a power capable of receiving them that is not embodied in matter.[126] Further, because we understand many things potentially, though not actually, we must have a power that stands in potentiality to intelligible things and possesses the capacity to reflect on them through judgment and discursive reasoning.[127] It is important to note that it is on the basis of this fact that Aquinas believes the soul is capable of subsisting separate from the body, although "to exist apart from bodies is an accidental competence [*convenit ... per accidens*] on the part of souls, since they are naturally forms of bodies."[128] In a disembodied state, however, the soul "understands in a different manner" than when the soul is united to the body, which is its proper

---

124. Although the possible intellect is a "quasi-passive power" (*De Virt.* 1.9), St. Thomas is careful to distinguish the *intellectus possibilis* from the *intellectus passivus* (which is the term Aristotle uses for the cogitative power). See *ScG* II.60; *QD De anima*, q. 13.

125. *De ver.*, q. 10, a. 6, *ad 7* (emphasis added).

126. See, e.g., *ScG* II.50. Here Aquinas is following the modus principle (*ScG* II.50.6). Pasnau critiques this argument in "Content Fallacy." Cf. Wood, *Thomas Aquinas on the Immateriality of the Human Intellect*.

127. *ST* I.54.4. In a contemporary context, it is probably most helpful to think of intelligible species as something akin to competencies developed over time by the possible intellect. The more I observe, interact with, and use a hammer, the more I grasp the universal "hammer" that I then deploy intellectually in a variety of ways (practically, literally, metaphorically, analogically, etc.). Aquinas is not imagining that we simply walk around zapping things with our agent intellects, instantaneously abstracting perfect universal forms. But he does believe that we are capable of grasping something true and real about things in a way that transcends their pluriform material conditions.

128. *ScG* II.91.2.

mode of being.¹²⁹ Because the intellect is the highest power of the human soul, it is often used by synecdoche as a synonym for the soul, which highlights how central this understanding is for Aquinas' conception of the human person.¹³⁰

Cognition and Metaphysics

To argue, as I have, that our metaphysical presuppositions will have ramifications for our understanding of human cognition is not to say that we simply read off a cognitive theory straight from the fundamental structures of being. Rather, a wide range of inquiry is involved that encompasses not only various philosophical loci but also phenomenology, biology, neuroscience, and so on. Nonetheless, our conception of being provides the fundamental structures and terms for our understanding of these actions of knowing and, in that way, proves decisive for how we conceive of cognition and intellection. As a result, I would like to discuss four interrelated metaphysical principles and how they bear upon this picture of cognition.

First, one of the key elements in a participatory approach is the principle of formal causation. If "act" is what is received, and "potency" is that which receives, then we can understand essences as the limiting potency of being. Understanding act and potency in terms of participation undermines any absolute dichotomy between the two: both being and essence are given by God, and receiving being is not opposed to having an act of being that is one's own. The same goes for knowing. At each step of Aquinas' cognitive psychology, the active potentiality of the intellect is emphasized through both reception and causation. By distinguishing in both sensation and intellection between what [*quod*] is perceived, and that *by which* [*quo*] it is perceived, Aquinas is able to insist that the *res*, the thing itself, is the object of knowledge, even while the sensible species, phantasms, and intelligible species serve as the instrumental principles of the mind's reception of the object and indelibly shape the mind's grasp of it.¹³¹ While the senses are passive in

---

129. *ScG* II.80.12.

130. *De ver.* 10.1; *ST* I.79.1. It is worth noting that Aquinas conceives of the noetic effects of the fall in terms of disorder, rather than the loss or corruption of the powers of nature (*Comp. Theol.* 1, ch. 186). After the fall, human nature loses this proper ordering, but not its substantial parts, nor the capability of the mind to seek truth or the will's freedom of choice (*ST* I-II.85.2).

131. *ST* I, q. 85, a. 2 *s.c.* (emphasis added).

> The species should not be thought of as a pictorial image; rather it represents that characteristic feature of sensible things, which grounds the act of sense perception: it is an effect of the thing communicating itself according to its formal structure. This general view entails that the species in sensation is an instrumental principle, rather than the perceptual object itself. (Spruit, *Species*, 159, citing *ScG* II.75)

relation to the external world, they are actual powers that both receive input and produce species and phantasms to enable acts of intellectual cognition. Species and phantasms are instrumental principles grounding acts of sensation, they are not perceptual objects in themselves. Nonetheless, they retain the same formal structure as the object: *esse naturale* remains the foundation for both *esse sensibile* and *esse intelligibile*.[132]

Second, it is not only that what we know gets its intelligibility from its participation in God but also that human reason itself is a participation in the divine *Logos*: our rationality is what Aquinas calls a "participated likeness of the uncreated light, in which are contained the eternal types."[133] Key to this is the agent intellect, which Aquinas describes as an intellectual "light"[134] that has the power to abstract the intelligible species from the phantasm.[135] Not only does this call into question modern dichotomies between faith and reason or natural and supernatural revelation,[136] it also emphasizes the weight that theism lends to the coherence of realism, and vice versa. In other words, it is not an accident that the denial of the existence of proper essences for things and the ontological dimension of truth has gone hand in hand with the lapse of religious belief in modernity. It is important to note, however, that the agent intellect is not the Platonic anamnesis, for Aquinas insists with Aristotle that nothing is in the intellect that is not first in the senses. Nor is it the Cartesian postulation of God to secure the existence of the universe. Thomas is not attempting to traverse a bridge between sense and intellect; he is interested in the nature of thought as it transitions from sense to intellect, and he sees an important connection between this and how reality itself transitioned from (divine) intellect to material existence in creation. The active power of the intellect is given by the one who gave formal existence to all things.

Third, central to the meaning of "part-icipation" is the sense that to participate is to have a part, and not the whole, but it is to have that part truly. This holds

Cf. *De unitate intellectus*, ch. 3, §66; *In I De anima*, lect. 14, §418; *In Metaph*. bk. 5, lect. 7, §860; *ST* I, q. 83, a. 3 *resp.* See discussion in De Anna, "Aquinas on Sensible Forms and Semimaterialism," 43–63; Pasnau, *Theories of Cognition in the Later Middle Ages*, esp. 31–62.

132. *In De anima* II, VII, 310; cf. Spruit, *Species*, 158.

133. *ST* I, q. 84, a. 5. Cf. Davison, *Participation*, 310.

134. "Phantasms are actualized by the light of the agent intellect, which is a kind of participation of the light of superior substances" (*QD De anima*, a. 15 ad 19). Boland writes, "Saint Thomas speaks of the *intellectus agens* in terms of light since it is a capacity to illumine sense data and make them intelligible. As lumen intellectuale it is a participation in the uncreated light of which Psalm 4 speaks. The intellect is always in possession of this power which is nonnatural to it" (Boland, *Ideas in God*, 280). Cf. Scarpelli Cory, "Rethinking Abstractionism: Aquinas's Intellectual Light and Some Arabic Sources," 607–46.

135. See Scarpelli Cory, "Averroes and Aquinas on the Agent Intellect's Causation of the Intelligible," 1–60.

136. "Hence we must say that for the knowledge of any truth whatsoever man needs Divine help, that the intellect may be moved by God to its act" (*ST* I-II.109.1). See *ST* I.12.13.

true in both being and knowing. Receiving is the mode of having that is proper to creatures. This points to the fact that the limited nature of our knowledge both of God and creation does not result from a negative assessment of truth—as if the world were just chaos and thus largely unintelligible. As Étienne Gilson puts it, what "knowledge grasps in the object is something real, but reality is inexhaustible."[137] Aquinas' recognition of our limited knowledge comes from his understanding of the excess of intelligibility in the world, rather than its lack. There is too much truth, goodness, and beauty in creation for us to grasp it fully—it is our nature to grasp it in part.[138] If truth is, at root, about being, then it is effusive and boundless. Unlike antirealist idealism, a participatory metaphysic does not draw a radical separation between physical and intentional being. If beings are capable of communicating their being according to the formal structure of their essence, and our mind is capable of cognizing external objects according to the uniquely sensible and intelligible modes of being proper to our senses and intellect, it is unnecessary to make the mind the sole ground of reality. At the same time, the more positive idealism of Kant, focused on the "ideal" categories of our thought, is countered by Aquinas' understanding of the agent intellect, without undermining the role of sensation in every act of intellection. As Spruit notes, the agent intellect plays a normative function as the source of intelligibility within the mind, but does not itself contain species, which would make phantasms superfluous.[139] While a naïve realist insists that concepts conform to objects, and an idealist argues that objects conform to concepts, Aquinas argues for both. In grasping how things appear to us, we grasp something of the things in themselves, but we do so according to the active fashioning of our senses and intellect.

This leads us to the fourth point. Aquinas offers us a "realist" approach to knowledge, but it is by no means naïve. While the thing itself is the measure of truth, Aquinas does not think that phantasms move the intellect, as if the mind played no role in shaping our perception of the world. There is both activity and passivity involved in cognition, which grounds both the partiality and objectivity of knowledge. Aquinas' realism is not incompatible with a recognition that each of us is shaped by specific traditions of reasoning and habitual ways of inhabiting the world. We are habituated into patterns of thinking and acting, and those predilections both draw our attention to certain aspects of reality and not others, and they determine how we understand them. Participation allows us to understand this in terms of mode of being—to grasp something in part, according to *esse intentionale*, is not to create something out of thin air, nor is it to grasp it falsely. If being can be communicated according to the same formal structure in

---

137. Gilson, *Methodical Realism*, 102.
138. Davison, *Participation*, 316, 337.
139. *In De anima III*, lect. X, 739; *ST* I, q. 84, a. 3-4. "The intelligible species which are participated by our intellect are reduced, as to their first cause, to a first principle which is by its essence intelligible—namely, God. But they proceed from that principle by means of the sensible forms and material things, from which we gather knowledge" (*ST* I, q. 84, a. 4 *ad 1*).

qualitatively different modes, then truth can be grasped, even if only partially and slowly.

Three elements, in particular, of the foregoing are worth keeping in mind for the next chapter.[140] First, while knowledge pertains to universals, our acquisition of information and subsequent acts of reflection are always dependent on phantasms, which means that our knowledge is always conditioned, and thus limited in both mode and scope, by our particular geographical, historical, and cultural context. Second, there is a triangular relationship between external things, phantasms, and forms such that the conventional significations of our languages denote natural concepts within the mind, which themselves denote the natural things signified by language.[141] As Thomas Joseph White notes, "Language not only denotes but also draws our discriminating attention to various facets of reality."[142] Our language, concepts, and symbols do not simply proceed from our intellectual grasp of things, for "their cultural performance also initiates us to the act of grasping the things that they denote."[143] Furthermore, much of what we come to grasp is not simply natural but the result of human ingenuity, from political, religious, and philosophical customs to physical artifacts. Aquinas is no naïve realist, and he is insistent on the ways in which the physical conditions of knowing remain determinative for the acts of the intellect throughout the embodied life of the soul.[144] In this connection, he goes so far as to argue that divine revelation is given "under the species of phantasms," for the human has no other way of understanding.[145] Third, while the universality of knowledge allows us to affirm the real grasp of essences and insights into reality present in all cultures at all times, White maintains that "we must also recognize that there are cultures in which the *degree or intensity* of such insight differs in a given realm of understanding. And there are vastly different degrees of scientific, religious, philosophical, and moral insight (or ignorance) present in distinct cultures across time."[146] The affirmation of realism does not relativize cultural or historical difference, but upholds it, grounding it firmly in an understanding of the nature of human knowing.

It is beyond the scope of this study to elaborate in detail the implications of this picture for our understanding of "history" as an instance of knowledge. Nonetheless, it is worth noting the general shape such an approach would take. If history is about events and narratives, then the epistemic status of history as a form of knowledge depends on our access to those events and the relation between event

---

140. These are discussed by White, "The Infused Science of Christ," 620–2.

141. Aristotle, *De interpretatione* 1.1.16a3–6. As noted in White, "Infused Science," 621.

142. White, "Infused Science," 621. See discussion of the Sapir-Whorf hypothesis in Taylor, *The Language Animal the Full Shape of the Human Linguistic Capacity*, 320–31.

143. Ibid.

144. See *QD De anima*, a. 15 ad 20.

145. Here "species" means "category" or "aspect," rather than "under intelligible species." *De ver.*, q. 19, a. 1; *ST* I.84.7 *ad* 3; *ScG* II.73.38.

146. White, "Infused Science," 622.

and narrative.¹⁴⁷ Aquinas' cognitive theory suggests a third approach between the poles of historicism and postmodern constructivism. This approach would insist that events exist outside of the mind, but that our knowledge of them is shaped by our senses and intellect in a way that cannot be overcome methodologically. As a realist approach, it would insist that the world is not reducible to historical processes, and that the ontological makeup of reality is normative in important ways for the discipline of historiography. As a result, this historiographical approach would be cognizant of its metaphysical foundations and capable of openly debating them and accounting for a multiplicity of approaches grounded in competing metaphysical construals.¹⁴⁸ This approach would also be critical of the relativism of postmodern reader-response theories. A truly critical-realist historiography would be skeptical of the idea that historical narratives (such as "the Renaissance") exist in the past, but far from being content to lean into the constructed nature of such narratives, it would be chastened by this fact.¹⁴⁹ At the same time, Aquinas' understanding of habits and virtues could enable it to account for why good historians are frequently capable of making historical judgments that transcend the limitations of their methods.

Conclusion

In the centuries that have elapsed since Aquinas' time, we have made immense advances in our scientific understanding of the natural world and the human body. Many of those developments are relevant to the picture set out in this chapter and would do much to fill out, nuance, and critique certain elements of Aquinas' understanding. Take, for example, Aquinas' belief that the internal senses are localized in specific ventricles of the brain, an idea that was based on the anatomical discoveries of Galen that have since been disproven.¹⁵⁰ Thomas' conception of the sub-psychological systems of the brain is more crudely localized than our understanding today. There is no question that the intervening advances in biology, medicine, and even philosophy (especially certain approaches to phenomenology, psychology, and so on) have much to offer this conversation. However, it is equally important to recognize that on the level of our understanding of *being*, and of philosophical anthropology and its attendant ontological entailments, there is little reason to think that similar advancements have been made. A vastly more detailed grasp of our sub-psychological biological systems of information processing does little, in itself, to challenge the ontological

---

147. See Heringer, *History and Theology*, 9.

148. See ibid., xii. Unlike Wright's critical realism, this approach would be metaphysically realist, not just epistemologically realist.

149. Lonergan discusses elements of such an approach in *Method in Theology*.

150. *ST* I.78.4. See Kemp and Fletcher, "The Medieval Theory of the Inner Senses," 559–76.

framework of the psychological powers of the intellect laid out by Aquinas. For the purposes of thinking about historiography and Christology, the metaphysical insights Aquinas offers herein remain vital.[151] Various scholars have argued for the need to develop a robust philosophical anthropology—something they seem to have lost in the modern period—before we proceed into discussions of moral psychology and moral philosophy. My argument is that the same should be said for historiography and Christology.[152]

Our study of Aquinas has illustrated the detailed connections between metaphysics and epistemology, outlining his compelling, yet critical, case for metaphysical realism. Further, I have outlined the ways in which metaphysical presuppositions shape our conception of God and our understanding of philosophical anthropology such that they cannot be ignored if we want to talk responsibly about Christology. To this end, Aquinas has also provided us with a robust and nuanced cognitive theory that will provide the raw material for the theological discussions to come in the following chapters. With these elements in mind, we now turn to one of the central topics of twentieth-century Christology: the doctrine of Christ's knowledge.

---

151. For contemporary discussion and defense of various accounts of Aquinas' Anthropology and cognitive theory, see Braine, *The Human Person*; MacIntyre, *Dependent Rational Animals*; Moreland and Rae, *Body and Soul*; Lonergan, *Insight*; Lonergan, *Verbum*; Evans, "Separable Souls," 327–40; Feser, *Philosophy of Mind*; Oderberg, *Real Essentialism*; Klima, "Aquinas on the Materiality of the Human Soul and the Immateriality of the Human Intellect," 163–82; Madden, *Mind, Matter and Nature*; Klubertanz, *Philosophy of Human Nature*; Freddoso, "No Room at the Inn," 15–30; Pasnau, *Human Nature*; Simpson (ed.), *Neo-Aristotelian Perspectives*; Wood, *Immateriality of the Human Intellect*; and the work of Daniel De Haan Op. cit.

152. Anscombe, "Modern Moral Philosophy," 1–19; MacIntyre, *Dependent Rational Animals*; De Haan, *Vis Cogitativa*.

Chapter 5

DIVINE KNOWLEDGE: AN EXCURSUS ON MK 13:32

Early theological discussions of Jesus' knowledge were occasioned by his terse statement following the parable of the fig tree: "But concerning that day and hour no one knows [οὐδεὶς οἶδεν], not even the angels of heaven, nor the Son [οὐδὲ ὁ υἱός], but the Father only" (Mk 13:32).[1] Since the fourth century, this text has regularly been taken in hand as evidence of Jesus' ignorance and used to advance subordinationist, kenotic, or Ebionite Christological agendas. There is no doubt that, as Augustine writes, this text raises "a large question (*magna quaestio*)," and it has clearly disquieted many theological commentators.[2] Meanwhile, historical Jesus scholars have frequently appealed to patristic commentary on this passage as evidence of the ahistorical nature of classical Christian reflection on Jesus, regarding it as "defensive exegesis, as special pleading."[3] As Dale Allison Jr. writes, "the church fathers read the logion with presuppositions foreign to it, presuppositions that indeed contradict it. They found only what they wanted to find, reading their own christology into the Gospels so that Jesus might hand it right back to them."[4] Indeed, many biblical scholars, after encountering patristic exegesis on Mk 13:32/Mt. 24:36, have agreed with Allison's sense that "our theological tradition is full of tendentious, ahistorical readings of Gospel texts, readings that have served orthodox christological agendas instead of historical

---

1. Compare this text with its parallel in Matthew (it is absent from the parallel in Lk. 21:29-33):

Mk 13:32: Περὶ δὲ τῆς ἡμέρας ἐκείνης **ἢ τῆς** ὥρας οὐδεὶς οἶδεν, οὐδὲ οἱ ἄγγελοι **ἐν οὐρανῷ** οὐδὲ ὁ υἱός, εἰ μὴ ὁ πατήρ. Mt. 24:36: Περὶ δὲ τῆς ἡμέρας ἐκείνης **καὶ** ὥρας οὐδεὶς οἶδεν, οὐδὲ οἱ ἄγγελοι **τῶν οὐρανῶν** [οὐδὲ ὁ υἱός], εἰ μὴ ὁ πατὴρ **μόνος**.

2. Augustine, *Sermon 97* (PL 38:549).
3. Allison Jr., *The Historical Christ and the Theological Jesus*, 83.
4. Ibid.

truth."[5] Having freed themselves from the strictures of theological tradition, Allison considers modern biblical scholars to be uniquely positioned to read these texts historically and discern their meaning.

Allison's charge extends beyond the claim that patristic readings of this passage were insufficiently historical: he maintains that they are theologically problematic, for they preserve the divinity of Christ at the expense of his humanity, thereby advancing a docetic Christology.[6] He asks, "what then does it mean that, until relatively recent times, our dominant theologians have put Jesus into a christological straitjacket, that they have, despite their protests otherwise, been docetists of a sort, for whom Jesus' humanity was above all a philosophical problem?"[7] He continues:

> When one looks at how [orthodoxy's] advocates have, from ancient times, interpreted certain New Testament texts, one must object, at least if one has been trained to think historically. Again and again Jesus' deity has all but liquidated his humanity, making him a historically impossible figure. He has been a simulacrum, his humanity merely a doctrine to be believed, not a fact to be felt.[8]

This would, indeed, be a serious issue for orthodox Christianity, and those concerned with the truth of the gospels as historical texts will rightly worry about the implications of Allison's charge. And yet, while his diagnosis may be true of certain textbook treatments of conciliar Christology, it does not hold up in the face of the patristic sources themselves. It is true that the church fathers, by and large, did not approach the gospels in the same way that today's historians tend to. They possessed no criteria of authenticity and no developed discipline of form and redaction criticism.[9] They knew nothing of the Q community and had yet to learn the value of multicolored beads for democratically discerning the historicity of Jesus' sayings. However, that does not mean they were unconcerned with the historical human existence of Jesus of Nazareth, or that this historical concern did not play a significant role in their exegesis. If we revisit their interpretations of Mk 13:32/Mt. 24:36 with the appropriate Christological framework in mind, we will find that much of the patristic Christological tradition is a prolonged attempt to uphold the historical human existence of Jesus in the face of a variety of theological tendencies that threatened it. If the fathers were uncomfortable with this passage, it was because of the sheer scale of theological and philosophical presuppositions

---

5. Ibid., 84.

6. While historically "Docetism" is primarily a denial of Jesus' physicality, historical Jesus scholars typically use it to refer to a denial that Jesus was truly human. In this chapter, I will use it in this latter, nontechnical sense.

7. Ibid., 85.

8. Allison, *The Historical Christ*, 82.

9. For an early and trenchant critique of the criteria of authenticity, see Hooker, "Christology and Methodology," 480–7.

being brought to bear on the text from all sides. Complex questions had to be answered before adequate exegetical solutions became available, questions such as: to what extent, and in what ways, can a human nature be deified by grace and still be fully human? I would like to suggest that Aquinas offers a compelling exegetical solution that illustrates the strength of the patristic readings and provides a robust and unparalleled Chalcedonian affirmation of Jesus' humanity.

After a brief Christological prelude, I will begin by outlining key elements of patristic exegesis of this passage and showing how and why they have frequently been misinterpreted. I will then consider some philosophical and theological distinctions that Aquinas provides, which further illuminate the coherence of the patristic Christological approach. Finally, I will consider a Thomistic argument that upholds and strengthens the patristic readings of this pericope. I conclude with some reflections on the theological agenda undergirding the interpretations of this passage offered by Dale Allison and Bart Ehrman. I will suggest that patristic Christological readings of Mk 13:32 arose more from intertextual concerns than from abstract metaphysics, and their interpretation is no more dogmatic than Allison's own theological reading of this passage. Furthermore, Aquinas offers a framework within which the concerns of patristic exegesis on this passage can be upheld and extended to answer Allison's charges.

A Brief Christological Prelude

Before we begin, it will be helpful to state the patristic conundrum concisely by considering two theological principles that impact how we might understand Christ's knowledge to relate to his two natures. First, as we have seen, knowledge belongs to a person only by reason of their nature, which means that in the Incarnation we cannot attribute knowledge to the hypostatic union itself. We cannot say that there is a single knowledge on the part of the *person*, but that the person of Christ has knowledge in each of his natures. Nonetheless, there must be a certain degree of correspondence between these two distinct operations (i.e., divine and human knowledge). If Jesus' human will is an active, free instrument of his divinity, it cannot act out of ignorance. Doing so would either result in an antipathy between his divine and human wills, yielding a duality of persons, or it would render the human will passive, resulting in Docetism. Therefore, without positing a knowledge on the part of the union, we nonetheless have to inquire about the unified action of the person of Christ with reference to his twofold knowledge, a conception that requires a correspondence between the two natures that nonetheless maintains their qualitative difference. We cannot avoid enquiring about a kind of union in the order of knowledge in addition to hypostatic union in the order of being. In the Chalcedonian paradigm, we are forced to forgo easy answers that simply apply this or that element of knowledge to Jesus' divinity or humanity, with no consideration of the relation between the two. As we will see, a key question here is the nature and extent of this correspondence necessary to uphold the unity of personhood.

Second, the doctrine of divine simplicity entails that, if Jesus was fully God, then he must have possessed divine omniscience, along with every other divine predicate, which God possesses in the simple unity of his being. In one sense, then, the question of Jesus' divine knowledge appears relatively straightforward for those of orthodox Trinitarian persuasion, the affirmation or rejection of it tantamount to the avowal or refusal of his divinity. And yet, a further implication of divine simplicity is frequently overlooked. Because divine knowledge is identical with the divine essence, it cannot be possessed by a human mind. The act of divine knowing simply is the very essence of God; therefore, it cannot belong to another nature. This fact, in part, drove early thinkers such as Eunomius and Apollinarius toward monophysitism. As they saw it, human knowledge involves ignorance (*agnoia*), which, as the ancient Greeks argued, is the root of moral evil and, thus, is incompatible with Christ's sinlessness.[10] In their thinking, if divine knowledge could not belong to Jesus' human mind, then his divinity must have *replaced* his human soul or mind. The later Christological councils were primarily concerned with denying these trends and reaffirming Jesus' full humanity, including his mind and will—affirmations which made the question of Jesus' human possession of divine knowledge acute for the later tradition.

Patristic Exegesis Reconsidered

In the second and early third centuries, there is little evidence that Mk 13:32 provided discomfort to Christian theologians.[11] Responding to early Gnostics, Irenaeus (*c.* 130–202) appeals to this passage as an illustration of Jesus' humility, urging us to exhibit epistemological modesty in kind: "If, then, the Son was not ashamed to ascribe the knowledge of that day to the Father only, neither let us be ashamed to reserve for God those greater questions which may occur to us."[12] Origen of Alexandria (*c.* 185–255) offers an ecclesiological interpretation: "For so long as the church, which is the body of Christ, does not know that day and hour, so that he is understood to know it at the time that all his members also know it."[13] Both theologians appear relatively untroubled by this passage, emphasizing the ostensible focus of the pericope: the day of judgment.[14] However, since around the

---

10. See discussion in Aloys Grillmeier with Hainthaler, *Christ in Christian Tradition*, 363.

11. Adam G. Messer notes that we have no evidence of any church father taking issue with this passage until after the adoptionist controversy late in the third century ("Patristic Theology and Recension in Matthew 24:36," 127–88).

12. Irenaeus of Lyons, *Against Heresies* II.28 (ANF 1:401).

13. Origen, *The Commentary of Origen on the Gospel of St Matthew*, §55 (639).

14. Origen connects this passage to 2 Thess. 2:1-2, "We beg you, brothers and sisters, not to be quickly shaken in mind or alarmed, either by spirit or by word or by letter, as though from us, to the effect that the day of the Lord is already here" (Origen, *Gospel of St Matthew*, §55 [637]).

time of the adoptionist controversy, Mk 13:32 has persistently proven controversial as a pericope favored by Arians and kenoticists alike.[15]

In his 1968 monograph *Jesus God and Man,* Raymond Brown made much of Cyril of Alexandria's (*c.* 370–444) statement that "[The Word of God] has not refused to descend to such a low position as to bear all that belongs to our

---

15. Jerome notes the absence of οὐδὲ ὁ υἱός from the Greek copies of Matthew and suggests that *neque filius* was added to the Latin manuscripts (Jerome, *Commentarii in Evangelium Matthei* 4 in CCSL 77, 231-2). Ambrose even suggests that the Arians themselves may have interpolated the phrase into the holy Scriptures: "*Primum ueteres non habent codices graeci nec filius scit. Sed non mirum, si et hoc falsarunt, qui scripturas interpolauere diuinas*" (Ambrose, *De Fide* 5.16 *NPNF*² 10:298). The evidence we have today points strongly in favor of οὐδὲ ὁ υἱός being original to Mark's text: only one tenth-century Greek MS (codex X) and one late Vulgate MS drop οὐδὲ ὁ υἱός (See Wallace, "The Son's Ignorance in Matthew 24:36," 184). However, there is some reason to think that Jerome and Ambrose could be correct regarding Matthew's parallel (24:36). Bruce Metzger argues that although οὐδὲ ὁ υἱός is lacking "in the majority of the witnesses of Matthew, including the later Byzantine text," the best Western and Alexandrian representatives contain the phrase and "the omission of the words because of the doctrinal difficulty they present is more probable than their addition by assimilation to Mk 13:32" (Metzger, *A Textual Commentary on the Greek New Testament,* 51-2). The majority of scholars have (often uncritically) followed Metzger, including Bart Ehrman, who makes this the key text of his argument in *The Orthodox Corruption of Scripture.* Ehrman maintains that the omission arose as a proto-orthodox response to adoptionism, and suggests that "the reason [for the omission] is not hard to postulate; if Jesus does not know the future, the Christian claim that he is a divine being is more than a little compromised" (*Misquoting Jesus,* 204). However, as noted above, we have no evidence of any church father taking issue with οὐδὲ ὁ υἱός until after the adoptionist controversy (Messer, "Patristic Theology and Recension," 127–88). Further, Daniel Wallace has argued persuasively in favor of the shorter text of Matthew. He finds that the external evidence is sufficient to call into question Metzger's claim, and that the internal evidence heavily favors the view that οὐδὲ ὁ υἱός was a later addition to Matthew's gospel. The redactional evidence is strong: Wallace shows that Matthew always develops Mark's text in the direction of a more explicitly high Christology and that his addition of μόνος makes most sense as a *replacement* of οὐδὲ ὁ υἱός. Hence, the original text would have read: "But as for that day and hour no one knows [it]—not even the angels in heaven—except the Father *alone.*" Thus, Matthew's Jesus says implicitly what Mark's Jesus says explicitly: "it preserves his high Christology while not altering the basic point" (Wallace, *Son's Ignorance,* 203). Wallace suggests that, given the use of the codex in this period, it is likely that all four gospels would have been copied by the same scribe. Therefore, if they were editing Matthew for theological reasons, they would have altered Mark as well. Since they did not alter Mark, then the idea that others added οὐδὲ ὁ υἱός to Matthew would align with the much more widely attested tendency to harmonize the gospels, regardless of the theological implications (contra Metzger). As such, it is at least plausible that οὐδὲ ὁ υἱός, while original to Mark's gospel, may not be original to Matthew's.

nature, *included in which is ignorance* [ὧν ἕν ὑπάρχει καὶ ἡ ἄγνοια]."[16] Brown intended to establish a non-Nestorian approach to Christology that would allow for ignorance in Christ, and he viewed Cyril as providing a significant patristic precedent. And yet, he appears to have misunderstood the Patriarch of Alexandria. For, although Cyril recognized the distinction of natures, he maintained a strong emphasis on the unity of personhood in Christ.[17] This led him to qualify his affirmation of ignorance, contending that Christ's divine knowledge somehow cancels out his innate human ignorance. Thus, in commenting on Mk 13:32, Cyril contends that "Christ acts in accordance with the economy [of salvation], although he says that he does not know the hour, he is not truly ignorant."[18] Evidently, Cyril's avowal of ignorance refers to the human nature of the incarnate Christ in a counterfactual manner, *were it not united to the Word*, while insisting that in the hypostatic union Christ's human ignorance was overcome through his divine omniscience.

Brown is by no means the only scholar to make this kind of mistake in his reading of the fathers, and it is not difficult to see why. As Raymond Moloney has noted, "whenever theologians and exegetes speak of Christ's knowing or not knowing this or that, it is always salutary to pose the question, Who is the 'he' to whom this knowledge or lack of it is being ascribed?"[19] One of the strategies to answer this question is to employ reduplication (i.e., "X is F *qua* Y"). So, for example, we might say "Christ hungers and thirsts *qua* human," or "Christ is immutable *qua* divine." This mirrors the wording of the Formula of Union of 433, an important document in the development of Chalcedon: "As to the evangelical and apostolic phrases about the Lord, we know that theologians treat some in common, as of one person, and distinguish others, as of two natures, and interpret the God-befitting ones in connection with the Godhead of Christ, and the humble ones of the manhood."[20] This reduplication is implicit in much of what we say of Christ because most predicates are applied to him in virtue of one of his natures. In potential cases of ambiguity, we can make the reduplication explicit, and doing so will bring clarity to otherwise opaque passages of patristic exegesis.

---

16. Cyril, *Thesaurus on the Holy and Consubstantial Trinity* 22 (PG 75:369), as cited by Brown, *Jesus God and Man*, 102. See also Brown, *Introduction to New Testament Christology*, 28n28.

17. Cyril, *On the Incarnation of the Only-Begotten* (PG 75:1189–1253).

18. "Οἰκονομεῖ γάρ τοι Χριστός, μὴ εἰδέναι λέγων τὴν ὥραν ἐκείνην, καὶ οὐκ ἀληθῶς ἀγνοεῖ" (Cyril, *Thesaurus* 22 [PG 75:377D]. My translation). See Moloney, *Knowledge of Christ*, 43–4.

19. Moloney, *Knowledge of Christ*, 130. Properly speaking, "he" should refer only to a person, not a nature. But this language is not always consistent between patristic commentators and their interlocutors.

20. ET: *The Christology of the Later Fathers*, 356.

Let us now consider three common elements of patristic interpretations of Mk 13:32.[21] First, in the hands of the Arians, this pericope raised questions of an intra-Trinitarian nature, focused on the divinity of Christ and his equality with the father. Therefore, setting Jesus' words alongside Jn 1:3—"All things came into being through him, and without him not one thing came into being"—Hilary (315–368), Ambrose (337–397), Jerome (347–420), and Augustine (354–430) convey their misgivings that He in whom all things were made could be ignorant of anything (see Jn 16:15; 21:17).[22] Far from following an abstract metaphysical principle, this is an issue raised by the Gospels themselves and, indeed, by the entire biblical canon (Deut. 6:4). They are interested in affirming that "Christ *qua* divine," as the eternal only-begotten Word of God, is equal to the Father. They do not work out in detail in this context what this means for the person of Christ incarnate or how his omniscience relates to his human nature.[23] Insofar as their exegesis is occasioned by Arian readings of the text, it is difficult to claim at this stage that they are importing a foreign Christological paradigm so much as they are simply ruling out insufficient theological interpretations. In other words, it is the Arians who have imported a theological paradigm onto the text, one which these authors are rejecting primarily on intertextual grounds.

Second, expanding the discussion from a Trinitarian to an incarnational focus, Athanasius of Alexandria (d. 373) sets Mk 13:32 alongside Lk. 2:52, arguing that Jesus knew of the day and hour as the divine Word, but not as a human "by reason of the flesh."[24] Ambrose offers a similar interpretation, which seems to imply that Jesus was ignorant in some sense in his humanity, but not in his divinity.[25] Athanasius insists further that "it belongs to man to be ignorant," and thus it was fitting that Jesus "knew not in flesh, though knowing as Word."[26] Athanasius and Ambrose make explicit what had been implied in the first approach: that "Christ *qua* human" is ignorant in some sense while "Christ *qua* divine" is not. Although they are not entirely clear on what this means for the correspondence between his two knowledges, it seems that both are affirming that it is not by virtue of

---

21. All three of these can show up in a given author, so they are neither mutually exclusive nor diachronic. See related discussions in Wickham, "The Ignorance of Christ," 213–26; Moloney, "Approaches to Christ's Knowledge in the Patristic Era," 37–66; Moloney, *The Knowledge of Christ, Problems in Theology*, 41–52; Madigan, "*Christus Nesciens?* Was Christ Ignorant of the Day of Judgment?," 255–78.

22. Hilary, *De Trinitate*, 9.59, 2:438–39; Jerome, *Tractatus in Marci Evangelium*, 496; Ambrose, *De Fide*, 5.1.206–8; Augustine, *Sermon 97* (PL 38:549).

23. See also Ambrose, *De Spirito Sancto*.

24. Athanasius, *Contra Arianos*, III.43 (NPNF² 4:417).

25. See Ambrose, *De Fide* 5.16.194, p. 289. Ambrose argues that it is not specifies whether "*neque filius*" refers to the Son of Man, or the Son of God (*Expositio Evangelii secundum Lucam* in CCSL 14, ed. M Adriaen [Turnhout: Brepols, 1975], 9.34, p. 310).

26. Athanasius, *Contra Arianos*, III.45.

his human nature but through his divinity that he knows the day and the hour, but that the human Jesus does in fact know.[27] These authors make it clear that reading this text as an affirmation that the second person of the Trinity is less than the father due to ignorance requires importing some form of Monophysite Christology onto the passage, and they insist to the contrary that the focus of Jesus' words is his human knowledge. Here Ambrose and Athanasius affirm the reality and integrity of Jesus' humanity, and its transformation through personal union with God, though the details of the latter remain underexplained.

Third, connecting Mk 13:32 with Acts 1:7, "It is not for you to know times or seasons that the Father has fixed by his own authority," Ambrose contends that Jesus knew the day of judgment, but chose not to reveal it to his disciples.[28] Jerome follows suit and maintains that it was not expedient for the disciples to know, or as Hilary puts it, "he removed the weight of our anxiety by saying that no one knows that day."[29] Aloys Grillmeier refers to the notion at work here as *ignorantia de jure* (as opposed to de facto): "the special nature of such spiritual activity leaves Christ's native human ignorance open to being cancelled from within by his divine knowledge. All that remains is the 'right' to act from time to time as if he did not know."[30] Thus, Christ chooses to act like he does not know, because it is better for the disciples not to know. In other words, Christ *qua* divine—and, in some sense, Christ *qua* human—does know the day and hour, but because it is not *from* his human nature that he knows these things, he has the right to act as if he does not know for the sake of his fellow humans who need not know.[31] Hilary connects

---

27. Athanasius writes that "Since He has been made man, and it is proper to man to be ignorant ... in order that, having human ignorance in his body, He might present to the Father a humanity holy and perfect after having wholly redeemed and cleansed it" (*Second Letter to Serapion* 9 [PG 26:621-24]. ET: *Sources of Christian Theology, Christ and His Mission*, iii, 70–1). And yet, he also says that Jesus' "flesh" is "instructed" by the Word (*Contra Arianos* III.56-57 [PG 26:440–41]; ibid. III.38 [PG 26:404]; *Epist. Fest.* XIV.4 [PG 26:1421A]). "Such is the dominance, for Athanasius, of divine knowledge in Christ, that, at the end of the day, there does not seem to be any room left for real human ignorance in Christ" (Moloney, "Approaches," 43. Citing especially *Contra Arianos* III.48 [PG 26:424f]).

28. Ambrose, *Expositio Evangelii secundum Lucam* VIII.34 (CCSL 14.310).

29. Hilary of Poitiers, *Commentary on Matthew*, §26.4 (256). In his Matthew commentary, Hilary is open to some version of the idea that the Son did not know the day and hour, but he later rejects the possibility in *De Trinitate* 9.58-75 after becoming aware of the Arian uses of this passage. See also Jerome, *in Evangelium Matthei* 4, ET: *St. Jerome*, 277–8; *Tractatus in Marci Evangelium*, 496; Augustine, *Question 60* in *Ennarationes in Psalmos*, 6.1; Augustine, *De Trinitate*, 1.12.23; John Chrysostom, *The Gospel of Matthew* 77.2 (PG 58:703–4).

30. Grillmeier, *Christ in Christian Tradition*, vol. I, p. 315. As we will see, the crux of the issue is how we understand this idea of "cancelling from within."

31. Gen. 22:12 is often cited as a parallel: when God comes to know of Abraham's faithfulness, it is really that he has revealed it to Abraham. While it is highly implausible to render all three uses of οἶδα in Mk 13:32-37 as "reveal" ("For you do not *reveal* when the

this explicitly with the doctrine of accommodation, perceptively distinguishing between the gradual revelation of the plan of salvation and the full expression of God's purposes and power.³² Despite the difficulties with this third approach, it has the benefit of properly foregrounding the clear emphasis of the passage in its rhetorical and narrative context, which is an exhortation to Jesus' followers not to concern themselves with the day or hour of his return. The problem raised by this text does not stem from the importation of a foreign Christological paradigm, rather a Christological paradigm is offered to account for the intertextual problems raised by the text in light of Jesus' Messianic office and various passages regarding his role as eschatological judge (Mt. 11:27, 16:27, 25:31-32; Jn 5:22; Acts 17:31).

In response to Apollinarianism, Gregory Nazianzen (330–389) and Ambrose utilize the distinction between Christ "as human" and "as divine" in much the same way. Pointing to Christ's human knowledge as evidence of his finite soul, Gregory famously argues that "If anyone puts his trust in Him as man without a human mind [ἄνουν ἄνθρωπον], truly they are bereft of mind, and undeserving of salvation. For what is not assumed, cannot be healed [τὸ γὰρ ἀπρόσληπτον, ἀθεράπευτον]."³³ In this context, Mk 13:32 reveals to us the reality of Jesus' full humanity, in which ignorance is understood to subsist in some sense.³⁴ Likewise, Ambrose appeals to Lk. 2:52 as evidence that in his human nature, Christ had to grow in knowledge.³⁵ According to an anonymous document from the end of the sixth century, almost all of the fathers at Chalcedon affirmed ignorance in Christ,

time will come") the idea is not that it should be translated straightforwardly as "reveal," but that it has a different implication when placed in the mouth of God than it does in the mouth of humans—even when used of both in the same passage. This makes good sense in light of the fact that, as we have seen, God's knowledge is productive, rather than receptive, so that for him to "know" something is precisely for him to make it known (or to make it come into existence). For an alternative parallel, see 1 Cor. 2:2, "For I decided to know (εἰδέναι) nothing among you except Jesus Christ and him crucified."

32. Hilary, *De Trinitate* 1.30, 1.29. See also 9.62. Madigan notes that despite the promise of this approach, Hilary never actually uses it in his anti-Arian works (*Christus Nesciens*, 261).

33. Gregory of Nazianzen, *Letter to Cledonius* 101 (PG 37:181). Ambrose, *On the Mystery of the Lord's Incarnation*, Ch. 7, §68. ET: *Saint Ambrose*, 245). Gregory of Nyssa cites Heb. 4:15 and then comments, "the mind ... is not sin" (Nyssa, *Antirrheticus adversus Apolinarium*, 11; ET: *St. Gregory of Nyssa*, 127). Elsewhere he writes, "The Soul is not sin" *Contra Eunomium* 2.13 (*NPNF*² 5:127).

34. "Thus everyone must see that the Son knows as God, and knows not as man" (Gregory of Nazianzus, *Orationes* 30.15 [PG 36:124]; my translation).

35. Ambrose, *Mystery of the Lord's Incarnation* 7.72 (PL 16:837A):

> He increased in age and increased in wisdom, that is, human wisdom. So the Evangelist placed "age" first, that you might believe that it was said, according to man; for age does not belong to divinity but to the body. So, if He advanced in the age of man, He advanced in the wisdom of man, but wisdom advances according to the senses, because wisdom is from the senses. (ET: *Saint Ambrose*, 246)

though the textual evidence indicates that this was understood as ignorance "*qua human.*"[36] Given especially the influence of Cyril and Athanasius, this natural human ignorance is not understood to diminish the predominance of Jesus' divine knowledge.[37]

In these early discussions, a duality appears to emerge that calls into question the unity of Christ as a person: how can one subject experience both human ignorance and divine omniscience at the same time?[38] The distinction may help account for exegetical difficulties, but it raises a host of complicated theological issues that would grow in importance, especially in the hands of the Nestorians. However, if what I have argued is correct, these authors are almost universally contending that Jesus does not, in fact, experience both ignorance and omniscience.[39] They are simply acknowledging that Christ's humanity is a real humanity, and thus, *were it not united to the Word*, it would be ignorant. In the seventh century Maximus the Confessor (580–662) makes this explicit: "the humanity of the Lord, in so far as it was united with the Word, knew all things and displayed attributes proper to God. However, in so far as his human nature [χαθὸ δὲ φύσις ἀνθρωπεία] is considered as not united to the Word, it is said to be ignorant [ἀγνοείν]."[40] Or, as Pope St. Gregory the Great (590–604) put it, the fullness of Jesus' knowledge exists *in* his humanity, but not *from* his humanity.[41]

Without qualification, these statements bear a striking similarity to those of certain Monothelites.[42] The disciples of Severus of Antioch, for example, denied the presence of human knowledge in Christ's mind. Objecting to what they saw as the Nestorian implications of Chalcedon, they maintained that one universal divine knowledge and wisdom filled Christ's human soul.[43] However, without imposing undue precision on what remains a complex historical development,

---

36. *De sectis* X.3 (PG 86:1262–63). See Grillmeier, *Christ*, vol. 2/2, 493–502.

37. There were some exceptions to this within Antiochene theology, including Diodore of Tarsus (*c*. 330–394) and Theodore of Mopsuestia (*c*. 350–428).

38. Moloney writes: "That ignorance of a specific point ... should coexist in the same person with divine knowledge of the same point, is something which Athanasius has neither the language nor the insight to explain" ("Approaches," 42). Some of this perceived problem is mitigated by recalling the substantial account of personhood assumed by these authors, as opposed to one grounded in consciousness, as we discussed in Chapter 3.

39. By way of contrast, Calvin uses similar language but insists that Jesus does experience both ignorance and omniscience at the same time—something the patristic tradition would have almost universally considered to imply Nestorianism. Calvin, *Commentary on a Harmony of the Evangelists*, 3.36.

40. Maximus the Confessor, *Questions and Doubts*, Answer 66 (PG 90:840).

41. *Letter to Eulogius of August 600* (*Reg.* X.21) (CCSL 140A.852). Wickham, who remains unconvinced by these patristic approaches, notes that "they do not present a Christ who is a mere cipher or deprive the historical figure of his actuality. It would not be fair to say that the ancient theology only yields a sort of 'docetic' Christ" ("Ignorance of Christ," 226).

42. Monothelites maintained that Jesus had only one (divine) will.

43. See Grillmeier, *Christ*, vol. 2/2, 368.

the vital distinction appears to be between (a) divine knowledge *simpliciter* playing the only role in Christ's mental life (as the monothelites contend), resulting in a denial of Christ's human soul or mind, and (b) divine *revelation* proportioned to the human mind of Christ characterizing his *theandric* intellection.[44] Cyril speaks for the latter position when commenting on Mt. 24:36 that "he was not only the God-Logos, but became and was a human being who does not know the future according to his nature and the measure of humanity, *but often receives this from God's revelation* [ἀποκαλύψεως Θεοῦ]."[45] Here, divine omniscience itself does not crowd out human ignorance, as the monothelites contend. Rather, some form of revelatory illumination is afforded to Jesus' human mind by virtue of the hypostatic union. In this light, we can understand Maximus to be affirming that both the human and divine operations knew all things, but only by means of revelation from the divinity, not by the power of the human nature. Early medieval theologians took up the task of considering what form this revelation took.

It should be clear by now that the orthodox patristic commentary on this passage fit within a broader Christological discussion about the nature of Jesus' knowledge and questions of how to uphold his real humanity and divine personhood, as well as his apocalyptic role as Messiah and judge of all, *because these things were also taught in Scripture*. That is not to say that their exegetical solutions are necessarily compelling as they stand, or that they fully succeeded in their aims. But that does not mean that they were simply importing presuppositions into the text that explicitly contradicted it. Consider the following passages, for example: "All things came into being through him, and without him not one thing came into being" (Jn 1:3); "All things have been handed over to me by my Father" (Mt. 11:27); "The Son of Man is to come with his angels in the glory of his Father, and then he will repay everyone for what has been done" (Mt. 16:27). In light of this, and the broader theological vision of the biblical canon, what seems like a "straightforward" or "historical" interpretation of Mk 13:32 to Allison et al. requires a more complicated theological approach to the passages just listed, or vice versa. More often, when treated "historically," texts such as Jn 1:3 and Mt. 16:27 are simply ruled out. By contrast, rather than opting for a form-critical solution to difficulties within the text, these patristic authors sought a theological explanation that would hold together the incarnational claims of the New Testament with the

---

44. Michael Allen terms these "immediate" and "mediate" knowledge flowing from the hypostatic union in *The Christ's Faith*. See also Daley, "Divine Transcendence and Human Transformation," 497–506.

45. *Commentary on Matthew*, quoted in Grillmeier, *Christ*, vol. 2/2, 370 (emphasis added). John of Damascus (d. *c.* 750) writes, "[Christ's] human nature does not in essence possess the knowledge of the future, but the soul of the Lord through its union with God the Word Himself and its identity in subsistence was enriched ... with knowledge of the future as well as with the other miraculous powers" (*De Fide Orthodoxa* 3.21 [NPNF² 9]).

apparent implications of this pericope. That does not mean they are rejecting history and opting for metaphysics instead. I would like to suggest that certain philosophical developments in the thought of Thomas Aquinas might allow us to make some distinctions that both uphold this exegetical tradition and extend it in ways that do greater justice to the passage.

Patristic Exegesis Extended

While standing in doctrinal continuity with this tradition, Aquinas presents a number of significant advances both in conceptual clarity and philosophical rigor. As we have seen, Thomas affirms that Christ possessed divine knowledge. This "knowledge" is productive rather than receptive, eternal rather than successive, and unchangeable just as God's essence is immutable.[46] If one's mode of knowledge is appropriate to one's mode of being, then there is an infinite qualitative difference between divine and human modes of knowing. Therefore, the modes of knowing proper to creator and creature cannot be understood as mutually exclusive or plotted along a spectrum from knowledge of a little to knowledge of a lot. God's knowledge is not simply human knowledge writ large, expanded to include all possible facts and data. Rather, it is the extrinsic formal cause of all that is. In the Incarnation, the Word retains its divine operation and eternal governance of the universe. Because divine knowledge is identical with the divine essence, it is to this eternal mode of existence that his divine knowledge is proper.[47] This does not mean, however, that divine knowledge is irrelevant to the *theandric* activity of the Word made flesh, as we will see.

Once we move beyond questions of the equality of the eternal Son with God the Father and the integrity of the human nature Christ assumed in the Incarnation, the issue no longer has to do with the compatibility between Jesus' omniscience *qua* divine and his ignorance *qua* human. Divine omniscience and human ignorance are not two poles on a quantitative spectrum, so the difference for which we need to account is not a presence or lack of "knowledge" (whatever we mean by that term). Rather, it is between human and divine *modes of knowing*. In this way, Aquinas shifts the conversation by providing a detailed account of these two modes of knowledge and the relationship between them in the one person of Christ. Central to this account is the modus principle. Aquinas argues that created knowledge is part of human nature, and "nothing natural was wanting in Christ."[48] In the *tertia pars*, Thomas attempts to account for the specifically human

---

46. *ST* I.14.

47. "Christ is always engaged in the act of thinking [*considerationem*] according to His uncreated knowledge. But, since the two activities belong to Him by reason of two natures, this [act of thinking] does not therefore exclude that he had the additional consideration [*considerationem*] of created knowledge" (*De ver.* q. 20, a. 1 *ad* 6).

48. Ibid. See *ST* III.5; *De ver.* 20.1 *ad* 2.

ways of knowing that must have been operative if Jesus was truly human, arguing that, had there been no other knowledge besides the divine in Christ, "the soul of Christ ... would have known nothing; and thus it would have been assumed to no purpose."[49] Therefore, as we saw in Chapter 3, he outlines three modes of human knowledge possessed by Jesus: acquired knowledge, prophetic knowledge, and the beatific vision.

Turning to Aquinas' exegesis of Mk 13:32, it is immediately clear that his affirmation of Jesus' acquired knowledge does not lead Thomas to argue that Jesus did not know the day or hour. He comments that:

> [Christ] is said, therefore, not to know the day and the hour of the Judgment, because He does not make it known, since, on being asked by the apostles (Acts 1:7), He was unwilling to reveal it ... But the Father is said to know, because He imparted this knowledge to the Son. Hence, by saying *but the Father*, we are given to understand that the Son knows, not merely in the Divine Nature, but also in the human, because, as Chrysostom argues, if it is given to Christ as man to know how to judge—which is greater—much more is it given to Him to know the less, that is, the time of Judgment.[50]

Here Thomas upholds the third element of the patristic approaches outlined above, which suggests that Jesus (*qua* human) in fact knew the day of judgment but chose not to reveal it to the disciples. However, he also provides tools for a more nuanced Christological explanation. The doctrine of accommodation should give us pause before we object too strongly to the idea that Jesus withheld knowledge from his disciples that he himself possessed. As any good teacher knows, unleashing the full unadulterated depths of one's knowledge on a group of unwitting students does not provide them with a clear path toward understanding. Nevertheless, this passage becomes tricky for the way Jesus appears to mislead his disciples by not only withholding information from them but by claiming not to know it in the first place. The focus of the passage is, of course, on eschatology rather than Christology: Jesus is saying this to dissuade his followers from fixating on the timing of the Parousia, rather than to make a point about his own ontological and psychological constitution. But he does make a claim that appears to circumscribe his knowledge in a way that is not easily squared with other biblical passages.

While Aquinas does not explicitly apply his distinction between acquired, infused, and beatific knowledge to Christ in his exegesis of this passage, various modern Thomists have done so and provided a compelling exegetical solution.[51] The vision of God is a direct, intuitive grasp of the divine essence, and all things as they are in God (rather than through species of how they are in themselves), which is itself wholly inexpressible. And yet, Aquinas maintains that the blessed

---

49. *ST* III.9.1.
50. *ST* III.10.2 *resp.* 2.
51. See discussion in Gaine, *Did the Savior See the Father?*, 156.

"can from his vision of the divine essence form in himself the likenesses of things which are seen in the divine essence."[52] In like manner, Christ's soul was able to "form likenesses of the things which it sees,"[53] thereby expressing in a limited and finite way what he sees of created reality in the divine essence. In light of this, we might say that in his human mind, in terms of articulable, explicit acquired knowledge, Jesus did not know the day or the hour, even though he saw it in his inexpressible vision of God. It would not be untruthful for him to say that he did not know it, even if, given the right processes of reflection, he could have come to know and express it in concrete terms. Anyone who has answered that they do not know the solution to a complex mathematical equation, even though they technically have the intellectual tools to solve it, will be on similar footing. This fits well with the broader theme in Mark's gospel of Jesus deflecting attention away from himself and toward the father—not, in order to make an ontological point about his own divine essence but because pointing people to God the father is central to his Messianic mission.

Aquinas' approach enables us to appreciate the patristic interpretations of this passage by providing a more nuanced philosophical framework through which to explicate their theological insights. This is not to say that each of them had precisely this solution in mind, or that they would have necessarily agreed with this Thomistic interpretation. However, it does provide one possible way in which the dominant strands of patristic exegesis might be understood and extended forward. Rather than rejecting their approach outright, it allows us to engage sympathetically with the theological and exegetical concerns operative in their commentary. Aquinas considers his interpretation to be a faithful representation of the patristic commentary tradition, and insofar as he is correct, he allows us to affirm this tradition as deeply anti-docetic and concerned with upholding the historical human life of Christ, through which his divine personhood was made manifest in history.

Conclusion

All of this suggests that the occasional caricatures of patristic Christology as dehumanizing of Jesus are rather far off the mark.[54] The same goes for those who see classical Christology simply advocating "divine knowledge" in Jesus.[55]

---

52. *ST* I.12.9 *ad* 2.

53. *De ver.* 20.3 *ad* 4.

54. In addition to Allison's comments, N. T. Wright speaks of "the Jesus who wanders around with a faraway look, listening to the music of the angels, remembering the time when he was sitting up in heaven with the other members of the Trinity" (Wright, *Challenge*, 164–5).

55. Gordon Fee claims that classical theologians "vigorously affirm the humanity of [Christ's] bodily functions, but often just as vigorously deny humanity to his thought

In the end this is what the defenders of Chalcedon argued against. Furthermore, interpretations of Mk 13:32 that emphasize Jesus' "ignorance," in some broad sense, over against a wide array of other passages that speak to his extraordinary knowledge (e.g., Mk 2:8-12; Mt. 9:4-8; 11:27; Jn 1; 8:19; 10:38; 14:6-10) are not inherently more "historical," however well they fit the metaphysical or theological presuppositions of contemporary historians.[56] Arguably, a non-theological reading of the passage would restrict itself to eschatology, which is the evident focus of Jesus' statement. But as soon as Christological implications are raised, there is no reason that the Chalcedonian reading must be ruled out, unless we are committed to Ebionitism as the only possible historical approach. For the church fathers, Jesus' humanity is not a philosophical problem, but its status as an instrument of the Word poses a theological conundrum. What are the limits of the grace that can be afforded to a human nature in its sanctifying union with God, and in what way does that grace transform the knowledge proper to humans?

Because Aquinas insists that "grace does not destroy nature but perfects it," he considers the revelatory illumination of Christ's human mind to make him more fully human, not less so. The grace of knowledge is granted to Christ's human mind by virtue of the hypostatic union in the form of infused species and beatific vision, and, as we will see in the chapters to come, this knowledge is instrumental in maintaining the unity of his personhood and the hypostatic synergy of his two wills. While "ignorance" in a broad sense is incompatible with such a picture, that does not mean that Christ did not know certain things in qualitatively distinct modes, some of which he would not have possessed with an explicit conscious awareness in his human mind.

One benefit of thinking in terms of qualitative modes of knowing rather than a quantitative spectrum between ignorance and omniscience is that it helps us see that, even if we took this passage according to what many contemporary exegetes consider to be its literal sense, it does not have the Christological implications they frequently discover therein. If Jesus simply does not know the day or hour,

---

processes" (Fee, "The New Testament and Kenosis Christology," 25n1). He maintains that many who hold to classical Christology "hold a kind of naive docetism, where Jesus appeared as a real person, but who was God in such a way that it superseded anything truly human about him except for the accidents of his humanity—basically his bodily functions: eating, talking, sleeping, and so on" (ibid.).

56. There is nothing inherently "historical" about an approach that allows these texts to undermine divine simplicity. Any reading with implications for the doctrine of God is a theological reading that enfolds the text into a larger metaphysical and doctrinal framework, as Allison himself seems to acknowledge: "[historical questions] are observer-dependent and reflect internalized metaphysical and historical assumptions … Additional factors are involved, including one's historical sagacity and/or (as with a miracle) one's philosophical disposition and/or (as with Gregory of Nyssa and the tenth plague) one's moral sense" (ibid., 39).

then there is a single instance in which Jesus' human mode of knowledge does not extend to encompass the full depths of his divine knowledge. As Origen put it, "there is nothing strange if, out of all things, it is only this he does not know, that is the day and hour of the consummation."[57] In fact, Aquinas already affirms that there are things Jesus does not know in his human mind, even in the beatific vision:

> Now it is impossible for any creature to comprehend the Divine Essence ... seeing that the infinite is not comprehended by the finite. And hence it must be said that the soul of Christ nowise comprehends the Divine Essence.[58]

Maintaining that Jesus (*qua* human) did not, in any sense, know the precise details of God's foreordained eschatological inbreaking into human history—surely a unique category of knowledge—does nothing to prove that Jesus was simply "ignorant" and, therefore, not divine, as Barth Ehrman appears to argue.[59] Neither is it proof of Trinitarian subordinationism, as Allison claims, because it pertains to the supernatural revelation afforded to Jesus' human mind by grace.[60] It tells us nothing about his "divine knowledge," which is identical with the divine essence and thus shared equally with the Father and the Spirit from all eternity. Only if one imports a Monophysite Christology into the passage—by denying Jesus a distinctly human mode of knowing and directly attributing his ignorance to his divinity[61]—does it deliver what Ehrman and Allison take it to mean. Ultimately, the Christological reasons for insisting that Jesus did know the day and hour, if only inexpressibly through his vision of God, rest not on ontology but on Jesus' Messianic office and his role as eschatological judge of all.[62] The argument is primarily intertextual, it is not simply metaphysical. Allison's suggestion that the patristic authors sought to resolve a competition between Jesus' humanity and divinity in favor of his divinity is revealing, because his advocacy for a "historical" approach to these texts veils a dogmatic agenda to resolve this perceived competition in favor of Jesus' humanity. The patristic and medieval solution is instead to insist that divinity and humanity

---

57. Origen, *Gospel of St Matthew*, §55 (637).

58. *ST* III.10.1. Cf. *ST* I.12.7.

59. "If Jesus does not know the future, the Christian claim that he is a divine being is more than a little compromised" (Ehrman, *Misquoting Jesus*, 204).

60. "[The quest of the historical Jesus] has accomplished what the exegetical arguments of the Arians, Socinians, and Unitarians, who rightly insisted that Matt. 24:36 = Mark 13:32 subordinates the Son to the Father, were unable to accomplish" (Allison, *The Historical Christ*, 83).

61. In other words, to read the text in this way, one must assume that any and all predicates applied to Christ automatically apply to his divinity, which, as we saw in our discussion of reduplication above, is only the case if he has only one nature.

62. They are not arguments from necessity, but fittingness.

do not exist in a competitive relationship, an idea which depends for its coherence on the doctrine of divine simplicity.

Patristic exegesis assumes a theistic metaphysic and strives to understand the gospels within a canonical hermeneutic. There is nothing inherently ahistorical, let alone Docetic, about this approach. By comparison, the arguments of Ehrman and Allison belie Monophysite or Ebionite dogmatic assumptions. There is no reason why they should not be able to advance such readings, but neither is there reason to accept that what they are doing is "history" while the church fathers simply advanced predetermined dogma.

Chapter 6

ACQUIRED KNOWLEDGE

As we saw in Chapter 1, when historians approach Jesus as a historical figure, their task often centers on questions to do with his knowledge: who did Jesus think he was? What did he intend to accomplish with his characteristic words and actions, and what motivated him to undertake specific actions at key points in his life? It should be clear by now that the frameworks of knowledge that the historian brings to bear on these questions are by no means neutral. This fact is amplified when they consider it within their purview to adjudicate whether or not Jesus knew he was God. To elucidate how questions of Jesus' knowledge are intertwined with fundamental questions about his identity, we now turn to consider Aquinas' doctrine of Jesus' knowledge, equipped with the frameworks of metaphysics and cognitive theory necessary to grasp how the argument unfolds. In this chapter, I will outline Aquinas' novel argument that Jesus possessed "acquired" or "empiric" knowledge and the implications of this argument for historical Jesus research. I will then connect Aquinas' theological argument with his exegetical treatment of Jesus' priestly office, highlighting how narrative and history coalesce alongside ontology to fill out Aquinas' understanding of Jesus' identity.

I will argue that it is not Jesus' "divinity" in itself that causes problems for historians. Rather, it is the perfection of his human nature: the invisible mission of the Spirit to the humanity of the incarnate Son by virtue of the hypostatic union.[1] This problem arises because of the role of analogy in historical method, an issue we introduced in Chapter 1. The question we must ask is, what are human beings? What are the limits to their capacity for sanctification and union with God, and what is the role of grace in the perfection of their nature? If we cannot speak of a perennial essence of humanity, and if we cannot understand that essence in terms of its ultimate end, then our affirmation of Jesus as "fully human" becomes something other than what is intended by the Christian tradition.[2] The question this chapter raises is whether historical methods are capable of engaging with a

---

1. To put it in a Trinitarian register, their problem is not with the Son of God but with the Holy Spirit.

2. By speaking of a "perennial essence," I am not intending to take a position in relation to the evolutionary mutability of species. Rather, I am arguing that underlying the various economic states of human nature there is something that is collectively the same. For a Thomistic discussion of the former issue, see, e.g., Andrew Davison, "'He Fathers-Forth

picture of humanity perfected by grace, and whether historiography might not depend on metaphysics and theology to fill out the arguments for plausibility that drive much historical Jesus research, particularly within the "third quest."

Acquired Knowledge

Aquinas argues not only that Jesus possessed divine revelation proportioned to his human mind but that he acquired empirical knowledge through his physical senses.

> It is necessary to say that in Christ there were intelligible species received in the possible intellect by the action of the agent intellect—which means that there was acquired knowledge [*scientiam acquisitam*] in Him, which some call empiric [*experimentalem*]. And hence, although I wrote differently, it must be said that in Christ there was acquired knowledge, which is properly knowledge in a human mode, both as regards the subject receiving and as regards the active cause. For such knowledge springs from Christ's agent intellect, which is natural to human nature.[3]

Aquinas is said to be the first medieval theologian to affirm that Christ possessed acquired knowledge,[4] an issue about which he changed his mind, having denied the possibility in his early commentary on the *Sentences*.[5] Simon Gaine has pointed out that Aquinas was led to this conclusion because of his philosophical anthropology, which distinguished between the agent and possible intellect.[6] Thomas argues that the agent intellect—the power by which we abstract intelligible species from phantasms—is a constitutive element of human nature. Thus, for Jesus to be fully human he must have possessed, and made use of, an agent intellect.[7] Empiric knowledge is structured and indelibly shaped by physical

---

Whose Beauty Is Past Change,' but 'Who Knows How?': Evolution and Divine Exemplarity," 1067–102.

3. *ST* III.9.4.

4. "Comme on le sait, Thomas a été le premier des médiévaux à admettre pleinement cette science acquise chez le Christ" (Torrel, *Recherches Thomasiennes*, 202). The question is discussed by Alexander of Hales, Albert the Great, and Bonaventure, but "Mais même ces deux demiers sont encore assez loin d'une véritable science expérimentale" (ibid.). See Torrel, "Le savoir acquis du Christ selon les théologiens médiévaux," 355–408.

5. *In III Sent.*, D, xiv, a. 3; D, xviii, a. 3.

6. Gaine, "Christ's Acquired Knowledge According to Thomas Aquinas," 255–68 at 262–3.

7. Given Aquinas' Aristotelian prioritization of act over potency—"everything is on account of its operation"—he sees particularly clearly the necessity that Jesus must not only have possessed certain powers in his hypothetical "nature," but that he must have made use of them in his historical human existence (*ST* III, q. 9, a. 1 *resp.*).

processes of knowing, involving the five external senses embodied in physical organs and the four internal senses—common sense, memory, cogitation, and imagination—embodied in the brain. Affirming that Christ possessed acquired knowledge involves emphasizing Christ's physicality and animality, the processes of maturation and learning appropriate to all humans, and the communal, social, and linguistic webs of dependency and meaning that constitute the frameworks of human knowing.

This affirmation provides Christological reasons to pursue the historical study of Jesus and has positive methodological implications for the discipline. Most notably, it validates inquiry into "worldviews" and "mindsets" for the task of historical Jesus studies. As N. T. Wright notes, worldviews are something we look *through*, not *at*, relating, as they do, to the "presuppositional, pre-cognitive stage of a culture or society."[8] On an ontological level, the culturally limited nature of human knowing is attributed to the role of phantasms in human cognition. By affirming that, to be fully human, Jesus must have possessed empiric knowledge, Aquinas provides a Christological argument for the relevance of this level of historical research in relation to Jesus. Furthermore, as Thomas Joseph White notes, from a theological perspective, the culture that conditioned Jesus of Nazareth's human knowledge was unique, resulting as it did from supernatural revelation to the patriarchs and prophets of Israel. Jesus continually appealed to this prophetic lineage, presenting his teaching as an authoritative interpretation of the revelation that preceded him.[9] "What this means," argues White,

> is that, just as we can study the books of the Bible simultaneously as fonts of divine revelation and as products of human agency in a given time and place, so also we can analyze, for lack of a better term, the "theology" of the historical Christ insofar as it is an especially inspired, theologically ultimate human interpretation of the word of God.[10]

While historians have frequently attributed significant creativity to the authors of the gospels, they have been less willing to allow the same for Jesus himself. As C. H. Dodd pointed out, while we have little to go on regarding what forgotten

---

8. Wright, *NTPG*, 122. See also, e.g., Witherington III, *The Christology of Jesus*; Caird, *New Testament Theology* (Oxford: Clarendon, 1995), ch. 9. However, Wright's method for dealing with the conflicts that arise between competing worldviews leaves much to be desired. See, e.g., critical assessments in Heringer, *Worlds Colliding*, 100–3; Johnson, "A Historiographical Response to Wright's Jesus," 207–24.

9. Inspired interpretation of earlier prophecy played a major role in the OT prophetic tradition. See Blenkinsopp, *A History of Prophecy in Israel*.

10. White, "Infused Science," 623. White cites Ben Witherington III, George B. Caird, and Wright as advocates of this approach. Similarly, Anthony Giambrone argues that "we concretely encounter the mind of Christ in and through Israel's Scriptures" ("Scripture as *Scientia Christi*," 274–90 at 275).

masterminds may have stood behind the first decades of the church, "the New Testament itself avers that it was Jesus Christ himself who first directed the minds of His followers to certain parts of the scriptures as those in which they might find illumination upon the meaning of His mission and destiny."[11] If some approaches to Christology have encouraged us to distance Jesus from his Jewish setting in order to universalize his teaching, Aquinas returns us firmly to the Old Testament as the context for understanding Christ. Attending to Jesus' interpretation of this tradition is the way we come to understand what he had to say, because it is this tradition that structured both his thinking and his teaching.[12]

This emphasis also provides a fruitful avenue for unpacking the dogmatic significance of Jesus' Jewishness.[13] As Pope John Paul II stated:

> Those who regard the fact that Jesus was a Jew and that his milieu was the Jewish world as mere cultural accidents, for which one could substitute another religious tradition from which the Lord's person could be separated without losing its identity, not only ignore the meaning of salvation history, but more radically challenge the very truth of the incarnation.[14]

Not only was the cultural-historical matrix of the Jewish people God's chosen vehicle for prophetic revelation and divine blessing to the world, it is also the distinctly human way-of-being-in-the-world that he took up in the Incarnation (Rom. 9:5). Whereas Schleiermacher viewed the historical conditioning of

---

11. Dodd, *According to the Scriptures*, 110. Schweitzer says something similar in *The Quest of the Historical Jesus*, 348, and Wright expands on this argument in *JVG*, 479.

12. As we will see, Aquinas attributes infused species to Christ (i.e., prophetic knowledge), but since the possible intellect is always "turned toward the phantasms," cooperating with the imagination and cogitative power to perform intellectual acts of deliberation, judgment, and reasoning, these culturally conditioned phantasms substantively shape Jesus' knowledge. See *ST* III.11.2 *ad* 3, where Aquinas argues that, while Jesus could understand without turning to phantasms, he could also choose to turn to phantasms.

13. While this concept is contested, I am using "Jewishness" to refer to membership in the people of Israel by way of halakic relationship to Temple, Torah, and the one God. See, e.g., discussion in Langer, "Jewish Understandings of the Religious Other," 255–77; Schwartz, *Imperialism and Jewish Society, 200 BCE to 640 CE*.

14. John Paul II, "Address of His Holiness Pope John Paul to a Symposium on the Roots of Anti-Judaism." http://www.vatican.va/holy_father/john-paul-ii/speeches/1997/October/documents/hf_jpii_spe_19971013_com-teologica_en.html Liberia Editrice Vaticana, 1997 (accessed May 4, 2020). Karl Barth made a similar argument shortly after the Second World War, see *Dogmatik im Grundriß*, 88ff. J. Kameron Carter argues that the racial imagination of Western modernity has its origin in "Christianity's quest to sever itself from its Jewish roots," which included distancing Christ from his Jewish flesh (*Race: A Theological Account*, 4).

Jesus' culture as corrosive to his development of God-consciousness,[15] Aquinas recognizes the vitality and fittingness of this lineage for Christ's mission as teacher and savior.[16] Barbara Meyer maintains that this is not the case more broadly in Christian thought, arguing that "there is no traditional theological category for the Jewishness of Jesus and no developed discourse of its theological meaning," lamenting the fact that "Jewishness" has, at most, been a qualification of Jesus' human nature.[17] Sensitive to Meyer's critique, Kayko Driedger Hesslein has argued that a true union of natures in Christ requires that both natures relate in "mutual formativity" such that Jesus' Jewish humanity "must formatively influence his divine nature and the one person."[18] While her emphasis on multicultural theory leaves the ontological implications somewhat vague, it appears that Driedger Hesslein's approach needlessly undermines divine simplicity in an attempt to argue that Jesus' Jewishness "influenced his divinity."[19] Her insistence that such a conception is requisite for non-supersessionist Christology is simply a category mistake. "Jewishness" characterized the human mode of being that the eternal Word took up in the incarnation, such that the *theandric* thoughts and actions of Christ were those of a first-century Jew (therefore, the divine *person* of the Word is Jewish, *qua human*). And yet, because of the qualitative difference that remains between divinity and humanity, the divine *nature* is no more Jewish than it is male, heterosexual, tall, or hungry. The God of Abraham, Isaac, and Jacob is being itself, not *a* being to which racial or cultural predicates can be meaningfully applied.[20]

When Aquinas argues that divine revelation is given "under the species of phantasms," he means that the only way of saying something that means anything—even if it is universally true—is to say it through the stories, symbols, and praxis of a particular culture at a particular time in history.[21] Not only did

---

15. As Kayko Driedger Hesslein notes, "Schleiermacher argues that the religious context that constitutes him [Jesus] must be set aside in order for Christ to function as the sinless Ideal Human. Jesus must be freed from the 'detrimental influences' of his historical context that would lead him to resist God's activity within him" (*Dual Citizenship*, 46–7, citing Schleiermacher, *The Christian Faith*, 387).

16. E.g., *ST* III.31.2, *In Epist. ad Hebr.* passim.

17. Meyer, "The Dogmatic Significance of Christ Being Jewish", 144–56, at 144.

18. Hesslein, *Dual Citizenship*, 11–12. See my full review in *Reviews in Religion and Theology*, 86–8.

19. Ibid., 126. She goes so far as to suggest that "as the Son of God is Jewish, so is the Father" (ibid.).

20. See Barbara U. Meyer's discussion of Jesus' continuing Jewishness in *Jesus the Jew in Christian Memory*, esp. 66–97. Meyer discusses Dietrich Ritschl's arguments on this score (see Ritschl, *Memory and Hope*), and argues that "the proclamation that Jesus *is* Jewish is not a Jewish but a Christian statement of faith. It relies on Jewish memory that Jesus was Jewish and on Christian belief that Jesus Christ is alive today" (Meyer, *Jesus the Jew*, 68–9).

21. *De ver.* q. 19, a. 1 *resp.*; *ST* I.84.7 *ad* 3; *ScG* II.73.38.

Jesus teach in this way, he also thought in this way.[22] For this reason, we have real historical work to do if we are to understand his teaching, given the hermeneutical distance between his time and culture and our own. That does not, however, mean that his thought and teaching do not have universal relevance and meaning. As White notes, "rightly understood, a philosophy of the agent intellect allows us to understand that all modes of human thought have overt degrees of universality to them."[23] If the light of the agent intellect is capable of abstracting intelligible species from phantasms, and if these are the universal forms of things, which not only originated in the mind of God but act as the formal principles of the particular existence of individual substances, then rational thought is universal in its mode and signification. Biblical scholars have regularly insisted that taking into account the role of human agency in the production of Scripture does not mitigate the possibility that it constitutes divine revelation,[24] and yet historical Jesus scholars have not often allowed that the same could be true for Jesus. Situating Jesus' "theology" within the cultural matrix of Second-Temple (Hellenistic) Judaism does nothing to undermine it as a font of revelation. Theologically, there is no incompatibility between the limited horizon of a given culture and the universal scope of truth revealed in and through that culture's people and history.[25] The same goes for Christ, whose human acts of knowing are conditioned by the language, stories, symbols, and praxis of his particular culture, and who, through these cultural artifacts, comes to reveal universal truths of salvation to all of humanity. We might refer to this as the hermeneutics of the hypostatic union, and it reveals the Chalcedonian framework as a bulwark against the use of dehistoricization as a means of universalizing Jesus' teaching.

As a result of his complex Aristotelian anthropology, Aquinas offers a rich understanding of the rational animality and development of Jesus in relation to passages such as Lk. 2:52: "And Jesus increased [προέκοπτεν] in wisdom [σοφία] and in years [ἡλικίᾳ] and in divine and human favor [χάριτι]."[26] Given

---

22. See White, "Infused Science," 624; Lonergan, *De Verbo Incarnatio*. ET: *The Incarnate Word*, 593.

23. White, "Infused Science," 624.

24. See, e.g., Enns, *Inspiration and Incarnation*. Ben Witherington III critiques Enns' Christological analogy while affirming the basic point that "the situatedness of the biblical record should not pose a problem for the definition of revelation" (*The Living Word of God*, 38).

25. Pace Kant, *Religion within the Limits of Reason Alone*, bk. 3, §6.

26. See Lonergan, *Incarnate Word*, 697. Increase in ἡλικίᾳ can refer either to years or stature and, in reference to a twelve-year-old, we may assume both are in view. Here χάριτι apparently refers back to v. 47, while the entire verse parallels 1 Sam. 3:19-20, a chapter invoked repeatedly at the outset of Luke's gospel. It is, of course, the increase in σοφία that has occasioned the most Christological reflection, alongside the increase in χάριτι with God. Note v. 40 "And the child grew and became strong, filled with wisdom (σοφίᾳ). And the favor (χάριτι) of God was upon him."

his hylomorphism, Aquinas insists that "the soul, since it is part of the body of a human being, is not the whole human being and my soul is not I."[27] We not only have, but *are*, our animal bodies. As Alasdair MacIntyre notes, "Human identity is primarily, even if not only, bodily and therefore animal identity and it is by reference to that identity that the continuities of our relationships to others are partly defined."[28] While Aquinas does not reflect on the animality of Christ, his approach offers helpful principles for us to do so. MacIntyre explains that, by emphasizing the distinctly rational nature of humanity, Aristotle (and Aquinas after him) was not arguing that rationality separates humans from their animality; rather, rationality is itself an animal property. While our uniqueness from nonhuman animals is important, appreciating our commonality helps us understand what it means to be human.[29] It also helps us unpack some of what is implied by the fact that Jesus developed from infancy, for, as Aquinas argues, "The Lord has done nothing that does not suit his age."[30] As Lonergan argues, citing Lk. 2:52, "with the growth of his natural acts, his supernatural acts were able to grow, since they had something successively different to complete and perfect in a supernatural way."[31] Furthermore, what it means to be human is, in part, to be dependent on others, especially in infancy, but in some ways throughout our lives, and that, as we see in the gospels, this dependence characterized Jesus' life as well.

Two Axioms of Fittingness

Aquinas receives from the fathers an approach to Christology that is driven by soteriological concerns, and his reflections on the person of Christ follow on the belief that "God was made man, that man might be made God."[32] As such, Aquinas

---

27. *In I Epist. ad Cor.*, ch. 15, lect. 2, §924.

28. MacIntyre, *Dependent Rational Animals*, 8. See Aquinas' argument that the soul of Christ did not have omnipotence with regard to his own body (*ST* III, q. 13, a. 3). For an evocative reflection on Jesus' physical body, see Moss, "The Man with the Flow of Power," 507–19.

29. We share with nonrational animals the functions of the internal and external senses and, though our cogitative power is transformed by our grasp of universals while their estimative power acts primarily by instinct, there is a significant overlap in our functions of practical rationality.

30. *ST* III.12.3 *ad 3*.

31. Lonergan, *Incarnate Word*, 697.

32. *ST* III.1.2, quoting Augustine. See Eusebius, *Ecclesiastical History* 5.20. ET: *The Ecclesiastical History of Eusebius*; Irenaeus of Lyon, *Against Heresies* 5 (Preface), in *Ante Nicene Fathers* 1. Aquinas does not think that, by taking up the universal form of human nature, Christ deifies it, because Aquinas does not believe that Platonic forms exist. "The incarnate Son of God is the common savior of all, not by a generic or specific community, such as is attributed to the nature separated from the individuals, but by a community of cause, whereby the incarnate Son of God is the universal cause of human salvation" (*ST* III,

recognizes that we are dealing with divine revelation and cannot proceed by means of demonstration governed by necessity. Rather, our interest lies in the verification of fittingness (*conveniens*), which is a kind of conditional necessity in view of salvation history.[33] Thus, while it was within the absolute power of God to do otherwise, the Incarnation of the Son is "supremely fitting" (*convenientissimum*). In relation to the person of Christ, there are two principles in particular that govern this notion of fittingness. The first is well known and, as articulated by Gregory Nazianzen, it is central to the patristic Christological tradition: the unassumed is not healed. This principle ensured Docetism would not attain an enduring place within Christian orthodoxy. The second, the principle of the maximum, is less well known, and not widely appreciated in contemporary thought. This participatory principle states that the cause of something must be first in its genus, and when employed soteriologically it entails that salvation is accomplished by the full and perfect humanity assumed in the incarnation.[34] In light of these, Aquinas proceeds by asking whether it was fitting for Christ to have assumed this or that perfection or defect of the body and soul for the purpose of his saving mission.[35]

These soteriological axioms have ontological implications that, as I have shown, should be welcome to historians, emphasizing as they do the integral reality of

q. 4, a. 4 *ad 1*). He would not, however, concur with Harnack's critiques, for this was always understood by the Eastern Fathers to happen in and through the cross (see discussion in Hart, *In Him Was Life*, 1–114).

33. "A thing is said to be necessary for a certain end in two ways. First, when the end cannot be without it ... Second, when the end is attained better and more conveniently (*convenientius*)" (*ST* III, q. 1, a. 2 *resp.*). Narcisse, *Les Raisons de Dieu*, shows that the frequency of the vocabulary of fittingness in the *Tertia Pars* is far greater than in any other part of the *Summa*.

34. See *ST* III.56.1. For this principle, Aquinas draws on *Metaphysics* 2, 1, 993b24–25. Simon Gaine writes that

> a class of things that possess the same actuality or perfection, where the members of the class vary in how far they possess that perfection, and are thus internally ordered in terms of relative priority among themselves. The very first in the genus, which need not be first in a temporal sense but is first in terms of the actuality or perfection, Aquinas takes to possess that perfection maximally or pre-eminently or most excellently, such that all else in the genus has the perfection derivatively from the first member, and is nearer to the first insofar as it has the perfection to a greater degree. The first Aquinas calls the "measure" of all else in the genus, and it is the cause of the others in at least the sense of an exemplary cause (e.g., *DV*, q. 3, a. 8.). While the first has the perfection *per* or *propter se* or through its essence, the others have it through another or by participation. (Gaine, "The Beatific Vision and the Heavenly Mediation of Christ," 116–28, at 122, citing Emery, *A Christology of Communication*)

35. *ST* III.4–15; III.46.6. See Gaine, *Did the Saviour See*, 193.

Jesus' full humanity. However, they also have what we might call "economic" implications—consequences for the *way* that Jesus lived his human life—which stand in tension with current historiography. In Chapter 1, I noted Aquinas' axiom that "grace does not destroy nature but perfects it."[36] This notion stands at the center of one of the most significant theological debates of the twentieth century, which was instigated by Henri de Lubac's argument that the final end of the human person must be a supernatural one.[37] Without adjudicating the highly technical arguments that followed in the wake of de Lubac's book, it is worth briefly outlining the state of this question in Aquinas' writings and how it bears on our discussion.[38]

Aquinas distinguishes between the human essence and the economic modes in which it subsists. To do so, he made hypothetical use of the concept of *pura naturalia*: that is, human nature considered in terms of its own limits and powers apart from grace.[39] For Thomas, this hypothetical concept of the human essence is necessary in order for us to evaluatively compare its various economic states, without necessarily affirming that "pure nature" in itself ever actually exists.[40] He maintains that humanity was originally created in a state of grace, which he calls original justice: "This rectitude consisted in reason being subject to God, the lower powers to reason, and the body to the soul."[41] Each element of this proper ordering was due to a supernatural endowment of grace, such that humanity's intrinsic natural economic mode depended on an extrinsic gift from God. Aquinas also considers two states of nature in abstraction from grace: integral nature and corrupted nature. Integral nature also refers to the state of Adam before the fall, but does so without reference to innocence or original justice. "In the state of integrity, as regards the sufficiency of the operative power, man by his natural endowments could wish and do the good proportionate to his nature such as the good of acquired virtue; but not surpassing good, as the good of infused virtue."[42]

---

36. *ST* I.1.8.
37. Lubac, *Surnaturel*.
38. For further discussion see Feingold, *Natural Desire to See God*.
39. Jean-Pierre Torrell notes that Aquinas does not use *natura pura*, which became common after his time. See "Nature and Grace in Thomas Aquinas," 155–88, at 155.
40. White extends this point through dialogue with Aristotle, arguing that "coherent narratives of change of any kind simply to be logically coherent in themselves as forms of discourse must evaluate change in terms of stable forms of identity (essences) that undergo or are the subjects of history, and in terms of teleological grammar." He continues, "if one is committed to a narrative history of dynamic development, change in view of progress and of fulfillment in some overarching teleological mode, then one is committed to a concept of perennial nature, and indeed, we might even add, to an understanding of human nature that employs the classical four causes (formal, material, efficient, and final)" (*Incarnate Lord*, 156, 159).
41. *ST* I.95.1.
42. *ST* I-II.109.2.

This is the prelapsarian state of humanity endowed with the natural privileges bestowed at creation but considered in isolation from sanctifying grace.[43]

Corrupted nature, on the other hand, refers to the state of fallen humanity despoiled of both the gratuitous gifts of sanctifying grace and the natural gifts. Aquinas writes:

> The good of human nature is threefold. First, there are the principles of which nature is constituted, and the properties that flow from them, such as the powers of the soul, and so forth. Secondly, since man has from nature an inclination to virtue, as stated above, this inclination to virtue is a good of nature. Thirdly, the gift of original justice, conferred on the whole human nature in the person of the first man, may be called a good of nature.[44]

Through sin, the first good was retained, the second was lessened but not abolished, and the third good was entirely destroyed.[45] As Thomas puts it, "human nature is not altogether corrupted by sin, so as to be shorn of every natural good."[46] What belongs to the essence of human nature, including its substantial parts, rational ability to seek truth, and free will, are not lost because of sin.[47] But neither is humanity, through the fall, returned to some hypothetical state of pure nature. Humanity enters a state of corruption that requires the intervention of grace to realign its natural capacities and lead it to its telos, which stands beyond that of which it is naturally capable. In other words, corrupted nature stands in need of being both healed and elevated by grace. When we do the good proportionate to our nature, we do so by grace, and when we attain our ultimate good, which stands beyond the capacity of our nature, we are carried there by grace.

The coherence of this taxonomy of the various economic states of human nature depends on a concept of pure nature. As White argues:

> This means in turn that human beings can exist without grace (because it is a gift), but also that they cannot be fully themselves (naturally) without that gift, and that in its absence (in the wake of sin) they suffer devastating intrinsic effects to their nature, both personally and collectively. Underlying the states of integral, fallen, redeemed, and Christic (Christ's own) human nature, there is something that is collectively the same [that is, pure nature].[48]

---

43. Torrell, "Nature and Grace," 171.
44. *ST* I-II.85.1.
45. *ST* I-II.85.1-2.
46. *ST* I-II.109.2.
47. "Sin cannot entirely take away from man the fact that he is a rational being, for then he would no longer be capable of sin" (*ST* I-II.85.2).
48. White, *Incarnate Lord*, 167.

It is worth noting that, while it is essential to affirm that human beings *could* exist without grace, because otherwise grace would be purely intrinsic or natural to humanity, that does not mean that they do so. And even if they did, their existence in that state would still depend moment by moment on the underlying act of God who holds them in being by participation. In that sense, even a hypothetical "pure nature" does not stand on its own.[49]

This discussion bears on our question in multiple ways.[50] First, it highlights the possibility of establishing perennial aspects of human nature philosophically. Much of our discussion in Chapter 4 had to do with these elements of anthropology, and this creates an important meeting point between Christian and non-Christian approaches. Insisting on a purely theological conception of humanity reduces our discourse to assertion and counter-assertion based on our reception or rejection of biblical revelation. Aquinas recognizes the fruitlessness of such an approach and avoids closing off nature entirely within the realm of grace. Second, it emphasizes that, while this hypothetical concept of pure nature is of use in certain contexts, it is not something we encounter in history, and it requires elucidation in terms of the states in which we do encounter it. Therefore, to understand nature fully, we must query the role of grace in enabling it to function toward its end, which requires a concept of final causation. Third, it highlights the fact that affirming the humanity of Christ ontologically does not necessarily involve the idea that, in the incarnation, Christ took on the same economic state as us. In fact, one of the central claims of the Christian tradition is that Christ was without sin, and thus existed in a different state than we do (1 Jn 3:5; Heb. 4:15). Jesus' unlikeness to us plays a paradigmatic role in Christology: denying this is just as problematic as denying his likeness.[51] To suggest that by existing in a different state from us, Jesus would not be human is, as Michael Waddell puts it, to misunderstand the relationship between nature and grace "by failing to see that the limits of our natural human capacities are not the limits of human existence."[52]

Historical Jesus scholars appear to assume that affirming Jesus as fully human entails his existence in a state of pure nature, conceived in terms of our state of corrupted nature. In other words, they suppose that we already know what being *truly* human looks like, and that true human nature exists in a state of disorder, devoid of grace. By contrast, when the Christian tradition affirms Jesus' full humanity, the idea of a real essence of human nature is integral to this affirmation,

---

49. *ST* I-II.109.2.

50. White provides a related discussion in chapter two of *The Incarnate Lord*. See p. 149.

51. When Chalcedon says that Christ was "like us in all things except sin" it must be referring to the general makeup of human nature, not the individual perfections Christ possessed. See Ols, "Réflexions sur l'actualité de la Christologie de Saint Thomas," 58–71, at 64–7; Koester, *Hebrews*, 283. "For example, he was conceived of the Holy Spirit, was uniquely anointed by that Spirit, worked miracles by means of human touch and taught with an unparalleled authority" (Gaine, *Did the Savior See*, 144).

52. Waddell, "Aquinas on the Light of Glory," 105–32 at 118.

along with the belief that the intelligibility of a nature is derived from its end and that it is healed to its natural end and elevated to its supernatural end by grace. The historical Jesus scholars' denial of this position amounts to either a denial of the existence of a human "essence" as such, or a denial that God is the telos of humanity (or both).[53] The former is a result of the implication that ontology is not relevant, only the economic historical state of "being human" like us. The latter stems from their labeling the grace and perfections of Christ's humanity as "docetic." This reveals just how far their opposition to "Docetism" stands from a defense of the classical Christian perspective.[54] To put this argument succinctly: the Christian tradition affirms that Jesus assumed a "human nature," which in ontological terms is the same as ours, but that his humanity existed in a different economic state due to the grace that flowed to him from the Holy Spirit by virtue of the hypostatic union. Historical Jesus scholars, on the other hand, affirm that Jesus possessed the same economic historical human condition as us, but implicitly deny that any ontological essence of "humanity" exists, or that it could be understood in terms of its end or the grace imparted to it in varying economic states. As Frederick Beiser argues, the central thesis of historicism is

> that everything in the human world—culture, values, institutions, practices, rationalism—is made by history, so that nothing has an eternal form, permanent essence or constant identity which transcends historical change. The historicist holds, therefore, that the essence, identity or nature of everything in the human world is made by history, so that it is entirely the product of the particular historical processes that brought it into being.[55]

This implicit metaphysic results in explicit doctrinal claims advanced as if they are innocuous and obvious to any honest observer. When historians say Jesus is fully human, they mean that Jesus' human existence was entirely the product of mundane historical processes. More often than not, when the term "historical" is used as an antonym to "theological" to describe claims about the past, it does not signify whether or not something happened. Rather, it indicates whether or not

---

53. In other words, while nominalism and a view of pure nature do not necessarily entail one another, they become problematically correlated within a historicist metaphysic.

54. Kathryn Tanner writes that "what is of theological interest about it [human nature] is its lack of given definition, malleability through outside influences, unbounded character, and general openness to radical transformation" (*Christ the Key*, 1). While Aquinas' understanding of substantiality can help us mitigate some of this language, the point about human nature being inherently open to radical transformation stands.

55. Beiser, *Historicist Tradition*, 2. This position has strong affinities with Heraclitus. Aristotle argues to the contrary that there is both continuity and change, and that the principle of continuity that organizes change is "nature" (Aristotle, *Physics*, Bk II [192b5–200b5]).

the events in question are interpreted in the naturalistic metaphysical terms of historicism.

Martin Kähler raised this question regarding the economic state of Jesus' human nature, and his critique has not been resolved so much as ignored by historical Jesus scholars. "Sinlessness is not merely a negative concept," wrote Kähler, "The inner development of a sinless person is as inconceivable to us as life on the Sandwich Islands is to a Laplander."[56] Kähler expresses this in terms of form and content: the form of Jesus' life was like ours, but his sinlessness meant that the content of his life was utterly unlike ours. He contends that historical analogy is only possible if the form and content are qualitatively the same. Because that is not the case with Jesus, Kähler argued, we must base our understanding of Christ on our kerygmatic experience of him, *rather than* historical reconstruction from the gospels. The main problem with Kähler's solution, besides his insufficient articulation of the relationship between nature and grace, is that he assumed that historical reconstruction must be done in the terms of enlightenment historiography—that it must remain constrained by the metaphysical presuppositions that shaped the discipline in his day, and continue to in ours.[57] I would suggest to the contrary that, in order for historiography to illuminate the figure of Jesus, it must reckon with the theological principles that undermine its use of analogy. In other words, the elements that lend plausibility to a given historical reconstruction are not limited to source material and reconstruction of the original context but also include metaphysics and theology. If a story about the past interpreted through the lens of a particular metaphysic does the best job of making sense of the data, it cannot be ruled out as ahistorical simply because it is not framed in terms of nineteenth-century German idealism, twentieth-century existentialism, or modern Western secular atheism. None of these are inherently more "historical," let alone metaphysically neutral, compared with classical theism and Christian orthodoxy.

To conclude this discussion, it is worth noting that this recognition of the unique economic state of Jesus' human existence leads Aquinas to qualify his understanding of Jesus' acquired knowledge in two ways. First, arguing from fittingness in light of Jesus' role as teacher (*magister*), he maintains that Jesus did not learn from others.[58] Second, Aquinas contends that Christ's acquired

---

56. Kähler, *Historical Jesus*, 53.

57. As both Heringer (*Worlds Colliding*, 58–65) and Rowlands (*Historical Jesus*, 157) rightly note.

58. *ST* III.12.3. Simon Gaine argues: "I do not think we need to suppose that this means that Christ never found out anything from his parents or anyone else, only that he always obtained a scientific knowledge of what he was presented with ahead of any attempts by others to convey any knowledge to him at this scientific level" (Gaine, "Christ's Acquired Knowledge According to Thomas Aquinas," 255–68 at 264. See Lonergan, *Incarnate Word*, 703). Because some scholars have been concerned to establish the basic continuity and commensurability between Israel's Scriptures (or, more specifically, some subset of a Second-Temple Jewish worldview) and the self-professed "vocation" of Jesus, they have often argued that Jesus discovered his calling and identity in the Scriptures (see, esp. Wright,

knowledge reached perfection; that, over time, he came to know all things "such as are knowable by the light of man's active intellect."[59] Various commentators have taken issue with Aquinas' argument on this score, including Simon Gaine, who suggests that Aquinas' own concept of relative perfection (as opposed to absolute perfection) would be more appropriate to this context. In this way, one might say that Christ's knowledge was perfect relative to his situation, without having to posit that he had reasoned his way to knowing all possible things.[60] Aquinas' soteriological arguments from fittingness, based on the principle of perfection, do not undermine the insights we have outlined in this section regarding how his ontological affirmation of Christ's full humanity legitimates and encourages a historical approach. As Lonergan notes, the medieval question of habits is not the same as the modern question of the cognitional acts that constitute a life.[61] In other words, to affirm the perfection of Christ's acquired knowledge is not to suggest that it would have been discernable to his contemporaries. The point is ontological, for reasons of soteriology. These arguments highlight the different modes of reasoning typically employed between theological and historical reflection on the person of Christ. They also show how philosophical and theological arguments may be necessary to fill out our historical reconstructions and lend further plausibility to the picture of Jesus painted by our sources. To further illustrate how ontological, theological, and historical arguments coalesce for Aquinas, we now turn to the relationship between acquired knowledge and Jesus' priestly vocation.

A Priest Forever in the Order of Melchizedek

"If anything is incontrovertible from the Jesus material," writes Jürgen Becker, "it is that there is not the slightest connection between Jesus and the theological self-understanding of the Jerusalem priesthood."[62] As Crispin Fletcher-Louis comments, "this fairly states a scholarly consensus."[63] It is unsurprising given the Western ideal

---

JVG, 479, 576). The assumption is that, if Jesus' self-understanding is compatible with the Jewish tradition, then said tradition must constitute its source. Highlighting and exploring this continuity is valuable, but by conflating correlation with causation, Wright ends up making explicitly Christological arguments about the nature of Jesus' knowledge that are highly problematic and unnecessary for his project. By contrast, Giambrone argues that we should take Jesus' engagement with the scriptures as an event of *anagnorisis* (recognition), rather than *anamnesis* (remembrance) or, we might add, *heuriskō* (discovery) ("Scripture as *Scientia Christi*," 283).
    59. *ST* III.12.1 *ad* 3.
    60. Gaine, "Acquired Knowledge," 266. See also White, "The Infused Science of Christ," 617–64 at 622–3.
    61. Lonergan, *Incarnate Word*, 593.
    62. Becker, *Jesus of Nazareth*, 215.
    63. Fletcher-Louis, "Jesus as the High Priestly Messiah: Part 1," 155–75.

of separation of church and state and the predominance of Protestantism in biblical scholarship, that the role of priesthood in Jesus' messianic self-understanding has been largely ignored in historical Jesus scholarship.[64] Julius Wellhausen's contempt of priestly material in the Pentateuch stands as representative of a long-held bias in Old Testament scholarship that has only been overcome relatively recently. As for historical Jesus scholarship, Fletcher-Louis points out that while reflection on the role of the Temple in the Judaism of Jesus' day has been revitalized by E. P. Sanders, this has not resulted in a corresponding emphasis on priesthood.[65]

And yet, if we attend to the canonical theology of the Hebrew Bible and the political and eschatological views prevalent in first-century Judaism, it becomes apparent that priesthood played a central role in both the relevant understandings of Israelite government and the varieties of messianic expectation in Jesus' day. As Nicholas Perrin argues, "in many a first-century mind the ultimate significance of the promise of Davidic restoration lay not in its implications of political autonomy (as important as autonomy might be) but in its cultic entailments, for as pressing as the problem of Roman occupation might have been, even more acute was the festering defilement of the temple."[66] Unlike the king, provided as an accommodation to the demands of Israel (1 Sam. 8), the priest was ordained by God as a mediator to his chosen people in tabernacle and temple: a microcosm of the role Israel was called to play for all of creation (Exod. 19:6; Isa. 61:6). The widespread fixation on *royal* messianism fails to grasp the evidence for the varieties of first-century messianic expectation. According to Fletcher-Louis, this expectation came in three distinct forms: (1) one anointed high priest alone, (2) an anointed priest who is also a king, or (3) the joint rule of an anointed priest and anointed king.[67] It should surprise us if any serious messianic figure had nothing to say about this.[68]

In the thirteenth century, theologians were similarly silent on the priesthood of Christ, due largely to the fact that Peter Lombard did not include it as a distinction in his *Sentences*. Torrell points out that "Thomas appears to be the only one among his contemporaries to have treated this question."[69] It is clear that Aquinas' detailed commentary on Hebrews influenced his treatment of Christ's priesthood in the *Summa Theologiae* and provided him answers to a number of questions raised by the gospel portraits of Jesus' priestly vocation.[70] As Levering has shown, Aquinas

---

64. See Jenkins, *The New Anti-Catholicism*.
65. Fletcher-Louis, "Messiah: Part 1," 156–7.
66. Perrin, *Jesus the Priest*, 7.
67. Fletcher-Louis, "Messiah: Part 1," 164–6.
68. "The absence of a purely royal messianism and the ubiquity of the priestly alternative in the political theology of the later years of the Second Temple should not surprise us. *This is the picture presented by the Hebrew Bible*" (ibid., 167).
69. Torrell, "Le sacerdoce du Christ dans la *Somme de théologie*," 75–100, at 76.
70. See Berceville, "Le sacerdoce du Christ dans le *Commentaire de l'Épître aux Hébreux* de saint Thomas d'Aquin," 143–58.

locates his understanding of Jesus firmly within the context of ancient Israel.[71] The objections Aquinas considers in this section of the *Summa* compare Christ's Spiritual priesthood with that of the Hebrew Temple. Citing Heb. 5:1, Aquinas notes that "the office proper to a priest is to be a mediator between God and the people."[72] Throughout his Hebrews commentary, Aquinas comments on Christ's excellence over Old Testament mediators. He explains that "the priesthood of the old law was a figure of the priesthood of Christ," just as the law itself was a figure of the law of the Spirit, which would be circumcised on the hearts of God's people.[73] It was fitting that Christ not be born of the tribe of Levi—"of the stock of the figurative priests"—because his priesthood differs from theirs "as truth from figure."[74] Instead, his priesthood is "according to the order of Melchizedek" (Heb. 5:6) who foreshadowed the excellence of Christ's priesthood over that of the Levites, having "received tithes (*decimas*) from Abraham, in whose loins the priesthood of the Law was tithed (*decimatus*)."[75] Jesus is a priest greater than Aaron, the descendent of Levi, for he is a mediator of the law of the Spirit, which is circumcised on to the hearts of his people.

Aquinas connects this priestly office with Jesus' acquired knowledge by quoting Heb. 5:8: "Although he was a son, he learned obedience through what he suffered [Greek: ἔπαθεν; Latin: *passus*]." Thomas references a gloss that says "through what he experienced [*expertus est*]" (a gloss that accords well with the more active sense of πάσχω).[76] The author of Hebrews argues that a true high priest must be able to "deal gently with the ignorant and wayward, since he himself is subject to weakness" (5:2). In order that Christ might be such a high priest, "he assumed a human nature in which he would suffer and even have compassion" and this required "knowledge gained by experience, according to which he learned obedience."[77]

71. Levering, *Torah and Temple*.
72. *ST* III.22.1. See *In Epist. ad Hebr.* ch. 5, lect. 1. Torrell highlights Aquinas' emphasis on mediation here in his discussion. *Christ and Spirituality in St. Thomas Aquinas*, esp. 131–7.
73. *ST* III.22.1 *ad* 2.
74. Ibid.
75. *ST* III.22.6.
76. *ST* III.9.4 *s.c.* Gaine takes issue with Aquinas' exegesis here because Thomas maintained that Jesus reached the perfection of his acquired knowledge *before* his passion (*ST* III.12.2 *ad 1*; III.39.3 *ad* 3). Even noting the active gloss, Gaine restricts the reference of Aquinas' citation to the passion, noting that "it is far from clear that this fresh experience of immense suffering shows Christ acquiring *scientia* as such" ("Acquired Knowledge," 265). It may well be that Thomas' argument requires alternative exegetical grounding. However, I wonder if it is necessary to think that Aquinas would restrict the reference of the passage to the passion. Recall that he titled his entire treatment of Christ's life as those things he "did and suffered" (*acta et passa*). This suggests to me that this passage could apply to Christ's life as a whole. In other words, human life is marked from the beginning by suffering, and Christ acquired knowledge of obedience through what he experienced/suffered. Even if this is not what Thomas had in mind, it may be a preferable approach.
77. *In Epist. ad Hebr.* ch. 5, lect. 2, §259.

Through this obedience, the invisible sacrifice of Christ became efficacious for all of humanity. He is our true mediator because he learned obedience in the way that we do, through the physical working of his senses and imagination in concert with his intellect. Here we see Aquinas' philosophical commitments, which lead to certain ontological entailments in his Christology (i.e., Jesus' acquired knowledge), being affirmed by his close attention to the history of Israel and Jesus' economic fulfillment of the priest's role as mediator between God and creation. Far from setting ontological, speculative, and historical arguments off against each other, Aquinas integrates them into a thematic whole, which allows them mutually to inform one another in fruitful ways.

Conclusion

Our discussion in this chapter shifts the focus of the historical questions in some interesting ways. If the Chalcedonian tradition and historical Jesus scholars agree about Jesus' full humanity—including even his human knowledge and will—then their differences turn rather on metaphysics and anthropology. Here we have a metaphysics of pure nature at odds with a conception of nature that is always dependent on grace and is intelligible in light of its end. From the Christological perspective, for historical analogy to function properly, the economic state of human nature should be taken into account, which means that metaphysics and theology must be included in the realm of issues brought to bear on the plausibility of our historical accounts. Because of Jesus' role as the priest of the New Law, he assumed and made use of the faculties of knowing operative in acquired knowledge: the external and internal senses embodied in physical sense organs and the brain. In this way, his knowledge was shaped in fundamental ways by his historical and cultural context. This argument provides vital theological resources for supporting and encouraging historical study of Jesus, and it reveals the way in which ontology and narrative are mutually informative within a properly incarnational Christology.

Chapter 7

PROPHETIC KNOWLEDGE

Those who encounter Jesus in the Gospels most frequently identify him as a prophet.[1] We find this in the shared synoptic material, Matthew and Luke's special material (plus Acts 3:22), and John.[2] Jesus even refers to himself in such terms in all four Gospels (Mt. 13:57; Mk 6:4; Lk. 4:24; 13:33; Jn 4:44). And yet, outside of this, there is nothing in the New Testament about Jesus as a prophet.[3] If the early Christians moved away from this category in their discussions of Jesus, its centrality to the Gospel portraits is all the more striking. The prophetic picture of Jesus fits well within first-century Judaism, especially in relation to popular movements of the period[4] and makes good sense of his relationship to John the Baptist.[5] It is for this reason that so many historical Jesus scholars, especially within the third quest, agree that Jesus was considered, and considered himself to be, a prophet of some kind.[6]

---

1. For treatments of Jesus' prophetic identity and message, see, e.g., Evans, "Prophet, Sage, Healer, Messiah, and Martyr," 1217–44; Herzog II, *Prophet and Teacher*, 99–124; Dunn, *Jesus Remembered*, 655–66; Theissen and Merz, "Jesus the Prophet," 240–80; Becker, *Jesus of Nazareth*, 186–224; Hooker, *The Signs of a Prophet*; Wright, *JVG*, 147–97; Allison, *Constructing Jesus*.

2. Mt. 13:57/Mk 6:4; Mk 8:28/Mt. 16:14/Lk. 9:19; Mk 6:14-16/Mt. 14:1-2/Lk. 9:7-9; Mk 14:65/Mt. 26:68/Lk. 22:64; Mt. 21:11; 21:46; Lk. 7:16; 7:39-50; 13:33; 24:19; Jn 1:21; 6:14; 4:19; 7:52; 9:17.

3. See *JVG*, 165.

4. This, despite some streams of rabbinic Jewish tradition held that prophecy had ceased in the time of Ezra (Boring, "Prophecy [Early Christian]," 5:495; Sommer, "Did Prophecy Cease?," 31–47). On the varieties of prophecy present in the Second-Temple period, see Webb, *John the Baptizer and Prophet*, ch. 9.

5. See Meyer, *The Aims of Jesus*, ch. 6.

6. "If there is anything that is virtually uncontested in the highly contested world of Jesus scholarship, it is the conclusion that Jesus likely spoke and acted in ways that identified him as a prophet" (Pitre, *Jesus and the Last Supper*, 53. See, Boring, "Prophecy," 497). The major alternative, common among members of the "new quest" such as Burton Mack and J. S. Kloppenborg, is to see Jesus as a Cynic sage or teacher of aphoristic wisdom.

The varieties of prophetic activity in the first century complicate this picture, and there is no universal agreement as to what *kind* of prophet Jesus was. There are prophetic types, such as those labeled clerical prophets, sapiential prophets, and popular prophets, and there are subtypes, like leadership popular prophets or solitary popular prophets, some of which lead movements of liberation while others announced impending doom.[7] There are also prophetic exemplars, each of which is evoked in the Gospel portraits of Jesus: Moses, the prophet of God's deliverance,[8] Jonah and Amos, who proclaimed God's judgment on Israel,[9] Ezekiel, who predicted God's abandonment of the temple,[10] and Jeremiah, who foresaw its destruction.[11] The synoptics present John the Baptist as the new Elijah,[12] a theme that Jesus picks up prominently in his own self-portrayal.[13] To understand the picture of Jesus painted by our historical sources, it is important to attend to these nuances without moving too quickly to fit Jesus into the mold of just one type or exemplar.[14] At the very least, we can say Jesus is likely to have been perceived as one who announced a prophetic message and inaugurated a movement of renewal, following in the footsteps of John the Baptist if also quickly overshadowing him.

All of this is not to say that historical Jesus scholars affirm that Jesus actually *was a prophet*, or that he possessed prophetic knowledge. In this chapter, I would like to consider the difference that a theological conception of prophecy might make for our historical understanding of Jesus. I will begin by outlining Aquinas' understanding of prophecy as "infused science" and then consider Jesus' eschatological predictions of an imminent Parousia as a test case for how a theological consideration of prophecy might transform perennial historical conundrums about Jesus' teaching. A discussion of the Gospel portrayals of Jesus' knowledge of the thoughts of others will illustrate further the crucial connection between Jesus' vocation, his narrative identity, and his knowledge. I will conclude with a brief discussion of Jesus' relation to *the* prophet foretold in Deuteronomy 18. As Collin Blake Bullard argues, according to the narrative presentations of the Gospels, "what Jesus knows and how he knows it are fundamental features of his identity."[15] My argument in this chapter is twofold. First, affirming Jesus' possession of supernatural prophetic knowledge does nothing to undermine the integrity of

---

7. See Robert Webb, *John the Baptizer*.

8. Deut. 18. See Jn 1:21, 6:14, 7:40.

9. Jon. 3:4. See Mt. 12:38-42/Lk. 11:29-32. Amos 5:18-20. See Lk. 19:41-44; Mk 13:24.

10. Ezek. 10:1-5, 15-22; 11:22-23. See Mt. 23:38/Lk. 13:35.

11. Jer. 6:2-5; 7:11. See Mt. 21:12-13/Mk 11:15-19/Lk. 19:45-48.

12. Mt. 3:1-12/Mk 1:2-8/Lk. 3:1-20; Mt. 17:12-12/Mk 9:13.

13. Lk. 4:25-27; 7:11-17. This also points to Jesus as the new Elisha. See Brown, "Jesus and Elisha," 85–104; Bostock, "Jesus as the New Elisha," 39–41; and Brodie, "Jesus as the New Elisha: Cracking the Code," 39–42.

14. It is also worth noting again how much of Jesus' prophetic language creatively adapts the pronouncements of earlier prophets.

15. Blake Bullard, *Jesus and the Thoughts of Many Hearts*, 15.

his humanity, unless we are also committed a priori to discounting Israel's ancient prophetic tradition as a form of Docetism. Second, while the principle of perfection leads Aquinas to affirm, on the register of speculative Christology, certain things about Christ that set him apart from all other humans (such as the perfection of his acquired knowledge or universal extension of his infused knowledge), these do nothing to undermine his real, historical human existence. While Aquinas affirms that Christ received infused species of all things, he insists that Jesus possessed this knowledge habitually (not actually) in a manner univocal with our knowledge. The modus principle, grounded in Aquinas' participatory metaphysics, holds fast, returning us again to the integrally human mode of Jesus' incarnate life. While the topic of Chapter 8 is Jesus' possession of the beatific vision, we will find that, much like his prophetic and messianic vocations, Jesus' infused and beatific knowledge are not so easily isolated from one another, and the latter will play a notable role in this chapter as well.

Infused Science

Aquinas argues that it was fitting that the soul of Christ should be wholly perfected by the reduction of each of its powers to act, and that therefore there was knowledge imprinted or infused (*indita vel infusa*) in the soul of Christ. Thomas understands infused science as a supernatural form of insight, resulting not from the natural activities of the senses and agent intellect but received directly from God in a prophetic fashion.[16] Through infused science, God teaches the prophet to participate uniquely in divine knowledge. While a human teacher can represent things to a student through signs of speech, she cannot enlighten the student inwardly, which requires an act of judgment in the agent intellect. But when God confers the gift of prophecy, he provides both the representation of things through imprinting or coordinating phantasms or intelligible species *and* the prophetic light of judgment.[17] Aquinas notes that God can present sensible forms to the senses (citing Dan. 5:25) or the imagination (Jer. 1:13),[18] or he can impress

---

16. See esp. *ST* II-II.171-74; *De ver.* q. 12; *ScG* III.154; *In Matt.* I.5. See an introduction to Aquinas on prophecy in Bonino, "Charisms, Forms, and States of Life (IIa IIae, qq. 171-189)," 341-6. Aquinas uses Aristotle's naturalistic explanation in *De divinatione* 1-2, 462b1–464b19 to contrast biblical prophecy from that found in pagan literature (*De ver.* 12.5 *ad 4*).

17. *ST* II-II.171.2. See discussion of this twofold *acceptio* and *iudicium* in Garceau, *Judicium, Vocabulaire, Sources, Doctrine de Saint Thomas d'Aquin*, 38-9. See also Gaine, "The Veracity of Prophecy and Christ's Knowledge," 44-62 at 56.

18. "When prophetic revelation is conveyed by images in the imagination, abstraction from the senses is necessary lest the things thus seen in imagination be taken for objects of external sensation" (*ST* II-II.173.3). See *De ver.* 12.9. Aquinas notes that such abstraction is not necessary in any other case of prophetic revelation.

intelligible species directly into the possible intellect (as he did for Solomon and the apostles). If images are presented without understanding, as happened to Pharaoh (Gen. 41:1-7) and Nebuchadnezzar (Dan. 4:1-2), then such men are not considered prophets. On the other hand, if the light of judgment is present without the forms or species, as was the case for Joseph (Gen. 41:25-36), one is considered a prophet. But, as Augustine says, "Especially is he a prophet who excels in both respects."[19] By infusing the intellectual light and the various types of species, God allows the prophet to participate in divine knowledge in a higher way than he can by the light of the agent intellect.

Aquinas maintains that "the gift of prophecy, as all the other charismatic graces, is ordained to the building up of faith," and to this end it provides the soul with an understanding of things beyond the scope of natural human reason.[20] This gift is a work of the Spirit that remains a transient impression, rather than an abiding form or habit.[21] Prophets do not prophecy whenever they choose, "because no prophecy ever came by human will, but men and women moved by the Holy Spirit spoke from God" (2 Pet. 1:21).[22] At given moments, prophets passively receive prophetic insights: charisms ordered to sanctifying grace and the common good of the ecclesial body that are historically and culturally conditioned, understood through or in conjunction with phantasms, and communicated by the prophet in words and actions within a particular time and place for a specific purpose.

Thomas Joseph White highlights three theological questions that surface when the question of prophecy is raised in relation to Jesus: the scope or extension of the infused science, its actual occurrence at any given moment, and its compatibility with Jesus' historically limited acquired knowledge. "We might characterize the maximalist perspectives here by the threefold claim that (1) Christ as man knew through infused science all things possible for man to know, (2) that he knew them actually at every given moment, and (3) that he knew them in a way that transcended and was unconditioned by his historically acquired knowledge."[23] Aquinas does not avow this maximalist perspective, instead providing principles for a more balanced approach.[24] He argues, following Col. 2:3, that for the perfection of the soul of Christ, which was in potency to all intelligible things,[25]

---

19. *Gen ad lit.* xii, 9, as quoted in *ST* II-II.171.2. See *De ver.* 12.7.

20. *In Epist. ad Rom.* 12.2 §978. See *De ver.* 12.2. Aquinas develops his "divine" understanding of prophecy in distinction from Maimonides' "natural" understanding (see *De ver.* 12.3; *The Guide of the Perplexed*, II, ch. 32-48; Altmann, "Maimonides and Thomas Aquinas," 1-19 at 7). Unlike "natural" prophecy, "divine" prophecy does not require any particular capacity or moral perfection on the part of the prophet, but is a matter of unmerited grace (*De ver.*, 12.4-5).

21. *ST* II-II.171.2; *De ver.*, 12.1.

22. Quoted in *De ver.*, 12.3 s.c.1.

23. White, "Infused Science," 628.

24. Aquinas accepts the first point, but not the second and third.

25. See Aristotle, *de Anima* III, 432.

the Word imprinted intelligible species of all things into Jesus' possible intellect, much the same as he did for the angels.[26] However, this knowledge "was univocal with our knowledge," which means that it was habitual, rather than actual.[27] While other prophets passively received infused species on an occasional basis by the work of the Spirit, Christ possessed infused species habitually, and could reduce them to act "by the command of the will [*ad imperium voluntatis*]" through the strength of the divinely infused light of prophecy.[28] In other words, Christ can turn freely to his extraordinary knowledge in a way the other prophets could not, but, as a habit, this knowledge lies in potency until actuated in given instances.

All of this means that Jesus is not like the "fact psychic" Claude Sylvanshine from David Foster Wallace's unfinished final novel, *The Pale King*. When Sylvanshine tastes a Hostess cupcake, he "knows where it was made; knows who ran the machine that sprayed a light coating of chocolate frosting on top; knows that person's weight, shoe size, bowling average, American Legion career batting average; he knows the dimensions of the room that person is in right now. Overwhelming."[29] This profusion of detail that traces the exponential web of causation spiraling out from each human event cannot add up to meaningful insight. "*The length and average circumference of Defense Secretary Caspar Weinberger's small intestine.*" As Sylvanshine's IRS trainer says, "information per se is really just a measure of disorder." Knowledge and wisdom have more to do with selection and arrangement than they do with simply compiling facts and details. "*How many people faced southeast to witness Guy Fawkes's hanging in 1606.*" Sylvanshine is simultaneously an illustration of a certain approach to literary realism and a cautionary parable for an internet age. "*The exact (not estimated) height of Mount Erebus.*" For Sylvanshine, this accumulation of trivia is oppressive, "ephemeral, useless, undramatic, distracting," and he experiences it as an affliction or disability. "One reason [his] gaze is always so intent and discomfiting is that he's

---

26. *ST* III.9.3. This is a gift of wisdom and prophecy that actualizes both the natural and obediential powers of the soul, and it includes whatever can be known naturally by the active intellect and all things made known by divine revelation (*ST* III.11.1). This knowledge extends to all things existing at any time, but not to all possible things, nor to the divine essence. Because he was not only wayfarer but also comprehensor (i.e., he possessed the beatific vision), Jesus' infused *scientia* included knowledge of all singulars, as it does for the angels, rather than just universals, as is typically the case for the possible intellect of humans (*ST* III.11.1 *ad* 2). However, the intelligible species received by Christ are diverse, which means that his knowledge was distinguished by different habits (*ST* III.11.6). In all this, we see the principle of perfection again at work. But note that the perfection of the possible intellect requires a habit, not an act. Because he possessed infused species habitually, Aquinas says Jesus was a prophet, but also more than a prophet (*In Ioan.* 4, lect. 6).

27. *ST* III.11.5.

28. *ST* III.11.5 *ad* 2. This is a habitual grace, a work of the Holy Spirit and a supernatural habit that raises human nature to share in God's nature. See *ST* I-II.110.2.

29. Wallace, *The Pale King*, 121. All quotations from pp. 119–21.

trying to filter out all sorts of psychically intuited and intrusive facts." "*The metric weight of all the lint in all the pockets of everyone at the observatory in Fort Davis TX on the 1974 day when a scheduled eclipse was obscured by clouds.*" Above all, the essence of his power is abundance, and abundance in itself is debilitating. "*What Cointreau tasted like to someone with a mild head cold on the esplanade of Vienna's state opera house on 2 October 1874.*"

There is nothing particularly "divine," let alone helpful or advantageous, about the full, simultaneous conscious awareness of such a cacophony of trivial data within the human mind. For this reason, Aquinas is concerned not so much with the maximal extension of Jesus' knowledge as with its integrity.[30] In other words, it matters that what Jesus does and says constitute divine revelation. As he writes,

> The mode of knowledge impressed on the soul of Christ befitted [*fuit conveniens*] the subject receiving it. For the received is in the receiver according to the mode of the receiver. Now the connatural mode of the human soul is that it should understand sometimes actually, and sometimes potentially. But the medium between a pure power and a completed act is a habit.[31]

The soul of Christ did not actively know all things at once, nor over time did he necessarily reduce to act infinite things in his intellect. Rather, his habitual infused knowledge served "the due end of [his] will ... as the matter in hand and the time require[d]."[32] A teleological understanding of knowledge allows Aquinas to situate Jesus' prophetic insight within his saving mission, emphasizing its economic

---

30. Although it largely remains in potency during his incarnate life, the full extension of Jesus' infused knowledge

> is of decisive importance eschatologically, in the resurrected and glorified state of Christ, where his infused science does *now* have a much broader extension of purpose of range. We should not say, for example, that a military scientist who is praying today to Christ in English about the moral decision of making a nuclear warhead is *unintelligible* to the risen Christ in his human mind. On the contrary, precisely because Christ in his glory is able to assist such a person with the gift of his grace, the situation of that person must be not only divinely but also humanly intelligible, and in the light of Christ's own understanding. We might conclude, then, that Aquinas's characterization of the habitual character of the infused science of Christ allows us to understand why the exercise of his prophecy should be both of a limited, even if utterly consequential, kind during his human historical life among us, on the one hand, and of a far more radiant extension in the mystery of the resurrection, on the other, as we see indeed in the New Testament itself in the risen Lord's prophecies given to the seven churches of Asia in the Book of Revelation (Rev 2:1–3:22). (White, "Infused Science," 631)

31. *ST* III.11.5.
32. *ST* III.11.5 *ad* 2.

function over its simple extension. Thus, his prophetic knowledge was related to the revelation of his identity and mission, and its actualization contained nothing extraneous to this purpose. While Aquinas affirms that intelligible species of all things were infused into the soul of Christ, he denies that Christ actively knew all things, because that is not how human knowing works.

Aquinas insists that Christ could know by his infused knowledge things that transcend the physical, such as separate substances, and therefore that he could know in this mode without turning to phantasms.[33] Nonetheless, it was fitting for Christ to turn to phantasms as we do, making use of his senses for both physical and intellectual purposes.[34] The key implication we can draw from this is that Jesus' infused knowledge was therefore conditioned by his acquired knowledge. Furthermore, Aquinas also maintains that there was collative and discursive knowledge in Christ, given the fact that "the proper operation of a rational soul consists in comparison and discursion from one thing to another."[35] While Christ did not *acquire* intelligible species in this way, because they were already divinely infused, these processes of knowing marked his *use* of the knowledge he possessed. Discursive cognition is proper to human rationality and is employed even by those who already know the relevant conclusions. Reginald Garrigou-Lagrange likens this to theologians who deduce from one revealed truth another truth that has been otherwise revealed.[36] Furthermore, his habitual knowledge would be actualized and engaged by sense impressions. Aquinas' theological treatment of Jesus' infused knowledge raises a significant question when considered in light of the historical picture of Jesus' prophetic vocation. Could his infused knowledge be in error? And if not, what does that mean for his eschatological predictions of the immanent Parousia?

The Eschatological Prophet

This, then, is the knowledge of the prophet. To consider the impact a theological understanding of prophecy might have on historical questions, let's now consider a test case. In *The Quest of the Historical Jesus*, Schweitzer outlines what he sees as the three great dichotomies in historical Jesus studies: "The first was laid down by Strauss: *either* purely historical *or* purely supernatural. The second had been worked out by the Tübingen school and Holtzmann: *either* Synoptic *or* Johannine. Now came the third: *either* eschatological *or* non-eschatological!"[37] He attributes

---

33. *ST* III.11.2.
34. *ST* III.11.2 *ad* 3. "Anyone who does not make use of phantasms is not using effable knowledge" (Lonergan, *Incarnate Word*, 713).
35. *ST* III.11.3.
36. Garrigou-Lagrange, *Christ the Savior*, 382. Aquinas cites Mt. 17:24-25 as an example of this in action.
37. *The Quest*, 237.

the third to Johannes Weiss (b. 1863), who revived Reimarus' oft-ignored emphasis on the eschatological nature of Jesus' preaching.[38] While Weiss' Jesus was a mere herald of the coming kingdom, Schweitzer's Jesus was its agent and cause who attempted to force God's eschatological hand and was crushed in the process.[39] Both take Jesus' words in Mk 9:1 as a misguided eschatological prediction: "There are some standing here who will not taste death until they see that the kingdom of God has come with power."[40] By the time Wrede and Schweitzer published their competing accounts at the start of the twentieth century, the dichotomy was set in stone: thoroughgoing skepticism vs. thoroughgoing eschatology. The former sought, through form-critical criteria and other literary methods, to extract the kernel of historical fact from the "dogmatic" husk of the Gospels, the latter found a path to treating more of the Gospel accounts as genuine history by foregrounding eschatology in their understanding of Jesus. The result was a Christological Catch-22: either we cannot trust the Gospels as historical sources or we cannot trust Jesus, who was mistaken in his immanent expectation of the final judgment.[41] As Schweitzer quips: *Tertium non datur*.[42]

In historical Jesus scholarship today, there are three basic positions on the issue of Jesus as an eschatological/apocalyptic prophet.[43] (1) There are those who affirm

---

38. Weiss, *Die Predigt Jesu vom Reiche Gottes*.

39. Schweitzer, *Quest*, 349–50.

40. It is worth noting that this is arguably not the strongest reading of Mk 9:1. The reading common among the church fathers and Aquinas takes Jesus' words as a reference to the transfiguration in Mk 9:2. As Cranfield maintains, "τὴν βασιλείαν τοῦ θεοῦ ἐληλυθυῖαν ἐν δυνάμει is a not unfair description of what the three saw on the mount of Transfiguration" (Cranfield, *Mark*, 288). Aquinas adds a second reading, "In another way, it can be said that the kingdom of God is the Church. So there is someone who *will not taste death*, like John, *till they see the Son of man coming in his kingdom*, i.e., until the Church is widespread, for he lived so long that he saw the Church widespread, and many churches built" (*In Matt*. 16.3).

41. See Mt. 10:23; 16:27-28; 24:34; 26.64; Mk 8:38–9:1; 13:30-37; 14:62; Lk. 9:26-27; 21:32; 22:69. As Hays notes, "the principle [sic] problem with saying that Jesus was wrong about his imminent expectation of the consummation of the eschaton is that the imminence of the kingdom of God was central to Jesus' message" (Hays in collaboration with Gallagher, Konstantinovsky, Ounsworth OP, and Strine, *When the Son of Man Didn't Come*, 259–60).

42. Ibid., 335. Schweitzer maintains that "the whole history of 'Christianity' down to the present day, that is to say, the real inner history of it, is based on the delay of the Parousia, the non-occurrence of the Parousia, the abandonment eschatology, the progress and completion of the 'de-eschatologising' of religion which has been connected therewith" (358). For criticism of Schweitzer's role in historical Jesus' scholarship, see esp. T. F. Glasson, "Schweitzer's Influence," 289 ff.

43. "Apocalyptic" (from the Greek ἀποκάλυψις, meaning "unveiling, revelation, disclosure") primarily denotes a literary genre—but can also refer to a worldview or movement—in which heavenly realities are revealed to a seer, providing insight into present and future worldly affairs. Eschatology refers to the study of last things (ἔσχατα). Apocalyptic literature can be eschatological or non-eschatological, and eschatology can,

the picture of Jesus as an eschatological prophet who (mistakenly) expected the immanent eschatological consummation of all things;⁴⁴ (2) there are those who reject the picture of Jesus as an eschatological prophet;⁴⁵ (3) and there are those who consider Jesus a non-eschatological apocalyptic prophet. The latter conceive of apocalyptic as a mode of describing this-worldly sociopolitical events by means of tropes of cosmic destruction, and they interpret Jesus' apocalyptic claims as references to mundane historical events, such as the destruction of the temple in AD 70.⁴⁶ This third position, associated most with N. T. Wright, has been highly influential, but has yet to convince in every detail. As Richard Hays notes, "in the Old Testament, the language of cosmic destruction can indeed be applied to the mundane overthrow of a single city or nation, as in Ezek. 32:7; Amos 8:9; Zeph. 1:15. Still, it has been argued that this very motif aims to apply language of final destruction proleptically to mundane events that prefigure that destruction."⁴⁷ While Jesus' apocalyptic statements appear to invest coming historical events with cosmic significance, they are not all so easily stripped of their eschatological horizon.⁴⁸

A collaborative project authored by the Oxford Postdoctoral Colloquium on Eschatology has suggested, in line with the first position, that Christ did prophesy his return within a generation, but that this prophecy should not be considered erroneous, despite the fact that the Parousia did not come about within the expected timeframe.⁴⁹ The authors argue that "the delay of the Parousia is entirely

but need not be, apocalyptic. See Collins, *The Apocalyptic Imagination*; Rowland, *The Open Heaven*, esp. 23–9, 47–8. This should not be confused with the contemporary movement called "Apocalyptic Theology," which traces its influence from the Reformation through Kierkegaard, Barth, Bonhoeffer, T. F. Torrance, and J. Louis Martyn. See Adams, *The Reality of God and Historical Method*, 152–71; Campbell, *The Deliverance of God*, 190–1; Martyn, *Galatians*.

44. See esp. Allison Jr., *Jesus of Nazareth*, 1–171; Allison Jr., *Constructing Jesus*, 31–220; and Ehrman, *Jesus*, 125–62, 83–219.

45. In particular, those connected with the Jesus' seminar. See, e.g., Funk, *Honest to Jesus*; Crossan, *The Historical Jesus*. This position depends heavily on the *Gospel of Thomas* and a particular "layer" of Q (known as Q1), which lacks eschatological sayings.

46. Most notably, Wright, *JVG*, 354–8; France, *The Gospel of Mark*, 541–3. This allows them to deny the need to ascribe any extraordinary knowledge to Jesus in these passages. For example, Wright notes that Jesus' prediction of his own death "did not, actually, take a great deal of 'supernatural' insight, any more than it took much more than ordinary common sense to predict that, if Israel continued to attempt rebellion against Rome, Rome would eventually do to her as a nation what she was now going to do to this strange would-be Messiah" (*JVG*, 610).

47. Hays, *Son of Man*, 9n31.

48. Dale Allison questions Wright's simple dichotomy between two understandings of apocalyptic ("Jesus & the Victory of Apocalyptic," 129).

49. Hays, *Son of Man*, 259–60.

consonant with the way ancient prophecy works and with the operations of the God that Christians worship."[50] The coming of the Lord, they maintain, depends to some degree on human response, for the triune God cooperates with his creation. They begin this argument by setting Jesus' eschatological prophecies within the broader context of "prophetic non-fulfillments, partial-fulfillments, and deferrals" in Israel's history, and highlighting the conditional nature of biblical prophecy.[51] Both partial fulfillment—such as the limited return from exile in the time of Ezra and Nehemiah—and conditional fulfillment—like the prophecies of Jonah that were averted by the repentance of the Ninevites—are central to the biblical tradition of prophecy, and explicit reflection on these two traits of prophecy can be found in both Jewish and Christian texts.[52]

The authors highlight two divergent approaches to prophecy in the OT: (1) Deut. 18:22: "If a prophet speaks in the name of the LORD but the thing does not take place or prove true, it is a word that the LORD has not spoken," and (2) Jeremiah 18:

> At one moment I may declare concerning a nation or a kingdom, that I will pluck up and break down and destroy it, but if that nation, concerning which I have spoken, turns from its evil, I will change my mind about the disaster that I intended to bring on it. And at another moment I may declare concerning a nation or a kingdom that I will build and plant it, but if it does evil in my sight, not listening to my voice, then I will change my mind about the good that I had intended to do to it. (Jer. 18:7-10)[53]

In the former paradigm, the prophet whose prediction does not come true is put to death; in the latter, the failure of a prophet's prediction to come about is a mark of his success. For Jeremiah, the purpose of prophecy is to influence behavior. C. A. Strine, lead author of Chapter 3, argues that the Jeremianic view would have been the dominant view in ancient times and remained prevalent in the Second-Temple era.[54]

Hays applies this distinction to the Gospels, showing that Jesus' prophecy was of the Jeremianic, conditional kind. For example, he suggests that the flexible timing of Jesus' prediction is implied by the prayer Jesus' bequeathed to his disciples: "thy kingdom come" (Mt. 6:10; Lk. 11:2). This reading is supported by the fact that the Lord's Prayer was frequently invoked in the early church in the explicit hope of "hastening the coming of the day of God" (2 Pet. 3:12).[55] The close connection between Jesus' eschatological proclamations and his instructions concerning behavior and mission suggests that the outcome of his prediction is dependent on

---

50. Ibid., 20 [italics deleted].
51. Ibid., 20. See pp. 23–78.
52. See, e.g., Daniel 9, 4 Ezra, 2 Pet. 3:3-4, 8-10. See ibid., 23–38.
53. Ibid., 39–44.
54. Ibid., 47–50.
55. Hays, *Son of Man*, 84. See Lk. 13:6-9.

how his listeners respond: an interpretation that is corroborated by texts like Rom. 2:3-4 and Acts 3:19-21.[56] However, Jesus' prophecies differ from both Jeremiah and Jonah in that repentance and obedience are understood to hasten, rather than evade, the predicted outcome (see Jer. 18:9-10).[57] As Jesus says in Mt. 24:14, "And this good news of the kingdom will be proclaimed throughout the whole world, as a testimony to all nations; and then the end will come [καὶ τότε ἕξει τὸ τέλος]." Hays argues that the veracity of Jesus' prophecy does not depend only on whether or not the end came when predicted. "His prophecy about the timing of the end assumed that the people would respond rightly to his instructions about how to act in light of God's impending judgment."[58] That the end did not come is the result of the people's failure to respond in obedience, opting instead to reject his teaching and agitate for his execution.

Simon Gaine has written an article discussing and extending the findings of the Oxford study. In it, he asks why Jesus' mistaken assumption about how people would respond to his instructions does not affect the veracity of his proclamation.[59] Gaine notes that Hays et al. appear to conflate the veracity of a prophecy with its success, thereby obscuring two distinct issues: the truthfulness of a prophecy and its purpose. In other words, if the success of a prophecy is all that matters, then it need not be true to be effective. At the same time, a prophecy may well be true but nonetheless fail to influence behavior. In order to tease these apart, Gaine turns to Aquinas, who is "a happy source for such a discussion because, as we shall see, he makes a distinction in terms of the working of prophecy in relation to the divine mind that can be mapped neatly onto the authors' own distinction between the Mosaic and the Jeremianic."[60] In the *Summa Theologiae*, Aquinas asks whether prophecy can be false: can genuine revelation from God be untruthful or deceptive?[61] As Gaine reminds us, prophecy for Aquinas is in the first place *knowledge*, so the question is not primarily about outcome, but about how prophetic knowledge conforms to reality.[62] "If the prophet's knowledge is a similitude of the divine knowledge, given through divine teaching, then prophetic knowledge shares in its truth and is not subject to falsehood."[63] Real prophecy, by its very nature, must conform truly to reality. Therefore, to account for these passages, Aquinas notes a distinction between two ways in which future contingents are known by God.

---

56. Ibid., 87–99.
57. Hays locates this understanding in Justin Martyr, Tertullian, and Cyprian (ibid., 100–2).
58. Ibid., 83.
59. Gaine, "Veracity of Prophecy," 53.
60. Ibid.
61. *ST* II-II.171.6.
62. Gaine, "Veracity of Prophecy," 54.
63. Ibid., 57.

In his simple, eternal knowledge of all things, God knows contingents both in their undetermined causes and as determined outcomes in themselves.[64] For example, God knows of a speeding car both that its current velocity and trajectory will result in death and that in the end it spins harmlessly into a ditch, having been knocked off course by a sudden bump in the road.[65] As Gaine notes,

> Aquinas supposes that while both kinds of knowledge exist eternally in the simplicity of the infinite divine mind, an individual instance of prophecy as a finite impression made by God on the prophetic mind does not match up to the whole of God's power, and hence does not encompass both kinds knowledge at once: impressions made by agents do not always match the agent's power. Sometimes then prophets may have revealed to them God's knowledge of some contingent as it is determined in itself in its presentness. At other times, however, he may imprint on their minds a similitude of his knowledge by way of causes, and this is what we have in the cases of Isaiah, Jeremiah and Jonah.[66]

God knows by way of causes that Nineveh's sinfulness will lead to their destruction, but knows it in such a way that a different outcome is not excluded. Because the prophetic knowledge of Jonah is a knowledge of causes, rather than of outcome, his prophecies are not subject to error when they do not come about. When such prophecy manages to influence behavior, the changed outcome does not undermine divine immutability, because God's "repentance" is metaphorical: it is the unfolding of a "single, unchanging divine plan, which through divine omniscience takes account of all creaturely responses to prophetic exhortation."[67] Gaine suggests that Aquinas' distinction maps onto the division between Mosaic prophecy (knowledge of outcome) and Jeremianic prophecy (knowledge of causes).

Despite the fact that Aquinas treated Jesus' prophecy as Mosaic in character, taking the coming of the Son of Man in Mt. 10:23 as a reference to the resurrection, Gaine argues that we can use Aquinas' principles as the basis for an alternative exegetical approach.[68] If we instead take Jesus' prophetic knowledge of that which

---

64. See Goris, *Free Creatures of an Eternal God.*
65. *ST* I.14.13.

> Now God knows all contingent things not only as they are in their causes, but also as each one of them is actually in itself. And although contingent things become actual successively, nevertheless God knows contingent things not successively, as they are in their own being, as we do; but simultaneously. The reason is because His knowledge is measured by eternity, as is also His being. (Ibid.)

66. Gaine, "Veracity of Prophecy," 59.
67. Ibid., 60.
68. *In Matt.* 8.2, 16.3.

pertains to eschatological proclamations as Jeremianic in character, then affirming its veracity would require more than just the assumption of the people's repentance. As Gaine notes, "what is required is that there were indeed around the time of the prophecy 'causes' of the particular timespan of his return in question."[69] Jesus would have been prophesying that there were conditions present at that point in his ministry that, if they continued to the end of the present generation, would bring about an early Parousia. While we cannot know precisely what those causes were, they can be inferred from their subsequent absence. If people responded to Jesus' teaching with repentance and further preaching of the kingdom early in his ministry but then abandoned such obedience by the end, then the delay of the Parousia can be explained by the latter without undermining the veracity of Jesus' prophecy in the order of causes.[70] If Jesus did in fact foretell the eschatological return of the Son of Man within the lifespan of those present, the non-fulfillment of his pronouncement places him in a long tradition of Hebrew prophets who foresaw future contingents through their causes in a manner that was determined to influence the behavior of their hearers.[71] My purpose here is not to suggest that there is a tidy theological way of sidestepping each and every problem raised by historical scholarship, no matter how the relevant texts are interpreted. Rather, I am attempting to illustrate again how theological forms of reasoning transform the nature of the historical questions. If historical Jesus scholars insist on considering only those historical solutions that reject Jesus' claims to the possession of extraordinary knowledge, then there will always be a chance that they are ignoring elegant solutions for dogmatic reasons.

Aquinas argues that prophecy is not the only kind of extraordinary knowledge Jesus possessed, for he also had the perfect, inexpressible, immediate vision of God. In this light, his apocalyptic unveiling of history may have less to do with his prophetically infused species and more to do with the beatific vision. In the Gospels, there is a notable element of Jesus' knowledge that does not belong to the prophets of Israel: his knowledge of what is in people's hearts. The presence of such privileged knowledge points beyond Jesus' prophetic vocation to something more.

69. Gaine, "Veracity of Prophecy," 61.

70. This does not refer simply to the crowds who variously hail Jesus' arrival and agitate for his crucifixion. See, e.g., Eklund, "From 'Hosanna!' to 'Crucify!,'" 21–42.

71. Because of Aquinas' affirmation that Jesus possessed infused species of all things that can be known, he would affirm that Jesus *also* knew by way of determined outcome that the people would not respond appropriately in the end. But that need not keep him from prophesying by way of causes in a manner determined to influence behavior. In other words, even if he knew things both in their undetermined causes *and* in their outcomes, it would not be untruthful or misleading to speak based on the current state of undetermined causes as an encouragement to continue apace. Though, again, it is worth reiterating that this is something Aquinas would not support, since the need to explain Jesus' words with reference to the Parousia arises from a rejection of the historicity of the transfiguration.

The Knowledge of Hearts

We do well to avoid focusing on the simple extent of Jesus knowledge by directing our attention instead to its personal dimensions as depicted in the gospels. It is never the mere magnitude of Jesus' knowledge that makes an impact on those he encounters, but its specificity, and his ability to speak to the particular situation of his hearers. As Ian McFarland notes, Jesus knows others "in such a way that they become known to themselves."[72] A theological consideration of one of the most distinctive aspects of Jesus' knowledge highlights key elements of his narrative identity as presented in the Gospels that both affirm and transcend his prophetic vocation.

One of the most striking elements of the Gospels is Jesus' first-hand knowledge of the thoughts of others: "When Jesus perceived [ἐπιγνούς] their thoughts [διαλογισμός], he answered them, 'Why do you raise such questions in your hearts?'" (Lk. 5:22).[73] Among biblical scholars, those who have considered the implications of this motif for Jesus' identity have typically chosen one of three interpretive options.[74] Jesus' knowledge of human thoughts is understood as (1) extraordinary human discernment,[75] (2) prophetic discernment,[76] or (3) divine knowledge.[77] I would like to suggest that Aquinas' offers a fourth option—the beatific vision—which stands between the second and third, and better accounts for the role that knowledge of hearts plays in Scripture while also allowing that, unlike "divine knowledge" itself, this was something Jesus possessed humanly. This also allows us to draw a distinction between the kind of insight into the actions or

---

72. McFarland, *From Nothing*, 144.

73. See also Lk. 4:22-24; 5:21-22; 6:7-8; 7:39-40; 9:46-47; 10:29-36; 11:15-17,38-39; 11:53-12.3; 14.3; 16:14-15; 20:23; 24:38; Mt. 9:20-22; Jn 9:1-38.

74. See Bullard, *Thoughts*, 12–17.

75. See, e.g., Fitzmyer, *The Gospel according to Luke*, 584; Marshall, *The Gospel of Luke*, 214.

76. Johnson, *The Gospel of Luke*, 56, 95, 102, 129; Green, *The Gospel of Luke*, 242, 311.

77. For those who opt for the third category, the key question is whether this ability is considered with reference to Hebrew or Greco-Roman literature. Rudolf Bultmann famously argued that "the idea is widespread in pagan and Christian Hellenism; the ability to recognize and to read the thoughts of those whom one meets characterizes the θειος ἄνθρωπος" (Bultmann, *The Gospel of John*, 102n1. See Bultmann, *The History of the Synoptic Tradition*). By contrast, Collin Blake Bullard argues for the third option but undermines Bultmann's supposed Hellenistic parallels and establishes an alternative Jewish background (Bullard, *Thoughts of Many Hearts*, 30–63). After a survey of the Greco-Roman sources, Bullard concludes that "if Luke were attempting to make the character of Jesus more palatable to a Hellenistic audience by introducing elements of extraordinary or even supernatural knowledge which were ostensibly familiar to them, then it is remarkable that Jesus' knowledge of thoughts bears so little resemblance to depictions of extraordinary knowledge in Greco-Roman literature" (ibid., 40).

intentions of others that is occasionally granted to the prophets and apostles, and the ability to overhear thoughts that Jesus possesses.

In his book *Jesus and the Thoughts of Many Hearts*, Colin Blake Bullard begins by noting the Lukan motif of Jesus' knowledge of the inner dispositions of others (uniquely referred to as διαλογισμός) and inquires as to its narrative function in the third Gospel. Situating the narrative presentation of Jesus within the thematic framework of Simeon's oracle to Mary (Lk. 2:34-35), he highlights the fact that one of the consequences foretold of Jesus' coming is revelation of the thoughts of many hearts.[78] Bullard considers the attributes of prophetic knowledge in the LXX and Second-Temple Jewish (STJ) literature and finds that "no prophet in the OT or STJ is depicted as overhearing the interior monologue of other characters."[79] Rather than locating the relevant parallels in 1 Sam. 9:15-20 or 2 Kgs 5–6,[80] he suggests that the closest literary parallels for the Lukan motif of Jesus' knowledge of thoughts are found in Gen. 17:15-20 and 18:1-15, where God "overhears" Abraham and Sarah's internal doubts about God's promise that they will bear a son. Knowledge of the heart is uniquely attributed to God in the OT—not to the prophets[81]—and is closely connected with the theme of divine judgment.[82]

> The connotation in these contexts is that Yahweh's knowledge extends to the depths of the human heart, searching and exposing every secret and sinful part of the human person. As a corollary, God's knowledge of the heart and the thoughts of humankind often functions as an expression of God's ability to judge righteously. That is, God is able to repay justly and equitably each according to his or her works because God knows the heart of each person.[83]

---

78. Bullard, *Thoughts of Many Hearts*, 7.
79. Ibid., 62.
80. In 1 Samuel 9, rather than directly overhearing the thoughts of Saul, Samuel appears to be promising to tell Saul about what is to come based on a previous prophetic revelation from God. As for 2 Kings 6, Bullard comments that "Nothing is mentioned concerning Elisha's knowledge, and this is not, strictly speaking, knowledge of the heart, but it would seem to be the case that Elisha possesses in his spirit some power of perception which is beyond normal human ability" (Bullard, *Thoughts of Many Hearts*, 49). See discussion of Mt. 26:67, Lk. 7:39, 22:64, and Jn 4:19 in ibid., 52.
81. "We are not arguing that it is, in principle, impossible for a prophet to be endowed with the ability to know the heart. We are arguing that, in practice, it is rarely—if at all—attested" (Bullard, *Thoughts of Many Hearts*, 49). Extending Bullard's argument from a historical to a theological register, I am suggesting that it is not part of the prophetic vocation or the supernatural grace afforded to the prophets for them to know directly the hearts of others in the same way that Jesus does.
82. On the connection between divine knowledge of the heart and divine judgment, see Pss. 7:8-9; 44:20-21; 94; 1 Kgs 8:38-39; 1 Chron. 28:9-10; Jer. 17:9-10; Isa. 66:12-24; Prov. 24:12.
83. Bullard, *Thoughts of Many Hearts*, 55.

Bullard maintains that if Jesus' extraordinary knowledge was concerned with external realities in order to authenticate his credentials, then it would properly be deemed "prophetic."[84] But because it is concerned with inner thoughts and intentions for the purpose of judgment, then it must be read in line with the tradition of divine knowledge of the heart.

One of the weaknesses of Bullard's study is the way in which he seems to set prophetic and divine knowledge over against each other, as if attributing prophetic knowledge to Christ might undermine his divine identity by ruling out his possession of divine knowledge.[85] Although he notes that Jesus' identity as a prophet and as Lord are not mutually exclusive, he limits Jesus' prophetic vocation primarily to suffering and fails to connect it with Jesus' extraordinary knowledge and ministry more broadly. Nevertheless, Bullard has expertly highlighted the way in which Luke weaves his Christology into the form of his narrative. The very way the story is told reveals Luke's fundamental belief that "an encounter with the Lord would involve an exposure of the heart."[86]

In both his Commentary on 1 Corinthians and the *Summa Theologiae*, Aquinas attributes the prophets' and apostles' knowledge of the secrets of hearts (*occulta cordis*) to prophecy or infused species, citing 1 Cor. 14:24-25: "But if all prophesy, an unbeliever or outsider who enters is reproved by all and called to account by all. After the secrets of the unbeliever's heart [κρυπτὰ τῆς καρδίας] are disclosed, that person will bow down before God and worship him."[87] In his Commentary on this passage, Aquinas notes that the secrets of the heart can be disclosed in multiple ways. First, they can literally be made known by someone who has "the grace to know the secrets of the heart and the sins of men," such as Peter in Acts 5.[88]

---

84. As we have seen, other aspects of Jesus' extraordinary (prophetic) knowledge do just this.

85. It is worth noting how, when discussion strays into Christological territory, a lack of any robust Christological framework leads Bullard to speak of Jesus' "divine knowledge" as if that were something he possessed humanly. As we saw in Chapter 5, there are myriad problems with this kind of language, as it tends toward Apollinarianism. A better Christological framework would have offered him more nuanced categories for this historical discussion, enabling him to forgo, for example, the strong dichotomy between prophetic and divine knowledge.

86. Bullard, *Thoughts*, 181.

87. See *In I Epist. ad Cor.* c. 14, lect. 5, §864 and *ST* II-II.171.3 s.c.

88. *In I Epist. ad Cor.* c. 14, lect. 5, §864. The scene in Acts 5 evokes the events of Joshua 7, and neither Joshua nor Peter is said to know what is in the heart of Achan or Ananias. Rather, they discern that these men have deceived God's people. In this sense, 2 Kings 6 is a fitting parallel, while Gen. 17:15-20 is not. If Luke is the author of Acts, then it is also noteworthy that he does not refer to the διαλογισμός of Ananias and Sapphira, but to the *deeds* they contrived in their hearts: ἔθου ἐν τῇ καρδίᾳ σου τὸ πρᾶγμα τοῦτο (Acts 5:4). While Peter certainly chastises them for the state of the heart evidenced by their actions, the object of his knowledge is their actions. Furthermore, it strikes me as significant that, in his commentary on 1 Corinthians 14, Aquinas refers to Peter instead of Jesus as the relevant

Second, when a preacher touches on the things that someone carries in their heart, those things can be said to have been disclosed when that person is convicted about them. In other words, the secrets of one's heart can be "disclosed" by being made known to others, or by being made known to oneself. In a third sense, the "secrets of the heart" can refer to one's doubts, which are addressed and overcome by the teaching of the church. Aquinas seems to think that Paul has each of these possibilities in mind here.[89]

When it comes to Jesus' own knowledge of hearts, however, Aquinas consistently attributes it not to infused species but to the beatific vision. In an early work, *Disputed Questions on Truth*, Aquinas explicitly denies that Jesus' knowledge of hearts is a function of prophecy. He argues that there are certain things that natural knowledge cannot grasp, including "the divine essence, future contingents, [and] the secret thoughts of men's hearts [*cogitationes cordium*]."[90] In his human soul, Christ did not know these things through acquired knowledge, "but knew them in the Word" (i.e., the beatific vision).[91] Aquinas writes that Christ also "did not know them by the knowledge of prophecy, since prophecy is an imperfect participation of that sight by which things are seen in the Word. And, since this knowledge was perfect in Christ, the imperfection of prophecy had no place there."[92] In his discussion of angelic knowledge in that same work, Thomas gives further clues as to why this might be. He notes that the angels do not have direct knowledge of the thoughts of the heart by impressed species, because knowledge involves the will moving the mind to act. "Now, an angel cannot naturally know the motion in the will of another person," writes Thomas, "because he naturally knows by means of forms that have been given him, and these are likenesses of things existing in nature. The motion of the will, however, has no dependence on or connection with any natural cause. It is the divine cause alone that can influence the will."[93] Aquinas notes that knowing the heart is not just about intelligible species, but about the motion of the will. As a result, it cannot be known by a similitude of natural things, but only in the divine essence.

Later, in the *tertia pars*, Aquinas extends Jesus' infused knowledge to include not only "whatever can be known by force of a man's active intellect" but also "all

parallel. If he considered the phenomenon under discussion to be similar to Jesus' own knowledge of hearts, why not refer to far more obvious texts in the Gospels instead of, or at least alongside, Acts? What Aquinas has in mind here is far different than Jesus' ability to directly overhear the thoughts of others.

89. Bullard takes this passage as evidence of the fact that early Christians associated encounter with the risen Christ in worship with exposure of the heart (*Thoughts of Many Hearts*, 183–4).

90. *De ver.* 20.6.
91. Ibid. See *ST* III.10.
92. *De ver.* 20.6.
93. *De ver.* 8.13.

things made known to man by Divine revelation."[94] As a result, it now includes knowledge of the future, but Aquinas says nothing about the knowledge of hearts. Rather, Aquinas argues again that Jesus' knowledge of hearts is a function of the beatific vision, though without explicitly denying that Jesus knew it by infused species. Citing Jn 5:27, Aquinas notes that Christ has been appointed judge of all because he is the Son of Man, "and therefore the soul of Christ knows in the Word all things existing in whatever time, and the thoughts of men, of which He is the Judge."[95] In this way, he is said to know "what was in man" (Jn 2:25) not only in his divine knowledge but in his human knowledge "in the Word."[96] At various points, Aquinas comments on the fact that God alone knows the secrets of the heart and connects Jesus' knowledge of hearts in the gospels directly to his divine identity.[97] As Bullard highlights, there is a distinctly apocalyptic cast to this knowledge, which is ordered toward judgment and the unveiling of that which is hidden. Jesus' revelation of what is in the heart is a foretaste of the eschaton when the hearts of all will be laid open and judged. In this sense, Jesus' knowledge of hearts fits well with the apocalyptic nature of the beatific vision, as we will see in the following chapter.

While he does not explicitly thematize this distinction between two kinds of *cogitatio cordis*, Aquinas describes the prophetic ability to discern duplicity and deceit in others as a work of the Spirit by the gift of infused species. Aquinas would affirm Christ's possession of this knowledge, though he never mentions it explicitly.[98] At the same time, Aquinas consistently attributes Jesus' ability to directly overhear the internal monologue of others to the beatific vision. In fact, I know of no instance where he attributes Jesus' knowledge of hearts to infused species. While I have used different terms to describe these two forms of insight into the heart, Aquinas refers to both as *cogitatio cordis*. Nonetheless, he is aware that while God may grant the prophet limited insight into the hidden actions or

---

94. *ST* III.11.1. He extends infused species beyond what can be known by natural reason because the agent of infused species is not the agent intellect but the Holy Spirit (*ad* 1). He also extends them to include "things of which there are no phantasms" because Christ possessed the beatific vision (*obj.* 2). "Before His Passion, Christ was not merely a wayfarer but also a comprehensor; hence His soul could know separate substances in the same way that a separated soul could" (*ad* 2). Finally, he argues that infused species include future things, which pertain to singulars, because they are required for the perfection of the intellective soul in practical knowledge (*ad* 3).

95. *ST* III.10.2 *resp.*

96. *ST* III.10.2 *resp.*

97. "It is not for man to judge of another man's goodness or wickedness: this belongs to God alone, who searches the secrets of the heart" (*ScG* IV.77); *ST* I.57.4 (citing 1 Cor. 2:11); *In Ioan.* c. 2, lect. 3, §422 (citing Prov. 15:11); *In Ioan.* c. 13, lect. 3, §1792 (citing Jer. 17:9).

98. "By this knowledge [of infused species] Christ knew all things made known to man by Divine revelation, whether they belong to the gift of wisdom or the gift of prophecy, or any other gift of the Holy Spirit" (*ST* III.11.1).

intentions of another person, there is no figure in Scripture besides God himself who possesses the ability to overhear and judge the inner thoughts of others the way Jesus does.[99]

Bullard does not address the theological question of Jesus' human possession of this uniquely divine knowledge, but his argument is easily extended using Aquinas' Christological framework. As a prophet, Christ possessed limited insight into the intentions of others. And yet, he also possessed a direct, intuitive knowledge of the heart that is different in kind from that of the prophets. This is fittingly attributed to his immediate vision of God: his knowledge of all things "in the Word," which he possessed as the Messiah and judge of all. This is not an argument from metaphysical necessity, but from fittingness according to the pattern of God's dealings with his people and Jesus' climactic fulfilment of Israel's prophetic office. As such, it suggests that prophetic and acquired knowledge are not sufficient to account for some of the most distinctive elements of the narrative presentation of Jesus' identity and vocation in the Gospels.[100]

---

99. Thomas Joseph White and Simon Gaine both maintain that, for Aquinas, Jesus' knowledge of hearts is a function of his infused knowledge (White, *Incarnate Lord*, 336; Gaine, *Did the Saviour See*, 152). As we have seen, Aquinas came to affirm that "the secrets of hearts" (*occulta cordis*) taken broadly can be known by infused species and, in this sense, I agree with Gaine and White that Christ possessed this knowledge. And yet, Aquinas' usage suggests that he considered it most fitting to attribute Jesus' unique perception of διαλογισμός to his vision of God. Gaine suggests that "in the *Summa* he extended [infused species] to knowledge of human hearts and of the future," citing *ST* III.11.1 (*Did the Saviour See*, 152). While it is true that Aquinas extends infused knowledge to include the future (*ad 3*), he says nothing about the knowledge of hearts. His explicit rejection of the possibility from *De Veritate* is missing here, but so is any avowal of it, here or elsewhere in his writings. Even if Aquinas came to reject his metaphysical argument that the knowledge of hearts *could not* be mediated by infused or impressed species, he evidently continued to think that Jesus' unique knowledge of hearts was most fittingly attributed to the beatific vision. To my mind, Aquinas' approach warrants a distinction between two kinds of *cogitatio cordis*: one to be taken in a broad sense, which is mediated by infused species to the prophets, while the other is a unique, intuitive, direct knowledge of the heart, which is possessed by Christ through the vision of God. As Bullard has shown, this distinction is also warranted exegetically: something fundamentally different is happening in Acts 5 than in Luke 5.

100. In two sources from early Jewish-Christian literature, *Pseudo-Clementine Homilies* and *Recognitions*, knowledge of hearts is put forward as a key trait of the True Prophet. But Bullard notes that "Knowledge of thoughts is not a trait borrowed from the prophets and attributed to the True Prophet; rather, it is a trait that is attributed to Jesus most likely on the basis of the canonical Gospels and is incorporated into Jesus' exalted status as True Prophet" (Bullard, *Thoughts of Many Hearts*, 38).

"I Will Raise Up for Them a Prophet"

Discussion of Jesus' prophetic vocation cannot proceed for long without coming to the question of whether he was perceived to be, or considered himself to be, *the* prophet foretold in Deuteronomy 18. "I will raise up for them a prophet like you from among their own people; I will put my words in the mouth of the prophet, who shall speak to them everything that I command. Anyone who does not heed the words that the prophet shall speak in my name, I myself will hold accountable" (Deut. 18:18-19). The Torah ends with the declaration that this promise had yet to be fulfilled (Deut. 34:10-11), and it stood at the center of Jewish hope for a new Exodus, which pervades the OT prophetic literature.[101] Most notably, various scholars have argued that the "suffering servant" of the book of Isaiah is deliberately modeled after the figure of the new Moses.[102]

The most explicit connections between Jesus and Deuteronomy 18 come from John and Acts,[103] but the deepest resonances are to be found in the synoptics.[104] Take, for example, Jesus' feeding of the multitude (Mt. 14:13-23/Mk 6:32-45/Lk. 9:11-17/Jn 6:1-15). Having instructed the *twelve* disciples (Lk. 22:30) to organize the crowds into groups (Mk 6:40-41; Exod. 18:25-26), Jesus' miraculous provision of bread in the wilderness when "the Passover ... was near" (Jn 6:4) could not help but evoke both Moses' distribution of manna in the desert and the new exodus foretold by the prophets.[105] In John's Gospel, it does precisely that: "When the people saw the sign that he had done, they began to say, 'This is indeed the prophet who is to come into the world.' When Jesus realized that they

---

101. Hos. 2:14-15; Mic. 7:11-15; Jer. 23:5-8; Isa. 43:15-19. This section is particularly indebted to discussion in Pitre, *Jesus and the Last Supper*, ch. 2.

102. See, e.g., Clements, "Isaiah 53 and the Restoration of Israel," 47–54; Allison Jr., *The New Moses*, 68–71. This expectation is present in early Jewish literature including the Dead Sea Scrolls and Josephus.

103. Jn 1:21, 6:14, 7:40; Acts 3:22.

104. Wright suggests that "the best evidence for Jesus being seen as *the* prophet, on the lines of Deuteronomy 18, is not in the synoptic gospels ... There is no reason why this should not be historical ... but the great bulk of the relevant evidence does not point to Jesus being seen in terms of Deuteronomy 18" (*JVG*, 163). However, consider the following parallels: Lk. 11:20 and Exod. 8:19; Mt. 19:28/Lk. 22:30 and Num. 1:1-16, 11:16-30; Mt. 12:39-42/Lk. 11:29-32/Mk 8:12 and Deut. 1:35; Mt. 14:13-21/Mk 6:30-44/Lk. 9:10-17/Jn 6:1-15 and Exod. 16:1-31; Mt. 26:27-28/Mk 14:23-24/Lk. 22:20 and Exod. 24:1-11. See Pitre, *Last Supper*, 54–5; Allison, *Constructing Jesus*, 270–3; Keener, *The Historical Jesus of the Gospels*, 244–5; McKnight, *Jesus and His Death*, 197–200; O'Toole, "The Parallels between Jesus and Moses," 22–9.

105. Aquinas writes that the boy who brought the five barley loaves symbolizes Moses (*In Ioan.* 6.1, §854), while "mystically, the five loaves signify the teachings of the law; 'with the bread of life and understanding, she will feed him' (Sir 15:3). The two fishes bring in the teaching of the Psalms and the prophets" (*In Matt.* 14.2, §1243. See Lk. 24:44).

were about to come and take him by force to make him king, he withdrew again to the mountain by himself" (Jn 6:14-15).[106] Or consider Jesus' words at the last supper, "take, eat; this is my body" and "this is my blood of the [new] covenant" (Mt. 26:20-28/Mk 14:17-24/Lk. 22:14-30/Cor. 11:24-25), which evoke the bread of Presence (Exod. 25:30) and the sacrificial blood on Mount Sinai:[107] "Behold the blood of the covenant that the LORD has made with you" (Exod. 24:8).[108] All of this leads Brant Pitre to suggest that "at the Last Supper, Jesus, as a new Moses, was not only inaugurating the eschatological covenant spoken of by the prophets; he may also have been instituting the new bread and wine of his own presence."[109] In this light, Jesus considered himself *the* prophet like Moses, and his actions were intended as miraculous symbolic fulfillments of the eschatological hopes centered on Deuteronomy 18.

Aquinas traces Jesus' prophetic lineage, following Matthew's genealogy, back to Abraham, the first of the Hebrew prophets (Gen. 20:7).[110] And just as Moses was both priest (citing Gen. 15:9) and prophet, so is Christ, who brings to fulfillment the promised blessing that was to come from the seed of Abraham (Gen. 22:18; Gal. 3:16).[111] At the same time, Aquinas maintains that Deut. 18:15 refers to Christ.[112] Like Moses, Christ was the lawgiver, teaching God's precepts to his people. But his teachings consist of the New Law, which is the fulfillment of the Old Law in both its literal and figurative senses. Aquinas maintains that, while the end of the Old Law was the justification of humanity, it "could not accomplish this: but foreshadowed it by certain ceremonial actions, and promised it in words."[113] Citing Rom. 8:3-4, Aquinas writes that the New Law fulfills the Old "by justifying men through the power of Christ's passion."[114] Far from abolishing the commandments, Jesus shows what true obedience looks like in light of the supernatural end of the law. Through his teaching, which is confirmed by miracles, and ultimately in his passion, Christ reconciles humanity to God and invites them to participate in this reconciliation

---

106. Arguments against the historicity of this event often turn on the fact that the parallel is so incredibly precise. For arguments in favor of historicity, see Pitre, *Last Supper*, 78–90.

107. Aquinas discusses the similarities and differences between Moses and Jesus in his commentary on this passage (*In Matt.* 26.4, §2202).

108. See Allison, *Constructing Jesus*, 272; Keener, *Historical Jesus*, 300. These words also allude to the death of the Isaianic suffering servant (Isa. 42:1-9; 49:5-9. See Pitre, *Last Supper*, 100–4). Aquinas connects the sacraments of the New Law to Jesus' priestly vocation in *In Matt.* 26.3, §2175.

109. Pitre, *Last Supper*, 147.

110. *ST* III.31.2.

111. *ST* III.31.2.

112. *In Ioan.* 4.6 §667.

113. *ST* I-II.107.2.

114. *ST* I-II.107.2. For a nuanced discussion of Aquinas on the Law, including questions of supersessionism in relation to the possible ongoing theological significance of Jewish observance of ceremonial law, see Tapie, *Aquinas on Israel and the Church*.

by the grace of the Holy Spirit.[115] In this way, the Sermon on the Mount reveals the supernatural end of the Law and proleptically inaugurates the new Exodus. Aquinas maintains that "Christ's doctrine, which is 'the law of the Spirit of life' (Rom. 8:2), had to be 'written, not with ink, but with the Spirit of the living God; not in tables of stone, but in the fleshly tables of the heart,' as the Apostle says (2 Cor. 3:3)."[116]

Like the later prophets, Christ prophesied and performed miracles, but like Moses, the core of his prophetic office was to redeem God's chosen people. As Matthew Levering explains, "Christ is most fully a prophet when he is carrying out his saving work on the cross. Christ enlightens humankind through his passion because, by suffering out of love for us, Christ enables us to receive of his fullness of grace."[117] Unlike the Old Law, the Law of the New Moses is written on the heart: it is the grace of the Holy Spirit, the indwelling presence of God among his people. The prophet like Moses, foretold in Deuteronomy and evoked throughout the prophetic tradition, was a messianic figure who was expected to bring about the new Exodus and redeem God's people from exile. The coherence of Jesus' priestly and prophetic vocations is found in his kingship, as the Messiah, the son of David. As Aquinas writes of the crowds in John's Gospel: "they believed that Jesus was not only a prophet, [but] he was also the *Lord of the prophets*."[118]

Conclusion

A prophet is only truly a prophet if they receive the divine light of judgment from God. The exact purpose of such revelation differs widely, but it is the veracity and provenance of a prophet's teaching that matter most. By refusing the possibility that Jesus possessed this light of judgment (either explicitly or implicitly), historical Jesus scholars are not opposing "Docetism."[119] Rather, they are inadvertently removing Jesus from his Jewish setting and distancing him from a worldview that very much believes that God raises up prophets through whom he communicates to his people. This is not to claim that, just because many first-century Jews believed in prophecy, therefore prophecy exists. Rather, I am arguing that far from removing him from his historical setting, which is what many historical Jesus scholars claim is accomplished by classical Christology, the prophetic knowledge

---

115. *ST* I-II.108; III.43.1; III.42.4.
116. *ST* III.42.4 *ad* 4.
117. Levering, *Torah and Temple*, 76. Citing *ST* III.7.9; Jn 1:16. See *ST* III.7.1.
118. *In Ioan.* 6.2, §867. See *In Epist. ad Hebrews* 1.1, §19.
119. As Lonergan puts it, "when God is known mediately [e.g., by infused species], some creature is known first and God is known only by the mediation of the known creature … So then, just as it does not surpass the proportion of created intelligence to know a creature, neither does it surpass the proportion of created intelligence to know God mediately" (*Word Incarnate*, 669).

attributed to Christ is drawn directly from his historical context and the terms in which the historical sources speak of him.

Extending the range of infused species received into Christ's intellect and possessed habitually does nothing to undermine the continuity between his human prophetic office and the human prophets who came before. There are also elements of Jesus' knowledge and vocation that point beyond his prophetic calling. The true prophet is also the suffering servant, the long-awaited Messiah. The one who knows the hearts of others, who overhears their thoughts and judges their innermost intentions, is not a mere prophet. All of this is not to say, as if on an apologetic register, that these theological principles prove the historicity of the theological claims of the Christian tradition. Rather, it is to note that classical Christological discourse, at least in the hands of Aquinas, arises from and preserves the narrative presentation of Jesus present in the Gospels. It places Jesus firmly within his Jewish context and takes seriously the historical and theological claims of the Jewish scriptures, which illuminate Jesus' identity and the meaning of his teachings. One need not deny Jesus' extraordinary knowledge to protect him from Docetism and beginning with such a denial can amount to nothing other than dogmatic Ebionitism. Again, there is no reason in principle that a historian should not be able to deny Jesus' extraordinary knowledge, provided that they acknowledge and defend the dogmatic claims they are advancing and the metaphysical presuppositions that underpin them.

Chapter 8

THE BEATIFIC VISION

One of various plausible scenarios in Second-Temple Jewish expectation was that Israel's God would act through a mediator to bring about a great victory over the pagan nations in a manner that evoked the enthronement scene of Daniel 7.[1] Central to these expectations was the belief that the Messiah would represent, establish, and/or enact God's divine kingship on earth, and this prospect was frequently expressed in apocalyptic language involving heavenly thrones, beasts, clouds of flame, and the like. Furthermore, as Wright notes, "according to some texts from this period, when YHWH acted in history, the agent through whom he acted would be vindicated, exalted, and honored in a quite unprecedented manner."[2] In the Second-Temple period there is an intriguing connection between apocalyptic literature and messianic expectation, which suggests that the true king would enact God's own cosmic justice, and that a true grasp of God's justice requires a vision of reality that transcends both the mundane and the prophetic.

In the New Testament, Jesus is presented as both revealer and revealed: a twofold emphasis captured well in the ambiguous opening of Revelation: Ἀποκάλυψις Ἰησοῦ Χριστοῦ, "the Revelation of Jesus Christ."[3] At his baptism, Jesus, like other apocalyptic visionaries (Ezek. 1:1; 2 Bar. 22; Rev. 4) sees the heavens open, and he is both the recipient and content of this vision: "You are my Son, the Beloved; with you I am well pleased" (Mk 1:11). As the eschatological agent of redemption, he is subject and object of divine revelation, and his apocalyptic knowledge is essential to his messianic identity.

The parallels with Aquinas' own treatment of this theme are striking. Citing Rom. 1:3, "concerning his Son, who was descended from David according to the flesh," Aquinas maintains that Christ's kingship is founded upon his possession of the beatific vision in his human soul.[4] This is how "he that was born King of the

---

1. Daniel 7 adapts this from the vision of the divine throne in Ezekiel 1. See, e.g., *1 En.* 14:14-25.

2. *JVG*, 624. See *3 Enoch, Testament of Job,* and discussion in Hengel, *Studies in Early Christology*, 119–226.

3. As noted by Baynes, "Jesus the Revealer and the Revealed," 15. Cf. Beale, *The Book of Revelation*, 183–4.

4. *ST* III.31.2; *ST* III.58.4 *ad* 2.

Jews" shares in the Father's rule.[5] Central to this rule is his knowledge of hearts. As Simeon foretold, "this child is destined for the falling and the rising of many in Israel, and to be a sign that will be opposed so that the thoughts from many hearts [ἐκ πολλῶν καρδιῶν διαλογισμοί] will be revealed" (Lk. 2:35). Part of Jesus' rule and judiciary power as the messianic king is that he knows what is in the hearts of others (e.g., Lk. 5:22; 11:17), so that he might "[order] all things according to his justice."[6] And yet, as we have seen, "to know and judge the secrets of hearts [*occulta cordium*], of itself belongs to God alone."[7] Jesus' human possession of such knowledge comes from "the overflow of the Godhead into Christ's soul"—i.e., the beatific vision—through which "it belongs to Him also to know and to judge the secrets of hearts."[8] Here Aquinas cites Rom. 2:16: "God, through Jesus Christ, will judge the secret thoughts of all."[9] As we saw in the previous chapter, this is not prophetic knowledge, but that does not mean it is not caused by the Holy Spirit. Aquinas explains that because he is the Word incarnate, Christ as man receives the "whole Spirit," which flows from the Word and imparts to his soul the supernatural *habitus* of the light of Glory "under which" (*sub quo*)[10] he sees the essence of God directly, and thereby, the hearts of others.[11] This is divine knowledge possessed in a human manner in Christ's soul: the received is in the receiver according to the mode of the receiver. In this way, Christ, as man, holds a human royal office, but reigns therein as the divine king—and this can be traced to the invisible mission of the Spirit to his human soul *by virtue* of the divine Word to whom he is hypostatically united in person.[12]

In this chapter we will consider Aquinas' argument that Jesus possessed the direct vision of the divine essence in his human soul. This is the highest form of supernatural human knowledge that Thomas attributes to Christ, and it is essential to both his messianic office and personal identity. I will begin by outlining Aquinas' understanding of the doctrine of the beatific vision—a central element of classical Christian eschatology—and his application of it to the incarnate Christ. Essential to this argument is the role of the vision of God in securing both Christ's impeccability and the instrumental unity of his wills. I will then consider two

---

5. *ST* III.36.8.

6. Levering, *Torah and Temple*, 73. Compare with, e.g., *1 En.* 61:8, "And the Lord of Spirits placed the Elect one on the throne of glory. And he shall judge all the works of the holy above in the heaven, and in the balance shall their deeds be weighed."

7. *ST* III.59.2 *ad 3*.

8. Ibid.

9. Ibid.

10. *ST* I.12.5.

11. *ST* III.10. Cf. *ST* III.10.2.

12. The connection between Jesus' kingship and beatific vision fits well with the emphasis on interiority in the Gospels. In the Sermon on the Mount (Mt. 5–7), we discover that intention and desire, more than external observance, pertain to holiness and obedience. Thus, the one who can judge justly must be able to know what is in the heart.

objections: one that challenges Aquinas' argument from fittingness for the grace and perfection of Jesus' humanity and one that stems from the intellectual humility attributed to Christ in the New Testament. My argument in this chapter is that the affirmation of Christ's possession of the beatific vision upholds the unity of his personhood without undermining the integrity of his human nature. Because it flows from the hypostatic union, as a work of the Holy Spirit, the beatific vision preserves the historical human life of Christ without undermining his divine personhood. It also creates continuity between Jesus and the apocalyptic figures that preceded him, placing him firmly within his Jewish context.

The Vision of God

While Scripture and the Christian tradition use a variety of metaphors to speak of the eschatological relationship with God that constitutes the human telos, the one they have privileged in particular is vision.[13] As Hans Boersma notes, the language of vision does not fully or adequately describe this eschatological relationship, but it is uniquely appropriate to the task and, therefore, holds a prominent place in theological reflection on this theme.[14] This stems especially from the biblical promise that "For now we see in a mirror, dimly, but then we will see face to face. Now I know only in part; then I will know fully, even as I have been fully known" (1 Cor. 13:12).[15] The audacity of the claim that "when he is revealed, we will be like him, for we will see him as he is" (1 Jn 3:2) is heightened by the recurring biblical teaching that "no one has ever seen or can see [God]" (1 Tim. 6:16).[16] In the new Jerusalem, writes John, "they will see his face, and his name will be on their foreheads. And there will be no more night; they need no light of lamp or

---

13. Hans Boersma outlines an array of such metaphors: the sowing of seed (Mt. 13:1-9; 13:31-32), leaven hidden in flour or treasure hidden in a field (Mt. 13:33), a budding fig tree (Mk 13:28-31 and parallels), a bride and bridegroom (Rev. 21:2), and so on (*Seeing God*, 2-3).

14. Boersma, *Seeing God*, 2. Charles Taylor discusses the way that, by decentering the doctrine of the beatific vision, Reformation thinkers contributed to the occlusion of transcendence and, thereby, the secularization of Western culture. He considers their efforts at the "sanctification of ordinary life" to have aided in reducing the telos of humanity to immanent flourishing (*A Secular Age*, esp. 179, 222).

15. See Job 19:26-27; Mt. 5:8; Jn 17:24; 2 Cor. 5:7; 1 Jn 3:2; Rev. 21:23-24, 22:4-5.

16. See Exod. 33:20; Jn 1:18; 1 Jn 4:12. Aquinas, commenting on 1 Timothy 6, says:

> If this refers to being comprehended, it is absolutely true, even for the angels, because God alone comprehends himself. But if it refers to the vision by which he is reached bodily, then it is true in three ways: first, because no one sees him with his bodily eyes; second, according to the essence in the mind's eye: then no one living in the flesh, except Christ, can see him ... (Exod. 33:20); third, no one sees what God is in himself citing Matt. 11:27 and Matt. 16:17. (*In I Epist. ad Tim.* c. 6, lect. 3, §270)

sun, for the Lord God will be their light" (Rev. 22:4-5). For Aquinas, this promise is the telos of human existence.[17]

Aquinas argues that, because God is incorporeal, "he cannot be seen by the senses or the imagination, but only by the intellect."[18] As we saw in Chapter 4, the method by which we come to know the nature of a thing is to follow this chain: objects → operations → powers → nature.[19] Not only are creatures distinguished by their highest powers, it is also by means of such powers that they are brought to their final end.[20] In other words, although "the good that is proper to a thing may be received in many ways," blessedness consists in grasping the greatest good through one's highest power, which means that "the end [*finis*] of the intellectual creature [is] to understand God [*est intelligere Deum*]."[21] In a strikingly pastoral section of the *Summa Contra Gentiles*, Aquinas considers various types of goods and explains why they are incapable of constituting humanity's ultimate happiness.[22] External goods, bodily goods, goods of the sensitive soul, and even the moral and intellectual virtues are insufficient to constitute ultimate happiness because they are uncertain, relative, and ordered to other things as ends. Aquinas does not deny that many of these goods will attend the ultimate felicity of the human, but he insists that they do not constitute beatitude itself. In much the same way that we saw the forms of accidental union flowing *from* substantial union in Christ, so other goods (what Aquinas calls *redundantia*) flow *from* the ultimate good of the intellectual vision of God.[23]

---

17. ScG II.23.10, III.25.6; *In Epist. ad Rom.*, §947.
18. *ST* I.12.3.
19. *ST* I.77.3.
20.

> Now, of all the parts of man, the intellect is found to be the superior mover, for the intellect moves the appetite by presenting it with its object; then the intellectual appetite, that is the will, moves the sensory appetites, irascible and concupiscible … and finally, the sense appetite, with the advent of consent from the will, now moves the body. Therefore, the end of the intellect is the end of all human actions. (ScG III.25.10)

See *ST* I.12.1; *ScG* III.25.1.

21. *ScG* III.24.7, III.25.1, III.25.3.
22. *ScG* III.27–37. See also *ST* II-II.3.2-6.

> Nevertheless, the operations of the senses can belong to happiness, both antecedently and consequently: antecedently, in respect of imperfect happiness, such as can be had in this life … [consequently], because at the resurrection, "from the very happiness of the soul," as Augustine says "the body and the bodily senses will receive a certain overflow [*refluentia*], so as to be perfected in their operations." (*ST* I-II.3.3)

23. *ST* I-II.3.3 *ad* 3.

Despite this language of vision, Thomas argues that the divine essence cannot be grasped by means of sensible or intelligible species. This is because "the essence of God is His own very existence ... which cannot be said of any created form," and because God's essence is uncircumscribed, while every created similitude is necessarily finite and limited.[24] As we saw in Chapter 4, the intellect of God and its object, along with the intelligible species and the act of understanding are all one and the same.[25] God understands himself through himself and comprehends himself, for, in being free from all matter and potentiality, he is most fully and perfectly knowable.[26] "In this way," notes Thomas, "through one intelligible species, which is the divine essence, and through one understood intention, which is the divine Word, God can understand many things."[27] For Aquinas, this suggests an avenue for understanding how God grants the vision of his essence to humans. In order to see God as he is, God must be not only the object of knowledge but also the means of knowing: "In such a vision the divine essence must be both what is seen and that whereby it is seen."[28] By uniting himself to the intellect of the creature, the divine essence becomes the intelligible species by which the creature understands.[29] This is only possible, notes Aquinas, because God's being "is such that it [can] be participated by another thing."[30] Thus God is efficient and formal (and, of course, final) cause of this vision: the object, means, and agent of the operation by which the created intellect comes to see the divine essence.[31] This vision is accomplished through the *lumen gloriae*, a supernatural disposition added to the human intellect by grace, which illuminates it and makes the human *deiform*.[32] As the Psalmist writes, "In your light we shall see light" (Ps. 36:9).[33] This light is not a similitude of the divine essence or a supplement to its intelligibility. Rather, it is a perfection of the created intellect that raises it to a disposition above its nature so that it might grasp the divine essence, which is itself most fully and perfectly intelligible.[34] The mode of the knower is perfected by the light of glory, raised up to a "great and sublime height" and enabled to receive the very essence of God as its intelligible form.[35]

While the vision of God, the "font and principle of all being and of all truth," is sufficiently beatifying in itself, God nonetheless grants to those who see him a

---

24. *ST* I.12.2. See *ScG* III.49.6–8.
25. *ST* I.14.4.
26. *ST* I.14.3; *ScG* I.47.
27. *ScG* I.53.5.
28. *ScG* III.51.2.
29. *ScG* III.51.4. See *In 1 Epist. ad Cor.* ch. 13, lect. 4, §800.
30. *ScG* III.51.4.
31. *ScG* III.52.2.
32. *ST* I.12.5. Citing Rev. 21:23 and 1 Jn 3:2.
33. Quoted in *ST* I.12.5 *s.c.* See *In Epist. ad Hebr.* ch. 8, lect. 3, §409.
34. *ST* I.12.5 *ad 2*.
35. *ST* I.12.5.

vision of all things that exist by participation in him. Because the human intellect is adapted to possess (or "become") the forms of all things, Aquinas holds that the end of the human consists not in the delineation of the order and causes of the universe, as some philosophers contend, but in the vision of God, "for, as Gregory says: 'What is there that they do not see who see Him who sees all things?' "[36] As pilgrims (*viatores*) in this life, we see the first cause through his effects in creation; as *comprehensores* in the life to come, we shall see the effects through their cause.[37] Thus, while denying that in seeing the divine essence, the created intellect will see all that God does or can do, for to do such would be to comprehend God entirely,[38] Aquinas nonetheless affirms that "of what God does or can do any intellect can know the more, the more perfectly it sees God."[39] The secondary objects of this vision are not known successively, but simultaneously, as "when many things can be understood by the one idea, they are understood at the same time."[40] Here, Thomas quotes Augustine: "Our thoughts will not be unstable, going to and fro from one thing to another; but we shall see all we know at one glance."[41] This is an immediate, intuitive vision of all things at once through a direct apprehension of the ground of their being.[42]

The Son's Beatific Vision

Aquinas maintains that Christ possessed this vision from the first moment of his conception, and he grounds this claim first and foremost in soteriology.[43]

> Man is in potentiality to the knowledge of the blessed, which consists in the vision of God; and is ordained to it as to an end ... Now men are brought to this end of beatitude by the humanity of Christ (Heb. 2:10) ... And hence, it

---

36. *De ver.* 2.2. On textual issues regarding Thomas' quotation of Gregory, see Davison, *Participation*, 121n28.

37. *ST* I.12.8; *ScG* III.47.9. Note the important difference between the verb *comprehendere*—to comprehend—and the verbal noun *comprehensor*—possessor (of the beatific vision). See *ST* I.14.2.

38. *ST* I.12.7. "God is called incomprehensible not because anything of Him is not seen; but because He is not seen as perfectly as He is capable of being seen" (*ST* I.12.7 *ad* 2).

39. *ST* I.12.8.

40. *ST* I.12.10.

41. Augustine, *De Trinitate*, xvi. Quoted in *ST* I.12.10 *s.c.* However, we, like the angels, retain a secondary form of intellectual movement, because we remain finite (*ST* I.12.10 *ad* 2).

42. *ScG* III.60. Citing Jn 17:3, "And this is eternal life, that they may know you, the only true God, and Jesus Christ whom you have sent," Aquinas claims that by the beatific vision the created intellect becomes a partaker of eternal life. As he puts it, "acts are specified by their objects ... therefore this vision is in eternity, or, rather, is eternity itself" (*ScG* III.61.3).

43. Compare *ST* III.33.2 with *ST* I.118.

was necessary that the beatific knowledge, which consists in the vision of God, should belong to Christ preeminently since the cause ought always to be more efficacious than the effect.[44]

Contrary to those who argue that Aquinas simply follows a "principle of perfection" here, Thomas actually employs the principle of the maximum in a soteriological form.[45] His concern is salvation, not the abstract perfection of Jesus' humanity.[46] Christ cannot bestow what he does not possess, and thus, in his humanity, he only brings us to our end through his preeminent possession of that end in himself. Importantly, this vision does not constitute Jesus' divine personhood, because "this light does not unite the created intellect with God in the act of being, but only in the act of understanding."[47] However, as we will see, it plays a vital role as the medium by which the unity of his personhood is maintained in and through the duality of his natures.

The beatific vision is the ground of the impeccability of Christ: by the grace of the *lumen gloriae*, Christ does not experience the separation between intellect and will that characterizes our fallen human existence. As Maximus puts it, Christ possesses a natural will, but not a gnomic will.[48] The permanent rectitude of the human will depends on the immediate vision of God, for "the will of him who sees the essence of God, of necessity, loves whatever he loves in subordination to God ... And this is precisely what makes the will right."[49] If sin is the turning of the

---

44. *ST* III.9.2. See *Comp. Theol.* c. 216; *In Epist. ad Hebr.* ch. 2, lect. 3, §128.

45. Recall that the principle of the maximum states that the cause of a given perfection must possess it preeminently in itself such that all others can receive it by participation (*ScG*, 2.28.5). It is not that Aquinas simply thinks Jesus must be perfect in every way because he's God. Rather, Christ took up those perfections (and defects) necessary to bring us to salvation.

46. Mansini, "Understanding St. Thomas on Christ's Immediate Knowledge of God," 91–124. See *ST* III.7.1. Mansini points out that Aquinas also argues on the basis of Jesus' teaching in the gospels (*In Ioan.* ch. 7, lect. 2 §1065).

47. *ScG* III.54.9. As we saw in Chapter 4, Aquinas follows Aristotle in arguing that by possessing the forms of things, the intellect "becomes" that which it knows: "intellect in act is what it understands; the form of the object is the form of the mind in act" (*In III De anima*, §788). When the form of something is united to the intellect, the person does not become that thing according to the determined act of existence proper to it. Rather, it has "become" it in an act of understanding according to an intentional mode. Jonathan Edwards rejects the traditional understanding of the beatific vision as a direct vision of the divine essence, arguing instead that in the eschaton, the vision of God is mediated by Christ, in part because an immediate and intuitive vision of the divine essence would entail a "union of personality," a personal union with God (Edwards, "Happiness of Heaven is Progressive," 18:427. Discussed in Boersma, *Seeing God*, 369). Here Edwards confuses these two realms—the act of being and the act of understanding.

48. *Opusculum* III, 45D.

49. *ST* I-II.4.4.

will away from God, it must stem in part from a faulty perception of Him, for "the will of the man who sees God in His essence of necessity adheres to God."[50] Those who see God immediately in glory will derive impeccability from an unimpeded apprehension of him, and only such impeccability is proper to the personal identity of the divine son. Were we to affirm faith in Christ rather than vision, we could not uphold Christ's impeccability in a truly human mode.[51] Thus, we would be left undermining the integrity of his human nature or else dogmatically imputing sin to him. As McFarland notes, "thus, insofar as impeccability is intrinsic to the person of the Word (since God cannot sin), and insofar as a human being may be impeccable only by virtue of enjoying the beatific vision, it is necessary for Jesus to have had from conception an unimpeded vision of the divine will," which is for Christ, as for all humans, a gift of the Holy Spirit.[52]

Furthermore, this vision unites Christ's human and divine wills in a hypostatic synergy such that his every human action just is that of the eternal Word.[53] On this score, White argues that "if the human action of Jesus is to be the personal action of the Son of God, it must be immediately subject to the activity of the divine will which it expresses. This requires that the human intellect of Jesus possesses the vision of God."[54] If the human will of Jesus is truly an instrument of the divine Word, it too must inhabit a filial mode of being such that Jesus' human operations are expressive of his divine personhood.[55] The only way this can happen while retaining the freedom of the human will is through the medium of direct knowledge.[56]

In question eighteen of the *tertia pars*, Aquinas considers a quotation from John Damascene: "To will in this or that way belongs not to our nature but to our intellect, i.e., our personal intellect."[57] Thomas responds that:

---

50. *ST* I.82.2. Cf. *ScG* III.116.3.

51. Michael Allen attempts to account for Jesus' impeccability by means of a Spirit Christology (*The Christ's Faith*, 135–42).

52. *Word Made Flesh*, 134–5. See *ST* I.12.5; *In Ioan*. ch. 7, lect. 5, §1092.

53. Aquinas does not make this latter argument explicitly, but it is an evident conclusion to be drawn from the basic principles of his Christology. It has been articulated most recently by Thomas Joseph White, following the work of Herman Diepen, Jacques Maritain, and Jean Miguel Garrigues (White, *Incarnate Lord*, 236–76).

54. White, *Incarnate Lord*, 239. White responds decisively to the objections to Thomas' theory of Jesus' possession of the beatific vision advanced by Galot ("Le Christ terrestre et la vision," 429–50) and Weinandy ("Jesus' Filial Vision of the Father," 189–201).

55. Healy, "*Simul Viator et Comprehensor*," 341–55.

56. Again, the reason to preserve Jesus' human will is not because it is its own person—rather we are accounting for an instrumental form of causality that neither bypasses nor incapacitates the will, but moves it in a manner proper to its free, rational operation. This is unique as an instance of primary causation working through second causes because it is perfectly expressive of divine personhood in a way that other secondary causation is not.

57. *ST* III.18.1 *obj* 4. Citing *De Fide Orth*. iii, 14.

When we say "to will in a certain way," we signify a determinate mode of willing. Now a determinate mode regards the thing of which it is the mode. Hence since the will pertains to the nature, "to will in a certain way" belongs to the nature, not indeed considered absolutely, but as it is in the hypostasis. Hence the human will of Christ had a determinate mode from the fact of being in a Divine hypostasis, i.e., it was always moved in accordance with the bidding of the Divine will.[58]

In other words, what the person of the Son wills in his human nature is expressive of his personal identity because the will, which belongs to nature, exists *in the hypostasis*. Similarly, the divine will cannot be absent from the personal action of the Son of God, and this requires that Christ be humanly conscious of his divine will in all of his actions.[59] As White argues, this cannot happen only occasionally, for it is indicative of the unity of his person and must therefore be stable, perfect, and indefectible.[60] It is not the perfect ideal of human nature that is at stake here, but "the very unity of the operations of Christ in his practical actions."[61] The properly human nature of Christ's will is to be affirmed, but in the hypostatic mode proper to his identity as Son.[62]

In light of this fact, and because the movement of the will follows upon knowledge,[63] White argues persuasively that:

> It is only if Christ's human intellect is continuously and immediately aware of his own divine will (by the beatific vision, and not merely by infused knowledge and by faith), that his human will can act in immediate subordination to his divine will as the 'assumed instrument' of his divine subject. Only such knowledge will assure the operative unity (in and through two distinct natures) of Christ's personal actions, because this knowledge alone gives the mind of the man Jesus an evidential certitude of the will he shares eternally with the Father.[64]

---

58. *ST* III.18.1 *ad* 4.

59. Noting the single will of the Trinity, White maintains that "if the Son is going to adequately manifest the mystery of the Holy Trinity in his human decisions and choices, then he must be humanly aware of what the Father who sent him wills and of what he wills with the Holy Spirit, so that he can express this in his human actions and choices" (*Incarnate Lord*, 255).

60. Ibid. Otherwise, "Christ would be the Word incarnate, but he might act as if he were a subject distinct from the Word, because he would not be aware of sharing in one will with the Father" (ibid.).

61. Ibid., 256.

62. Note that Aquinas can use "mode" in two distinct ways here in relation to both nature and personhood. In his human nature, the person of the Word wills in a distinctly human mode. Similarly, his human will has a determinate mode according to his divine personhood.

63. *ST* I-II.9.1.

64. White, *Incarnate Lord*, 257.

White notes that infused species do not permit Christ an immediate human knowledge of his divine identity and will, because those who know by infused species are still united to God by faith. In that paradigm, Jesus[65] would only have access to his own transcendent personhood by continued acts of faith, believing obscurely in his divine will and hoping that he was acting according to his own divine ends.[66] As White notes, those who wish to affirm in Christ the existence of both faith and a divine identity/will must consider the question: "how are these two phenomena capable of producing *a unity of personal action* that belongs to the Son of God as its principal source?"[67] He does not consider this dilemma capable of resolution without adverting to kenotic Christology, which upholds the unity of Christ's personhood at the expense of his divine immutability. Thus, the beatific vision is necessary in order to raise Christ's human spiritual operations to attain to his divinity and bear its mark in their activities. This vision is unique compared to that possessed by the angels and the saints because of its filial nature: Christ does not see the Trinity "as a subject ontologically distinct from himself," notes White, rather, this vision "permits the Son to know *himself* 'objectively' and to understand his own filial personhood in a certain and evidential way."[68] This stands contrary to

---

65. Note how this way of speaking already forces us into Nestorian-sounding turns of phrase: "Jesus" becomes a distinct subject from his divine personhood, which he accesses through certain actions.

66. On the incompatibility of faith and vision, see *ST* I-II.67.5; *ScG* III.40. For discussions of this issue in relation to the debate surrounding the Pauline phrase *pistis Christou* (Rom. 3:22, 26; Gal. 2:16, 20; 3:22; Phil. 3:9; Eph. 3:13), see especially *The Faith of Jesus Christ* and a defense of Aquinas' position in Gaine, *Did the Saviour See the Father?*, 105–28. For his part, Aquinas often follows the third view, taking the genitive adjectivally as "Christ-faith" or "the Christian faith." See a recent defense of this view in Grasso, "A Linguistic Analysis of πίστις χριστοῦ," 108–44. Michael Allen has written, in line with the subjective reading, a theological defense of Jesus' possession of faith (Allen, *Christ's Faith*). Without discussing in detail his misinterpretations of Aquinas (on, e.g., the compatibility between infused species and faith [ST II-II.171.5], the nature and role of arguments from fittingness, the priority of act over potency, and his suggestion that Aquinas does not emphasize the importance of Christ's life), it is worth noting that the core of Allen's argument is that "obedience pleases the triune God only insofar as it flows from faith in God" (Allen, *Christ's Faith*, 189). The upshot of such an argument is that the telos of humans subverts their ability to please God by means of obedience, as if humanity outside of a state of separation from God cannot obey him. It seems to me that the shortcomings of this position fundamentally undermine his claim that Christ must have been ignorant and exercised faith as a result of "the axiomatic place of faith grounding all other forms of creaturely obedience," rendering his argument somewhat tautological (Allen, *Christ's Faith*, 6).

67. Ibid., 261.

68. Ibid., 262. "By 'objectively' I do not mean 'notionally' (since the vision is an intuitive, *immediate* knowledge), but 'pertaining to true knowledge of reality'" (ibid., 262n47). See Gaine, *Did the Savior See*, 81–2.

much twentieth-century Christology, which attempted to ground Christ's divine sonship in his unique knowledge of the Father.[69]

The beatific vision is not in competition with infused species because its object is the divine essence, which cannot be known by finite species. Jesus' knowledge of the secondary objects of the beatific vision is intuitive and inexpressible because they are all known under the single aspect of the divine essence, rather than through their own individual intelligible species. For this reason, a number of Thomists, influenced by the seventeenth-century commentator John of St. Thomas, have argued that infused species are necessary to "translate" what Jesus knows in the beatific vision, to make it intelligible and expressible.[70] However, Aquinas disagrees that these species must be infused, for he recognizes that when the Apostle Paul had an ecstatic vision of God, "and he heard things that cannot be told, which man may not utter" (2 Cor. 12:4), he was able to remember and communicate many of the things he saw in the state of rapture.[71] This is not

---

69. As we saw in Chapter 3, various theologians attempted to reinterpret the question of Jesus' understanding of his divine identity in relational terms: what Jesus knows or comes to know is his unique mission and relationship to the Father, he does not have direct knowledge of his "divinity." Friedrich Schleiermacher writes, "It would interfere with all human treatment of the subject and Christ would be a completely ghostly figure if we were to ascribe to him ... a parallel awareness of his divinity and his humanity" (*The Life of Jesus*, 269). Similarly, Jon Sobrino: "Here 'person' represents the end of a long process of self-reconciliation in which the subject surrenders his self to another ... Through this concrete, historical surrender to the Father, Jesus becomes the Son in a real rather than an idealistic way" (*Christology at the Crossroads*, 387). N. T. Wright argues that Jesus was conscious of a vocation "given him by the one he knew as 'father', to enact in himself what, in Israel's scriptures, God had promised to accomplish all by himself" with the caveat that "awareness of vocation is by no means the same thing as Jesus having the sort of 'supernatural' awareness of himself, of Israel's God, and of the relation between the two of them" such as those who hold to a "Docetic" high Christology (*JVG*, 653). Adolf von Harnack can be felt in the background here, writing that "The consciousness which he possessed of being *the Son of God* is, therefore, nothing but the practical consequence of knowing God as the Father and as his Father. Rightly understood, the name of Son means nothing but the knowledge of God" (*What Is Christianity?*, 128). "The Gospel, as Jesus proclaimed it, has to do with the Father only and not with the Son" (ibid., 144).

70. As Gaine explains, if the divine essence is not known under *species impressa* then our mind cannot produce *species expressa* of it ("Is There Still a Place for Christ's Infused Knowledge in Catholic Theology and Exegesis?" 601–15 at 606). For arguments about the role of species in "translating" the vision, see, e.g., Maritain, *On the Grace and Humanity of Jesus*, 72–3, 89–97, 104; Garrigou-Lagrange, *Christ the Savior*, 355–7; Durand, "La science du Christ," 497–503.

71. *ST* I.12.9 *obj. 2*. Aquinas notes that the light of glory can be shared as an abiding form, as in the vision of the blessed, or "by way of a transitory passion; and in this way that light was in Paul when he was in rapture" (*ST* II-II.175.3 *ad* 2). See also *In II Epist. ad Cor.* ch. 12, lect. 2, §458–63.

surprising, given that our cognitive faculties are capable of forming images on the basis of things conceived (e.g., the imagination can fashion a golden mountain from the images of gold and mountains, and the intellect can form the concept of species from the ideas of genus and difference). "Thus Paul, or any other person who sees God," writes Thomas,

> by the very vision of the divine essence, can form in himself the similitudes of what is seen in the divine essence, which remained in Paul even when he had ceased to see the essence of God. Still this kind of vision whereby things are seen by this likeness thus conceived, is not the same as that whereby things are seen in God.[72]

Hence, Christ can form finite similitudes of the secondary objects of his vision, including what is in the hearts of others. As Thomas argues elsewhere, "from the fact that [the soul of Christ] sees in the Word, it can form for itself likenesses of the things it sees."[73] Gaine contends that this is how the beatific vision can explain "how the earthly Christ could be the Teacher of divine realities of which knowledge cannot be acquired through the natural human route ... leading us all to share ultimately in his own vision of the Father."[74] It is also the ground of his ability to reign humanly as the divine king.

Far from removing Jesus from his historical context, attributing the beatific vision to Christ places him more firmly within his first-century Jewish milieu by incorporating the apocalyptic nature of his teaching into our doctrinal treatment of his knowledge.[75] Ernst Käsemann famously maintained that "apocalyptic was the mother of all Christian theology."[76] While this is an evident exaggeration, the apocalyptic picture of Jesus' teaching has emerged with increasing clarity as

---

72. *ST* I.12.9 *ad* 2.

73. *De ver.* q. 20, a. 3 *ad* 4.

74. Gaine, "Infused Knowledge," 603. See esp. Garrigou-Lagrange, *Our Savior and His Love for Us*, 143–71; Mansini, "Understanding St. Thomas on Christ's Immediate Knowledge of God," 91–124; Wilkins, "Love and Knowledge of God in the Human Life of Christ," 77–99.

75. Here I am assuming John J. Collins' definition of apocalyptic as "a genre of revelatory literature with a narrative framework, in which a revelation is mediated by an otherworldly being to a human recipient, disclosing a transcendent reality which is both temporal, insofar as it envisages eschatological salvation, and spatial insofar as it involves another supernatural world" ("What Is Apocalyptic?" 2). A later addition to the definition notes that apocalypse is "intended to interpret present, earthly circumstances in light of the supernatural world of the future, and to influence both the understanding and the behaviour of the audience by means of divine authority" (ibid., 5–6). However, as Collins himself notes, to specify the function of apocalyptic is problematic, as its form can serve a variety of purposes.

76. Käsemann, "The Beginnings of Christian Theology," 17–46 at 40.

our knowledge of apocalyptic literature has grown.[77] As Stephen Cook shows, unlike the prophets, apocalyptic visionaries "assert extraordinary illumination in understanding the world and its fate."[78] This stems from their unique vision of the heavens mediated by an otherworldly being, such as an angel.[79]

First Enoch, one of the classic apocalyptic texts, opens with the following words: "Enoch a righteous man, whose eyes were opened by God, saw the vision of the Holy One in the heavens, which the angels showed me, and from them I heard everything (πάντας), and from them I understood as I saw."[80] Here we have a vision of God mediated to a human figure by angels. As the vision unfolds, we see that it has granted Enoch a cosmic understanding of history (or, as Moltmann emphasizes, a historical understanding of the cosmos) viewed from an eschatological perspective.[81] It is striking how closely this maps onto the concept of the beatific vision in Aquinas. The angels, who possess the vision of God, mediate this vision to a seer, and unlike the specificity of what is received by the prophets, this vision is expansive and characterized by synthesis, the reverse aspect of the secondary objects of the beatific vision: Enoch now sees history through the lens of its final cause and ground of being.[82] Unlike Enoch, Jesus is unique in that he fills the role not just of the apocalyptic visionary but of the angelic mediator, and he possesses this apocalyptic vision continually, rather than in a fleeting state of rapture.[83] Because he possesses the immediate vision of God himself, he can mediate this vision to his followers.

There are those who object that the possession of the beatific vision makes Jesus something other than human.[84] However, this objection rests on a problematic understanding of the ways that grace raises nature to participate in that which belongs to God. In the patristic idiom, this is *theosis* or *deification*,

---

77. See, e.g., *The Jewish Apocalyptic Tradition and the Shaping of New Testament Thought*; Collins, *The Apocalyptic Imagination*.

78. Cook, "Apocalyptic Prophecy," 19–33 at 22.

79. Collins, "Introduction," 1–20.

80. *1 Enoch* 1:1.

81. Moltmann, *Theology of Hope*, 137.

82. Note that providing a theological explanation for the kind of knowledge at work in this text is not the same as insisting or proving that Enoch had this kind of knowledge as a matter of historical fact.

83. "The occasions in the Gospels where Jesus plays the part of the human recipient of revelation are succeeded by his acting in a more commanding role as the supernatural revealer, functioning much like an *angelus interpres*" (Baynes, "Revealer and Revealed," 17). Baynes discusses Jesus revealing and concealing mysteries in his parables in a way that strongly evokes apocalyptic literature (ibid., 17–23). Markus Bockmuehl refers to the transfiguration as an "apocalyptic preview for the saints" (*Revelation and Mystery in Ancient Judaism and Pauline Christianity*, 39).

84. E.g., Rahner, "Current Problems in Christology," 149–200 at 168; Urs von Balthasar, *The Glory of the Lord*, 328n141; O'Collins and Kendall, "The Faith of Jesus," 403–23 at 409.

the working out of the biblical promise that "we will be like him, because we will see him as he is" (1 Jn 3:2).[85] As Aquinas puts it, "glory perfects nature, it does not destroy it."[86] It is also worth noting that Aquinas suggests that the bodily effects (*redundatia*) of beatification were withheld from Christ during his incarnate life, such that the vision of God did not interfere with his ability to suffer and experience the trials of human existence in his life and sacrificial death.[87] Thomas writes that:

> From the natural relationship which is between the soul and the body, glory flows into the body from the soul's glory. Yet this natural relationship in Christ was subject to the will of His Godhead, and thereby it came to pass that the beatitude remained in the soul, and did not flow into the body; but the flesh suffered what belongs to a passible nature; thus Damascene says (*De Fide Orth.* iii, 15) that, "it was by the consent of the Divine will that the flesh was allowed to suffer and do what belonged to it."[88]

In his intellect, Christ apprehends the divine essence and experiences the joy appropriate to the beatific vision, but in his external and internal senses, he experiences and apprehends bodily pain and suffering.[89] Gaine notes that, "For Aquinas, there is no competition for 'space' in Christ's soul between joy and sorrow, for they have very different objects, and they can perfectly well co-exist, the former in the intellectual and the latter in the sensory appetite."[90] This vision does not take away from the truly human life of Christ, but it allows him to live it in a way proper to his identity as the Son of God: impeccably in line with his divine will such that his every action is expressive of his divine personhood.[91]

The Logic of Assumption and Grace

Aquinas' arguments for the supernatural knowledge of Christ—infused and beatific—do not stem from absolute metaphysical necessity but rather from

---

85. See *In Epist. ad Phil.* ch. 3, lect. 3, §145.

86. *In IV Sent.* 49.2.3 *ad* 8. "Even though the glory had in heaven does not destroy nature, it elevates it to a level which it could not reach by itself, namely, that level where it can see things through God's very essence without any likeness acting as a medium in this vision" (*De ver.* 8.5 *ad* 3).

87. See Gaine, *Did the Saviour See*, 179–201.

88. *ST* III.14.1 *ad* 2.

89. For an insightful discussion of Jesus' relation to and transformation of the laments of Hebrew Scripture, see Eklund, *Jesus Wept*.

90. Gaine, *Did the Saviour See*, 189.

91. See also Crowe, "Eschaton and Worldly Mission in the Mind and Heart of Christ," 193–234.

fittingness [*conveniens*].⁹² But that does not mean they are peripheral or inconsequential. As we have seen, Aquinas' participatory metaphysic allows him to establish the substantial divine personhood of Christ without undermining the finite integrity of his human nature because he does not consider Christ's divinity to result from the application of divine predicates to his human nature or the transformation of his humanity into something else. But he insists further that it was fitting for Christ to assume certain human perfections for the purpose of his saving mission. I would like to consider one argument against Aquinas' understanding on this score, to highlight why the logic of fittingness cannot be ignored or confused with arguments from necessity, and how this impacts historical treatments of Jesus.

Edwin Christian van Driel has written an article attempting to defend classical Christology by making it more palatable to proponents of kenotic Christology.⁹³ To accomplish this, he opposes Aquinas' arguments for the maximal grace and beatific vision of Christ, arguing that the reasons for affirming these are "independent of the classical theory of assumption and hypostatic union itself."⁹⁴ The crux of his argument is the idea, which he develops from Duns Scotus, that any "substance nature," be it intellectual or not, could be assumed by the Word.⁹⁵ Van Driel maintains that because the Word could assume a non-intellectual nature, the perfection of the intellect must be entirely distinct from assumption and must be argued for on separate grounds. He is correct to note that classical Christology "is not an account of cognitive or voluntary influence of one nature on the other."⁹⁶ Recalling our discussion of personhood in Chapter 3, such cognitive

---

92. See *ST* III.1.2; *ST* I.32.1 *ad* 2; Davison, "Christian Systematic Theology and Life Elsewhere in the Universe," 447–61; Gondreau, "Anti-Docetism in Aquinas's *Super Ioannem*," 254–76 at 272; Brown, "'Necessary' and 'Fitting' Reasons in Christian Theology," 211–30; Baker, "Convenient Redemption," 96–113; Bauerschmidt, *Thomas Aquinas*, 160–88; Narcisse, "Les Enjeux Épistémologiques de l'Argument de Convenance selon Saint Thomas d'Aquin," 143–67.

93. Van Driel, "The Logic of Assumption," 265–90.

94. Ibid., 285.

95. Scotus, *The Quodlibetal Questions*, , q.19, sec. 19.61, 19.62 (pp. 432–3). As van Driel notes, Aquinas affirmed in his commentary on the Sentences that it is technically within the power of God to assume any nature (*In III Sent* 2.1.1 *ad* 1). However, in the *Summa Theologiae* Thomas defines assumability explicitly in terms of fittingness, and thus argues that only rational natures are capable of being assumed (*ST* III.4.1). Van Driel writes: "I do not read this as a rejection of the earlier position in the *Scriptum*, only as an incomplete summary" ("Logic," 281). While it may not be a "rejection" of his earlier position, Aquinas has clearly shifted his position regarding the appropriate frame of reference for the question, and he argues unambiguously that "a thing is said to be assumable according to some fitness for such a union" (*ST* III.4.1). Van Driel's simple dismissal of arguments from fittingness is neither consonant with Aquinas' position in the *ST* nor is it sufficient to refute his position therein.

96. Van Driel, "Logic," 277.

influence is not sufficient to ground the union of natures, it must flow *from* a truly hypostatic union. But van Driel suggests further that Christology is *only* about the ontological dependence of a nature grounded in the person: it is not about the communication of some power or influence and, furthermore, any such influence would be inappropriate in a Chalcedonian paradigm.[97]

There are several complications to this argument that are not addressed in the article. To begin with, simple ontological dependence is not sufficient to account for the instrumental unity of Christ's two wills necessary to maintain the unity of his personhood. The fact that a divine person's assumption of a non-rational nature would not involve any influence on the intellect of that nature (because it would not have an intellect) does nothing to prove that the same would be true of God's assumption of a rational nature, or that such a lack of influence would be fitting. The fact that van Driel concludes with the work of N. T. Wright as a possible solution is telling.[98] Wright offers precisely the view we have been critiquing throughout this study: that in Jesus' human mind, he believed he had a special calling to do and be what only God could do and be for the people of Israel. If everything Jesus does comes from a position of inference, hope, and faith—knowing that "he could be making a terrible, lunatic mistake" but doing his best nonetheless[99]—in what sense can we say that his every word and action is that of the divine Word? Either we must posit that the Word surreptitiously directs his human will without involving his human intellect (a kind of miraculous voluntarism, perhaps), thereby undermining his human freedom and resulting in Docetism, or else his human will is free to follow where his ignorance leads, which surely includes paths contrary to the will of the Word, resulting in Nestorianism. The act of being of the person of the Son cannot be abstracted to the simple fact of his existence in two natures—it must connect to the very lived actions of Jesus in his historical human life: actions that are attributable to no one other than the eternal Word of God.

Even granting that the soteriological reasons for the grace and perfection of Christ's human nature are governed in important ways by a different set of theoretical considerations than the reasons for the classical theory of assumption, that does not mean that there are not good and bad answers to the former in light of the latter. Unfortunately, Van Driel's argument simply misrepresents Aquinas' position. For example, he suggests that classical Christology makes Jesus' humanity "as godlike as is possible" in the same way that kenoticists make his divinity as humanlike as possible.[100] Van Driel asserts that the divinization of Jesus'

---

97. He suggests that it would not be wise for classical theologians to affirm the distribution of these latter gifts to the humanity of Christ (see ibid., 286), though the justification for this argument is not clear. For a contrary perspective, see Gaine, *Did the Saviour See*, 129–58.

98. Van Driel, "Logic," 288–9.

99. Wright, "Jesus' Self-Understanding," 59.

100. Van Driel, "Logic," 287. Given that he is focused on Aquinas throughout the article as the example of a classical Christology that insists on the cognitive perfections of Jesus' humanity, this is evidently aimed at Thomas, though van Driel does not say so explicitly.

humanity is a "change of the nature," as if sanctification transforms humanity into something nonhuman—in other words, as if grace destroys nature.[101] Thomas' arguments for the perfections of Jesus' humanity do not stem from an inability to make sense of the hypostatic union without homogenizing Jesus' two natures. His arguments are soteriological: the perfections assumed in the Incarnation were those fitting for Christ to bring us to salvation.[102] And as we have seen, far from requiring that his natures be similar, Aquinas insists on the qualitative difference between divinity and humanity in the hypostatic union as the necessary grounds for personal union. Furthermore, drawing any kind of equivalence between humanizing divinity and divinizing humanity makes little sense metaphysically or soteriologically. The divine nature cannot be transformed such that it becomes the subject of creaturely predicates, whereas the very telos of the creature is to share in the life of God. To insist that, in the personal union of divinity and humanity in Christ, the divine nature (and thus person) should exert no influence on the human nature in the order of grace is to ignore the entire biblical and theological tradition that insists that the very presence of God transforms humans.[103] As Aquinas writes, "For the nearer any recipient is to an inflowing cause, the more does it partake of its influence. Now the influx of grace is from God, according to Ps. 83:12: 'The Lord will give grace and glory.' And hence it was most fitting that His [Christ's] soul should receive the influx of Divine grace."[104] To insist to the contrary is to ignore or misconstrue the dignity of the person of Christ, which can only be manifest in a human life in the order of grace. And as Lonergan notes, "Life according to grace does not take away this human living but supposes it, implants itself in it, completes it through another order of acts, and also, in the sense of its natural perfection, perfects it."[105] Or as Aaron Riches puts it, "The result of the Chalcedonian formulation was to realize very clearly that 'the proximity of the divine' does not threaten or compromise 'the integrity of the human,' but in fact establishes it."[106] A human life is most human when it manifests divine grace, whereas the divine nature would not become more Godlike were it to relinquish divine properties.

Van Driel's argument is instructive for highlighting the ways in which classical Christology problematizes the seemingly tidy solution offered by a focus on strict metaphysical possibility. Much of my argument thus far has focused on the logic of ontological dependence and how the doctrine of the hypostatic union does not undermine the historical humanity of Jesus. Insofar as van Driel is arguing similarly, we are in common cause. But, as we have seen especially in Chapters 6 and 7, it is not the case that absolute metaphysical necessity is the only relevant

---

101. Ibid. Cf. *ST* I.1.8.
102. *ST* III.7; III.9.2.
103. See, e.g., 2 Pet. 1:4; 2 Cor. 3:17-18; Jn 17:22; Phil. 3:21.
104. *ST* III.7.1.
105. Lonergan, *Incarnate Word*, 695.
106. Riches, *Ecce Homo*, 61. Quoting George, *The Difference God Makes*, 4.

consideration. Just because something is technically possible from a metaphysical perspective does not make it a good theological argument, or, for that matter, a plausible reading of Scripture. To ignore arguments from fittingness or confuse them with arguments from necessity is theologically disastrous. When Aquinas maintains that the grace and perfection of Christ's human nature is fitting, he does not mean that his comments are tangential to the coherence of his Christology. Along with the entire patristic tradition, while allowing metaphysical necessity to govern the terms of his doctrine in important ways (divine simplicity, for example), Aquinas argues primarily in light of soteriology, and he considers these arguments to be essential. I see no way for a Christology that denies the divine nature/person's influence on the human nature to account for the unity of personhood in the historical life of Jesus. Such a Christology is simply an abstraction, one which has no resources for understanding Jesus' human existence as expressive of his divine identity.

Intellectual Humility

Another objection to Jesus' possession of the beatific vision stems from the humility attributed to Christ, which Christians are called to imitate.[107] How can Jesus practice humility of mind if he knows all things through a direct vision of the divine essence? As Michael Allen argues, "a spacious account of the life of Jesus Christ depicts his journey as undertaken in humble submission, marked by deep faith in the midst of the world's terrors and misery."[108] Is a life of humility necessarily marked by faith, rather than vision? In his letter to the Philippians, Paul presents Christ's humility of mind as exemplary for the Christian life, calling the Christians of Philippi to be of the same mind by imitation.

> Let the same mind [φρονεῖτε] be in you that was in Christ Jesus,
> who, though he was in the form of God,
> did not regard equality with God
> as something to be exploited,
> but emptied [ἐκένωσεν] himself,
> taking the form of a slave,
> being born in human likeness.
> And being found in human form,
> he humbled [ἐταπείνωσεν] himself
> and became obedient to the point of death—
> even death on a cross (Phil. 2:5-11).[109]

---

107. See, e.g., Mt. 11:29; Mt. 21:1-12/Zech. 9:9; Phil. 2:5-11. I have chosen this objection, in part, because Sjmon Gaine does not discuss it.

108. Allen, *Christ's Faith*, 212.

109. See *In Epist. ad Phil.* ch. 2, lect. 2, §51–58.

As we saw in Chapter 1, this passage has frequently been interpreted in ways that conceive of God divesting himself of his divine properties in order to live and act humanly in the Incarnation, or else in ways that historicize God by defining divinity in terms characteristic of human existence. This emphasis on limitation, privation, and divestiture has had a related impact on understandings of the New Testament concept of intellectual humility, particularly as it relates to Christ. In his book *The New Testament and Intellectual Humility*, Grant Macaskill points out that much of the work on intellectual humility has focused on fostering open-mindedness through cognizance of limitations and deficiencies.[110] This focus pairs well with *kenotic* readings, which, as Macaskill puts it, tend to suggest that "humility necessarily brings about a divestment of fullness. It is not possible, ultimately, to be humble and retain the perfections of God. In the terms of our text [Phil. 2:5-11], humility means that the form of God must be *exchanged* for the form of a servant. If God is humble, he must cease to be God."[111] Conceptions of humility that focus on limitation appear to rely on a philosophical anthropology that denies the power of grace to perfect, rather than destroy nature. This suggests that the same problematic metaphysical presuppositions that underlie kenotic and historicizing Christologies might also underlie the truncated conceptions of humility applied to Christ.[112]

Macaskill notes that a classical Christological approach requires an understanding of the virtue of humility that "maintains plentitude and competency" and centers a concept of intellectual servanthood that has nothing to do with deficiency or limitation.[113] To begin with, Macaskill points out that in Philippians 2, humility is not the effect of Christ's self-emptying, but its cause. "It is the state of attitude that *leads to* Christ emptying himself, rather than the condition that proceeds from this."[114] The action designated by the verb κενόω expresses the eternal humility of the Word of God, it does not engender it anew. "Humility of mind is not a position of weakness or simple subordination, for it is something that characterizes the mind of God himself."[115] Here, humility has to do with a low concern for status, rather than the ownership of limitations,[116] but Macaskill notes that it also "involves a redemptive purpose that ultimately re-affirms the status of the one who descends."[117] Ultimately, the emptying of

---

110. See Whitcomb, Battaly, Baehr, and Howard-Snyder, "Intellectual Humility," 1–31.

111. Macaskill, *The New Testament and Intellectual Humility*, 154.

112. For a discussion of how participation impacts our understanding of ethics on this score, see Davison, *Participation*, 348–66.

113. Ibid., 136.

114. Ibid., 148.

115. Ibid., 170.

116. Thus matching more closely to Robert C. Roberts and W. Jay Wood's definition of intellectual humility as a disposition toward "a low level of concern to be well regarded by other people for one's intellectual accomplishments or prowess" (*Intellectual Virtues*, 236).

117. Macaskill, *Intellectual Humility*, 159.

the Son serves the purpose of salvation—a sharing of God's wisdom with those who lack it.[118] This humility is not a kind of subservience but an empowering and powerful act.[119] Intellectual humility is the antithesis of intellectual vices such as arrogance, vanity, conceit, grandiosity, domination, and egotism. It refuses the positioning and power granted to those with knowledge, instead serving others and sharing wisdom with them for their own sake.

Aquinas has a more specific understanding of the nature of the virtues, and especially of the virtue of humility. He argues that humility has to do with the appetite rather than the estimative power, and that its role is "to temper and restrain the mind, lest it tend to high things immoderately."[120] It is a complement to magnanimity, which "urges the mind to great things in accord with right reason."[121] For Aquinas, this does involve knowledge of one's limitations, recognizing one's "disproportion to that which surpasses his capacity."[122] For this reason humility is fitting to God "not as regards His divine nature, but only as regards His human nature."[123] God does not possess an irascible appetite, nor can he immoderately tend to what is above him. Nevertheless, Aquinas' understanding could be extended to account for Macaskill's insights, which have to do with intellectual humility in a more expansive sense. The eternal Word exhibits humility metaphorically by not considering his position something to be exploited: he radically demonstrates the opposite of arrogance, vanity, and grandiosity by sacrificially taking on the form of a slave. Aquinas notes that intrinsic humility happens when, for example, "a man, considering his own failings, assumes the lowest place according to his mode."[124] God need not temper himself from immoderation according to his mode of being,

---

118. See Cessario, "Incarnate Wisdom and the Immediacy of Christ's Salvific Knowledge," 334–40.

119. See Pardue, *The Mind of Christ*.

120. *ST* II-II.161.1; 161.2 *s.c.*

121. *ST* II-II.161.1 *ad 3*.

122. *ST* II-II.161.2.

123. *ST* II-II.161.1 *ad 4*.

> The manner and the sign of his humility is obedience, whereas it is characteristic of the proud to follow their own will, for a proud person seeks greatness. But it pertains to a great thing that it not be ruled by something else, but that it rule other things; therefore, obedience is contrary to pride. Hence, in order to show the greatness of Christ's humility and passion, he says that he became "obedient"; because if he had not suffered out of obedience, his passion would not be so commendable, for obedience gives merit to our sufferings. But how was he made "obedient"? Not by his divine will, because it is a rule; but by his human will, which is ruled in all things according to the Father's will: "nevertheless, not as I will but as you will" (Matt. 26:39). (*In Epist. ad Phil.* ch. 2, lect. 2, §64–66)

124. *ST* II-II.161.1 *ad 1*.

but he can display an utter lack of regard for status by taking on a new humble mode of being, which is what he has done in the incarnation.

It is precisely through his possession of the vision of God that Christ humanly manifests intellectual humility. Perfect creaturely humility is carried out "in dependence and submission to God."[125] It does not come from limitation, ignorance, self-effacement, or modesty. Rather, it is a positive virtue of freedom that is manifest most among the wise (Prov. 11:2); it is a virtue that exhibits knowledge most fully and appropriately by directing it to its proper ends without improper concern for the regard of others.[126] Just as someone is most humble when their will is most aligned with God's will for them, so Jesus is perfectly humble through the instrumental unity of his human will with his divine will. Furthermore, if intellectual humility involves sharing wisdom for the building up of others rather than hoarding it for oneself, this is exactly what the apocalyptic visionary does, and none more so than Christ. The beatific vision completes and perfects humility in the creature.[127] To suggest otherwise is to maintain that the very telos of humanity subverts their virtue.

Conclusion

Through the possession of the beatific vision in his human soul, Christ's two wills maintain an unbroken instrumental unity that allows his human life to express his divine personhood perfectly. This direct vision of God provided him with the means to teach divine things in a human way, such that his words and actions genuinely constitute divine revelation (see Jn 3:34).[128] The eschatological nature of this knowledge is consistent with his Messianic vocation, and its apocalyptic aspect places him in continuity with an influential line of Jewish thought, while also highlighting his superiority over the prophets of Israel who foretold his coming. It is by virtue of his direct vision of God that Christ enacts YHWH's divine kingship on earth, fulfilling the promise that His kingdom would be established forever through a descendent of David.[129] The value of this argument for our purposes

---

125. Macaskill, *Intellectual Humility*, 170. As Aquinas puts it, humility "regards chiefly the subjection of man to God, for whose sake he humbles himself by subjecting himself to others" (*ST* II-II.161.1 *ad 5*).

126. See *ST* II-II.162.3 *ad 1*.

127. It is worth noting that I am not arguing for the intradivine humility of the Son in the way that Karl Barth does (*Church Dogmatics* IV/1, §59, 192–210). My argument here has to do with expanding the metaphorical meaning of humility in order to account for this biblical passage, not with applying a privative notion of humility to God. See Mansini, "Can Humility and Obedience be Trinitarian Realities?," 71–98; White, "Intra-Trinitarian Obedience and Nicene-Chalcedonian Christology," 377–402.

128. *ScG* IV.54. See Sherwin, "Christ the Teacher in St. Thomas's Commentary on the Gospel of John," 173–93; Dauphinais, "Christ the Teacher."

129. 2 Sam. 7:12-14. See Psalm 2; Isa. 11:1-5; and Ps. 132:11 (cited in *ST* III.31.2).

is not to prove the Messianic claims of the Christian tradition, or to establish Jesus' divinity by historical means. Rather, it is to illustrate the fact that there are philosophical and theological categories of human thought and intention that far outstrip those commonly employed in historical Jesus scholarship. This discussion shows the frailty of arguments, which suggest that Jesus' extraordinary knowledge either undermines his humanity or removes him from his first-century Jewish milieu. It also reveals the dogmatic aspect of many concepts implicitly assumed by historians: concepts of divine causality, the relationship between nature and grace, virtues such as humility, the intelligibility of the divine essence, and the deifying impact of God's presence on creatures.

Most importantly, I have argued that the denial of Jesus' possession of a certain kind of *knowledge* (i.e., the beatific vision) fundamentally undermines claims about his divine *personhood* and messianic office. *Pace* van Driel, to deny Jesus such knowledge, as many of the historians we discussed in Chapter 1 have done, is to rule out the possibility of his divine personhood. Claims about what Jesus did or did not know are not theologically neutral, nor do they stem from genuinely historical arguments. Rather, they are assumed on the basis of precommitments to alternative metaphysical and theological frameworks. Here it is impossible to ignore the manifest influence of naturalism. To state whether or not Jesus "knew he was God" requires a vast array of philosophical and theological judgments, which should be supported by philosophical and theological arguments. Fortunately, these forms of reasoning provide an expanded range of tools to enable the historian in their work. Homogenizing the varieties of knowledge witnessed to in ancient sources blinds historians to the unique claims being made therein by limiting the scope of possibility to the horizon created by naturalistic metaphysics. They need not affirm the veracity of these claims, but to deny them from the outset is to overstep their purview as historians.

CONCLUSION: RIVAL TRADITIONS OF HISTORICAL ENQUIRY

The horizon concern of this study is what counts as a "historical" perspective when it comes to Jesus and why. I have shown that in contemporary historical Jesus scholarship, a historical perspective is typically considered to be one that subordinates historical evidence to the horizon of metaphysical naturalism.[1] Nowhere is this more apparent, and methodologically significant, than in the area of knowledge and self-understanding. I have argued, by contrast, that Aquinas provides us with the principles for a rigorously historical treatment of Jesus that is not confined to the same metaphysical limits. In this way, historical Jesus scholarship and classical Christology should be seen as rival traditions of historical enquiry. Central to Aquinas' argument has been his use of the modus principle and his insistence that grace does not destroy but perfects nature. With these two principles in hand, understood in light of a metaphysics of participation, we have seen how the ontological affirmation of Jesus' divinity upholds both the finite integrity of his humanity and the unity of his personhood, and how Aquinas' approach offers vital resources for contextualizing Jesus' human life within his historical and social setting, insisting on the ways he was shaped by the language, stories, symbols, and praxis of his particular culture. Central to this accomplishment are Thomas' substantial account of personhood, his Incarnational Christology of substantial union, and his Chalcedonian "Spirit Christology."

Within this concern, the principal question this book has attempted to address has been what the implications of classical Christology are for thinking about Jesus as a historical figure: what resources does it provide for the task and what space does it open up for Christians to engage with history? My answer is that classical Christology, particularly in the hands of Thomas Aquinas, allows us properly to order a wide range of diverse enquiries into a coherent whole, without truncating or ruling out questions that provide vital perspective on the historical figure of Jesus. By comparison with historical Jesus scholarship, the classical Christian tradition provides a more expansive and consistent approach to the relevant issues in play. Here, history, metaphysics, and theology coalesce into a lucid and instructive investigation into the identity, purpose, and significance of Jesus of

---

1. This would be a necessary but not sufficient condition.

Nazareth. Ontology and narrative illuminate one another, and they, in turn, provide valuable categories for understanding historical questions about aims, intentions, and personal identity.

My argument began with the history of Jesus scholarship and a discussion of the way in which the methods of the discipline coalesce around a focus on the interiority of historical figures: intention, motivation, and self-understanding. Historians' answers to these questions reveal that they are working with a severely limited set of concepts, and that they are driven by philosophical and theological presuppositions, not just by historical investigation. This is illustrated well by discussions of "Docetism" in the literature, which belie three particular objections: that affirming Jesus' "divinity" undermines historians' access to the "inside" of history; that high Christology undercuts the historical emphasis on context and falls into anachronism; and that source material which they take to reflect these tendencies—"narrative Docetism"—should be discounted. I have argued that the classical Christological tradition, at least as represented by Thomas, does nothing to undercut our emphasis on context or lead us into anachronism. Nonetheless, I have shown that Jesus need not possess the same epistemic limitations as his contemporaries in order for him meaningfully to share their historical perspective. Jesus' identity does, however, present challenges to the way we access the "inside" of history.[2] From this perspective, Jesus' very uniqueness requires that theological forms of reasoning be brought to bear on this question if we are to provide fully formed answers. However, opting for a theological solution to explain historical events is no less "historical" than explaining the events away using source-critical methods. The upshot of this argument is that the tendency to discount source material that evidences "narrative Docetism" is not itself a refusal of Docetism but a dogmatic advancement of Ebionitism. This fact should lead to a renewed engagement with John's gospel, in particular, as an ancient witness to the historical Jesus.[3]

---

2. Paul Merkley points out that the New Questers misappropriated Collingwood by papering over the distance between the inside of Jesus' life and our own with an existentialist bridge that Collingwood himself would never have accepted. Merkley's reflections suggest to me the positive work to be done by a theological argument, which complicates our historical access to the "inside" of Jesus' life (though Merkley instead advocates a return to the more strictly Rankean approach to historiography as exemplified by Albert Schweitzer). See Merkley, "New Quests for Old," 205.

3.
> What most Johannine scholars have notably failed to take seriously is that the Gospel's theology itself requires a concern for history. The theological claim of John's prologue that "the word became flesh and dwelt among us" presupposes that Jesus was a real human person in real history. This is not negated by the degree of reflective interpretation that the author incorporates—certainly a greater degree than in the Synoptics—because the interpretation is in search of the profoundest meaning of what Jesus said and did. We should not expect the history to have

The simple assertion that Jesus was fully human does nothing to establish that his knowledge must have been limited to those ways of knowing assumed within post-enlightenment naturalistic historiography. There is nothing Docetic or ahistorical about attributing to Jesus prophetic knowledge or an apocalyptic vision of God. Rather, these forms of knowing clash with the assumptions of metaphysical naturalism. The question we are left with is whether the historical evidence is being given due weight by these historians, or whether their naturalistic assumptions are hegemonic, defeating anything that does not fit within what they expect to find. Insofar as the latter is the case, historical Jesus scholarship should be categorized in the end as a tradition with normative philosophical and theological assumptions that create a particularly rigid hermeneutical horizon for engagement with the past.[4] The fact that the tenets of this dogma are widely held among secular Western societies does not mean that they are objective or neutral, let alone true. As such, we cannot say that any Jesus not sufficiently grounded in the historical Jesus *as he can be reconstructed by historical Jesus scholars* is necessarily Docetic or in any way problematic.[5] Critical historiography needs to be more critical about its own philosophical presuppositions, and academic historical study of Jesus should make space for rival traditions of historical enquiry. At the same time, theologians should be invested in critical historical investigation of Jesus but should do so without allowing metaphysical naturalism to dictate the terms of their investigation.[6] One implication of this is that "history" cannot primarily be about discovering by supposedly objective scientific methods whether or not Christian truth claims are accurate.[7]

been lost behind the interpretation but rather to have been highlighted by the interpretation. (Bauckham, *The Testimony of the Beloved Disciple*, 10)

I take Bauckham's reference to Jesus as "a real human person" not as a technical ontological point (as if to deny the *anhypostasis* of Christ's humanity) but as a historical one: Jesus lived a truly human life.

4. See Howard, *Religion and the Rise of Historicism*.

5. Otherwise, as Kant recognized, "under this system, historical faith must finally become mere faith in Scriptural scholars and their insight" (*Religion within the Limits*, bk. 3, §6 [p. 105]).

6. Far from defending fideism, I am arguing that metaphysical understandings should be argued for on philosophical grounds, whereas historical understandings should be argued for on historical grounds, and doing the latter critically requires accounting for and defending the metaphysical presuppositions assumed within one's methods. In other words, an uncritical acceptance of metaphysical naturalism as a component part of historiography is its own form of fideism.

7. N. T. Wright, for example, refers to himself as a "scientific historian" in "Whence and Whither Historical Jesus Studies in the Life of the Church?", 115–60 at 126. See Louth's robust criticism of the ways history has mistakenly attempted to "ape the sciences" in *Discerning the Mystery*.

The fact that these forms of enquiry are constituted by traditions does not mean that they are without recourse for critical engagement with one another. For my part, I conceive of this task in much the same way that MacIntyre outlines in *Whose Justice? Which Rationality?* I refer the reader to that volume for a detailed discussion, but it is worth noting one central facet of that conversation here. MacIntyre contends that in order for the protagonists of two rival traditions to understand one another, they need not necessarily share the same standards of rational evaluation. Indeed, central to his argument is that "rationality" is always embodied within and receives its standards from a particular tradition. And yet, he does not affirm either relativism or perspectivism. The task of adjudicating between two rival and incompatible traditions does not involve judging their claims from some neutral position, for such neutrality does not exist. Rather, it requires that protagonists of each tradition contend for the overall strength and coherence of their tradition over/against its rivals and show both *that* the rival tradition falls short of its own standards and *why* it does so. Part of my task has been to show that historical Jesus scholarship falls short of its own standards of philosophical and theological neutrality,[8] and that it does so because it lacks a coherent framework and developed discourse for interrogating and theorizing about the philosophical and theological assumptions that underpin its methods and approaches.

I cannot adequately unpack how history will be done differently if it takes critical account of the metaphysical and theological baggage it has carried with it, and I would not want to foreclose the possibilities by venturing an overly prescriptive answer. But I would like to gesture toward the implications of my argument in ways that I believe will help with that work. This discussion illustrates the fact that historical events can and do shape our understanding of reality, and that our understanding of reality shapes our interpretation of historical events. The task of theology requires not only that we construct coherent frameworks of description and evaluation but also that we regularly suspend those frameworks in order to consider their contingency and limitations. Critical history is therefore vital to the theological task because it gives us the tools to contextualize the metaphysical and theological claims being made both by us and by the historical figures we study. Refusing to take theological and philosophical concepts as methodologically given opens up greater possibilities that the historical task itself might constructively challenge contemporary philosophical and theological frameworks. Even the act of accepting something as timelessly or universally true is a historical act.[9] But the theological intuition is that our commitment to certain values need not be undermined by our understanding of their historical contingency. At the same time, the assumption is often made that adopting the metaphysical presuppositions of modern Western culture provides historians with a "neutral"

---

8. Seth Herringer's work contributes a significant amount to this task as well.

9. See discussion in Joas, *The Sacredness of the Person*, 128. Cited in Aspray, "Employing Genealogies Responsibly in Theology."

setting within which to situate historical events. I have argued to the contrary that these presuppositions are far from neutral, and they leave an indelible imprint on the historical subjects under consideration.

Darren Sarisky argues for a construal of faith as "a readerly capacity rather than a prejudice with a pious gloss."[10] I have argued for something similar when it comes to doctrine. Far from having to deny the claims of Chalcedon in order to study Jesus as a genuine historical figure, I have shown that the classical tradition of Christological reflection provides resources for expanding and deepening our understanding of the relevant historical texts. As we have seen, to take the metaphysical and theological claims of the text seriously as descriptions of reality can provide genuine insight into the historical claims being made—not by forcing us to accept those claims as true but by deepening our grasp of the significance and implications of those claims beyond the social and political. Furthermore, Sarisky maintains that "better than repudiating history is seeing it as having an 'intrinsic openness to something greater.'"[11] Theological approaches to the gospels are not ahistorical simply because they refuse to foreclose the possibility that the words and actions of Jesus might have profound implications. In order for theologians and religious communities to engage positively with critical history, there must be a way of interrogating the past that does not foreclose this "intrinsic openness" as a genuine possibility. I have argued that simple rhetorical openness cannot accomplish this. It is not enough for a historian to *say* that they are open to this possibility; it requires significant reflection on the metaphysical presuppositions built into one's methods. To insist on the importance of history for theology is not to accept that history can deliver all that it has promised. Historical Jesus scholarship has tended to hold an overinflated sense of its own capacities as a discipline. In particular, both the positive and the negative *theological* claims of historical Jesus scholars stem more from metaphysical presuppositions than from historical argumentation. They typically begin with certain theological ideas and then construct a Jesus that fits within them, which is precisely what they have tended to accuse theologians of doing. To say that Jesus did not or could not know that he was God in the manner that historical Jesus scholars have done is simply to state one's philosophical and theological presuppositions as if they were historical conclusions. What their methods require is that, to some degree, Jesus shared the same historical perspective as his contemporaries, and we have seen that classical Christology agrees that he did. That does not mean that he therefore shared the same epistemic limitations as his contemporaries, or that he could not have known things that they did not.[12]

---

10. Sarisky, *Reading the Bible Theologically*, 290.
11. Ibid., 241. Quoting Joseph Ratzinger.
12. On a practical note, we might hope that in narrowing their ambitions, historical Jesus scholars could also chasten the confidence of authors pandering to popular audiences with mass market books about the historical Jesus.

This argument also has implications for New Testament scholarship more broadly. Assumptions about the historical Jesus play a vital role in the broader discipline, even for those uncomfortable with the current state of historical Jesus studies. Pauline studies, for example, assume a range of answers to questions about Jesus, Paul's relationship to Jesus, the disciples, and the earliest Christian communities. Even if study of the Pauline or Catholic Epistles is less beholden to form criticism and criteria of authenticity, their findings are inescapably linked to the questions raised and answered by historical Jesus scholarship.

On a theological register, I have argued in defense of the dyothelitism of the classical Christian tradition as a way forward for contemporary Christological reflection. Having defended both Aquinas' substantial account of personhood and the centrality of personal union in his Christology, I have advanced Thomas' argument for the fourfold knowledge of Christ by highlighting the ways in which his ontological categories reflect those within the biblical narrative that speak to Jesus' identity and purpose. Paying attention to the varieties of knowledge presented in these ancient sources and interpreting them ontologically in light of our philosophical anthropology allows us to bring greater specificity to the claims being made about who Jesus is. And this, in turn, leads to greater attention to narrative and history, not less. According to the narrative presentations of the Gospels, "what Jesus knows and how he knows it are fundamental features of his identity."[13]

In arguing that Aquinas' Christology should be considered a genuine tradition of historical enquiry, my purpose has not been to defend a simple return to the thirteenth century or a retreat from historical questions into dogma. Rather, I have argued that attending to metaphysics will allow us to coordinate the insights of various disciplines so that they can speak constructively to both historical and theological questions, such as the identity and purpose of Jesus of Nazareth. As Jeremy Wilkins puts it, "by anticipating and relating the contents to be known through inquiry, metaphysics is also a structure for interrelating methods of inquiry."[14] Far from arguing that we should do metaphysics *instead of* history, I am suggesting that a failure to attend to metaphysics has contributed to the current state of discord between the disciplines of theology and history. A more metaphysically aware approach to historiography would make it harder to conflate uncritical metaphysical or theological presuppositions with historical conclusions. In the same way, a historically aware approach to theology will be less likely to smuggle in uncritical historical presuppositions under the guise of theology. Furthermore, a nonnaturalistic approach to historiography would better allow theologians to engage constructively with critical historical research. As such, I am advocating for theologians to pay more attention to history, not less.

It may be the case that certain historians will not be happy until theologians accept an Ebionite Christology, but we should not make the mistake of thinking

---

13. Bullard, *Thoughts of Many Hearts*, 15.
14. Wilkins, *Before Truth*, 179.

that they are doing so for historical reasons. The fact is that metaphysics and theology are always in play, shaping the very task of historical investigation. At the same time, the resistance of theologians to the aims of historical Jesus studies should not necessarily be confused with a rejection of history. At its best, it is a denial of naturalism. The classical Christian tradition possesses a powerful theological vocabulary that enables us to speak of the personal active presence of God within the historical human life of Jesus without corrupting the integrity of his humanity or invalidating the importance of his historical and cultural context. In the end, arguments about whether or not Jesus "knew he was God" cannot be answered by means of historical method alone, for they necessarily include reference to philosophical anthropology, cognitive theory, and concepts such as the limits to the human capacity for sanctification and union with God, and the role of grace in the perfection of human nature. It is not Jesus' "divinity" that causes problems for historians, but the grace which perfects his humanity. Aquinas provides vital resources for interrogating these issues critically, and his approach offers more precise conceptual tools than those currently employed in the literature. For Thomas, Christ possessed divine knowledge and three modes of human knowledge: acquired knowledge, prophetic knowledge, and the apocalyptic vision of God. By means of his acquired knowledge, Jesus was formed and shaped by his environment that he might teach divine things in a *human* way. His infused and beatific knowledge were instrumental in the unity of his personhood, such that his genuinely human words and actions were those of none other than the divine Word, they enabled him to teach *divine* things in a human way, and they were instrumental in bringing humanity to salvation. This theological framework coordinates the insights of various modes of inquiry, allowing history, doctrine, and ontology to speak coherently to the identity of Christ, and pointing us continually back to a historical encounter with Jesus of Nazareth.

BIBLIOGRAPHY

For works of Thomas Aquinas, see table on page x.

Adam, A. K. M. "Why Historical Criticism Can't Protect Christological Orthodoxy: Reflections on Docetism, Käsemann, and Christology." In *Faithful Interpretation: Reading the Bible in a Postmodern World*. Edited by A. K. M. Adam, 37–56. Minneapolis, MN: Fortress, 2006.

Adams, Marilyn McCord. *What Sort of Human Nature? Medieval Philosophy and the Systematics of Christology*. The Aquinas Lecture, 1999. Milwaukee, MN: Marquette University Press, 1999.

Adams, Samuel V. *The Reality of God and Historical Method: Apocalyptic Theology in Conversation with N. T. Wright*. Downers Grove, IL: InterVarsity, 2015.

Aland, Barbara and Johannes Karavidopoulos Kurt, Carlo M. Martini, and Bruce M. Metzger, eds. *Novum Testamentum Graece*. 28th revised edition (NA28). Stuttgart: Deutsche Bibelgesellschaft, 2012.

Allen, R. Michael. *The Christ's Faith: A Dogmatic Account*. London: T&T Clark, 2009.

Allison Jr., Dale C. *Constructing Jesus: Memory, Imagination, and History*. Grand Rapids, MI: Baker Academic, 2010.

Allison Jr., Dale C. *The Historical Christ and the Theological Jesus*. Grand Rapids, MI: Eerdmans, 2009.

Allison Jr., Dale C. "Jesus & the Victory of Apocalyptic." In *Jesus and the Restoration of Israel: A Critical Assessment of N. T. Wright's Jesus and the Victory of God*. Edited by Carey C. Newman, 126–41. Downers Grove, IL: IVP Academic, 1999.

Allison Jr., Dale C. *Jesus of Nazareth: Millenarian Prophet*. Minneapolis, MN: Fortress Press, 1998.

Allison Jr., Dale C. *The New Moses: A Matthean Typology*. Eugene, OR: Wipf & Stock, 1993.

Allison Jr., Dale C. *The Resurrection of Jesus: Apologetics, Criticism, History*. New York, NY: Bloomsbury, 2021.

Allison Jr., Dale C. "The Secularizing of the Historical Jesus." *Perspectives in Religious Studies* 27 (2000): 135–51.

Altmann, Alexander. "Maimonides and Thomas Aquinas: Natural or Divine Prophecy?" *Association for Jewish Studies Review* 3 (1978): 1–19.

Ambrose. *On the Mystery of the Lord's Incarnation*. ET: *Saint Ambrose: Theological and Dogmatic Works*. Translated by Roy J. Deferrari. Washington, DC: Catholic University of America Press, 1963.

Anderson, Paul N. *The Fourth Gospel and the Quest for Jesus: Modern Foundations Reconsidered*. London: T&T Clark, 2007.

Anderson, Gary A., and Markus Bockmuehl, eds. *Creation Ex Nihilo: Origins, Development, Contemporary Challenges*. Notre Dame, IN: University of Notre Dame Press, 2018.

Anscombe, G. E. M. "Modern Moral Philosophy." *Philosophy* 33 (1958): 1–19.

Anselm. *Proslogion*. Edited by M. J. Charlesworth. Oxford: Oxford University Press, 1965.

Aristotle. *The Complete Works of Aristotle*. The Revised Oxford Translation. Edited by Jonathan Barnes. 2 vols. Princeton, NJ: Princeton University Press, 1984.

Aristotle. *Metaphysics*, in *Complete Works*. The Revised Oxford Translation. Edited by Jonathan Barnes. Princeton, NJ: Princeton University Press, 1991.

Aristotle. *Posterior Analytics*, in *Complete Works*. The Revised Oxford Translation. Edited by Jonathan Barnes. Princeton, NJ: Princeton University Press, 1991.

Ashley, Benedict M. "The Extent of Jesus' Human Knowledge According to the Fourth Gospel." In *Reading John with St. Thomas Aquinas: Theological Exegesis and Speculative Theology*, ed. Matthew Levering and Dauphinais Michael, 241–53. Washington, DC: Catholic University of America Press, 2005.

Aspray, Silvianne. "Employing Genealogies Responsibly in Theology: A Proposal." *Modern Theology* 39:4 (2023): 627–38.

Augustine. *Confessions*. Translated by Henry Chadwick. Oxford: Oxford University Press, 1992.

Augustine. *City of God*. Translated by William S. Babcock. Hyde Park, NY: New City Press, 2013.

Augustine. *De Trinitate*. Translated by Edmund Hill. New York: New City Press, 1991.

Augustine. *The Literal Meaning of Genesis*. Translated by Edmund Hill. The Works of Saint Augustine: A Translation for the 21st Century I/13. Edited by John E. Rotelle. Hyde Park, NY: New City, 2002.

Averroes. *Averrois Cordubensis Commentarium magnum in Aristotelis De anima libros*. Edited by F. Stuart Crawford. Corpus Commentatorioum Averrois in Aristotelem VI-1. Cambridge, MA: The Mediaeval Academy of America, 1953.

Avicenna. *Liber de anima seu sextus de naturalibus*. Edited by S. Van Reit. Louvain-Leiden: E. J. Brill, 1968.

Ayres, Lewis. *Nicaea and Its Legacy: An Approach to Fourth-Century Trinitarian Theology*. Oxford: Oxford University Press, 2004.

Baker, Anthony D. "Convenient Redemption: A Participatory Account of the Atonement." *Modern Theology* 30:1 (2014): 96–113.

Balla, Peter. "What Did Jesus Think about His Approaching Death?" In *Jesus, Mark and Q: The Teaching of Jesus and Its Earliest Records*. Edited by M. Labahn and A. Schmidt, 239–58. London: T&T Clark, 2001.

Baltuta, Elena. "Aquinas on Intellectual Cognition: The Case of Intelligible Species." *Philosophia* 41 (2013): 589–602.

Barber, Kenneth F., ed. *Individuation and Identity in Early Modern Philosophy: Descartes to Kant*. Albany, NY: State University of New York Press, 1994.

Barnes, Corey L. "Albert the Great and Thomas Aquinas on Person, Hypostasis and Hypostatic Union." *The Thomist* 72 (2008): 107–46.

Barnes, Corey L. *Christ's Two Wills in Scholastic Thought: The Christology of Aquinas and Its Historical Contexts*. Toronto: Pontifical Institute of Medieval Studies, 2012.

Barnes, Jonathan, ed. *The Complete Works of Aristotle*. The Revised Oxford Translation. 2 vols. Princeton, NJ: Princeton University Press, 1984.

Barth, Karl. *Church Dogmatics* 3/2. Translated by Geoffrey W. Bromiley and Thomas F. Torrance. Edinburgh: T&T Clark, 1960.

Barth, Karl. *Dogmatik im Grundriß*. Zurich: Evangelischer Verlag, 1947.

Barth, Karl. *Erklärung Des Philipperbriefes*. 6th ed., 1947. ET: *The Epistle to the Philippians*. Translated by James W. Leitch. London: SCM, 1962.

Barth, Karl. "Gospel and Law." In *Community, State, and Church: Three Essays*. Garden City, NY: Anchor Books, 1960.

Bauckham, Richard. *Jesus and the God of Israel: God Crucified and Other Studies on the New Testament's Christology of Divine Identity*. Grand Rapids, MI: Eerdmans, 2008.

Bauer, D. R. "Son of David." In *Dictionary of Jesus and the Gospels*. Edited by Joel B. Green, Scot McKnight, and I. Howard Marshall, 766–9. Leicester: InterVarsity, 1992.

Bauer, D. R. *The Testimony of the Beloved Disciple: Narrative, History, and Theology in the Gospel of John*. Grand Rapids, MI: Eerdmans, 2007.

Bauerschmidt, Frederick Christian. *Thomas Aquinas: Faith, Reason, and Following Christ*. Oxford: Oxford University Press, 2013.

Baym, Nina. *Norton Anthology of American Literature*. Vol. 2: *1865 to the Present*. London: W. W. Norton, 2008.

Baynes, Leslie A. "Jesus the Revealer and the Revealed." In *The Jewish Apocalyptic Tradition and the Shaping of New Testament Thought*. Edited by Benjamin E. Reynolds and Loren T. Stuckenbruck, 15–30. Minneapolis, MN: Fortress Press, 2017.

Bazán, Carlos. "The Human Soul: Form *and* Substance? Thomas Aquinas' Critique of Eclectic Aristotelianism." *Archives d'Historie Doctrinale et Littéraire du Moyen Age* 64 (1997): 95–126.

Beale, G. K. *The Book of Revelation: A Commentary on the Greek Text*. NIGTC. Grand Rapids, MI: Eerdmans, 1999.

Becker, Jürgen. *Jesus of Nazareth*. Translated by James E. Crouch. New York: De Gruyter, 1998.

Behr, John, ed. *The Case against Diodore and Theodore: Texts and Their Contexts*. Oxford Early Christian Texts. Oxford: Oxford University Press, 2011.

Beiser, Frederick C. *The German Historicist Tradition*. Oxford: Oxford University Press, 2011.

Berceville, Gilles. "Le sacerdoce du Christ dans le *Commentaire de l'Épître aux Hébreux* de saint Thomas d'Aquin." *Revue Thomiste* 99 (1999): 143–58.

Bieler, Martin. "The Theological Importance of a Philosophy of Being." In *Reason and the Reasons of Faith*. Edited by Paul J. Griffiths and Reinhard Hütter, 295–326. London: T&T Clark International, 2005.

Bird, Michael F. *Are You the One Who Is to Come? The Historical Jesus and the Messianic Question*. Grand Rapids, MI: Baker Academic, 2009.

Bird, Michael F., and Preston Sprinkle, eds. *The Faith of Jesus Christ: Exegetical, Biblical, and Theological Studies*. Grand Rapids, MI: Baker Academic, 2009.

Bird, Michael F., and Craig A. Evans, eds. *How God Became Jesus: The Real Origins of Belief in Jesus' Divine Nature*. Grand Rapids, MI: Zondervan, 2014.

Blenkinsopp, Joseph. *A History of Prophecy in Israel*. Revised edition. London: Westminster John Knox, 1996.

Blondel, Maurice. *The Letter on Apologetics & History and Dogma*. Translated by Alexander Dru and Illtyd Trethowan. Grand Rapids, MI: Eerdmans, 1994.

Blowers, Paul M. *Drama of the Divine Economy: Creator and Creation in Early Christian Theology and Piety*. Oxford: Oxford University Press, 2012.

Bockmuehl, Markus. "Creatio Ex Nihilo in Palestinian Judaism and Early Christianity." *Scottish Journal of Theology* 65 (2012): 253–70.

Bockmuehl, Markus. *Revelation and Mystery in Ancient Judaism and Pauline Christianity*. Tübingen: Mohr Siebeck, 1990.

Boersma, Hans. *Heavenly Participation: The Weaving of a Sacramental Tapestry*. Grand Rapids, MI: Eerdmans, 2011.

Boersma, Hans. *Nouvelle Théologie & Sacramental Ontology: A Return to Mystery*. Oxford: Oxford University Press, 2009.

Boersma, Hans. *Scripture as Real Presence: Sacramental Exegesis in the Early Church.* Grand Rapids, MI: Baker Academic, 2017.

Boersma, Hans. *Seeing God: The Beatific Vision in Christian Tradition.* Grand Rapids, MI: Eerdmans, 2018.

Boethius. *The Consolation of Philosophy.* Translated by S. J. Tester. LCL 74. Cambridge, MA: Harvard University Press, 1973.

Boethius. *Contra Eutychen* in *Theological Tractates and the Consolation of Philosophy.* Edited by Jeffrey Henderson. Translated by H. F. Stewart, E. K. Rand, and S. J. Tester. LCL 74. Cambridge, MA: Harvard University Press, 1973.

Boland, Vivian. *Ideas in God According to Saint Thomas Aquinas.* Leiden: Brill, 1996.

Bond, Helen K. *The Historical Jesus: A Guide for the Perplexed.* London: T&T Clark, 2012.

Bonino, Serge-Thomas. "Charisms, Forms, and States of Life (IIa IIae, qq. 171–189)." In *The Ethics of Aquinas.* Edited by Stephen J. Pope, 340–52. Washington, DC: Georgetown, 2002.

"Book of Enoch." In *The Apocrypha and Pseudepigrapha of the Old Testament.* Vol. 1: *The Apocrypha.* Edited by R. H. Charles. Oxford: Clarendon Press, 1963.

Borg, Marcus J. "Portraits of Jesus." In *The Search for Jesus: Modern Scholarship Looks at the Gospels.* Edited by Hershel Shanks, 83–108. Washington, DC: Biblical Archaeology Society, 1994.

Borg, Marcus J. *Jesus a New Vision: Spirit, Culture, and the Life of Discipleship.* San Francisco, CA: HarperSanFrancisco, 1987.

Borg, Marcus J. *Jesus in Contemporary Scholarship.* Valley Forge, PA: Trinity Press International, 1994.

Boring, M. E. "Prophecy (Early Christian)." In *Anchor Bible Dictionary.* Edited by David N. Freedman, 5:495–502. 6 vols. New York: Doubleday, 1992.

Boring, M. E. *Sayings of the Risen Jesus: Christian Prophecy in the Synoptic Tradition.* Cambridge: Cambridge University Press, 1982.

Bostock, D. Gerald. "Jesus as the New Elisha." *Expository Times* 92 (1980): 39–41.

Bower, Jeffrey E., and Susan Brower-Toland. "Aquinas on Mental Representation: Concepts and Intentionality." *Philosophical Review* 117 (2008): 193–243.

Boyle, John F. "The Twofold Division of St. Thomas's Christology in the *Tertia Pars*." *The Thomist* 60 (July 1996): 439–47.

Braine, David. *The Human Person: Animal and Spirit.* Notre Dame, IN: University of Notre Dame Press, 1994.

Brodie, Thomas L. "Jesus as the New Elisha: Cracking the Code." *Expository Times* 93 (1981): 39–42.

Brown, Colin. *Dictionary of Jesus and the Gospels.* Downers Grove, IL: InterVarsity Press, 1992.

Brown, Colin. "Historical Jesus, Quest Of." In *Dictionary of Jesus and the Gospels.* Edited by Joel Green, Scot McKnight, and I. Howard Marshall, 326. Downers Grove, IL: InterVarsity Press, 1992.

Brown, Colin. *Jesus in European Protestant Thought: 1178–1860.* Studies in Historical Theology 1, edited by David C. Steinmetz. Durham, NC: Labyrinth Press, 1985.

Brown, David. "'Necessary' and 'Fitting' Reasons in Christian Theology." In *The Rationality of Religious Belief: Essays in Honour of Basil Mitchell.* Edited by William J. Abraham and Steven W. Holtzer, 211–30. Oxford: Clarendon Press, 1987.

Brown, Raymond E. "Did Jesus Know He Was God?" *Biblical Theology Bulletin* 15 [April 1985]: 74–9.

Brown, Raymond E. "Jesus and Elisha." *Perspective* 12 (1971): 85–104.

Brown, Raymond E. *Jesus God and Man: Modern Biblical Reflections*. London: Geoffrey Chapman, 1968.

Brown, Raymond E. *Introduction to New Testament Christology*. New York: Paulist Press, 1994.

Brox, Norbert. "'Doketismus'—Eine Problemanzeige." *Zeitschrift für Kirchengeschichte* 95 (1984): 301–14.

Bullard, Collin Blake. *Jesus and the Thoughts of Many Hearts: Implicit Christology and Jesus' Knowledge in the Gospel of Luke*. Edited by Chris Keith. London: T&T Clark, 2015.

Bultmann, Rudolf. "The Christological Confession of the World Council of Churches." In *Essays: Philosophical and Theological*. Translated by James C. G. Greig, 273–90. London: SCM Press, 1955.

Bultmann, Rudolf. "The Problem of Natural Theology." In *Faith and Understanding: Collected Essays*, 313–31. SCM Press, 1969,

Bultmann, Rudolf. *Jesus and the Word*. New York, NY: Scribner's, 1958 (1926).

Bultmann, Rudolf. *Kerygma and Mythos*. Edited by Hans Werner Bartsch. Second edition. Hamburg: Reich, 1951.

Bultmann, Rudolf. *New Testament and Mythology and Other Basic Writings*. Edited and translated by Shubert M. Ogden. Philadelphia, PA: Fortress Press, 1984.

Bultmann, Rudolf. *The Gospel of John: A Commentary*. Oxford: Blackwell, 1971.

Bultmann, Rudolf. *The History of the Synoptic Tradition*. Translated by John Marsh. New York: Harper & Row, 1963.

Burkett, Delbert. *The Son of Man Debate: A History and Evaluation*. Cambridge: Cambridge University Press, 1999.

Burrell, David. "The Act of Creation with Its Theological Consequences." In *Creation and the God of Abraham*. Edited by David B. Burrell, Carlo Cogliati, Janet M. Soskice, and William R. Stoeger, 40–52. Cambridge: Cambrige University Press, 2010.

Burrell, David. *Analogy and Philosophical Language*. New Haven, CT: Yale, 1973.

Burrell, David, Carlo Cogliati, Janet M. Soskice, and William R. Stoeger, eds. *Creation and the God of Abraham*. Cambridge: Cambridge University Press, 2010.

Bynum, Caroline Walker. "Material Continuity, Personal Survival, and the Resurrection of the Body: A Scholastic Discussion in its Medieval and Modern Contexts." In *Fragmentation and Redemption: Essays on Gender and the Human Body in Medieval Religion*. Edited by Caroline Walker Bynum, 239–97. New York: Urzone Publishers, 1991.

Bynum, Caroline Walker. *The Resurrection of the Body in Western Christianity, 200–1336*. New York: Columbia University Press, 1995.

Caird, G. B. *New Testament Theology*. Oxford: Clarendon, 1995.

Cajetan. *De Nominum Analogia*. Edited by P. N. Zammit and P. H. Hering. Rome: Angelicum, 1951. ET: *The Analogy of Names and the Concept of Being*. Pittsburgh, PA: Duquesne University Press, 1953.

Calvin, John. *Commentary on a Harmony of the Evangelists: Matthew, Mark, and Luke*. Translated by William Pringle. Edinburgh: Calvin Translation Society, 1846.

Calvin, John. *Institutes of the Christian Religion*. Translated by F. Battles. Philadelphia, PA: Westminster Press, 1960.

Campbell, Douglas A. *The Deliverance of God: An Apocalyptic Rereading of Justification in Paul*. Grand Rapids, MI: Eerdmans, 2009.

Capps, Donald. *Jesus: A Psychological Biography*. Nashville, TN: Chalice Press, 2000.

Carmody, J. M., and T. E. Clark, eds. *Sources of Christian Theology, Christ and His Mission*. Westminster, MD: The Newman Press, 1966.

Carmody, J. M., and T. E. Clarke, eds. *Word and Redeemer*. Glen Rock, NJ: Paulist Press, 1960.

Carter, J. Kameron. *Race: A Theological Account*. Oxford: Oxford University Press, 2008.

Casey, Maurice. *Jesus of Nazareth: An Independent Historian's Account of His Life and Teaching*. New York, NY: T&T Clark, 2010.

Casey, Maurice. *Son of Man: The Interpretation and Influence of Daniel 7*. London: SPCK, 1979.

Cessario, Romanus. "Incarnate Wisdom and the Immediacy of Christ's Salvific Knowledge." In *Atti Del IX Congresso Tomistico Internazionale*, 334–40. Vatican City: Libreria Editrice Vaticana, 1991.

Chang, Ha-Joon. *23 Things They Don't Tell You About Capitalism*. London: Penguin, 2011.

Childs, Hal. *The Myth of the Historical Jesus and the Evolution of Consciousness*. Edited by Mark Allan Powell. Atlanta, GA: Society of Biblical Literature, 2000.

Clarke, W. Norris. "Causality and Time." In *The Creative Retrieval of Saint Thomas Aquinas: Essays in Thomistic Philosophy, New and Old*, 27–38. New York: Fordham University Press, 2009.

Clarke, W. Norris. "The Meaning of Participation in St. Thomas." *Proceedings of the American Catholic Philosophical Association* 26 (1952): 147–57.

Clarke, W. Norris. "What Cannot Be Said in Saint Thomas's Essence-Existence Doctrine." In *The Creative Retrieval of Saint Thomas Aquinas: Essays in Thomistic Philosophy, New and Old*, 117–31. New York: Fordham University Press, 2009.

Clarke, W. Norris. *The One and the Many: A Contemporary Thomistic Metaphysics*. Notre Dame, IN: University of Notre Dame Press, 2001.

Clarke, W. Norris. "The Limitation of Act by Potency." In *Explorations in Metaphysics: Being, God, Persons*, 65–88. Notre Dame, IN: University of Notre Dame Press, 1994.

Clements, R. E. "Isaiah 53 and the Restoration of Israel." In *Jesus and the Suffering Servant: Isaiah 53 and Christian Christian Origins*. Edited by William H. Bellinger Jr. and William R. Farmer, 39–54. Harrisburg, PA: Trinity Press International, 1998.

Coakley, Sarah. "The Person of Christ." In *The Cambridge Companion to the Summa Theologiae*. Edited by Philip McCosker and Denys Turner, 222–39. Cambridge: Cambridge University Press, 2016.

Colish, Marcia L. "Christological Nihilianism in the Second Half of the Twelfth Century." *Recherches de Théologie et Philosophie Médiévales* 63 (1996): 146–55.

Collingwood, R. G. *The Idea of History*. Oxford: Oxford University Press, 1971 [1946].

Collins, John J. "Introduction: Towards the Morphology of a Genre." *Semeia* 14 (1979): 1–20.

Collins, John J. "What Is Apocalyptic Literature?" In *The Oxford Handbook of Apocalyptic Literature*. Edited by John J. Collins, 1–17. Oxford: Oxford University Press, 2014.

Collins, John J. *The Apocalyptic Imagination: An Introduction to Jewish Apocalyptic Literature*. Second edition. Grand Rapids, MI: Eerdmans, 1998.

Cook, Stephen L. "Apocalyptic Prophecy." In *The Oxford Handbook of Apocalyptic Literature*. Edited by John J. Collins, 19–33. Oxford: Oxford University Press, 2014.

Crawford, F. Stuart, ed. Averrois Cordubensis *Commentarium magnum in Aristotelis De anima libros*. Corpus Commentatorioum Averrois in Aristotelem Volume VI-1. Cambridge, MA: The Mediaeval Academy of America, 1953.

Crossan, John Dominic. "Jesus at 2000 Debate." HarperSanFrancisco. Last modified 1996. Accessed April 12, 2018. http://www.markgoodacre.org/xtalk/debate.html.

Crossan, John Dominic. "Straining Gnats, Swallowing Camels: A Review of *Who Was Jesus?* By N. T. Wright." *Bible Review* 9 (August 1993): 10–11.

Crossan, John Dominic. "What Victory? What God? A Review Debate with N. T. Wright on Jesus and the Victory of God." *Scottish Journal of Theology* 50 (1997): 345–58.

Crossan, John Dominic. *The Historical Jesus: The Life of a Mediterranean Jewish Peasant*. San Francisco, CA: Harper Collins, 1991.

Crowe, Frederick E. "Eschaton and Worldly Mission in the Mind and Heart of Christ." In *Appropriating the Lonergan Idea*, 193–234. Toronto: University of Toronto Press, 2006.

Crowley, Paul G. "*Instrumentum Divinitatis* in Thomas Aquinas: Recovering the Divinity of Christ." *Theological Studies* 52 (1991): 451–75.

Cudworth, Ralph. *The True Intellectual System of the Universe Wherein all the Reason and Philosophy of Atheism is Confuted and Its Impossibility Demonstrated*. London: J. F. Dove, 1820.

Cyril of Alexandria. *Thesaurus on the Holy and Consubstantial Trinity*. In *Patrologia Graeca*. Edited by Jacques-Paul Minge, vol. 75. Paris, Imprimerie Catholique, 1857–66.

Daley, Brian E. "'A Richer Union': Leontius of Byzantium and the Relationship of Human and Divine in Christ." *Studia Patristica* 24 (1993): 239–65.

Daley, Brian E. "Divine Transcendence and Human Transformation: Gregory of Nyssa's Anti-Apollinarian Christology." *Modern Theology* 18 (2002): 497–506.

Dauphinais, Michael. "Christ the Teacher: The Pedagogy of the Incarnation According to Saint Thomas Aquinas." PhD Diss., University of Notre Dame, 2000.

Davison, Andrew. "'He Fathers-Forth Whose Beauty Is Past Change,' but 'Who Knows How?': Evolution and Divine Exemplarity." *Nova et Vetera*, English edition, 16 (2018): 1067–1102.

Davison, Andrew. "Christian Systematic Theology and Life Elsewhere in the Universe: A Study in Suitability." *Theology and Science* 16 (2018): 447–61.

Davison, Andrew. "Looking Back toward the Origin: Scientific Cosmology as Creation Ex Nihilo Considered 'from the Inside.'" In *Creatio Ex Nihilo: Origins and Contemporary Significance*. Edited by Markus Bockmuehl and Gary Anderson, 367–89. Notre Dame, IN: University of Notre Dame Press, 2017.

Davison, Andrew. *Participation in God: A Study in Christian Doctrine and Metaphysics*. Cambridge: Cambridge University Press, 2019.

De Anna, Gabriele. "Aquinas on Sensible Forms and Semimaterialism." *Review of Metaphysics* 54 (2000): 43–63.

De Haan, Daniel. "Hylomorphic Animalism, Emergentism, and the Challenge of the New Mechanist Philosophy of Neuroscience." *Scientia et Fides* 5 (2017): 9–38.

De Haan, Daniel. "Linguistic Apprehension as Incidental Sensation in Thomas Aquinas." *Proceedings of the American Catholic Philosophical Association* 84 (2011): 179–96.

De Haan, Daniel. "Perception and the *Vis Cogitativa*: A Thomistic Analysis of Aspectual, Actional, and Affectional Percepts." *American Catholic Philosophical Quarterly* 88 (2014): 397–437.

De Libera, Alain. "When did the Modern Subject Emerge?" *American Catholic Philosophical Quarterly*, 82 [2008]: 181–220.

de Lubac, Henri. *Surnaturel: Études historiques*. Paris: Aubier, 1946.

Deferrari, Roy J., trans. *Saint Ambrose: Theological and Dogmatic Works*. Washington, DC: Catholic University of America Press, 1963.

Deferrari, Roy J. *A Lexicon of Saint Thomas Aqinas Based on the Summa Theologica and Selected Passages of His Other Works*. Washington, DC: Catholic University of America Press, 1948.

Deloria Jr., Vine. *God Is Red: A Native View of Religion*. Golden, CO: Fulcrum, 2003.

Denton Jr., Donald L. *Historiography and Hermeneutics in Jesus Studies: An Examination of the Work of John Dominic Crossan and Ben F. Meyer*. Journal for the Study of the Historical Jesus Supplement Series 262. London: T&T Clark, 2004.

Denzinger, Heinrich, Peter Hünermann, Robert Fastiggi, and Anne Englund Nash. *Enchiridion symbolorum definitionum et declarationem de rebus fidei et morum, Compendium of Creeds, Definitions and Declarations on Matters of Faith and Morals*. San Francisco, CA: Ignatius, 2012.

Deryck Chalenor Barson. *A Divine Person in the Theology of Thomas Aquinas*. PhD Diss., Westminster Theological Seminary, 2019.

Dewan, Lawrence. "St. Thomas and Analogy: The Logician and the Metaphysician." In *Form and Being: Studies in Thomistic Metaphysics*, 81–95. Washington, DC: Catholic University of America Press, 2006.

Dodd, C. H. *According to the Scriptures: The Sub-Structure of New Testament Theology*. London: Collins, 1965 [1952].

Dodd, C. H. *The Parables of the Kingdom*. Revised edition. London: Nisbet, 1936.

Dodds, E. R. *Proclus: The Elements of Theology*. Oxford: Oxford University Press, 1963 [1933].

Doolan, Gregory T. "Aquinas on Esse Subsistens and the Third Mode of Participation." *The Thomist* 82 (2018): 611–42.

Doolan, Gregory T. *Aquinas on the Divine Ideas as Exemplar Causes*. Washington, DC: Catholic University of America Press, 2008.

Draper, Paul R. "God, Science, and Naturalism." In *The Oxford Handbook of Philosophy of Religion*. Edited by William J. Wainwright, 272–303. Oxford: Oxford University Press, 2005.

Dreyfus, François. *Did Jesus Know He Was God?* Translated by Michael J. Wren. Chicago, IL: Franciscan Herald Press, 1984.

Driedger Hesslein, Kayko. *Dual Citizenship: Two-Natures Christologies and the Jewish Jesus*. London: T&T Clark, 2015.

Dunn, James D. G., and James P. Mackey. *New Testament Theology in Dialogue*. London: SPCK, 1987.

Dunn, James D. G. *The Christ and the Spirit*. Vol. 1: *Christology*. Grand Rapids, MI: Eerdmans, 1998.

Dunn, James D. G. *Christology in the Making*. Philadelphia, PA: Westminster, 1980.

Dunn, James D. G. *Jesus and the Spirit*. London: SCM, 1975.

Dunn, James D. G. *Jesus Remembered: Christianity in the Making*. Vol. 1. Grand Rapids, MI: Eerdmans, 2003.

Duns Scotus, John. *The Quodlibetal Questions*. Translated by Felix Alluntis and Allan B. Wolter. Washington, DC: The Catholic University of America Press, 1975.

Durand, Alexandre. "La science du Christ." *Nouvelle Revue Theologique* 71 (1949): 497–503.

Eastman, Susan. "Participation in Christ." In *The Oxford Handbook of Pauline Studies*. Edited by Matthew V. Novenson and R. Barry Matlock, 441–54. Oxford: Oxford University Press, 2014.

Ebeling, Gerhard. *Word and Faith*. Translated by James W. Leitch. Philadelphia, PA: Fortress Press, 1963.

Edwards, Jonathan. "Happiness of Heaven is Progressive." In *The Works of Jonathan Edwards*, vol. 18, 427–34. New Haven, CT: Yale University Press, 1977–2009. Online: edwards.yale.edu.

Ehrman, Bart D. *How Jesus Became God: The Exaltation of a Jewish Preacher from Galilee*. New York: HarperOne, 2014.

Ehrman, Bart D. *Jesus: Apocalyptic Prophet of the New Millenium*. Oxford: Oxford University Press, 1999.

Ehrman, Bart D. *Misquoting Jesus: The Story Behind Who Changed the Bible and Why*. New York: HarperCollins, 2007.

Ehrman, Bart D. *The Orthodox Corruption of Scripture: The Effect of Early Christological Controversies on the Text of the New Testament*. Oxford: Oxford University Press, 1993.

Eklund, Rebekah. "From 'Hosanna!' to 'Crucify!': The Fickle Crowds in the Four Gospels." *Bulletin for Biblical Research* 26:1 (2016): 21–42.

Eklund, Rebekah. *Jesus Wept: The Significance of Jesus' Laments in the New Testament*. London: Bloomsbury T&T Clark, 2015.

Emery, Gilles. "The Personal Mode of Trinitarian Action in Saint Thomas Aquinas." *The Thomist* 69 (2005): 31–77.

Emery, Gilles. *The Trinitarian Theology of Thomas Aquinas*. Oxford: Oxford University Press, 2007.

Emery, Gilles. "Trinity and Creation." In *The Theology of Thomas Aquinas*. Edited by Rik Van Nieuwenhove and Joseph Wawrykow, 58–76. Notre Dame, IN: University of Notre Dame Press, 2010.

Emery, John. "A Christology of Communication: Christ's Charity According to Thomas Aquinas." Unpublished PhD Diss., Fribourg, Switzerland, 2017.

Enns, Peter. *Inspiration and Incarnation: Evangelicals and the Problem of the Old Testament*. Grand Rapids, MI: Baker, 2005.

Ernst, M. O., and H. H. Bülthoff. "Merging the Senses into a Robust Percept." *Trends in Cognitive Sciences* 4 (2004): 162–9.

Eusebius. *The Ecclesiastical History of Eusebius*. Translated by C. F. Cruse. London: George Bell and Sons, 1908.

Evans, C. Stephen. "Methodological Naturalism in Historical Biblical Scholarship." In *Jesus and the Restoration of Israel*. Edited by Carey C. Newman, 180–205. Downers Grove, IL: IVP Academic, 1999.

Evans, C. Stephen. "Separable Souls: Dualism, Selfhood and the Possibility of Life After Death." *Christian Scholars' Review* 34:3 (2005): 327–40.

Evans, C. Stephen, ed. *Exploring Kenotic Christology: The Self-Emptying of God*. Oxford: Oxford University Press, 2006.

Evans, Craig A. *Life of Jesus Research: An Annotated Bibliography*. Leiden: Brill, 1996.

Evans, Craig A. "Prophet, Sage, Healer, Messiah, and Martyr: Types and Identities of Jesus." In *Handbook for the Study of the Historical Jesus*. Edited by Tom Holmén and Stanley E. Porter, 1217–43. Leiden: Brill, 2011.

Fabro, Cornelio. "Actualite et originalite de l'"esse' thomiste." *Revue Thomiste* 56 (1956): 240–70.

Fabro, Cornelio. "The Intensive Hermeneutics of Thomistic Philosophy: The Notion of Participation." Translated by B. M. Bonansea. *The Review of Metaphysics* 27 (1974): 449–91.

Fabro, Cornelio. *La Nozione Metafisica Di Partecipazione: Secondo San Tommaso D'aquino*. Milan: Società Editrice, 1939.

Fabro, Cornelios. *Partecipazione E Causalità Secondo S. Tommaso D'aquino*. Turin: Società Editrice Internazionale, 1960.

Farrer, Austin. *Scripture, Metaphysics, and Poetry: Austin Farrer's* The Glass of Vision *with Critical Commentary*. Edited by Robert MacSwain. Burlington, VT: Ashgate, 2013 [1948].

Fasolt, Constantin. *The Limits of History*. Chicago: University of Chicago Press, 2004.

Fee, Gordon. "The New Testament and Kenosis Christology." In *Exploring Kenotic Christology: The Self-Emptying of God*. Edited by C. Stephen Evans, 25–44. Oxford: Oxford University Press, 2006.

Fee, Gordon. *Paul's Letter to the Philippians*. NICNT. Grand Rapids, MI: Eerdmans, 1995.

Feingold, Lawrence. *The Natural Desire to See God According to St. Thomas Aquinas and His Interpreters*. Ave Maria, FL: Sapientia Press, 2010.

Felton, Henry. *The Resurrection of the Same Numerical Body, and Its Reunion to the Same Soul; Asserted in a Sermon Preached before the University of Oxford, at St. Mary's on Easter-Monday, 1725. In Which Mr. Lock's Notions of Personality and Identity Are Confuted. And the Author of the Naked Gospel is Answered*. Printed at the Theatre and are to be sold by Steph. Fletcher, and Rich. Clements booksellers in Oxford; and Benj. Motte near the Middle Temple-Gate in London, 1725.

Ferrier, Francis. *What Is the Incarnation?* Translated by Edward Sillem. New York: Hawthorn Books, 1962.

Feser, Edward. *Philosophy of Mind: A Beginner's Guide*. Oxford: Oneworld Publications, 2006.

Finlan, Stephen. "Can We Speak of *Theosis* in Paul?" In *Partakers of the Divine Nature: The History and Development of Deification in the Christian Traditions*. Edited by Michael J. Christensen and Jeffrey A. Wittung, 68–80. Cranbury, NJ: Fairleigh Dickinson University Press, 2007.

Fiorenza, Elisabeth Schüssler. *Jesus and the Politics of Interpretation*. New York: Continuum, 2001.

Fitzmyer, Joseph A. *The Gospel According to Luke*. Anchor Bible, 28–28A. Garden City, NY: Doubleday, 1981.

Fletcher-Louis, Crispin H. T. "Jesus as the High Priestly Messiah: Part 1." *Journal of the Study of the Historical Jesus* 4 (2006): 155–75.

Flew, Antony. "Locke and the Problem of Personal Identity." In *Locke and Berkeley: A Collection of Critical Essays*. Edited by C. B. Martin and D. M. Armstrong, 155–78. Garden City, NY: Doubleday, 1968.

Forsyth, P. T. *The Person and Place of Jesus Christ*. London: Independent Press, 1909.

France, R. T. *The Gospel of Mark*. New International Greek Testament Commentary. Grand Rapids, MI: Eerdmans, 2002.

Franks, Christopher A. "The Simplicity of the Living God: Aquinas, Barth, and Some Philosophers." *Modern Theology* 21 (2005): 275–300.

Freddoso, Alfred. "Human Nature, Potency, and the Incarnation." *Faith and Philosophy* 3 (1986): 27–53.

Freddoso, Alfred. "No Room at the Inn: Contemporary Philosophy of Mind Meets Thomistic Philosophical Anthropology." *Acta Philosophica* 24:1 (2015): 15–30.

Funk, Robert. *Honest to Jesus: Jesus for a New Millennium*. New York: Macmillan, 1996.

Gaine, Simon Francis. "The Beatific Vision and the Heavenly Mediation of Christ." *TheoLogica* 2:2 (2018): 116–28.

Gaine, Simon Francis. "Christ's Acquired Knowledge According to Thomas Aquinas: How Aquinas's Philosophy Helped and Hindered his Account." *New Blackfriars* 96 (2015): 255–68.

Gaine, Simon Francis. *Did the Saviour See the Father? Christ, Salvation and the Vision of God*. London: T&T Clark, 2015.

Gaine, Simon Francis. "Is There Still a Place for Christ's Infused Knowledge in Catholic Theology and Exegesis?" *Nova et Vetera*, English edition, 16:2 (2018): 601–15.

Gaine, Simon Francis. "The Veracity of Prophecy and Christ's Knowledge." *New Blackfriars* 98 (2017): 44–62.

Galot, Jean. "Le Christ terrestre et la vision." *Gregorianum* 67 (1986): 429–50.

Galot, Jean. *La Conscience de Jésus*. Paris: Lethielleux, 1971.

Galot, Jean. *La Personne du Christ*. Duculot, 1969. ET: *The Person of Christ: A Theological Insight*. Translated by M. Angeline Bouchard. Rome: Gregorian University Press, 1981.

Garceau, Benoit. *Judicium, Vocabulaire, Sources, Doctrine de Saint Thomas d'Aquin*. Paris: Librairie philosophique J. Vrin, 1968.

Garrigou-Lagrange, Réginald. *Christ the Savior: A Commentary on the Third Part of St Thomas' Theological Summa*. Translated by Bede Rose. St. Louis, MO: B. Herder, 1950.

Garrigou-Lagrange, Réginald. *Our Savior and His Love for Us*. Translated by A. Bouchard. St. Louis, MO: Herder, 1951.

Garrigues, Jean-Miguel. "The 'Natural Grace' of Christ in St. Thomas." In *Surnaturel: A Controversy at the Heart of Twentieth-Century Thomistic Thought*. Edited by Serge-Thomas Bonino. Translated by Robert Williams and Matthew Levering, 103–15. Ave Maria, FL: Sapientia Press, 2009.

Geenen, Gottfried. "The Council of Chalcedon in the Theology of St. Thomas." In *From an Abundant Spring: The Walter Farrell Memorial Volume of "The Thomist"*, 172–217. New York: P. J. Kennedy, 1952.

Geenen, Gottfried. "En marge du Concile de Chalcédonie: Les textes du Quatrième Concile dans les œvres de saint Thomas." *Angelicum* 29 (1952): 43–59.

Geiger, Louis-Bertrand. *La Participation dans la Philosophie de S. Thomas d'Aquin*. Paris: J. Vrin, 1942.

George, Francis Cardinal. *The Difference God Makes: A Catholic Vision of Faith, Communion, and Culture*. New York: Crossroad Publishing Company, 2009.

Giambrone, Anthony. "Scripture as *Scientia Christi*: Three Theses on Jesus' Self-Knowledge and the Future Course of New Testament Christology." *Pro Ecclesia* 25 (2016): 274–90.

Gilson, Étienne. "Causality and Participation." In *Christian Philosophy: An Introduction*. Translated by Armand Maurer, 89–100. Toronto: Pontifical Institute of Mediaeval Studies, 1993.

Gilson, Étienne. *God and Philosophy*. Yale, CT: Yale University Press, 2002 [1941].

Gilson, Étienne. *History of Christian Philosophy in the Middle Ages*. New York: Sheed and Ward, 1955.

Gilson, Étienne. *Le Thomisme*. Sixth edition, 1965. ET: *Thomism: The Philosophy of Thomas Aquinas*. Translated by Laurence K. Shook and Armand Maurer. Toronto: Pontifical Institute of Mediaeval Studies, 2002.

Gilson, Étienne. "L'objet de la Métaphysique selon Duns Scot." *Mediaeval Studies* 10 (1948): 83–4.

Gilson, Étienne. *Methodological Realism: A Handbook for Beginning Realists*. San Francisco, CA: Ignatius, 2011.

Gilson, Étienne. *The Spirit of Mediæval Philosophy*. Translated by A. H. C. Downes. New York: Charles Scribner's Sons, 1940.

Gilson, Étienne. *Thomist Realism and the Critique of Knowledge*. Translated by Mark A. Wauck. San Francisco, CA: Ignatius Press, 1983 [1939].

Glasson, T. F. "Schweitzer's Influence—Blessing or Bane?" *Journal of Theological Studies* 28 (1977): 289–92.

Gleede, Benjamin. *The Development of the Term ἐνυπόστατος from Origen to John of Damascus*. Leiden: Brill, 2012.

Gondreau, Paul. "Anti-Docetism in Aquinas's *Super Ioannem*: St. Thomas as Defender of the Full Humanity of Christ." In *Reading John with St. Thomas Aquinas: Theological Exegesis and Speculative Theology*. Edited by Matthew Levering and Michael Dauphinais, 254–76. Washington, DC: Catholic University of America Press, 2005.

Gondreau, Paul. "The Humanity of Christ, the Incarnate Word." In *The Theology of Thomas Aquinas*. Edited by Rik Van Nieuwenhove and Joseph Wawrykow, 252–76. Notre Dame, IN: University of Notre Dame Press, 2005.

Gondreau, Paul. *The Passions of Christ's Soul in the Theology of St. Thomas Aquinas*. Münster: Aschendorff, 2002.

Gordon, James R. *The Holy One in Our Midst: An Essay on the Flesh of Christ*. Minneapolis: Fortress Press, 2016.

Goris, Harm. "The Angelic Doctor and Angelic Speech: The Development of Thomas Aquinas's Thought on How Angels Communicate." *Medieval Philosophy and Theology* 11 (2003): 87–105.

Goris, Harm. *Free Creatures of an Eternal God: Thomas Aquinas on God's Foreknowledge*. Leuven: Peeters, 1996.

Gorman, Michael. *Aquinas on the Metaphysics of the Hypostatic Union*. Cambridge: Cambridge University Press, 2017.

Gorman, Michael. "Uses of the Person–Nature Distinction in Thomas's Christology." *Recherches de Théologie et Philosophie Médiévales* 67 (2000): 58–79.

Gorman, Michael J. *Inhabiting the Cruciform God*. Grand Rapids, MI: Eerdmans, 2009.

Grasso, Kevin. "A Linguistic Analysis of πίστις χριστοῦ: The Case for the Third View." *Journal for the Study of the New Testament* 43 (2020): 108–44.

Green, Joel B. *The Gospel of Luke*. New International Commentary on the New Testament. Grand Rapids, MI: Eerdmans, 1997.

Gregory, Brad. *The Unintended Reformation: How a Religious Revolution Secularized Society*. Cambridge, MA: Belknap Press, 2012.

Greimas, Algirdas Julien, and Joseph Courtés. "The Cognitive Dimension of Narrative Discourse." *New Literary History* 8 (1976): 433–47.

Grillmeier, Aloys. *Christ in Christian Tradition*. Vol. 1. Translated by John Boweden. Atlanta, GA: John Knox Press, 1965.

Grillmeier, Aloys, and Theresia Hainthaler. *Christ in Christian Tradition*. Vol. 2/2. Translated by John Cawte and Pauline Allen. London: Mowbray, 1995.

Guite, Malcolm. *Waiting on the Word: A Poem a Day for Advent, Christmas and Epiphany*. Norwich: Canterbury Press, 2015.

Gumerlock, Francis X. "Mark 13:32 and Christ's Supposed Ignorance: Four Patristic Solutions." *Trinity Journal* 28 (2007): 205–13.

Gutwenger, Engelbert. "The Problem of Christ's Knowledge." In *Who Is Jesus of Nazareth: Dogma*. Edited by Edward Schillebeeckx, 91–105. New York: Paulist Press, 1966.

Hagner, Donald A. "An Analysis of Recent 'Historical Jesus' Studies." In *Religious Diversity in the Greco-Roman World: A Survey of Recent Scholarship*. Edited by Dan Cohn-Sherbok and John M. Court, 81–106. The Biblical Seminar 79. Sheffield: Sheffield Academic Press, 2001.

Haight, Roger. *Jesus Symbol of God*. New York: Orbis Books, 1999.

Haldane, John. "Aquinas and the Active Intellect." *Philosophy* 67 (1992): 199–210.

Haldane, John. "The Metaphysics of Intellect(ion)." *Proceedings of the ACPA* 80 (2007): 39–55.

Hanson, A. T. "Two Consciousnesses: The Modern Version of Chalcedon." *Scottish Journal of Theology* 37 (1984): 471–83.

Hardy, Edward R., ed. *The Christology of the Later Fathers*. Louisville, KY: Westminster John Knox, 2006 [1954].

Harnack, Adolf von. *What Is Christianity?* Translated by Thomas Baily Saunders. Philadelphia, PA: Fortress Press, 1957 [1900].

Hart, David Bentley. *That All Shall Be Saved*. New Haven, CT: Yale University Press, 2019.

Hart, Trevor. *In Him Was Life: The Person and Work of Christ*. Waco, TX: Baylor University Press, 2019.

Hartman, Lars. *Prophecy Interpreted: The Formation of Some Jewish Apocalyptic Texts and of the Eschatological Discourse Mark 13 Par*. Coniectanea Biblical Neotestamentica 1. Uppsala: Gleerup, 1966.

Harvey, Anthony E. *Jesus and the Constraints of History: The Bampton Lectures 1980*. London: Duckworth, 1982.

Hays, Christopher M. In collaboration with Brandon Gallagher, Julia S. Konstantinovsky, Richard J. Ounsworth OP, and C. A. Strine. *When the Son of Man Didn't Come: A Constructive Proposal on the Delay of the Parousia*. Minneapolis, MN: Fortress, 2016.

Hays, Richard B. "Knowing Jesus: Story, History and the Question of Truth." In *Jesus, Paul and the People of God: A Theological Dialogue with N. T. Wright*. Edited by Nicholas Perrin and Richard B. Hays, 41–61. Downers Grove, IL: IVP Academic, 2011.

Healy, Nicholas J. "*Simul Viator et Comprehensor*: The Filial Mode of Christ's Knowledge." *Nova Et Vetera* 11:2 (2013): 341–55.

Hengel, Martin. *Studies in Early Christology*. London: T&T Clark, 1995.

Heringer, Seth. "Worlds Colliding: A Theological Critique of the Historical Method." PhD Diss., Fuller Theological Seminary, 2016. Published as *Uniting History and Theology: A Theological Critique of the Historical Method*. Minneapolis, MN: Lexington Books/Fortress Academic, 2018.

Herzog, W. R. II. *Prophet and Teacher: An Introduction to the Historical Jesus*. Louisville, KY: Westminster John Knox, 2005.

Hochschild, Joshua P. *The Semantics of Analogy: Rereading Cajetan's De Nominum Analogia*. Notre Dame, IN: University of Notre Dame Press, 2010.

Hodge, Charles. *Systematic Theology*. Abridged edition. Grand Rapids, MI: Baker, 1988.

Hofer. Andrew, "Dionysian Elements in Thomas Aquinas's Christology: A Case of the Authority and Ambiguity of Pseudo-Dionysius." *The Thomist* 72 (2008): 409–42.

Hollenbach, Paul. "The Historical Jesus Question in North America Today." *Biblical Theological Bulletin* 19 (1989): 11–22.

Hooker, Morna D. "Christology and Methodology." *New Testament Studies* 17 (1970): 480–7.

Hooker, Morna D. "ΠΙΣΠΙΣ ΧΡΙΣΤΟΥ." *New Testament Studies* 35 (1989): 321–42.

Hooker, Morna D. *The Signs of a Prophet: The Prophetic Actions of Jesus*. Harrisburg: Trinity Press International, 1997.

Howard, Thomas Albert. *Protestant Theology and the Making of the Modern German University*. Oxford: Oxford University Press, 2006.

Howard, Thomas Albert. *Religion and the Rise of Historicism: W. M. L. de Wette, Jacob Burckhardt, and the Theological Origins of Nineteenth-Century Historical Consciousness.* Cambridge: Cambridge University Press, 2000.

Howard, V. "Did Jesus Speak About His Own Death?" *Catholic Biblical Quarterly* 39 (1997): 515–27.

Hume, David. *A Treatise of Human Nature.* Edited by L. A. Selby-Bigge. Oxford: Oxford University Press, 1888.

Hütter, Reinhard. "Attending to the Wisdom of God—from Effect to Cause, from Creation to God: A Relecture of the Analogy of Being According to Thomas Aquinas." In *The Analogy of Being: Invention of the Antichrist or the Wisdom of God?* Edited by Thomas Joseph White, 209–45. Grand Rapids, MI: Eerdmans, 2011.

Irenaeus of Lyons. *Against Heresies.* In *The Ante-Nicene Fathers.* Edited by Alexander Roberts and James Donaldson. Grand Rapids, MI: Eerdmans, 1953.

Israel, Jonathan I. *A Revolution of the Mind: Radical Enlightenment and the Intellectual Origins of Modern Democracy.* Princeton: Princeton University Press, 2003.

Jenkins, Philip. *The New Anti-Catholicism: The Last Acceptable Prejudice.* Oxford: Oxford University Press, 2003.

Jennings, Willie James. *Acts: A Theological Commentary on the Bible.* Louisville, KY: Westminster John Knox Press, 2017.

Jenson, Robert. *God After God.* Minneapolis, MN: Fortress Press, 1969.

Jerome. *Commentarii in Evangelium Matthei.* In CCSL 77. Edited by D. Hurst and M. Adriaen. Turnhout: Brepols, 1969.

Joas, Hans. *The Sacredness of the Person: A New Genealogy of Human Rights.* Translated by Alex Skinner. Washington, DC: Georgetown University Press, 2013.

John Paul II, "Address of His Holiness Pope John Paul to a Symposium on the Roots of Anti-Judaism." In *Visit to Israel of His Holiness Pope John Paul II.* Jerusalem: Israel Information Center, 2000. Available online at http://www.vatican.va/holy_father/john-paul-ii/speeches/1997/October/documents/hf_jpii_spe_19971013_com-teologica_en.html. Liberia Editrice Vaticana, 1997.

John Milbank, Catherine Pickstock, Graham Ward, eds. *Radical Orthodoxy: A New Theology.* London: Routledge, 1999.

Johnson, Luke Timothy. *The Gospel of Luke.* Sacra Pagina, 3. Collegeville, MN: Liturgical, 1991.

Johnson, Luke Timothy. "A Historiographical Response to Wright's Jesus." In *Jesus and the Restoration of Israel: A Critical Assessment of N.T. Wright's Jesus and the Victory of God.* Edited by Carey C. Newman, 207–24. Downers Grove, IL: InterVarsity, 1999.

Johnson, Luke Timothy. "The Humanity of Jesus: What's at Stake in the Quest for the Historical Jesus?" In *Contested Issues in Christian Origins and the New Testament: Collected Essays.* Supplements to Novum Testamentum 146, 1–28. Leiden: Brill, 2013.

Johnson, Luke Timothy. *The Real Jesus: The Misguided Quest for the Historical Jesus and the Truth of the Traditional Gospels.* San Francisco, CA: HarperSanFrancisco, 1995.

Jüngel, Eberhard. "The Dogmatic Significance of the Question of the Historical Jesus." In *Theological Essays II*, 82–119. London: T&T Clark, 2014.

Jüngel, Eberhard. *God as the Mystery of the World.* London: Bloomsbury, 2013.

Kähler, Martin. *The So-Called Historical Jesus and the Historic Biblical Christ.* Translated by Carl E. Braaten. Philadelphia, PA: Fortress Press, 1964 [1896].

Kant, Immanuel. *Religion Within the Limits of Reason Alone.* Translated by Theodore M. Greene and Hoyt H. Hudson. New York: HarperOne, 2008.

Käsemann, Ernst. "The Beginnings of Christian Theology." *Journal for Theology and the Church* 6 (1969): 17–46.

Käsemann, Ernst. "The Problem of the Historical Jesus." In *Essays on New Testament Themes*. Studies in Biblical Theology, 15–47. London: SCM Press, 1964.

Käsemann, Ernst. *The Testament of Jesus: A Study of the Gospel of John in the Light of Chapter 17*. London: SCM Press, 1968.

Keener, Craig S. *The Historical Jesus of the Gospels*. Grand Rapids, MI: Eerdmans, 2009.

Kemp, Simon, and Garth J. O. Fletcher. "The Medieval Theory of the Inner Senses." *American Journal of Psychology* 106 (1993): 559–76.

Kerr, Fergus. *Theology after Wittgenstein*. London: SPCK, 1997.

Kim, Jaegwon. "The American Origins of Philosophical Naturalism." *Journal of Philosophical Research* (2003): 83–98.

Klima, Gyula. "Aquinas on the Materiality of the Human Soul and the Immateriality of the Human Intellect." *Philosophical Investigations* 32:2 (2009): 163–82.

Klubertanz, George P. *The Philosophy of Human Nature*. Neunkirchen-Seelscheid: Editiones Scholasticae, 2014.

Klubertanz, George P. *St. Thomas Aquinas on Analogy: A Textual Analysis and Systematic Synthesis*. Chicago, IL: Loyola University Press, 1960.

Knox, John. *The Death of Christ: The Cross in New Testament History and Faith*. New York: Abingdon, 1958.

Koen, L. "Partitive Exegesis in Cyril of Alexandria's Commentary on the Gospel according to St. John." *Studia Patristica* 25 (1991): 115–21.

Koester, C. *Hebrews: A New Translation with Introduction and Commentary*. New York: Doubleday, 2001.

Koterski, Joseph W. "Boethius and the Theological Origins of the Concept of Person." *American Catholic Philosophical Quarterly* 78 (2004): 203–24.

Koterski, Joseph W. "The Doctrine of Participation in Thomistic Metaphysics." In *The Future of Thomism*. Edited by Deal W. Hudson and Dennis W. Moran, 185–7. American Maritain Association. Notre Dame, IN: University of Notre Dame Press, 1992.

Kretzmann, Norman. "Philosophy of Mind." In *The Cambridge Companion to Aquinas*. Edited by Norman Kretzmann and Eleonore Stump, 128–59. Cambridge: Cambridge University Press, 1993.

Langer, Ruth. "Jewish Understandings of the Religious Other." *Theological Studies* 64 (2003): 255–77.

Larsen, Kasper Bro. "Narrative Docetism: Christology and Storytelling in the Gospel of John." In *The Gospel of John and Christian Theology*. Edited by Richard Bauckham and Carl Mosser, 346–55. Grand Rapids, MI: Eerdmans, 2008.

Lash, Nicholas. "Up and Down in Christology." In *New Studies in Theology* 1. Edited by Stephen Sykes and Derek Holmes, 31–46. London: Duckworth, 1980.

Lee, Henry. *Anti-Skepticism: Or, Notes upon each Chapter of Mr. Lock's Essay concerning Humane Understanding. With an Explication of all the Particulars of which he treats, and in the same Order*. London: Printed for R. Clavel and C. Harper, 1702.

Lee, Patrick. "St. Thomas and Avicenna on the Agent Intellect." *The Thomist* 45 (1981): 41–61.

Legge, Dominic. *The Trinitarian Christology of Thomas Aquinas*. Oxford: Oxford University Press, 2017.

Leibniz, Gottfried W. *New Essays on Human Understanding*. Translated by Remnant and Bennett. Cambridge: Cambridge University Press, 1981.

Leo the Great. *Tome to Flavian*, in *Compendium of Creeds, Definitions, and Declarations on Matters of Faith and Morals*. Edited by Heinrich Denzinger, Peter Hünermann, et al. San Francisco, CA: Ignatius Press, 2012.

Leontius of Byzantium. *Deprehensio et Triumphus super Nestorianos*. In *Patrologia Graeca*. Edited by Jacques-Paul Minge, vol. 86. Paris, Imprimerie Catholique, 1857–66.

Levering, Matthew. *Christ's Fulfillment of Torah and Temple: Salvation According to Thomas Aquinas*. Notre Dame, IN: University of Notre Dame Press, 2002.

Levering, Matthew. *Engaging the Doctrine of Israel: A Christian Israelology in Dialogue with Ongoing Judaism*. Eugene, OR: Cascade, 2021.

Lietzmann, Hans, ed. *Appolinarius von Laodicea Aund seine Schule: Texte und Untersuchungen*. Tübingen: Möhr, 1904.

Liston, Greg. "A 'Chalcedonian' Spirit Christology." *Irish Theological Quarterly* 81 (2016): 74–93.

Loke, Andrew Ter Ern. "*Did the Saviour See the Father? Christ, Salvation and the Vision of God*. By Simon Francis Gaine." *Journal of Theological Studies* 68 (April 2017): 465–8.

Loke, Andrew Ter Ern. *A Kryptic Model of the Incarnation*. Burlington, VT: Ashgate, 2014.

LoLordo, Antonia. "Persons in Seventeenth- and Eighteenth-Century British Philosophy." In *Persons: A History*. Edited by Antonia LoLordo, 154–81. Oxford: Oxford University Press, 2019.

Lonergan, Bernard. *De Constitutione Christi Ontologica et Psychologica*. Translated by Michael G. Shields, vol. 7: *Collected Works of Bernard Lonergan*. Toronto: University of Toronto Press, 2002.

Lonergan, Bernard. *Insight: A Study of Human Understanding*. Edited by Frederick E. Crowe and Robert M. Doran, vol. 3: *Collected Works of Bernard Lonergan*. Toronto: University of Toronto Press, 1992 [1957].

Lonergan, Bernard. *Method in Theology*. London: Darton, Longman & Todd, 1972.

Lonergan, Bernard. *De Verbo incarnatio*. ET: *The Incarnate Word*. Translated by Charles C. Hefling Jr. Edited by Robert M. Doran and Jeremy D. Wilkins, vol. 8: *Collected Works of Bernard Lonergan*. Toronto: University of Toronto Press, 2016 [1964].

Lonergan, Bernard. *Verbum: Word and Idea in Aquinas*. Edited by Frederick E. Crowe and Robert M. Doran, vol. 2: *Collected Works of Bernard Lonergan*. Toronto: University of Toronto Press, 2005 [1968].

Losch, Andreas. "The Origins of Critical Realism," *Theology and Science* 7:1 (2009): 85–106.

Losch, Andreas. "Wright's Version of Critical Realism." In *God and the Faithfulness of Paul: A Critical Examination of the Pauline Theology of N.T. Wright*. Edited by Christoph Heilig, Thomas J. Hewitt, and Michael F. Bird, 101–14. Tübingen: Mohr Siebeck, 2016.

Louth, Andrew. *Discerning the Mystery: An Essay on the Nature of Theology*. Oxford: Oxford University Press, 1989.

Louth, Andrew. *Maximus the Confessor*. New York: Routledge, 1996.

Lyttkens, Hampus. *The Analogy between God and the World: An Investigation of Its Background and Interpretation of Its Use by Thomas of Aquino*. Translated by A. Poignant. Uppsala: Almqvist and Wiksells, 1952.

Macaskill, Grant. *The New Testament and Intellectual Humility*. Oxford: Oxford University Press, 2019.

Macaskill, Grant. *Union with Christ in the New Testament*. Oxford: Oxford University Press, 2013.

MacDonald, Paul. "Direct Realism and Aquinas's Account of Sensory Cognition." *The Thomist* 71 (2007): 348–78.
MacIntyre, Alasdair. *After Virtue: A Study in Moral Theory*. Third edition. Notre Dame, IN: University of Notre Dame Press, 2007 [1981].
MacIntyre, Alasdair. *Dependent Rational Animals: Why Human Beings Need the Virtues*. Chicago, IL: Open Court, 1999.
MacIntyre, Alasdair. *Ethics in the Conflicts of Modernity: An Essay on Desire, Practical Reasoning, and Narrative*. Cambridge: Cambridge University Press, 2016.
MacIntyre, Alasdair. *Three Rival Versions of Moral Enquiry: Encyclopaedia, Genealogy, and Tradition*. Notre Dame, IN: University of Notre Dame Press, 1994.
MacIntyre, Alasdair. *Whose Justice? Which Rationality?* London: Duckworth.
Mackey, James P. *Jesus, the Man and the Myth: A Contemporary Christology*. London: SCM Press, 1979.
Mackey, James P. *The Christian Experience of God as Trinity*. London: SCM Press, 1983.
Mackie, J. L. *Problems from Locke*. Oxford: Oxford University Press, 1976.
Mackintosh, H. R. *The Doctrine of the Person of Christ*. London: T&T Clark, 1912.
Madden, James. *Mind, Matter and Nature: A Thomistic Proposal for the Philosophy of Mind*. Washington, DC: Catholic University of America Press, 2013.
Madigan, Kevin. "*Christus Nesciens?* Was Christ Ignorant of the Day of Judgment? Arian and Orthodox Interpretation of Mark 13:32 in the Ancient Latin West." *Harvard Theological Review* 96:3 (2003): 255–78.
Mahoney, Timothy A. "A Note on the Importance of the Incarnation in Dionysius the Areopagite." *Diakonia* 35 (2002): 49–53.
Mansini, Guy. "Can Humility and Obedience Be Trinitarian Realities?" In *Thomas Aquinas and Karl Barth: An Unofficial Catholic-Protestant Dialogue*. Edited by Bruce L. McCormack and Thomas Joseph White, 71–98. Grand Rapids, MI: Eerdmans, 2013.
Mansini, Guy. "Understanding St. Thomas on Christ's Immediate Knowledge of God." *The Thomist* 59 (1995): 91–124.
Maritain, Jacques. *The Degrees of Knowledge*. Translated by Gerald B. Phelan. New York: Scribner, 1959.
Maritain, Jacques. *On the Grace and Humanity of Jesus*. Translated by Joseph W. Evans. London: Burns and Oates, 1969.
Marsden, George M. *Fundamentalism and American Culture*. Third edition. Oxford: Oxford University Press, 2022.
Marsh, Clive. "Quests of the Historical Jesus in New Historicist Perspective." *Biblical Interpretation* 5 (1997): 403–37.
Marshall, I. Howard. *The Gospel of Luke: A Commentary on the Greek Text*. NIGTC. Exeter: Paternoster, 1978.
Martin, Raymond, and John Barresi, *Naturalization of the Soul: Self and Personal Identity in the Eighteenth Century*. London: Routledge, 2000.
Martin, Raymond, and John Barresi. *The Rise and Fall of Soul and Self: An Intellectual History of Personal Identity*. New York: Columbia University Press, 2006.
Martyn, J. Louis. *Galatians: A New Translation with Introduction and Commentary*. The Anchor Yale Bible, vol. 33A. New Haven, CT: Yale University Press, 1997.
Mascall, E. L. *Via Media: An Essay in Theological Synthesis*. London: Longmans, Green, 1956.
Matthen, Mohan, ed. *The Oxford Handbook of Philosophy of Perception*. Oxford: Oxford University Press, 2015.

Maximus the Confessor. *Questions and Doubts*. In *Patrologia Graeca*. Edited by Jacques-Paul Minge, vol. 90. Paris: Imprimerie Catholique, 1857–66.

McCabe, Herbert. *God Matters*. London: Continuum, 1986.

McCormack, Bruce L. "Kenoticism in Modern Christology." In *The Oxford Handbook of Christology*. Edited by Francesca Aran Murphy and Troy A. Stefano, 444–57. Oxford: Oxford University Press, 2015.

McFarland, Ian A. *From Nothing: A Theology of Creation*. Louisville, KY: Westminster John Knox, 2014.

McFarland, Ian A. *The Word Made Flesh: A Theology of the Incarnation*. Louisville, KY: Westminster John Knox, 2019.

McGinnis, Andrew M. *The Son of God Beyond the Flesh: A Historical and Theological Study of the Extra Calvinisticum*. London: Bloomsbury, 2014.

McGrath, Alister. *The Making of Modern German Christology: From the Enlightenment to Pannenberg*. Oxford: Basil Blackwell, 1986.

McInerny, Ralph. *Aquinas and Analogy*. Washington, DC: Catholic University of America Press, 1996.

McKnight, Scott. *Jesus and His Death: Historiography, the Historical Jesus, and Atonement Theory*. Waco, TX: Baylor University Press, 2005.

McWhorter, Matthew R. "Aquinas on God's Relation to the World." *New Blackfriars* 94 (2013): 3–19.

Meier, John P. *A Marginal Jew: Rethinking the Historical Jesus*. Vol. 1: *The Roots of the Problem and the Person*. London: ABRL Doubleday, 1991.

Meier, John P. "The Present State of the 'Third Quest' for the Historical Jesus: Loss and Gain." *Biblica* 80 (1999): 459–87.

Merkley, Paul. "New Quests for Old: One Historian's Observations on a Bad Bargain." *Canadian Journal of Theology* 16 (1970): 203–18.

Messer, Adam G. "Patristic Theology and Recension in Matthew 24:36: An Evaluation of Ehrman's Text-Critical Methodology." In *Revisiting the Corruption of the New Testament: Manuscript, Patristic, and Apocryphal Evidence*. Edited by Daniel B. Wallace, 127–88. Grand Rapids, MI: Kregel Publications, 2011.

Metzger, Bruce M. *A Textual Commentary on the Greek New Testament*. Second edition. Germany: German Bible Society, 1994.

Meyer, Ben F. *The Aims of Jesus*. London: SCM Press, 1979.

Meyer, Ben F. *Critical Realism and the New Testament*. Allison Park, PA: Pickwick, 1989.

Meyer, Barbara U. "The Dogmatic Significance of Christ Being Jewish." In *Christ Jesus and the Jewish People Today: New Explorations of Theological Interrelationships*. Edited by Philip A. Cunningham, Joseph Sievers, Mary C. Boys, Hans Herman Henrix, and Svartvik Jesper, 144–56. Grand Rapids, MI: Eerdmans, 2011.

Meyer, Barbara U. *Jesus the Jew in Christian Memory: Theological and Philosophical Explorations*. Cambridge: Cambridge University Press, 2020.

Meyer, Paul. "Faith and History Revisited." *Princeton Seminary Bulletin* 10 (1989): 75–83.

Miller, John. *Jesus at Thirty: A Psychological and Historical Portrait*. Minneapolis, MN: Fortress, 1997.

Miner, Robert. *Thomas Aquinas on the Passions: A Study of Summa Theologiae 1a2ae 22–48*. Cambridge: Cambridge University Press, 2009.

Moloney, Raymond. "Approaches to Christ's Knowledge in the Patristic Era." In *Studies in Patristic Christology*. Edited by Thomas Finan and Vincent Twomey, 37–66. Dublin: Four Courts Press, 1998.

Moloney, Raymond. *The Knowledge of Christ (Problems in Theology)*. New York: Continuum, 1999.
Moltmann, Jürgen. *The Crucified God*. Translated by R. A. Wilson and John Bowden. Minneapolis, MN: Fortress Press, 1993 [1973].
Moltmann, Jürgen. *Theology of Hope: On the Ground and the Implications of a Christian Eschatology*. Minneapolis, MN: Fortress Press, 1993.
Mongeau, Gilles. "The Human and Divine Knowing of the Incarnate Word." *Josephinum Journal of Theology* 12 (2005): 30–42.
Montagnes, Bernard. *The Doctrine of the Analogy of Being According to Thomas Aquinas*. Translated by E. M. Macierowski. Milwaukee, WI: Marquette University Press, 2004.
Morard, Martin. "Thomas d'Aquin lecteur des conciles." *Archivum franciscanum historicum* 98 (2005): 211–365.
Moreland, J. P., and Scott Rae. *Body and Soul: Human Nature and the Crisis in Ethics*. Downers Grove, IL: Intervarsity Press, 2000.
Moss, Candida R. "The Man with the Flow of Power: Porous Bodies in Mark 5:25–34." *Journal of Biblical Literature* 129 (2010): 507–19.
Murphy, Francesca Aran. *God Is Not a Story: Realism Revisited*. Oxford: Oxford University Press, 2007.
Narciesse, Gilbert. "Les Enjeux Épistémologiques de l'Argument de Convenance selon Saint Thomas d'Aquin." In *Ordo Sapientiae et Amoris: Image et Message de Saint Thomas d'Aquin à Travers les Récentes Études Historiques, Herméneutiques et Doctrinales. Hommage au Professeur Jean-Pierre Torell OP à l'Occasion de Son 65e Anniversaire*. Edited by Carlos-Josaphat Pinto de Oliveira, 143–67. Fribourg: Éditions universitaires de Fribourg, 1993.
Neder, Adam. *Participation in Christ: An Entry into Karl Barth's Church Dogmatics*. Louisville, KY: Westminster John Knox, 2009.
Neill, Stephen and N. T. Wright. *The Interpretation of the New Testament 1861–1986*. Second edition. New York: Oxford University Press, 1988.
O'Collins, G., and D. Kendall. "The Faith of Jesus." *Theological Studies* 53 (1992): 403–23.
O'Neill, Colman. "The Problem of Christ's Human Autonomy." Appendix 3 in *Summa Theologiae*. Blackfriars edition, vol. 50. Translated by C. O'Neill. London: Eyre and Spottiswoode, 1965.
O'Neill, J. C. *Who Did Jesus Think He Was?* Biblical Interpretation Series 11. Leiden: Brill, 1995.
O'Rourke, Fran. *Pseudo-Dionysius and the Metaphysics of Aquinas*. Leiden: Brill, 1992.
O'Toole, R. F. "The Parallels between Jesus and Moses." *Biblical Theology Bulletin* 20 (1990): 22–9.
Oderberg, David. *Real Essentialism*. London: Routledge, 2007.
Ols, D. "Réflexions sur l'actualité de la Christologie de Saint Thomas." *Doctor Communis* 34 (1981): 58–71.
Origen. *The Commentary of Origen on the Gospel of St Matthew*. Translated by Ronald E. Heine. Oxford: Oxford University Press, 2018.
Owens, Joseph. "Aquinas on Cognition as Existence." *Proceedings of the American Catholic Philosophical Association* 48: Thomas and Bonaventure (1974): 74–85.
Owens, Joseph. "Aristotle: Cognition a Way of Being." *Canadian Journal of Philosophy* 6 (1976): 1–11.
Paget, James Carleton. "Quests for the Historical Jesus." In *The Cambridge Companion to Jesus*. Edited by Markus Bockmuehl, 138–55. Cambridge: Cambridge University Press, 2001.

Pannenberg, Wolfhart. *Jesus, God and Man*. Translated by Lewis L. Wilkins and Duane A. Priebe. Philadelphia, PA: Westminster Press, 1968.

Pannenberg, Wolfhart. *Systematic Theology*. Vol. 1. Grand Rapids, MI: Eerdmans, 1991.

Paolozzi, Bruce. "Hylomorphic Dualism and the Challenge of Embodied Cognition." In *Thomas Aquinas: Teacher of Humanity*. Edited by John P. Hitting and Daniel C. Wagner, 271–82. Cambridge: Cambridge Scholars Publishing, 2015.

Papineau, David. "Naturalism." *The Stanford Encyclopedia of Philosophy* (Summer 2021 edition). Edited by Edward N. Zalta. plato.stanford.edu/archives/sum2021/entries/naturalism/

Pardue, Stephen T. *The Mind of Christ: Humility and the Intellect in Early Christian Theology*. London: Bloomsbury, 2013.

Pasnau, Robert. "Aquinas and the Content Fallacy." *The Modern Schoolman* 75 (1998): 293–314.

Pasnau, Robert. *Theories of Cognition in the Later Middle Ages*. Cambridge: Cambridge Unviersity Press, 1997.

Pasnau, Robert. *Thomas Aquinas on Human Nature: A Philosophical Study of* Summa Theologiae *1a 75–89*. Cambridge: Cambridge University Press, 2002.

Pawl, Timothy. *In Defense of Conciliar Christology: A Philosophical Essay*. Oxford: Oxford University Press, 2016.

Pelikan, Jaroslav. *The Emergence of the Catholic Tradition (100–600)*. Chicago, IL: University of Chicago Press, 1971.

Perczel, Istvan. "The Christology of Pseudo-Dionysius the Areopagite: The *Fourth Letter* in Its Indirect and Direct Text Traditions." *Le Museon* 117 (2004): 409–46.

Perrin, Nicholas. *Jesus the Priest*. Grand Rapids, MI: Baker Academic, 2018.

Petrus Hispanus. *Pedro Hispano: Obras filosóficas* I. Edited by M. Alonso. Juan Flors: Barcelona, 1961.

Pickavé, Martin. "Human Knowledge." In *The Oxford Handbook of Aquinas*. Edited by Brian Davies, 311–23. Oxford: Oxford University Press, 2012.

Pieper, Josef. *Living the Truth*. San Francisco, CA: Ignatius Press, 1989.

Pieper, Josef. *The Silence of St Thomas: Three Essays*. Translated by John Murray, S.J. and Daniel O'Connor. Chicago, IL: Henry Regnery Co., 1957.

Pitre, Brant. *Jesus and the Last Supper*. Grand Rapids, MI: Eerdmans, 2015.

Pius XII. "Sempiternus Rex Christus." September 8, 1951. http://w2.vatican.va/content/pius-xii/en/encyclicals/documents/hf_p-xii_enc_08091951_sempiternus-rex-christus.html.

Pohle, Joseph. *The Divine Trinity: A Dogmatic Treatise*. St. Louis, MO: B. Herder Book Co., 1911.

Popkin, Richard H. "Spinoza and Bible Scholarship," in *The Cambridge Companion to Spinoza*, ed. Don Garrett. Cambridge: Cambridge University Press, 1996.

Powell, Mark Allan. *Jesus as a Figure in History: How Modern Historians View the Man from Galilee*. Louisville, KY: Westminster John Knox, 1998.

Przywara, Erich. *Analogia Entis: Metaphysics—Original Structure and Universal Rhythm*. Translated by John Behr and David Bentley Hart. Grand Rapids, MI: Eerdmans, 2013 [1962].

Rahner, Karl. "Current Problems in Christology." In *Theological Investigations*, vol. 1: *God, Christ, Mary and Grace*. Translated by C. Ernts, 149–200. New York: Seabury, 1961.

Rahner, Karl. "Dogmatic Reflections on the Knowledge and Self-Consciousness of Christ." *Theological Investigations V*. Translated by K.-H. Kruger, 193–215. London: Darton, Longman & Todd, 1966.

Rahner, Karl. "An Investigation of the Incomprehensibility of God in St Thomas Aquinas." In *Theological Investigations*, vol. 16: *Experience of the Spirit: Source of Theology*. Translated by D. Morland, 244–54. London: Darton, Longman & Todd.

Rahner, Karl. *The Trinity*. Translated by Joseph Donceel. New York: Herder & Herder, 1970.

Ramsey, Michael. *From Gore to Temple: The Development of Anglican Theology between Lux Mundi and the Second World War, 1889–1939*. London: Longmans, 1960.

Reimarus, H. S. *Von Dem Zwecke Jesu Und Seiner Jünger: Noch Ein Fragment Des Wolfenbüttelschen Ungenannten*. Edited by G. E. Lessing. Braunschweig: 1778. ET: *Reimarus: Fragments*. Edited by Charles H. Talbert. Translated by Ralph S. Fraser. *Lives of Jesus Series*. London: SCM Press, 1970.

Relton, Herbert. *A Study in Christology*. London: Society for Promoting Christian Knowledge, 1917.

Reynolds, Benjamin E., and Loren T. Stuckenbruck. *The Jewish Apocalyptic Tradition and the Shaping of New Testament Thought*. Minneapolis, MN: Fortress Press, 2017.

Riches, Aaron. *Ecce Homo: On the Divine Unity of Christ*. Grand Rapids, MI: Eerdmans Publishing Company, 2016.

Roberts, Robert C., and W. Jay Wood. *Intellectual Virtues: An Essay in Regulative Epistemology*. Oxford: Oxford University Press, 2007.

Robinson, James M. "Theological Autobiography." In *The Craft of Religious Studies*. Edited by Jon R. Stone, 117–50. New York: Palgrave, 2000.

Robinson, John A. T. "The Last Tabu? The Self-Consciousness of Jesus." In *Historical Jesus in Recent Research*. Edited by James D. G. Dunn and Scott McKnight, 553–66. University Park, PA: Eisenbrauns, 2005.

Rocca, Gregory P., O.P. *Speaking the Incomprehensible God: Thomas Aquinas on the Interplay of Positive and Negative Theology*. Washington, DC: Catholic University of America Press, 2004.

Rowe, C. Kavin. "Biblical Pressure and Trinitarian Hermeneutics." *Pro Ecclesia* 11:3 (2002): 295–312.

Rowe, C. Kavin. *One True Life: The Stoics and Early Christians as Rival Traditions*. New Haven, CT: Yale University Press, 2016.

Rowland, Christopher. *The Open Heaven: A Study of Apocalyptic in Judaism and Early Christianity*. Eugene, OR: Wipf and Stock, 2002.

Rowlands, Jonathan. *The Metaphysics of Historical Jesus Research: An Argument for Increasing the Plurality of Metaphysical Frameworks within Historical Jesus Research*. PhD Diss., University of Nottingham, 2019.

Runia, Klaas. *The Present-Day Christological Debate*. Leicester: Intervarsity Press, 1984.

Sanders, E. P. *The Historical Figure of Jesus*. London: Allen Lane, 1993.

Sanders, E. P. *Jesus and Judaism*. Philadelphia, PA: Fortress Press, 1985.

Sanders, E. P. "Jesus: His Religious 'Type.'" *Reflections* 87 (1992): 4–12.

Sanders, E. P. *Paul in Palestinian Judaism: A Comparison of Patterns of Religion*. London: SCM Press, 1977.

Sarisky, Darren. "Judgments in Scripture and the Creed: Reflections on Identity and Difference." *Modern Theology* (Online, 2020). https://doi-org.ezp.lib.cam.ac.uk/10.1111/moth.12657.

Sarisky, Darren. *Reading the Bible Theologically*. Cambridge: Cambridge University Press, 2019.
Scarpelli Cory, Therese. *Aquinas on Human Self-Knowledge*. Cambridge: Cambridge University Press, 2014.
Scarpelli Cory, Therese. "Averroes and Aquinas on the Agent Intellect's Causation of the Intelligible." *Recherches de Théologie et Philosophie Médiévales* 82 (2015): 1–60.
Scarpelli Cory, Therese. "Knowing as Being? A Metaphysical Reading of the Identity of Intellect and Intelligibles in Aquinas." *American Catholic Philosophical Quarterly* 91 (2017): 333–5.
Scarpelli Cory, Therese. "Rethinking Abstractionism: Aquinas's Intellectual Light and Some Arabic Sources." *Journal of the History of Philosophy* 53 (2015): 607–46.
Scarpelli Cory, Therese. "What Is an Intellectual 'Turn'? The *Liber de Causis*, Avicenna, and Aquinas's Turn to Phantasms." *Tópicos: Revista de Filosofía* 45 (2013): 129–62.
Schaff, Philip, ed. *The Creeds of Christendom*. Vol. 2. Grand Rapids, MI: Baker, 1877.
Schillebeeckx, Edward. *Interim Report on the Books "Jesus" and "Christ."* London: SCM Press, 1980.
Schillebeeckx, Edward. *Jesus: An Experiment in Christology*. New York: Crossroad, 1981 [1974].
Schillebeeckx, Edward. *Jesus in Our Western Culture: Mysticism, Ethics and Politics*. London: SCM, 1987.
Schleiermacher, Friedrich. *The Christian Faith*. Translated by Paul T. Nimmo. 2 vols. T&T Clark Cornerstones. London: Bloomsbury Academic, 2016.
Schleiermacher, Friedrich. *The Life of Jesus*. Philadelphia, PA: Fortress Press, 1975.
Schwartz, Seth. *Imperialism and Jewish Society, 200 BCE to 640 CE*. Princeton, NJ: Princeton University Press, 2001.
Schweitzer, Albert. *The Mystery of the Kingdom of God: The Secret of Jesus' Messiahship and Passion*. Translated by Walter Lowrie. London: A & C Black, 1925 [1901].
Schweitzer, Albert. *Von Reimarus Zu Wrede* (1906). ET: *The Quest of the Historical Jesus: A Critical Study of Its Progress from Reimarus to Wrede*. Third edition. Translated by W. Montgomery. London: Adam & Charles Black, 1954.
Schweizer, E. "Die Frage Nach Dem Historischen Jesus." *Evangelische Theologie* 24 (1964): 403–19.
The Shepherd of Hermas, in *The Apostolic Fathers*, vol. II. Edited by Bart D. Ehrman, 161–474. Cambridge, MA: Harvard University Press, 2003.
Sherwin, Michael. "Christ the Teacher in St. Thomas's Commentary on the Gospel of John." In *Reading John with St. Thomas Aquinas: Theological Exegesis and Speculative Theology*. Edited by Matthew Levering and Dauphinais Michael, 173–93. Washington, DC: Catholic University of America Press, 2005.
Shults, F. LeRon. "A Dubious Christological Formula: From Leontius of Byzantium to Karl Barth." *Theological Studies* 57 (1996): 431–46.
Silva, Moisés. *Philippians*. Second edition. Grand Rapids, MI: Baker Academic, 2005.
Simon, Yves. "An Essay on Sensation." In *Philosophy of Knowledge: Selected Readings*. Edited by Roland Houde and Joseph P. Mullally, 55–95. New York: J.B. Lippincott Company, 1960.
Simonetti, Manlio. *Ancient Christian Commentary on Scripture: Matthew 14–28*. Downers Grove, IL: InterVarsity, 2002.
Simpson, Benjamin I. *Recent Research on the Historical Jesus*. Sheffield: Sheffield Phoenix Press, 2014.

Simpson, William M. R., Robert C. Koons, and Nicholas J. Teh, eds. *Neo-Aristotelian Perspectives on Contemporary Science*. New York, NY: Routledge, 2018.

Slusser, Michael. "Docetism: A Historical Definition." *Second Century* 1 (1981): 163–72.

Smit, Peter-Ben. "The End of Early Christian Adoptionism? A Note on the Invention of Adoptionism, Its Sources, and Its Current Demise." *International Journal of Philosophy and Theology* 76 (2015): 177–99.

Sobrino, Jon. *Christology at the Crossroads: A Latin American Approach*. London: SCM Press, 1978.

Sommer, Benjamin D. "Did Prophecy Cease? Evaluating a Reevaluation." *Journal of Biblical Literature* 115 (1996): 31–47.

Soskice, Janet Martin. "*Creatio Ex Nihilo*: Its Jewish and Cristian Foundations." In *Creation and the God of Abraham*. Edited by David B. Burrell, Carlo Cogliati, Janet M. Soskice, and William R. Stoeger, 24–39. Cambridge: Cambridge University Press, 2010.

Soskice, Janet Martin. *The Kindness of God: Metaphor, Gender, and Religious Language*. Oxford: Oxford University Press, 2008.

Soskice, Janet Martin. "Athens and Jerusalem, Alexandria and Edessa: Is there a Metaphysics of Scripture?" *International Journal of Systematic Theology* 8 (2006): 149–62.

Spruit, Leen. *Species Intelligibilis: From Perception to Knowledge*. Vol. 1: *Classical Roots and Medieval Discussions*. Brill's Studies in Intellectual History 48. Leiden: Brill, 1994.

Stevenson, Austin. "'Concerning That Day and Hour': In Defence of Patristic Exegesis," *Journal of Theological Interpretation* (Accepted, forthcoming).

Stevenson, Austin. "The Self-Understanding of Jesus: A Metaphysical Reading of Historical Jesus Studies." *Scottish Journal of Theology* 72 (2019): 291–307.

Stevenson, Austin. "Trinitarian Spirit-Christology in Thomas Aquinas: Biblical Hermeneutics and the Munus Triplex." *Noesis Review* 5 (2018): 71–8.

Stevenson, Austin. "The Unity of Christ and the Historical Jesus: Aquinas and Locke on Personal Identity," *Modern Theology* 37:4 (October 2021): 851–64.

Stewart, Robert B. *The Quest of the Hermeneutical Jesus: The Impact of Hermeneutics on the Jesus Research of John Dominic Crossan and N. T. Wright*. Lanham, MD: University Press of America, 2008.

Stock, Michael. "Sense Consciousness According to St. Thomas." *The Thomist* 21 (1958): 415–86.

Strauss, David Friedrich. *Das Leben Jesu, kritisch bearbeitet*. 2 vols (1835 and 1836). ET: *The Life of Jesus Critically Examined*. Edited by Peter C. Hodgson. Translated from the fourth German edition by George Eliot. *Lives of Jesus Series*. London: SCM Press, 1973.

Stuart, Matthew. *Locke's Metaphysics*. Oxford: Oxford University Press, 2013.

Stump, Eleonore. *Aquinas*. New York: Routledge, 2003.

Sturch, Richard. *The Word and the Christ: An Essay in Analytic Christology*. Oxford: Oxford University Press, 1991.

Sykes, S. K. "The Strange Persistence of Kenotic Christology." In *Being and Truth: Essays in Honour of John Macquarrie*. Edited by Alistair Kee and Eugene T. Long, 349–75. London: SCM Press, 1986.

Tanner, Kathryn. *Jesus, Humanity and the Trinity: A Brief Systematic Theology*. Minneapolis, MN: Fortress Press, 2001.

Tapie, Matthew A. *Aquinas on Israel and the Church: The Question of Supersessionism in the Theology of Thomas Aquinas*. Eugene, OR: Pickwick, 2014.

Tatum, W. Barnes. *In Quest of Jesus: A Guidebook*. Revised edition. Nashville, TN: Abingdon Press, 1999.

Taylor, Charles. *The Language Animal: The Full Shape of the Human Linguistic Capacity*. London: Belknap Press, 2016.

Taylor, Charles. *A Secular Age*. Boston, MA: Belknap, 2007.

Te Velde, Rudi A. *Aquinas on God: The "Divine Science" of the Summa Theologiae*. Aldershot–Burlington, VT: Ashgate, 2006.

Te Velde, Rudi A. "God and the Language of Participation." In *Divine Transcendence and Immancence in the Work of Thomas Aquinas*. Edited by Harm Goris, Herwi Rickhof, and Henk Schoot, 19–36. Walpole, MA: Peeters, 2009.

Te Velde, Rudi A. *Participation and Substantiality in Thomas Aquinas*. Leiden: Brill, 1995.

Telford, William. "Major Trends and Interpretive Issues in the Study of Jesus." In *Studying the Historical Jesus: Evaluations of the State of Current Research*. Edited by Bruce Chilton and Craig Evans, 33–74. Leiden: Brill, 1994.

Theissen, Gerd, and Annette Merz. *The Historical Jesus: A Comprehensive Guide*. Minneapolis, MN: Fortress, 1998.

Theissen, Gerd, and Dagmar Winter. *The Quest for the Plausible Jesus: The Question of Criteria*, Translated by M. Eugene Boring. Louisville, KY: Westminster John Knox, 2002.

Thiel, Udo. *The Early Modern Subject: Self-consciousness and Personal Identity from Descartes to Hume*. Oxford: Oxford University Press, 2011.

Thiel, Udo. "The Trinity and Human Personal Identity." In *English Philosophy in the Age of Locke*. Edited by M. A. Stewart, 217–431. Oxford: Oxford University Press, 2000.

Thompson, Marianne Meye. *The Incarnate Word: Perspectives on Jesus in the Fourth Gospel*. Peabody, MA: Hendrickson, 1988.

Thompson, Thomas R. "Nineteenth-Century Kenotic Christology: The Waxing, Waning, and Weighing of a Quest for a Coherent Orthodoxy." In *Exploring Kenotic Christology: The Self-Emptying of God*. Edited by C. Stephen Evans, 74–111. Oxford: Oxford University Press, 2006.

Tomarchio, John. "Aquinas's Division of Being According to Modes of Existing." *Review of Metaphysics* 54 (2001): 585–613.

Torrell, Jean-Pierre. *Christ and Spirituality in St. Thomas Aquinas*. Translated by Bernhard Blankenhorn. Washington, DC: Catholic University of America Press, 2011.

Torrell, Jean-Pierre. "Nature and Grace in Thomas Aquinas." In *Surnaturel: A Controversy at the Heart of Twentieth-Century Thomistic Thought*. Edited by Serge-Thomas Bonino. Translated by Robert Williams. Translation revised by Matthew Levering, 155–88. Naples, FL: Sapientia Press, 2009.

Torrell, Jean-Pierre. *Recherches Thomasiennes: Études revues et augmentées*. Paris: Vrin, 2000.

Torrell, Jean-Pierre. "Le sacerdoce du Christ dans la *Somme de théologie*." *Revue Thomiste* 99 (1999): 75–100.

Torrell, Jean-Pierre. *Saint Thomas Aquinas*. 2 vols. Washington, DC: Catholic University of America Press, 2003.

Torrell, Jean-Pierre. "Le savoir acquis du Christ selon les théologiens médiévaux." *Revue Thomiste* 101 (2001): 355–408.

Torrell, Jean-Pierre. "La Science du Christ." In *Le Verbe Incarné*, 2:415–39. Paris: Cerf, 2002.

Troeltsch, Ernst. "The Dogmatics of the History-of-Religions School." In *Religion and History*. Edited by J. Adams and W. Bense, 87–108. Minneapolis, MN: Fortress Press, 1991 [1913].
Troeltsch, Ernst. *Gesammelte Schriften*. Tübingen: J. C. B. Mohr, 1913.
van Driel, Edwin Christian. "The Logic of Assumption." In *Exploring Kenotic Christology: The Self-Emptying of God*. Edited by C. Stephen Evans, 265–90. Oxford: Oxford University Press, 2006.
van Os, Bas. *Psychological Analyses and the Historical Jesus: New Ways to Explore Christian Origins*. London: T&T Clark, 2011.
Vass, George. *A Pattern of Doctrines 1: God and Christ*. Vol. 3: *Understanding Karl Rahner*. London: Sheed & Ward, 1996.
Vermes, Geza. *Christian Beginnings: From Nazareth to Nicaea (AD 30–325)*. London: Allen Lane, 2012.
Vermes, Geza. *Jesus the Jew: A Historian's Reading of the Gospels*. London: Collins, 1973.
Vermes, Geza. *The Religion of Jesus the Jew*. London: SCM, 1993.
von Balthasar, Hans Urs. *The Glory of the Lord: A Theological Aesthetics*. Vol. 1: *Seeing the Form*. Translated by E. Leiva-Merikakis. Edinburgh: T&T Clark, 1982.
von Balthasar, Hans Urs. *Theo-Drama: Theological Dramatic Theory*. Vol. 3: *Dramatis Personae: Persons in Christ*. Translated by G. Harrison. San Francisco, CA: Ignatius Press, 1987.
von Harnack, Adolf. *What Is Christianity?* Translated by Thomas Baily Saunders. Philadelphia, PA: Fortress Press, 1957 [1900].
Voorwinde, Stephen. *Jesus' Emotions in the Fourth Gospel: Human or Divine?* Library of New Testament Studies 284. New York: T&T Clark, 2005.
Waddell, Michael. "Aquinas on the Light of Glory." *Tópicos* 40 (2011): 105–32.
Wallace, Daniel B. "The Son's Ignorance in Matthew 24:36: An Exercise in Textual and Redaction Criticism." In *Studies on the Text of the New Testament and Early Christianity: Essays in Honour of Michael W. Holmes*. Edited by Daniel Gurtner, Juan Hernández Jr., and Paul Foster, 178–205. Boston, MA: Brill, 2015.
Wallace, David Foster. *The Pale King*. New York: Little, Brown, 2011.
Walters, Amy. "Elisabeth Schüssler Fiorenza and the Quest for the Historical Jesus." *Open Theology* 6:1 (2020): 468–74.
Ward, Keith. *Christ and the Cosmos: A Reformulation of Trinitarian Doctrine*. Cambridge: Cambridge University Press, 2015.
Warren, Andrew. "Narrative Modeling and Community Organizing in *The Pale King* and *Infinite Jest*." *Studies in the Novel* 44:4 (2012): 389–408.
Watts, Thomas A. "Two Wills in Christ? Contemporary Objections Considered in the Light of a Critical Examination of Maximus the Confessor's Disputation with Pyrrhus." *Westminster Theological Journal* 71 (2009): 455–87.
Weaver, Walter. *The Historical Jesus in the Twentieth Century: 1900–1950*. Harrisburg, PA: Trinity Press International, 1999.
Webb, Robert. *John the Baptizer and Prophet: A Socio-Historical Study*. Journal for the Study of the New Testament Supplement Series, vol. 62. Sheffield: Sheffield Academic Press, 1991.
Webster, John. "'Love Is also a Lover of Life': Creatio Ex Nihilo and Creaturely Goodness." *Modern Theology* 29, no. 2 (2013): 156–71.
Webster, John. "*Non Ex Aequo*: God's Relation to Creatures." In *God Without Measure: Working Papers in Christian Theology*, 115–26. London: Bloomsbury T&T Clark, 2017.

Wedeking, Gary. "Locke on Personal Identity and the Trinity Controversy of the 1690s." *Dialogue* 29 (1990): 163–88.
Weinandy, Thomas G. "The Beatific Vision and the Incarnate Son: Furthering the Discussion." *The Thomist* 70 (2006): 605–15.
Weinandy, Thomas G. *In the Likeness of Sinful Flesh: An Essay on the Humanity of Christ*. London: T&T Clark, 1993.
Weinandy, Thomas G. "Jesus' Filial Vision of the Father." *Pro Ecclesia* 13 (2004): 189–201.
Weiss, Johannes. *Die Predigt Jesu vom Reiche Gottes*. Göttingen: Vandenhoeck & Ruprecht. 1892.
Welch, Claud. *Protestant Thought in the Nineteenth Century*. Vol. 1. New Haven, CT: Yale University Press, 1972.
West, J. L. A. "Aquinas on Peter Lombard and the Metaphysical Status of Christ's Human Nature." *Gregorianum* 88 (2007): 557–86.
West, J. L. A. "The Real Distinction Between Supposit and Nature." In *Wisdom's Apprentice: Thomistic Essays in Honor of Lawrence Dewan, O.P.* Edited by Peter A. Kwasniewski, 85–106. Washington, DC: Catholic University of America Press, 2012.
Whitcomb, Dennis, Heather Battaly, Jason Baehr, and Daniel Howard-Snyder. "Intellectual Humility: Owning our Limitations." *Philosophy and Phenomenological Research* 91 (2015): 1–31.
White, Leo A. "The Picture Theory of the Phantasm." *Tópicos: Revista de Filosofía* 29 (2005): 131–56.
White, Leo A. "Why the Cogitative Power?" *Proceedings of the American Catholic Philosophical Association* 72 (1998): 213–27.
White, Thomas Joseph. "The Crucified Lord: Thomistic Reflections on the Communication of Idioms and the Theology of the Cross." In *Thomas Aquinas and Karl Barth: An Unofficial Catholic-Protestant Dialogue*. Edited by Bruce L. McCormack and Thomas Joseph White, 157–92. Grand Rapids, MI: Eerdmans, 2013.
White, Thomas Joseph. "Divine Simplicity and the Holy Trinity." *International Journal of Systematic Theology* 18 (2016): 66–93.
White, Thomas Josephs. "Dyothelitism and the Instrumental Human Consciousness of Jesus." *Pro Ecclesia* 17 (2008): 396–422.
White, Thomas Joseph. "How Barth Got Aquinas Wrong: A Reply to Archie J. Spencer on Causality and Christocentrism." *Nova et Vetera, English Edition* 7 (2009): 241–70.
White, Thomas Joseph. *The Incarnate Lord: A Thomistic Study in Christology*. Thomistic Ressourcement Series. Washington, DC: Catholic University of America Press, 2005.
White, Thomas Joseph. "The Infused Science of Christ." *Nova et Vetera*, English edition, 16:2 (2018): 617–64.
White, Thomas Joseph. "Intra-Trinitarian Obedience and Nicene-Chalcedonian Christology." *Nova et Vetera*, English edition, 6:2 (2008): 377–402.
White, Thomas Joseph. "The Voluntary Action of the Earthly Christ and the Necessity of the Beatific Vision." *The Thomist* 69 (2005): 497–534.
White, Thomas Joseph. *Wisdom in the Face of Modernity: A Study in Thomistic Natural Theology*. Ave Maria, FL: Sapientia Press, 2009.
Wickham, R. L. "The Ignorance of Christ: A Problem for the Ancient Theology." In *Christian Faith and Greek Philosophy in Late Antiquity: Essays in Tribute to George Christopher Stead*. Edited by L. R. Wickham and C. P. Bammel, 213–26. New York: Brill, 1993.
Wilken, Robert Louis. *The Spirit of Early Christian Thought: Seeking the Face of God*. New Haven, CT: Yale University Press, 2005.

Wilkins, Jeremy D. *Before Truth: Lonergan, Aquinas, and the Problem of Wisdom.* Washington, DC: Catholic University of America Press, 2018.

Wilkins, Jeremy D. "Love and Knowledge of God in the Human Life of Christ." *Pro Ecclesia* 21 (2012): 77–99.

Williams, Bernard. "Personal Identity and Individuation." In *Problems of the Self,* 1–18. Cambridge: Cambridge University Press, 1973.

Williams, C. J. F. "A Programme for Christology." *Religious Studies* 3 (1968): 513–24.

Williams, Rowan. *Christ the Heart of Creation.* London: Continuum, 2018.

Williams, Scott M. "Persons in Patristic and Medieval Christian Theology." In *Persons: A History.* Edited by Antonia LoLordo, 52–84. Oxford: Oxford University Press, 2019.

Wilson, A. N. *Jesus.* London: Sinclair Stevenson, 1992.

Wippel, John F. "Essence and Existence." In *The Cambridge History of Later Medieval Philosophy.* Edited by Norman Kretzmann, Anthony Kenny, and Jan Pinborg, 385–410. Cambridge: Cambridge University Press, 1982.

Wippel, John F. *The Metaphysical Thought of Thomas Aquinas: From Finite Being to Uncreated Being.* Washington, DC: Catholic University of America Press.

Wippel, John F. "Thomas Aquinas and the Axiom 'What Is Received Is Received According to the Mode of the Receiver.'" In *Metaphysical Themes in Thomas Aquinas II,* 113–22. Washington, DC: Catholic University of America Press, 2007.

Wippel, John F. "Thomas Aquinas and Participation." In *Studies in Medieval Philosophy.* Edited by John F. Wippel, 117–58. Washington, DC: Catholic University of America Press, 1987.

Witherington III, Ben. *The Christology of Jesus.* Minneapolis, MN: Fortress, 1990.

Witherington III, Ben. *Friendship and Finances in Philippi: The Letter of Paul to the Philippians.* Valley Forge, PA: Trinity, 1994.

Witherington III, Ben. *The Jesus Quest: The Third Search for the Jew of Nazareth.* Downers Grove, IL: InterVarsity Press, 1995.

Witherington III, Ben. *The Living Word of God: Rethinking the Theology of the Bible.* Waco, TX: Baylor University Press, 2007.

Wittman, Tyler R. "'Not a God of Confusion but of Peace': Aquinas and the Meaning of Divine Simplicity." *Modern Theology* 32 (2016): 151–69.

Wood, Adam. *Thomas Aquinas on the Immateriality of the Human Intellect.* Washington, DC: Catholic University of America Press, 2019.

Wrede, William. *Das Messiasgeheimnis in den Evangelein* (1901). ET: *The Messianic Secret.* Translated by J. C. G. Greig. Cambridge: James Clarke, 1971 [1901].

Wrede, William. "The Task and Methods of 'New Testament Theology.'" In *The Nature of New Testament Theology.* Edited by R. Morgan, 68–116. Naperville, IL: Allenson, 1973 [1897].

Wright, N. T. "A Biblical Portrait of God." In *The Changing Face of God: Lincoln Lectures in Theology,* 6–29. Lincoln: Lincoln Cathedral Publications, 1996.

Wright, N. T. *The Challenge of Jesus: Rediscovering Who Jesus Was and Is.* Downers Grove IL: InterVarsity, 2015.

Wright, N. T. "Doing Justice to Jesus: A Response to J. D. Crossan: 'What Victory? What God?'" *Scottish Journal of Theology* 50 (1997): 359–79.

Wright, N. T. *History and Eschatology: Jesus and the Promise of Natural Theology.* London: SPCK, 2019

Wright, N. T. "Jesus and the Identity of God." *Ex auditu* 14 (1998): 42–56.

Wright, N. T. *Jesus and the Victory of God.* Vol. 2: *Christian Origins and the Question of God.* Minneapolis, MN: Fortress, 1996.

Wright, N. T. "Jesus, Quest for the Historical." In *The Anchor Bible Dictionary*. Edited by David Noel Freedman, 796–802. New York: Doubleday, 1992.

Wright, N. T. "Jesus' Self-Understanding." In *The Incarnation: An Interdisciplinary Symposium*. Edited by Stephen T. Davis, Daniel Kendall, and Gerald O'Collins, 47–61. Oxford: Oxford University Press, 2002.

Wright, N. T. *The New Testament and the People of God*. Vol. 1: *Christian Origins and the Question of God*. Minneapolis, MN: Fortress, 1992.

Wright, N. T. "Response to Richard Hays." In *Jesus, Paul and the People of God: A Theological Dialogue with N. T. Wright*. Edited by Nicholas Perrin and Richard B. Hays, 62–5. Downers Grove, IL: IVP Academic, 2011.

Wright, N. T. "Whence and Whither Historical Jesus Studies in the Life of the Church?" In *Jesus, Paul and the People of God: A Theological Dialogue with N. T. Wright*. Edited by Nicholas Perrin and Richard B. Hays, 115–60. Downers Grove, IL: IVP Academic, 2011.

Yeago, David S. "The New Testament and the Nicene Dogma: A Contribution to the Recovery of Theological Exegesis." *Pro Ecclesia* 3:2 (1994): 152–64.

Young, Francis. *Biblical Exegesis and the Formation of Christian Culture*. Cambridge: Cambridge University Press, 1997.

Zachhuber, Johannes. *Theology as Science in Nineteenth-Century Germany: From F. C. Baur to Ernst Troeltsch*. Oxford: Oxford University Press, 2013.

Zahrnt, Heinz. *The Historical Jesus*. Translated by J. S. Bowden. London: Collins, 1963.

INDEX

accommodation 133, 137
act/potency 49, 103–5, 110–11, 116–19, 144 n.7, 198–90
Adam, A. K. M. 31
adoptionism 128–9
anachronism 32
analogy of being 53–7
angels 107–10, 177
anhypostasis/enhypostasis 61 n.10, 70, 74
Ankersmit, Frank 6
Allen, Michael 194 n.66, 202
Allison Jr., Dale 125–6, 139–40
Ambrose of Milan 129 n.15, 131–3
analogy 43, 53–7, 90
 of being 44, 56–7
 historical 31–2, 85, 143, 155, 159
anamnesis 120, 155 n.58
anthropology 112, 118–19, 149
apocalyptic 15–16, 21, 23, 135, 167–73, 178, 185, 196–7
apollinarianism 64, 70, 84 n.141, 128, 133, 176 n.85
Arianism 3, 129, 131, 140 n.60
Aristotle 28, 46, 103, 112, 120, 154 n.55
aseity 46
assumption 69, 74–5, 198–202
Athanasius of Alexandria 131
Aquinas, Thomas 3, 9–11
Augustine of Hippo 112 n.88, 131, 164
Averroes 112
Avicenna 112, 115 n.103

Barth, Karl 21, 36 n.98, 90 n.177, 146 n.14, 205 n.127
Barthes, Roland 6
Baur, F. C. 24 n.32
Bird, Michael 92
beatific vision 49 n.47, 110, 137–8, 140, 177, 185–206
Becker, Jürgen 156
Boersma, Hans 187

Boethius 62, 66, 106 n.48
Borg, Marcus 27
Bornkamm, G. 21
Brown, Raymond 26, 32, 129
Bullard, Colin Blake 175
Bultmann, Rudolf 21, 27, 89–91

causation 44–53, 119
 efficient 47–8
 exemplar 79, 105 n.43
 final 49, 153
 formal 48, 106 n.46, 119
 instrumental 85–9
 secondary 53
Chalcedon 5, 9 n28, 34, 59, 61
 rejection of 64, 69, 86, 95
Christology
 of accidental union 72–96 (*See also* Nestorianism)
 classical 3, 8, 60, 138–9, 154, 207
 consciousness 13, 64–6, 70
 of divine identity 83
 historicizing 39, 60 n.7, 77, 203
 kenotic 35–9, 125, 199, 203
 nihilianism 75 n.85
 "from below" 14, 59–60, 76, 78, 89, 95
 Spirit 60, 78–83
cognitive theory 57, 99–124, 213
Collingwood, R. G. 19, 20 n.5, 31, 208 n.2
common sense 115
conscience 63
consciousness 12–13, 62, 110 n.80
 mission 86, 89
contingency 46, 51 n.56, 106, 171–3, 177, 210
conveniens. See fittingness
communicatio idiomatum 36, 68, 78 n.100, 92–4, 130
creation 43–6
criteria of authenticity 23
Crowley, Paul 88, 94

Cudworth, Ralph 63
Cyril of Alexandria 129–30, 135

Damascene, John 192
Danto, Arthur 6
de Lubac, Henri 151
divine ideas 49, 103–7
divine simplicity 46 n.21, 49 n.40, 105 n.34, 107, 128, 139 n.56, 141, 147
divinization 80, 197–8
Docetism 30–5, 88–9, 94, 126–7, 150, 200, 208
doctrine 5, 7, 13, 202, 211, 213
Dodd, C. H. 145–6
dualism 111
Dunn, James 26
Dyothelitism 64, 68, 84–5, 127, 139, 192–3, 212

Ebionitism 3, 33, 95, 125, 139, 212
Edwards, Jonathan 191 n.47
Ehrman, Bart 26, 92–3, 140
Empedocles 103
epistemology 124
equivocity 55, 92, 112
eschatology 137, 167, 185, 205
essence/being 46, 71, 108
eternity 75 n.89, 106, 172, 190 n.42
  of creation 47 n.30
ethics 28–9, 72, 203 n.112
Eunomius 112 n.88
evil 49
existentialism 46 n.23, 77, 89, 93, 155, 208
extra Calvinisticum 37 n.101, 84

Fabro, Cornelio 43 n.9, 53
faith 86, 89, 192–4, 200–2. *See also pistis Christou*
fall 119 n.130, 152, 191
Farrer, Austin 38, 52
Fee, Gordon 138 n.55
Felton, Henry 67
Ferrier, Francis 65
fideism 209 n.6
First Enoch 197
fittingness (*conveniens*) 80, 85, 140 n.62, 149–56, 179, 187, 199–202
form criticism 23–5, 135, 168, 212
Formula of Union 130

Forsyth, P. T. 35
freedom 85
fundamentalism 1

Gaine, Simon 156, 171–2, 196
Galen 123
Garrigou-Lagrange, Reginald 167
Gilson, Étienne 100
Gorman, Michael 38 n.104, 66
grace 49–50, 93, 139, 143–4, 151–4, 198–203
  habitual 79–81, 85, 165 n.28
  of union 83, 85
Gregory Nazianzen 133, 150
Gregory the Great 134
Grillmeier, Aloys 9 n.28, 132

Haight, Roger 78–81
Hart, David Bentley 65 n.39
Hays, Richard 169–71
Hegel, G. F. W. 8 n.26, 39
Heraclitus 154 n.55
heresy 3 n.4
Heringer, Seth 5
hermeneutics 5, 141, 148
Hesslein, Kayko Driedger 147
Hilary of Poitiers 131–3
historical Jesus scholarship 2, 13–14, 19–40, 95, 167–8, 207–13
historicism 1, 4, 154
historiography 4 n.8, 209
history 6, 16, 19, 31, 210
Holtzmann, H. J. 20
Holy Spirit. *See* pneumatology
Hume, David 28
humility 202–5
hylomorphism 112, 149
hypostasis. *See* personhood
hypostatic union 61, 69, 72–95, 127

Idealism 6 n.14, 99–100, 121, 155
ignorance of Christ 85, 89, 125–40, 200, 205
imagination 82, 113–15, 118, 145, 163, 196
impeccability 29, 192
instrumentum divinitatis 71, 80, 85, 87–9, 94–5, 127, 139, 192, 200, 205, 213
intellect 108, 113, 118, 144, 148
Irenaeus 128

Jenson, Robert 39
Jeremias, J. 21
Jerome 129 n.15, 131–2
"Jesus Seminar" 21
"jewishness" 146–7
John of Damascus 85, 112 n.88, 135 n.45
John, Gospel of 208
John Paul II 146

Kähler, Martin 3, 6, 21, 155
Kant, Immanuel 8 n.26, 34, 64, 121, 148 n.25, 209 n.5
Käsemann, Ernst 21, 30, 33, 196
kenoticism. *See* Christology: kenotic
knowledge 99–100, 104
　acquired 137, 143–59
　divine 102–7, 136
　of hearts 174–9, 186
　historical 99, 122–3
　human 136–8
　infused (*See* species: infused)
　morning vs evening 110
　practical vs speculative 106 n.47
　prophetic 16, 81, 137, 161–83
Knox, John 27

language 55, 57, 122
Larsen, Kasper Bro 33
law 180–2
Legge, Dominic 78–9, 88
Leibniz 63 n.27
Leontius of Byzantium 66
Lessing, G. E. 23
light of glory (*lumen gloriae*) 189–91
likeness 48–57, 69 n.62, 79, 105, 120, 138, 177
Locke, John 62–4
Loke, Andrew Ter Ern 68 n.56
Lombard, Peter 74
Lonergan, Bernard 7, 99, 107, 156
de Lubac, Henri 151

Mackintosh H. R. 35
Macaskill, Grant 203
MacIntyre, Alasdair 2, 14, 28, 149, 210
Maimonides, Moses 44, 164 n.20
magnanimity 204
Maritain, Jacques 42 n.6, 100
Mascall, Eric 71

materialism 62, 101, 111
Maximus the Confessor 84–5, 134, 191
memory 63, 116, 145
Merkley, Paul 208 n.2
metaphor 56, 78, 172, 187, 204
McCabe, Herbert 48
McCord Adams, Marilyn 65 n.39
McFarland, Ian 192
McInerny, Ralph 53 n.70
Meier, John P 40 n.116
Messiah 25–7, 82 n.125, 94, 135, 179
Meyer, Barbara 147
missions, divine 79–83
modus principle 50, 54, 74, 83, 207
　and knowledge 103–4, 111, 118 n.126, 136, 163, 186
Moltmann, Jürgen 39, 197
monophysitism 3, 93, 128, 132, 140–1
monothelitism 88, 134
munus triplex 82–3
myth 90

naturalism 1, 5, 11–12, 206–7
natural/Gnomic will 84–5, 191
nature 73–4, 151–2
Nemesius 112 n.88
Nestorianism 60, 73–6, 89, 93, 127, 134, 200
Nominalism 62, 71 n.72

Old Testament 146
ontotheology 52 n.63
Origen of Alexandria 128, 140
Original Justice 151–2

Pannenberg, Wolfhart 6, 39
participation 14–15, 41–58, 105, 111, 119–23, 207
parousia 162, 167–73
passions 111 n.83
patristic exegesis 128–36, 141
Pauline studies 212
Perrin, Nicholas 157
personhood 60–72, 206
perspectivism 210
Peter of Spain 112
phantasms 108, 113–16, 122, 145–8
phenomenology 110 n.82
pistis Christou 194 n.66. *See also* faith

Pitre, Brant 181
Plato 105 n.43, 111–12, 120, 149 n.32
pneumatology 29, 80–3. *See also* Christology, Spirit
Pollard, T. E. 33 n.83
priesthood 156–9
processions, divine 79–83
prophet 161–84
prosopon 61
Pseudo-Dionysius 84, 107 n.53

Quest for the Historical Jesus. *See* Historical Jesus Scholarship

Rahner, Karl 64
realism 42 n.6, 100, 120–4
 critical 7, 40 n.116, 99–100
 literary 165
 naïve 100 n.3, 121–2
Reimarus, Samuel 20, 23–4
relativism 210
Renan, E. 20
res/modus distinction 56 n.89
revelation 122
Riches, Aaron 9 n.28, 61, 201
Romanticism 64
Rowe, Kavin 8 n.25
Rowlands, Jonathan 7, 155 n.57

Sanders, E. P. 157
Sarisky, Darren 5, 41, 211
Schillebeeckx, Edward 21, 61 n.10
Schleiermacher, Friedrich 27, 64, 71, 83, 146
Schweitzer, Albert 20–1, 59, 167
Scotus, John Duns 199
second temple Judaism 32, 148, 185
secrets of hearts 109, 175–9, 186
secularism 7, 90, 155, 187 n.14, 209
self-understanding 23–8, 32, 35 n.90, 157, 205
sensation 113–17, 145, 149 n.29
Severus of Antioch 134
similitude 45 n.18, 56 n.87, 103 n.19, 106, 117, 189, 196. *See also* likeness
Soskice, Janet 44
soteriology, 149–56, 159, 200
soul 62–3, 73, 80, 103, 112, 118–19, 149, 198

species
 impressed 109, 177, 179 n.99
 infused 83, 107–10, 139, 146 n.12, 162–7, 176–9, 194–5
 intelligible 103–22, 144, 148, 163, 164–7, 189, 195
Spruit, Leen 111
Spinoza, Benedict de 11
Strauss, D. F. 20, 24 n.32
subjectivity 68
subordinationism 125, 140
substance 66
supposit 62, 68, 70, 73–5, 81, 93

Tanner, Kathryn 39
Taylor, Charles, 187 n.14
teleology. *See* cause: final
temple 157–9
theological interpretation of Scripture 5
theosis. *See* divinization
St. Thomas, John of 195
Thompson, Marianne Meye 33
threefold office. *See munus triplex*
titles of Jesus 25–7
tradition 2, 14, 207–13
transcendence 39
transfiguration 37 n.102, 168 n.40, 173 n.71, 197 n.83
Trinity 32, 78–84
Troeltsch, Ernst 6
tropos 85
truth 101–2, 121, 148, 167, 171

univocity 38, 53–6, 104 n.29, 163, 165

Van Driel, Edwin Christian 199–201
vice 28–9, 204
virtue 28–30, 123, 151–2, 188, 203–6
vision of God. *See* Beatific Vision
voluntarism 200
von Balthasar, Hans Urs 89
von Ranke, Leopold 6

Wallace, David Foster 165
Ward, Keith 65
Weinandy, Thomas 93 n.191
Weiss, Johannes 20, 168
White, Hayden 6

White, Thomas Joseph 93 n.191, 145, 152, 164, 193–4
Williams, Rowan 9, 35 n.91, 42, 52, 69
Wilkins, Jeremy 212
Witherington, Ben 30, 35 n.90
worldview 145
Wrede, William 20
Wright, N. T. 6, 22, 26, 30, 34, 85–7, 123 n.148, 138 n.54, 145, 155 n.58, 200

www.ingramcontent.com/pod-product-compliance
Lightning Source LLC
Chambersburg PA
CBHW051519230426
43668CB00012B/1666